中国社会科学院老年学者文库

中国社会科学院
老年科研基金资助

中国社会科学院老年学者文库

中国粮食主产区
生态安全研究

李　周　【瑞士】克劳德·勒内·黑默/著

社会科学文献出版社
SOCIAL SCIENCES ACADEMIC PRESS (CHINA)

图书在版编目（CIP）数据

中国粮食主产区生态安全研究：中英文对照／李周，
（瑞士）克劳德·勒内·黑默著. -- 北京：社会科学文
献出版社，2021.11
（中国社会科学院老年学者文库）
ISBN 978 - 7 - 5201 - 8776 - 3

Ⅰ.①中… Ⅱ.①李… ②克… Ⅲ.①粮食产区 - 生
态安全 - 研究 - 中国 - 汉、英 Ⅳ.①F326.11

中国版本图书馆 CIP 数据核字（2021）第 158099 号

中国社会科学院老年学者文库
中国粮食主产区生态安全研究

著　　者／李　周　〔瑞士〕克劳德·勒内·黑默

出 版 人／王利民
组稿编辑／周　丽
责任编辑／徐崇阳
责任印制／王京美

出　　版／社会科学文献出版社·城市和绿色发展分社（010）59367143
　　　　　地址：北京市北三环中路甲29号院华龙大厦　邮编：100029
　　　　　网址：www. ssap. com. cn
发　　行／市场营销中心（010）59367081　59367083
印　　装／三河市龙林印务有限公司

规　　格／开　本：787mm × 1092mm　1/16
　　　　　印　张：22.5　字　数：404千字
版　　次／2021 年 11 月第 1 版　2021 年 11 月第 1 次印刷
书　　号／ISBN 978 - 7 - 5201 - 8776 - 3
定　　价／178.00 元

目　　录

CONTENTS

前　言

　　本书的目标读者为在国家层面、省级层面与农业可持续发展政策相关的所有人员，包括政策决策者、公务员和政策顾问。本书的主要作用是帮助相关人员更多地认识到影响农业生态系统的问题及其对应的解决方案，特别是认识到改善中国粮食主产区生态安全的重要性，以支持粮食的可持续生产。

　　在过去的40年里，中国经历了经济的快速增长，极大地提高了城乡居民的收入水平和生活水平。但也产生了一系列严重的生态和环境问题，例如，水资源污染、空气污染、水土流失、生态系统退化和生物多样性丧失。生态系统退化和环境污染已经威胁和破坏了中国经济和社会发展的可持续性。[①]

　　为了化解经济增长中的资源和环境约束，中国政府于2014年提出了绿色发展和建设生态文明的政策[②]，包括全面、科学和系统地协调人与自然的关系，它的目标是建立一个以自然规律、自然资源承载力和可持续发展为基础的资源节约型和环境友好型社会。在促进生态文明方面，政府也提出了一系列政策措施，涉及低碳发展、自然资源产权改革和严格控制环境污染物排放，制定了全国土地利用规划，并提出了各种生态补偿计划来控制土壤、水资源和空气污染。中国的政策制定者坚信，通过这些新的政策措

[①] Honggi Zhang and Erqi Xu, "An evaluation of the ecological and environmental security on Chinas, terrestrial ecosystems", Institute of Geographic Sciences and Natural Resources Research, Chinese Academy of Sciences; *Sci Rep*, April 2017, https://www.ncbi.nlm.nih.gov/pmc/articles/PMC5429794.

[②] 参见《中国共产党第十八届中央委员会第四次全体会议公报》。

施的实施,中国可以实现"绿色发展"的转型。中国的这些做法同联合国的"2030年可持续发展议程"(可持续发展战略目标)[①] 具有一致性。

由于家庭联产承包责任制、农业激励措施、技术改进和农田防护林等措施的成功实施,中国的粮食产量大幅增加,2017年粮食产量达到6.18亿吨。然而,在农业发展过程中,伴随的挑战也日渐显现,例如,化肥农药的过量施用,导致土壤、地下水和地表水的污染;土壤有机质和健康状况下降;可用于灌溉的地下水供应量减少;病虫害发生率提高;农田防护林的防护功能下降;气候变化对农业生产力造成不利影响的风险增加;等等。生态系统退化和环境污染,是当今中国粮食主产区农业可持续发展面临的最重要问题之一。

因此,要稳定并提高粮食主产区的农业生产力水平,不仅需要调整农业实践方式,例如,调减化肥农药的用量,减少农业非点源污染;提高灌溉效率;调整种植季节和选择抗旱抗虫的作物新品种;采用气候智能型农业概念。而且,更重要的是,必须制定互补的政策和制度,共同促进中国粮食主产区的生态安全。生态安全是指解决自然、经济和社会发展中可能会威胁人类生存、健康、基本权利、粮食安全和社会保障、社会秩序所需资源以及适应气候变化的能力。根据这一定义,生态安全取决于人口增长、经济发展、气候变化等带来的影响与生态系统之间的所有联系,如土地退化、森林砍伐、荒漠化、水资源和空气污染、能源短缺、温室气体、全球气候变化和人类安全。

促进粮食主产区的生态安全需要应对影响农业生产可持续性的挑战,尤其是要消除以下负面影响:

(1)农业化学品过量施用对土壤和地下水造成的持续污染;

(2)过度开发地下水资源导致灌溉用水不足;

(3)气候变化导致降水量分布不均、极端气候事件发生概率的增加;

(4)农田防护林的防护功能下降;

(5)粮食主产区周边的森林生态保护效应下降。

---

① 参见《胡锦涛在学习贯彻党的十七大精神研讨班开班式上的重要讲话》。

从可持续发展的角度来看，满足中国粮食主产区的生态安全要求（以及对整个中国农业部门的影响），将直接促进中国 2030 年可持续议程目标的实现，特别是：消除贫困（SDG 1）、消除饥饿（SDG 2）、确保包容和公平的优质教育（SDG 4）、实现性别平等（SDG 5）、提高用水效率（SDG 6）、获得体面工作（SDG 8）、采取可持续的消费和生产模式（SDG 12）、采取紧急行动应对气候变化及其影响（SDG 13）和遏制生物多样性丧失（SDG 15）。

本书包括六章。首先介绍中国的粮食安全的概念、现状和面临的挑战（第一章）。其次阐明当前生态安全问题对中国粮食安全的影响（第二章）。然后简要介绍中国解决粮食安全问题的农业政策和环境政策（第三章），以及中国改善粮食主产区生态安全应采取的技术措施（第四章）。再次分析制定粮食主产区生态安全战略需要考量的政策和要素（第五章）。最后论述了向生态安全投资对改善中国和其他国家粮食安全的重要性和一般意义（第六章）。

第一章　影响中国粮食安全的几大问题

第一节　中国的粮食安全概念和现状

一　全球粮食安全现状

根据联合国粮食及农业组织（FAO）的定义，粮食安全指的是所有人在任何时候都能在物质和经济上获得足够、安全和营养的食物，以满足饮食的需求，获得健康的生活。实现粮食安全需要同时满足以下四个基本维度："足够的供给""可买到""买得起""合意"。而第五个维度——"稳定性"，通常会被用以强调其他四个维度可持续的重要性。虽然每个维度对于整体粮食安全都是必要的，但与城市地区相比，各个维度在农村地区的权重可能不一样，并且在具有不同收入和净粮食贸易平衡的经济体之间也不尽相同。

"粮食安全"这一概念是 1972~1974 年世界粮食危机爆发时被首次提出的。1974 年 FAO 在《世界粮食安全国际约定》中指出，粮食安全从根本上讲是人类的一种"基本生活权利"，即"保证任何人在任何地方都能得到为了生存和健康所需的足够食品"。40 多年来，粮食安全的含义是逐步深化的，从发展进程看，是从基于数量的粮食安全走向基于质量的粮食安全，再走向基于产品安全、资源安全和生态安全三位一体的粮食安全。

现今，中国以不到世界 8% 的耕地面积养育着世界上大约 21% 的人口，其人均耕地面积不足 0.09 公顷。人口数量之大与耕地资源有限之间形成了强烈的反差，也为中国的粮食安全保障带来巨大的挑战。中国人均耕地面积一直较少，历史上，也曾因此出现过粮食短缺和饥荒。事实上，在过去的几个世纪中，中国虽经历了多次的粮食短缺，但又通过一系列措施得以缓解。

1984年以来，中国基本上解决了粮食总供给不足的问题，这得益于政策体系的完善和农业技术的改良，也是中国农业政策奏效的重要标志。1996年以后，为了进一步确保粮食安全，中国提出，国内的粮食产量至少要达到总供给量的95%。改革开放初期，中国农业生产开始实施"家庭联产承包责任制"，同时中央政府也提出了一系列战略改革。2004年的中央一号文件指出，调动了农民的种粮积极性，就抓住了粮食生产的根本；保护和提高了粮食主产区的粮食生产能力，就稳住了全国粮食的大局。2008年的中央一号文件提出，实施粮食战略工程，集中力量建设一批基础条件好、生产水平高和调出量大的粮食核心产区。由此可以看出，中国政府一直高度重视粮食生产。此外，中国共产党第十五届中央委员会第三次会议通过的《中共中央关于农业和农村工作若干重大问题的决定》明确指出，粮食核心生产区要起到保障粮食安全的重要作用，并在国家宏观调控下发挥市场对资源配置的基础性作用。加强和改善国家对粮食这一特殊商品的宏观调控，保护农民积极性，保证供给和价格基本稳定。中国有31个省（直辖市、自治区），其中有13个粮食主产省份[①]。粮食主产省份的粮食生产对中国粮食总产量具有举足轻重的影响。

从粮食安全的角度看，粮食主产区改革与发展的成果喜人。1949年和1952年，13个粮食主产省份的粮食产量占全国粮食总产量的比重分别为59.2%和65.3%。1978~2000年，13个粮食主产省份的粮食产量占全国粮食总产量的比重长期维持在70%左右。2000~2009年，13个粮食主产省份的粮食产量占全国粮食总产量的比重有较为明显的上升。2010年以来，粮食主产区的粮食产量占全国粮食总产量的比重提高到76%左右。1949~2015年，黑龙江省和河南省的粮食产量分别从578万吨和714万吨增加到6324万吨

① 13个粮食主产省份是河北、内蒙古、辽宁、吉林、黑龙江、江苏、安徽、江西、山东、河南、湖北、湖南、四川。

和 6067 万吨，分别增长了 9.9 倍和 7.5 倍。2015 年两省双双突破粮食产量 6000 万吨大关。两省粮食产量合在一起，超过了 1949 年和 1952 年的全国粮食总产量。

整体来看，中国的粮食产量从 1982 年的 3.54 亿吨增加到 2017 年的 6.18 亿吨，增长了 74%，超过了人口增长率约 34%[①]。中国三大谷类作物小麦、稻子和玉米的自给率约为 95%。相比之下，大豆、牛奶和食糖等其他农产品都有大量进口，其中大豆进口量占总消费量的 80%。中国的农业也是农村就业的重要引擎，吸收了 3.2 亿农民，并提供了收入。如果在全球范围进行比较，同期，中国粮食总产量占全球粮食总产量（28.18 亿吨）的比重稳定在 29% 左右。这表明中国现在已经成功地保证了粮食自给自足，并确保了近乎绝对的粮食供应安全，以满足其巨大的粮食需求[②]。但从某些方面看，目前中国的粮食生产似乎存在结构性供应过剩[③]。因此，未来保护粮食安全不仅要关注粮食主产区的粮食生产能力的保护，还要关注粮食的加工和消费端的保护。

目前，中国粮食总产量已经突破 6 亿吨的大关。随着可支付能力的持续增强，粮食净进口量也在增加。在这两类因素的共同作用下，国内市场上的粮食供需一直处于平稳状态。从长远来看，中国保障产品层面的粮食安全有一系列有利因素：①良种更新速度继续加快；②有效灌溉面积逐步增加；③地膜覆盖面积逐步增大；④综合机械化率不断提高；⑤粮食生产集中度逐步增强；⑥新型农业经营主体成长和农业规模经济形成。

中国农业在取得上述巨大成就的同时，也付出了沉重的代价，包括农用化学品投入过剩导致的农业非点源污染[④]、灌溉效率低下而导致的地下水

---

① Carter C. A., Zhong F., Zhu F., "Advances in Chinese agriculture and its global implications", *Appl. Econ. Perspect. Policy*, 2012（34），pp.1-36.

② Huang J. et al., "understanding recent challenges and new food policy in China", *Global Food Security,* 2017（12），pp.119-126.

③ Wang D., et al., "The implications on food security in China based on the reform of the agricultural supply–side structure", *Economist*，2017.

④ 农业非点源污染主要来源于过量施用的单元素化肥，其养分不能被作物有效地吸收利用。在过去三十年中，中国的化肥施用量增加了 3 倍，平均效率为 32%，但世界平均水平为 55%。

位下降等问题 [①]，以及过度使用化肥、农药、薄膜、秸秆焚烧、农机油耗等造成的越来越大的碳足迹问题。此外，由于机械和储运设施落后等原因，中国每年大约 1/6 的粮食在生产、加工和运输过程中被浪费。此外，中国高强度的粮食生产既带来了产量的提高，也导致了成本的提高，从而造成粮食价格的上升和国际竞争力的下降。如此高强度粮食生产伴随的严重生态环境问题则说明现有的粮食生产亟待结构性转型。

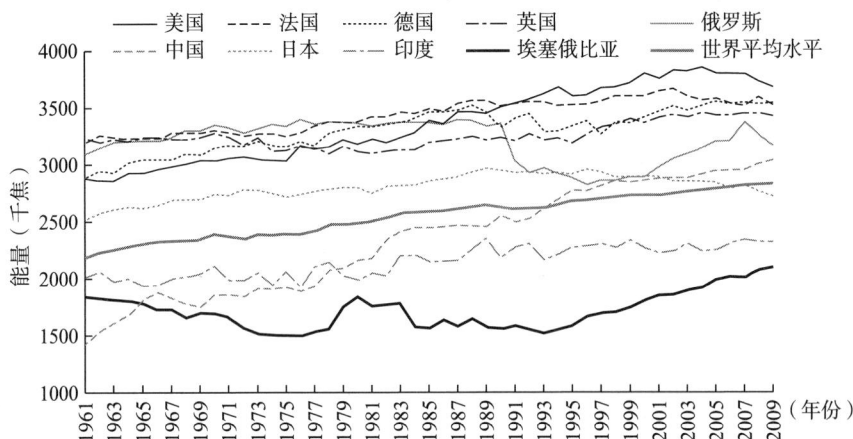

图 1-1　不同国家在 1961~2009 年粮食自我供应情况

资料来源：粮农组织统计数据库（FAOSTAT），http://www.fao.org/statistics/zh/。

二　产品层面的粮食安全

如今，中国在维护产品层面的粮食安全也面临一系列挑战，具体表现为劳动力价格、土地价格和化肥农药地膜等要素价格的不断提高，造成国内粮食竞争力的不断下降。这三个因素都将长期存在，这是我们必须正视的问题。

中国的食物需求已经跨越满足温饱的阶段，进入吃好和吃健康阶段。今后中国的粮食安全主要是食物的质量安全。为保证食物质量安全，中国

---

① 中国人均可用水量仅为 2050 立方米，占世界人均水平的 25%。农村作物灌溉用水量占中国总需水量的 60%，但是灌溉效率只有世界平均水平的 30%~40%，相较之下，发达国家能达到世界平均水平的 70%~80%。

应该做好以下几点。

首先，要将粮食生产最大限度地配置在肥沃的耕地上，这是生产出营养全面的优质食物的基本条件。

其次，要保障市场上的食物的新鲜度，走出过度运输、过度储存、过度加工的误区。

再次，要对食物生产标准做出严格规定，消除过度使用化肥、农药等化学品的行为。

最后，要开展有效的监管，让所有进入市场的食物都达到食物安全的最低标准，让所有国民都能吃上放心的食物，并逐步提高食物的质量标准。这是政府必须履行的职责。

三　土地资源层面的粮食安全

现实中的耕地非农化、非粮化对资源层面的粮食安全施加了负面影响。传统农业追求的是粮食产量最大化。主要做法有三种：①全面耕作，把能生产粮食的土地都开垦出来；②充分耕作，在能够种粮食的季节都进行粮食生产；③精耕细作，把土地生产力都挖掘出来。

然而，中国适宜粮食生产的土地是有限的，2014年，中国人均耕地面积约为 0.08 公顷，仅为世界平均水平的 40%[1]。此外，小农户拥有的农田小而分散，其中 60% 的农户耕地面积少于 0.1 公顷[2]。片面追求粮食产量去开垦边际土地和提高复种指数，必然造成粮食生产在水热条件匹配性差的地方和季节进行，并导致远距离调水和抽取深层地下水等问题。耕地的自然肥力是有限的，片面追求粮食产量最大化，就不得不多施化肥、农药来满足作物的肥力和健康需求，由此导致耕地、水体污染和土壤中营养物质减少等一系列问题。倘若产品层面的粮食安全要以地下水位下降、水体和耕地污染、土壤营养物质减少为代价，这种做法维持的时间越长，资源遭

---

[1] Ge D. et al., "Farmland transition in its influences in grain production in China", *Land Use Policy*, 2018（7）, pp. 94-105.

[2] Xiao Y. et al., "Optimal farmland conversion under double restraints of economic growth and resources protection", *Journal of Cleaner Production*, 2017（142）, pp.524-537.

受的破坏就越大。所以,我们要放弃"凡是能种粮食的土地都要开垦出来""凡是能种粮食的季节就要种植""土地的粮食产能都要挖掘出来"的传统观念,并改变把有利于维持土壤肥力的休耕扭曲为撂荒的说法。

从长远看,我们要从粮食生产潜力开发转向粮食生产能力保护,不必为了提高粮食产量而加大资源压力。粮食供给不足部分可以通过进口来解决。这种做法的实质是购买国外当年农地和水资源的使用权。

四 生态层面的粮食安全

生态系统的承载力和环境的自净能力都是有限的。倘若化肥、农药、地膜等造成的土壤污染、水体污染不断加重,受其影响的生态系统总有一天将无法继续作为人类的栖息地。这种结果决不会因为不观察或观察不清楚生态层面的粮食安全而改变。可持续的粮食安全,是有资源安全保障和生态安全保障的粮食安全。因此,不能只关注易观察到的产品层面的粮食安全,忽略不易观察到的生态层面的粮食安全。产品层面的粮食安全可以通过国内国外两个市场来实现,资源层面的粮食安全可以通过国内国外两种资源来实现,而生态层面的粮食安全必须依靠自己来实现。所以,生态层面的粮食安全是更重要的粮食安全,也是各级政府必须履行的重要责任。

五 消费层面的粮食安全

粮食安全还同消费有关。中国的粮食消费存在以下四个问题[①]。

自然损耗大。每年因遗撒、霉变、虫鼠害等因素造成的粮食损失高达250亿公斤,农民储粮损失175亿公斤。

加工损耗大。2011年全国稻谷产量为2008亿公斤,由于加工度过高,实际生产大米1202亿公斤,少产出195亿公斤大米;小麦的情况也一样。

变性损耗大。中国玉米深加工的总体产能每年稳定在775亿公斤左右,相当于国内玉米产量的47%。部分深加工把玉米变性为非粮食,把玉米中的一些营养物变为污染物,由此产生的高浓度有机废水污染又成为环境治

---

① 李周:《关注粮食安全的四个不同层面》,《中国社会科学报》,2014年4月20日。

理的重点。

消费损耗大。现在不仅宾馆、工厂、学校、机关中的食堂里粮食消费损耗大，家庭里的粮食消费损耗也大。假如相关措施都落实到位，全国每年可以减少粮食损耗835亿公斤，加上严格控制粮食变性加工措施，一年可以减少1200亿公斤的粮食消费。可见，节约粮食是每个公民都必须履行的责任。

第二节　生态安全在粮食安全方面的应用

中国农业生产中造成的环境问题目前引起了全世界的广泛关注。评估环境效率是反映农业生产对生态系统影响的直观方式，可以使政策制定者了解农业生产的环境成本，保证粮食的可持续生产。

粮食安全与生态安全具有一致性。生态安全是粮食安全的基础，粮食的长远安全取决于生态安全。生态安全要由粮食安全作为保障。粮食不安全，生态也不可能安全。所以粮食安全与生态安全必须协同，形成合力。用生态安全为粮食安全减负，用粮食安全为生态安全减压。

一　影响中国粮食安全的因素

在世界银行和联合国粮食及农业组织（FAO）的呼吁下，全世界约400名农业专家共同合作，经过为期6年的调查，于2008年发表了题目为《与农业开发相关的知识、科学和技术的国际认证》的报告。该报告指出，由化肥、农药、灌溉和转基因技术驱动的第二次农业"绿色革命"使粮食产量大幅提高，但也给生态环境造成了巨大破坏。

从这个角度来看，中国也不例外，中国农业存在类似的问题如下。

耕地非农化和非粮化。对18亿亩耕地红线[①]和16亿亩粮食种植面积造

[①] 中国政府关于生态保护红线的讨论可追溯到2011年。2017年初，中共中央办公厅国务院办公厅印发了《关于划定并严守生态保护红线的若干意见》，其中包括严格的污染防治政策规定，以保障生态系统服务功能，解决管理冲突。

成冲击。

水土流失。经测算,按照现在的水土流失速度,50年后东北黑土区1400万亩耕地的黑土层将流失掉,粮食产量将下降40%左右,35年后西南岩溶地区土地石漠化面积将翻一番。

过度灌溉。黑龙江三江平原近10年来地下水位平均下降2~3米,部分区域下降3~5米,华北平原已形成9万多平方公里的世界最大地下水开采漏斗区(包括浅层地下水和深层承压水)。

过量使用农用化学品。近年来与食品有关的重大公共安全事件接二连三地发生,食品不安全成为很多中国人担忧的一个问题。

中国粮食生产中普遍存在过量使用农用化学品的情况,并带来碳排放等"非合意产出"(Undesirable Output)。2011年,中国农业生产过程中产生的CO_2接近9000万吨。第一次全国污染源普查公报显示,农业污染源排放(流失)的总氮量(270.46万吨)占全国氮排放总量的57.2%;总磷量(28.47万吨)占全国磷排放总量的67.4%。然而,以往的农业生产效率测算未将"非合意产出"纳入分析框架,忽略了农业生产对环境的负面影响。

二 生态安全的概念

生态安全是指生态系统的完整性和健康水平。它可以通过结构、功能和景观的稳定性、可持续性,以及遭遇胁迫等指标来度量。生态安全的维护主要有两类措施,一类是通过保育化解它可能面临的生态风险,另一类是通过建设减轻它的生态脆弱性。

国际应用系统分析研究所给出的定义是:生态安全是指生态在人的生活、健康、安乐、基本权利、生活保障来源、必要资源、社会次序和人类适应环境变化的能力等方面不受威胁的状态,包括自然生态安全、经济生态安全和社会生态安全。生态安全与生态风险呈负相关,与生态健康呈正相关,所以生态安全可以从生态风险和生态健康两方面来定义。

1. 生态风险

生态风险是指生态系统遭遇风险、干扰或灾害对其结构与功能造成损害的可能性。特定风险对生态系统造成的损害同它的脆弱性相关。脆弱性受三个方面影响：一是生态系统承受风险的频率、强度；二是生态系统应对特定风险的内部恢复力；三是生态系统化解生态风险的外在恢复力。

2. 生态健康

生态健康指数（HI）= 系统活力（System Vigor）× 组织结构水平（Organizational Structure）× 系统恢复力（System Resilience）。公式中的系统活力表征系统功能，组织结构水平是指生态系统组分及途径的多样性，系统恢复力指系统受到胁迫时维持系统结构和功能的能力。系统恢复力可从四个方面度量：弹性（系统恢复到干扰前状态的时间）、可塑性（系统恢复后状态与干扰前状态可容许的差异程度）、振幅（系统受干扰后可恢复到原来状态的变化幅度）、滞后性（系统所受干扰消失后系统恢复的时间）。

生态安全是人类生存与发展的必备条件。生态安全程度有差异性，即各地的生态安全程度可以有所不同。生态安全程度具有动态性，即生态安全会随着社会发展和生态需求的提升而变化。生态安全具有调控性，人类可以通过保育和建设对其进行调控。生态安全维护需要成本。生态安全的威胁往往来自人类活动。化解由此造成的生态安全威胁需要大量投入。

生态安全具有多重特征，包括但不仅限于以下几点。

（1）整体性。局部生态破坏可能引发全局生态问题。

（2）综合性。生态安全因素会相互作用、相互影响。

（3）区域性。不同地域的生态安全影响因素和表现形式会有所不同。

（4）动态性。不同时期生态安全的影响因素会有所不同。

（5）战略性。生态安全关系经济社会可持续发展。

三　维护国家生态安全

生态安全纳入国家安全体系，是推进国家治理体系和治理能力现代化、实现国家长治久安的迫切要求。国家将生态安全纳入国家安全管理框架，有利于建立分工明确、协调统一的国家生态治理体系，促进生态治理现代化。为了将生态安全纳入国家安全体系，至少要在以下三个方面做出努力。

1. 加快国家生态安全体制机制建设

立足国家生态安全需求，健全生态安全法律体系。加强执法工作，确保任何活动都遵循红线或底线约束 ①。培育国民生态安全意识,形成良好的企业和个人行为。

2. 加快国家生态安全体制机制建设

提高系统性、整体性和协同性。整合相关组织机构,明确各部门职责。整合相关组织机构就要求生态保护、经济发展等部门要建立起沟通机制,以维护生态安全的底线。建立有效的监督考核与问责机制,确保国家生态安全战略实施效果。

3. 建立国家生态安全评估体系

构建国家生态安全综合数据库,分析、评估和预测国家生态安全情势并提出应对策略,保障中国生态安全。

简而言之,一方面,"生态红线"要应用在规范经济和社会活动中,另一方面,应加强激励机制,如生态补偿,鼓励经济实体和个人有意识地采取行动维护生态安全。生态安全也需要政策、技术、市场和公众参与等方面的协同配合,以减少各种威胁对生态系统可能造成的影响,例如过度使用农用化学品导致的问题等。

四　粮食安全与生态安全的协同

中国的经济发展已进入"新常态",粮食主产区不能只是不停地提高粮食产量,而忽略粮食主产区的生态保护。持续减少化肥和农药使用量,已经列入国家"十四五"发展规划和国家中长期发展规划,国家应尽快制定减少中国化肥和农药使用量的国家总体战略规划,形成减少化肥和农药使用的合力。制定和完善土地保育的相关法律、法规和政策,严格控制养殖业饲料中各类重金属和抗生素的添加,禁止重金属和抗生素含量超标的有机肥用于农田。

---

① 生态红线具有法律约束力。一是指国家划定的生态保护界线,例如,重点生态功能区的边界;二是指具有法律约束力的数值,例如,不可突破的基本农田面积和不可超过的水资源利用量;三是指受法律约束的行为,例如木材必须凭证采伐。生态底线不具备法律约束力。它是以前人经验、科学认知和生态承载力、生态阈值等为依据,使生态系统利用的范围、强度和方式不对生态系统演替造成破坏性冲击。它们的差异是:突破生态红线会受到法律惩罚,突破生态底线会终将遭到大自然的惩罚。

第二章　影响粮食主产区生态安全的因素

第一节　化肥

一　概述

肥料大致分为两种类型：一种是有机肥，也称天然肥料；另一种是无机肥，或称化肥或合成肥料。有机肥是天然存在的物质，包括生物肥、绿肥、有机粪肥和堆肥，这种肥料可以慢慢地将内含的营养元素释放到土壤中，以提高土地整体肥力。化肥是人造的化学物质组合，通常以不同的比例组合氮（N）、磷（P）、钾（K）、钙（Ca）、镁（Mg）和其他化学元素。化肥与有机肥不同，易于使用，并可立即释放出内含的营养元素。

化肥从 19 世纪末开始用于农业，它的应用为现代农业的发展铺平了道路。它因在短期内对作物产量有较大提升，而成为农业革命的核心。然而，化肥既不能像有机肥那样在被植物吸收之前先分解，也不能按照作物的养分需求同步释放相应的营养元素，所以在向作物提供所需养分的同时，也造成一定数量的养分流失，进而对环境造成长期的负面影响。

化肥中包含酸的成分，包括硫酸和盐酸。这些酸会溶解土壤中的成分，通过改变土壤的 pH 值来破坏它的天然结构，并杀死能将植物残余物转化为有机养分的有益微生物，而这些有益微生物可以使植物对疾病具有天然免疫力。化肥的长期使用，会使土壤出现板结，土壤板结后雨水就不易进入。

富含氮、磷等元素的化肥经雨水冲刷之后会进入河流、湖泊，甚至地下水，这会引起水体富营养化，扰乱水生生态系统。使用化肥会增加土壤中的硝酸盐浓度，经过食物进入人体内的硝酸盐有可能在微生物的作用下还原为亚硝酸盐，若与人体血液中的血红蛋白发生反应，就有可能导致高铁血红蛋白血症（也称为"蓝婴症"），对人体的血管和呼吸系统造成不良影响。所以，大量使用化肥生产的蔬菜和水果不太受民众欢迎。化肥的长期过量使用还会导致有毒化学物质，如镉、砷和铀在土壤中积累，最终可能会导致蔬菜和水果中的有毒化学物质超标。

化肥的过量使用已导致其成为农业非点源污染的主要来源。没有被植物吸收的那部分化肥污染了土壤和水体，不仅造成了环境问题，对农民来说也是金钱上的浪费。对此的解决方案是让工厂根据植物的需要生产适合的肥料，为植物提供均衡的营养，促进植物的快速生长，其叶子和残留物能保护土壤免受雨水侵蚀。

因此，化肥过量使用的问题需要进行更深入的探讨，要将其对环境造成的负面影响最小化，也要意识到维持粮食产量和保护农民收入的重要性。可能的解决方案包括使用缓释肥，采用生态农业管理实践，包括使用有机肥、堆肥、减耕、保护土壤、防止水土流失、农林复合经营等，高附加值作物，例如水果和蔬菜等，可以采用水肥一体化技术。

化肥过量施用是很多发达国家曾经面临的问题。它们在解决这个问题的过程中提出了每公顷耕地的安全施肥量为每年 225 公斤（折纯）/公顷的标准。有些学者根据中国的化肥施用量和总播种面积，求出中国平均每公顷耕地的化肥施用量，然后减去 225 公斤，得出中国农业的化肥过量施用量。这种做法具有警示价值，便于人们认识到过量施肥的严重性和危险性，但并不具备解决问题的价值。这是因为，只有谷物这样的中度耗肥作物适宜采用这个标准，蔬菜、水果等高耗肥作物采用这个标准有较大难度，而大豆等低耗肥作物无须采用这个标准。

二 化肥施用结构

农用化肥不仅用于耕地上的农作物，还用于园地和林地上的果树，草地上的人工种草，水面上的水产养殖和城市绿地。要弄清农作物生产中的化肥用量，首先要根据有关参数和有关部门的统计年鉴，把林业、牧业和渔业的化肥用量计算出来。

从表 2-1 可以看出，近 40 年，中国农用化肥的施用量由 1980 年的 1269.4 万吨增加到 2016 年的 5984.1 万吨，增长了 3.7 倍。复合肥施用量增长 80.1 倍，增长速度最快；钾肥施用量增长 17.4 倍，位居第二，磷肥施用量增长 2.0 倍，位居第三，氮肥施用量增长 1.5 倍，位居第四。

表 2-1　1980~2016 年中国农用化肥施用量

单位：万吨

年份	化肥施用量	氮肥施用量	磷肥施用量	钾肥施用量	复合肥施用量
1980	1269.4	934.2	273.3	34.6	27.2
1985	1775.8	1204.9	310.9	80.4	179.6
1990	2590.3	1638.4	462.4	147.9	341.6
1995	3593.7	2021.9	632.4	268.5	670.8
2000	4146.4	2161.5	690.5	376.5	917.9
2005	4766.2	2229.3	743.8	489.5	1303.2
2010	5561.7	2353.7	805.6	586.4	1798.5
2015	6022.6	2361.6	843.1	642.3	2175.7
2016	5984.1	2310.5	830.0	636.9	2207.1

资料来源：1981~2017 年的《中国统计年鉴》。

如表 2-2 所示，2015 年国内将近 80% 的化肥用量来自农业行业。

表 2-2　1999~2015 年中国的化肥施用量结构

单位：万吨

年份	全国	农业	林业	渔业	牧业
1999	4124.3	3359.2	501.7	170.9	92.5
2000	4146.4	3457.1	421.1	175.6	92.6
2001	4253.8	3575.3	406.1	179.8	92.6
2002	4339.4	3615.9	446.5	184.5	92.5
2003	4411.6	3684.5	447.1	187.6	92.4
2004	4636.6	3826.0	528.2	190.2	92.2
2005	4766.2	3966.6	510.9	196.7	92.0
2006	4927.7	4043.2	591.5	201.1	91.9
2007	5107.8	4166.2	704.6	145.1	91.9
2008	5239.0	4291.8	686.6	168.7	91.9

续表

年份	全国	农业	林业	渔业	牧业
2009	5404.4	4412.3	718.0	184.1	90.0
2010	5561.7	4525.2	760.4	188.4	87.7
2011	5704.2	4568.4	854.5	194.2	87.1
2012	5838.8	4635.6	919.4	202.5	81.3
2013	5911.9	4663.4	960.8	206.8	80.9
2014	5995.9	4563.2	1134.2	209.9	88.6
2015	6022.6	4736.7	996.9	212.7	76.3

注：林业化肥施用量主要包括山地果园和城市绿地的化肥施用量。牧业化肥施用量是指人工种草的化肥施用量。我国牧草种植面积平均每公顷化肥施用量在 105~130 公斤[1]，按该区间的中间数 117 公斤作为平均施用量。渔业化肥施用量为水产养殖化肥施用量，用《中国渔业年鉴》中历年池塘、水库和湖泊养殖面积分别乘以和它们的平均每公顷水面投肥量 600 公斤、57 公斤和 211 公斤的参数[2]算出。

资料来源：2000~2016 年《中国统计年鉴》《中国农业统计资料》《中国渔业年鉴》和《中国环境统计年鉴》。

三 中国谷物生产的化肥施用量的变化

表 2-3 所示为 1978~2012 年中国的农业化肥使用量分解。根据中国农产品成本收益资料汇编中的数据，计算高耗肥（蔬菜、棉花）、中耗肥（粮食）、低耗肥（大豆、油菜）作物的平均每公顷播种面积化肥施用量和农作物化肥施用总量。

表 2-3 1978~2012 年中国农业化肥施用量的分解

单位：万公顷、万吨、公斤 / 公顷

年份		1978~1982	1983~1987	1988~1992	1993~1997	1998~2002	2003~2007	2008~2012
播种面积	高耗肥	1018.4	1267.1	1590.2	1834.6	2227.2	2584.3	2748.2
	谷物	8206.7	8069.9	8346.4	8301.6	8128.8	7783.1	8635.1
	其他粮食	3503.4	3089.6	2826.9	2809.9	2778.8	2534.7	2313.5
	低耗肥	1968.9	1993.4	2004.1	2098.1	2439.6	2439.3	2328.2

---

[1] 李家康、林葆、梁国庆等：《对我国化肥使用前景的剖析》，《植物营养与肥料学报》2001 第 1 期，1~10 页。

[2] 李家康、林葆、梁国庆等：《对我国化肥使用前景的剖析》，《植物营养与肥料学报》2001 第 1 期，1~10 页。

续表

年份		1978~1982	1983~1987	1988~1992	1993~1997	1998~2002	2003~2007	2008~2012
化肥用量	高耗肥	122.3	213.2	326.0	612.7	804.5	1069.7	1175.4
	谷物	690.2	1017.6	1434.7	1799.0	2031.4	2152.8	2566.4
	其他粮食	176.9	235.1	293.5	347.0	371.7	386.3	391.8
	低耗肥	53.5	82.5	110.7	236.1	276.6	328.5	353.2
公顷耗肥	高耗肥	120.1	168.3	205.0	334.0	361.2	413.9	427.7
	谷物	84.1	141.7	171.9	216.7	249.9	276.6	297.2
	其他粮食	50.5	76.1	103.8	123.5	133.8	152.4	169.3
	低耗肥	27.2	41.4	55.2	112.5	113.4	134.7	151.7
未调整		321.2	369.6	417.5	403.3	416.6	425.4	449.0

注：未调整是指每个时期化肥用量加总数除以每个时期农作物播种面积的商。
资料来源：2000~2017年的《全国农产品成本收益资料汇编》，2000~2013年《中国统计年鉴》。

从表2-3中可以看出：① 2008~2012年谷物的平均每公顷播种面积化肥施用量为297.2公斤/公顷，比每公顷225公斤/公顷的安全水平高出32.1%。② 2008~2012年高耗肥作物的平均每公顷播种面积化肥施用量427.7公斤/公顷；③ 2008~2012年低耗肥作物和其他粮食的平均每公顷播种面积化肥施用量分别为151.7公斤/公顷和169.3公斤/公顷，还没有超出每公顷225公斤的安全水平。

表2-4　2002~2016年中国的谷物化肥施用量
单位：公斤/公顷、万公顷、万吨

年份	初始平均化肥施用量			播种面积			估计化肥施用量	实际化肥施用量	调整后平均化肥施用量		
	水稻	小麦	玉米	水稻	小麦	玉米			水稻	小麦	玉米
2002	317	309	314	2820	2391	2463	2405	2124	280	273	277
2003	315	284	314	2651	2200	2407	2214	2134	304	274	302
2004	293	287	282	2838	2163	2545	2170	2143	289	283	279
2005	313	324	276	2885	2279	2636	2369	2153	284	294	251
2006	309	333	301	2894	2361	2846	2537	2236	272	293	265
2007	323	341	313	2892	2372	2948	2664	2318	281	297	272
2008	309	344	305	2924	2362	2986	2625	2401	283	315	278
2009	309	348	321	2963	2429	3118	2761	2484	278	313	289
2010	323	377	338	2987	2426	3250	2977	2650	288	336	301

年份	初始平均化肥施用量			播种面积			估计化肥施用量	实际化肥施用量	调整后平均化肥施用量		
	水稻	小麦	玉米	水稻	小麦	玉米			水稻	小麦	玉米
2011	321	377	338	3006	2427	3354	3013	2718	290	340	305
2012	320	381	344	3014	2427	3503	3094	2786	288	343	310
2013	324	381	350.3	3031	2412	3631.8	3173.2	2853.4	291	343	315
2014	329	405	364.7	3031	2407	3712.3	3325.9	2950.2	292	359	324
2015	333	406	364.5	3022	2414	3811.9	3375.8	3018	298	363	326
2016	339	410	372.3	3018	2419	3676.8	3383.6	3040	305	368	334

资料来源：2000-2017 年的《全国农产品成本收益资料汇编》，2000-2013 年《中国统计年鉴》。

从表 2-4 可以看出，用三种谷物的初始平均化肥施用量和相应的播种面积估计出的化肥施用量要比实际化肥施用量高出 10% 左右。据分析，这很可能是农户把用于自家菜地、园地里的少量化肥也算做谷物用肥造成的。这当然不是做出这个调整的主要理由，做出这个调整的主要理由是笔者多年来组织并参与了多次大规模的农户调查，农户的每公顷谷物播种面积化肥施用量都不超过 1500 公斤，按 20% 折纯，约为 300 公斤。

化肥过量施用这个问题，要通过应用控缓施肥技术和测土配方施肥技术，以及采取有机肥替代化肥技术等一系列能够提高化肥利用率的精准施肥技术来解决，而绝不是简单地减量就可以奏效的。

做了这样的区分，解决农业化肥过量施用问题的任务就变得更加具体了。

第二节　农药

一　农药过量施用及其挑战

除草剂、杀虫剂、杀菌剂、灭鼠剂以及其他植物生长调节剂是农业生产中会使用的典型化学农药，目的是保护植物，并破坏可能会影响产量的其他不必要物质，如真菌、杂草、啮齿类动物或昆虫 [1]。除农业外，其他行

---

[1] 最新的数据信息显示，世界范围内，40% 的农药是除草剂，17% 为杀虫剂，10% 为杀菌剂。

业也会使用农药，如清除道路两旁的杂草、杀死入侵物种或控制水体中的藻类等。通过使用农药，农民能够最大限度地提高农作物产量并节省资金。杀虫剂还用于保护人类免受载体传播的疾病，如疟疾、登革热、血吸虫病等。

农药的应用在控制病虫害和确保粮食生产方面发挥着重要作用。据统计，化学农药应用的贡献率占世界粮食总产量的1/3。然而，农民普遍高估了病害虫可能造成的损失，因此不可避免地导致农药的过量使用。过量施用农药会污染农产品，农药残留会直接危害农民的健康和食品安全，也会导致害虫天敌灭绝、生物多样性减少、耕地退化和水质下降。

过量使用农药会产生诸多负面影响，导致环境和生态系统退化，特别是大气（挥发至空气中）、土壤和水污染，从而使生物群落退化。例如，农药污染水源可能导致鱼类和鸟类死亡。其他动物也会受农药污染的影响，如两栖动物遭受神经损伤，也可能导致其数量下降。有充足的科学证据表明，蜜蜂在食用了受农药污染的花粉、花蜜和水后会长期被毒害，从而影响其关键的授粉作用。[①]

此外，这些农药会通过食物链的方式最终进入人体，从而可能影响人类健康，导致癌症等[②]。事实上，农药的残留物可以在各种日常食品、饮料、动物饲料甚至母乳中找到。在人体和动物体内，农药可以代谢、排泄、储存和生物积累在体内脂肪中。从图 2-1 可以看出，从 1997 年到 2013 年，欧盟国家抽检的水果和蔬菜样本中含有多种农药残留的样本由接近 15% 提高到 27%，抽检样本中含有最高的农药数量由 8 个增加到 26 个。欧美国家的消费者食用的水果蔬菜中含有一定剂量农药残留，是他们近些年来重视食物安全的重要原因。

尽管农药对食物链和环境产生了负面影响，但全球各国对农药负面影响的关注程度差别很大[③]。例如，美国有许多法律规范商业上农药的使用（包括

---

① 根据联合国粮农组织的报告，提供世界粮食主要产量的 100 种作物中有超过 70 种是需要蜜蜂进行授粉的。报告详见：http://www.fao.org/news/story/en/item/384726/icode/。

② WHO:《农用化学品、健康和环境：资源目录》，http://www.who.int/heli/risks/toxics/chemicalsdirectory/en/index1.html。

③ WHO:《世卫组织推荐的农业中使用的农药分类》，WHO 官网，http://apps.who.int/iris/bitstream/handle/10665/44271/9789241547963_eng.pdf.jsessionid=1F8FD2E4A523131911C979DC2CF3EB1A?sequence=1.

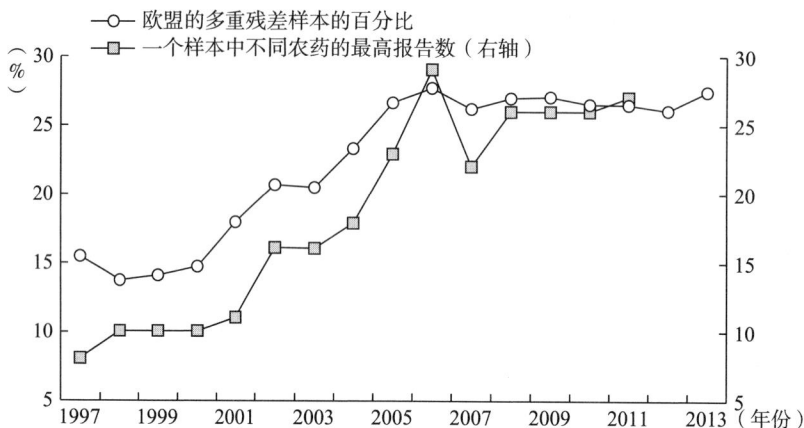

图 2-1　食物中的农药残留

资料来源：David Garthwaite et al.,"Collection of pesticide application data in view of performing Environmental Risk Assessments for pesticides", *EFSA Journal*, 2015, https://www.efsa.europa.eu/en/supporting/pub/846e.

《美国有毒物质控制法案》），但在环境和健康影响方面留下巨大的法律监管空白。欧盟已于 2012 年 3 月（欧盟 284/2013）采取了一项战略，要求通过设定食品和饲料中农药残留的限值来保护水生环境，确保农药使用有效且无害 ① 。然而，非政府组织批评此类农药立法中含有太多例外，而农药行业则认为这些例外是不可或缺的。至于农民，他们更关心与这些政策有关的经济影响和管理负担。在中国，1982 年颁布和实施了《农药安全使用条例》和《农药登记条例实施细则》。1989 年颁布的《农药安全使用标准》于 1990 年 2 月 1 日实施。2010 年颁布的《化肥使用环境安全技术导则》于 2010 年 5 月 1 日实施。

　　如今，农药的使用是政治家（和媒体）辩论的核心问题，一些研究人员主张，在符合粮食安全利益的情况下，使用农药是合乎逻辑的。然而，其他人则认为，这个理由根本不成立，尤其是考虑到对环境和人类健康的损害。目前对此问题不仅有诸多辩论，而且环境保护运动和公众对食品安全的关注意识也在日渐加强，迫使政府采取必要的措施规范农药的使用，以减少农药使用产生的负面影响。例如，要求农民只有当害虫风险最高时才能使

① 由于其对蜜蜂传粉的副作用，欧盟禁止所有农田使用世界上使用最广泛的杀虫剂（例如新烟碱类）。该禁令已经由所有成员国批准，并于 2018 年底生效。

用农药，而不是全年都使用；或通过轮作而不是单一作物栽培。生态农业
实践似乎是减少农药使用量的一个可令人信服的替代方案。在生态农业种
植实践中，农民使用天然肥料（例如粪肥和堆肥）并进行虫害生物防治。

二 中国粮食生产中的农药施用情况

中国农药施用量统计工作始于 1985 年。统计的是中国种植业的农药用
量，不包括林业、草原、草坪、卫生防疫等方面的农药用量。如表 2-5 所示
2010~2014 年中国种植业年平均农药用量为 31.73 万吨，其中，大田作物（包括水稻、
小麦、玉米、棉花、油料、糖料、薯类和豆类）的年平均农药用量为 19.81 万吨，
占种植业年平均农业用量的 62.4%；果蔬作物（不包括林业部门管理的果树）的
年平均农药用量为 9.25 万吨，占种植业年平均农业用量的 29.2%。其他农作物
年平均用药量为 2.67 万吨，占种植业年平均农业用量的 8.4%。生物农药的比重
为 7.83%。2012 年全国农户问卷调查显示，2011 年中国水稻、小麦和玉米这 3
种作物的农药施用量分别为 4.44 万吨、2.14 万吨和 3.97 万吨，平均用药量分别
为 14.8 公斤 / 公顷、8.8 公斤 / 公顷和 11.8 公斤 / 公顷。2017 年中国水稻、玉米、
小麦三大粮食作物农药利用率为 38.8%，比 2013 年提高了 3.8 个百分点。照此计
算，2017 年中国水稻、玉米、小麦三大粮食作物平均用药量为 14.2 公斤 / 公顷、
8.5 公斤 / 公顷和 11.4 公斤 / 公顷。平均每公顷谷物的化学农药施用量为 11.6 公斤。
与发达国家每公顷农药使用量（约 7~8 公斤 / 公顷）相比高出 50% 左右。

表 2-5　2010~2014 年中国种植业年平均农药使用量

单位：万吨，%

年份	2010	2011	2012	2013	2014	平均
农药使用量	31.28	32.26	32.44	31.72	30.92	31.73
大田作物农药使用量	20.13	19.37	20.53	19.82	19.18	19.81
果蔬作物农药使用量	8.56	10.27	9.18	9.16	9.07	9.25
其中生物农药比重	8.19	7.60	7.48	7.61	8.27	7.83

资料来源：束放、熊延坤：《我国农药生产应用现状及减量使用重要意义》，《营销界》2016 年第 7 期，
第 34~38 页。

三 粮食生产中农药施用的主要问题

农业劳动力成本的提高，使农民加大了对农药的依赖。农药价格下降

也促进了杀虫剂等农药的使用。[1] 农民存在不按药品说明配兑农药，随意加大农药施用剂量，增加施药次数和倾向于选用毒性较高、效果明显的农药等现象。[2]

政府存在农药残留标准不细、监管不力、安全用药宣传培训不够等问题。[3] Ryan E. Galt 指出，发展中国家的农药监管存在"双重标准"，即严格控制出口农产品的农药使用，以保证出口农产品通过发达国家的农药检测；而对国内农产品的农药使用监管不力。[4]

1. 施用器械方面的问题

从表 2-6 可以看出，粮食生产的病虫害防治主要采用农药利用率低的手工撒布和背负式喷雾器喷施（64.3%~74.3%），农药利用率较高和更高的背负式喷雾机和喷杆喷雾机分别为 300 万台和 60 万台。

表 2-6 中国农药施用器械的结构

农药施用器械	数量（万台）	防治比重（%）	雾滴直径（微米）	沉积份额（%）	农药利用率（%）
手工撒布		4.3			
背负式喷雾器	5800	60~70	400~500	20~40	30
背负式喷雾机	300	35.7~25.7	80~150	50~60	50
喷杆喷雾机	60		150~250	50~70	55

资料来源：《我国农药使用现状》，农药微信号，http://www.agroinfo.com.cn/other_detail_1833.html。

2. 经营规模方面的问题

从表 2-7 可以看出，经营规模越大，单位面积的农药施用量越少，经营规模越小，单位面积的农药施用量越多。中国大多数农户的经营规模小于 1 公顷，是农药施用量居高不少的原因之一。

---

[1] Pingali P. L.：《亚洲农业商业化在环境方面的后果》，《环境和经济发展》2001 年第 4 期，第 483-502 页。

[2] 李传义：《重庆市基地蔬菜农药残留污染现状及控制对策》，《农业环境科学》2005 年第 6 期，第 44-47 页。

[3] Ryan E.Galt：《美国食药局对进口蔬菜的农药残留和农药用量检测：实证发现和政策建议》，《食品政策》2009 年第 5 期，第 468-476 页。

[4] 宋稳成等：《中国农药残留监管现状及推进措施》，《农产品质量与安全》2010 年第 6 期，第 15-18 页。

表 2-7　2011~2013 年浙江省水稻生产农药施用统计表

单位：kg/ha

	数量（个）	经营面积（公顷）	2011	2012	2013	平均值
企业、合作社或农场	82	67.47~263.29	11.33	11.19	12.02	11.51
大户	114	19.39~22.67	11.82	15.57	11.35	12.91
散户	96	0.24~0.26	15.15	19.44	16.09	16.89
平均			12.91	15.41	13.02	13.78

资料来源：陆剑飞：《浙江省水稻农药使用状况调查与分析》，《农药》2014 年第 9 期，第 693~695 页。

四　中国农药施用与发达国家的差异

发达国家在农药施用方面的评估详见附件 1。通过这个评估可以看出，中国和发达国家农药施用的主要差异如下。

农药结构差异。发达国家除草剂（草甘膦）占 70% 以上，杀虫剂占比较低，中国除草剂占比为 33%，杀虫剂占比为 40.1%。

施药方式差异。发达国家注重预防，相当一部分农药用于土壤熏蒸、消毒和种子包衣等，中国农药主要用于防治有害生物危害。

农药利用率差异。发达国家大多采用大型喷杆喷雾设备或飞机喷洒，施药规模大，并由专业技术人员操作，农药利用率超过 50%；中国以农户使用小型施药机械打药为主，农药利用率为 30% 左右，近年来随着新型喷雾机械的使用和专业化统防统治的推行，农药利用率上升到 36% 左右。

农药使用管理差异。发达国家的农药生产、销售、使用等具有健全的法律法规、标准和严格的准入制度，中国在这方面的法律法规、市场管理和标准制定都不够健全。

单位面积用药量差异。发达国家重视综合防治，防治规模大、施药机械好，中国防治方式单一、防治规模小、施药机械差，最终表现为单位面积用药量形成差异。[①]

根据此评估，我们清楚地知道，应通过制定法律、法规和标准来加强

[①] 束放、熊延坤：《中国农药生产应用现状和农药减量使用的重要意义》，《中国农药》2016 年第 1 期。

农药的使用管理。同时要通过宣传和培训让农民获得有关农药使用、潜在风险等诸多知识和信息。

第三节　水资源

一　水资源过度耗用及挑战

粮食既是基于耕地的产品，更是基于水资源的产品。对中国来说，耕地占国土总面积的比例不到 15%，而农业耗用的水资源量占全国水资源耗用总量的 60% 以上。所以，要确保粮食安全，不仅要实行耕地保护政策，还要实行水资源可持续利用政策，做好农业水资源管理。

二　大部分粮食主产省份的粮食生产用水要靠抽取地下水灌溉

在中国 13 个粮食主产省份中，只有位于南部的江苏、江西、湖北、湖南和四川 5 个粮食主产省拥有充足的地表水资源，粮食生产用水不需要抽取地下水灌溉；位于北部的安徽、河南、山东、河北、内蒙古、辽宁、吉林和黑龙江 8 个粮食主产省区都面临水资源约束的挑战，都要靠抽取地下水来满足粮食生产的用水需求。例如，华北地区机井灌溉面积为 873 亿公顷，占灌溉总面积的 56%。东北地区机井灌溉面积为 409 万公顷，占灌溉总面积的62%，山东省机井灌溉面积 259 万公顷，占灌溉总面积的 57%。

这 8 个粮食主产省区不仅要靠抽取地下水来满足粮食生产的用水需求，而且对地下水的依赖程度不断提高。最为严重的是河北平原，其大部分农区的灌溉用水的 80% 以上取自地下水，黄淮海平原农业区抽取的地下水量占当地农业用水总量的 70% 以上。

三　地下水位下降成为这些地区最为突出的环境问题

中国地质调查局完成的《中国主要粮食基地地下水资源综合评价与合理开发研究》项目，对中国主要粮食基地灌溉农业对地下水的依赖程度和灌溉农业的地下水保障能力展开了调查和综合评价。主要结果如下。

第一，华北平原超采区的地下水位在主灌期呈"厘米"级（大于1.0厘米/天）下降、非灌溉期呈"毫米"级上升，"强降—弱升"的特征极为显著，由此说明灌溉是造成华北平原地下水位急剧下降的主要原因。

第二，华北平原农区因灌溉抽取的地下水量普遍在18万 $m^3/(a \cdot km^2)$ 以上，部分农区高达36万 $m^3/(a \cdot km^2)$ 以上，是该地区地下水可持续利用量的3倍；抽取的地下水量与地下水可持续利用量处于"严重不适应"或"极严重不适应"状态。

第三，农业灌溉抽取的地下水中，小麦等夏粮作物灌溉用水占50%以上，玉米等秋粮作物灌溉用水占10%~30%，蔬菜、水果作物灌溉用水占比急剧上升，有些地区已占20%。

总体来说，影响粮食主产区水资源过度耗用的原因有以下两个。

有效灌溉面积增多。很多人认为，灌溉农业是先进农业的代表，雨养农业是落后农业的代表，发展农业就是通过农业基础设施建设来最大限度地增加灌溉农业的比例。统计资料表明，中国的有效灌溉面积从1949年的1592.9万公顷增加到1978年的4496.5万公顷，增加了2903.6万公顷；2016年又进一步增加到6714.1万公顷，相较于1978年新增了2217.6万公顷。需要指出的是，1949~1978年增加的有效灌溉面积以利用地表水为主，它是互助社、合作社和人民公社期间农户共同努力的结果；1978~2016年增加的有效灌溉面积中相当一部分以利用地下水为主，它是农户各自努力的结果。其实，灌溉农业和雨养农业只有适宜范围的不同，并没有高下之分。按照这个理念发展农业，对于保障地下水的可持续利用，具有举足轻重的作用。

合作管理意识下降。1985年人民公社解体之后，除了极少数没有实行家庭联产承包责任制的村庄外，基于村庄的人民公社时期的农户合作形式不存在了，地表水灌溉体系因缺乏维护所需的农户合作规模而逐渐损坏了，农户不得不以打井的方式来解决灌溉用水问题。为了达到地下水利用所需的农户合作规模，出现了少数农户之间的合作，但这并不是地下水利用的主要方式。当然，打井技术的提升，电力供给的改进，管道重量的减轻，使得抽取地下水变得越来越容易，对农户选择井灌有重大影响；此外，井灌能最大限度地消除农户间的用水冲突，也是农户选择井灌的重要原因。

其实，要维护地表水灌区的可持续运行，农户家庭经营和农户合作经营是缺一不可的，放弃了合作经营，地表水灌区必然维持不下去。当然，由国有企业负责灌溉用水供给的大型灌区是能够维持下去的。

有些学者将中国现实中出现的资源过度利用同中国人均资源禀赋太少相联系，这显然是一种似是而非的解释。诚然，中国人均耕地面积和人均草地面积都为世界平均水平的 1/3，人均水资源拥有量和人均森林面积都为世界平均水平的 1/4。然而，中国的人均水资源拥有量无论如何也不可能达到世界平均水平，中国现有草地 4 亿公顷，占国土面积的 40% 以上，现有森林 2.58 亿公顷，占国土面积 27%，即使所有国土（9.6 亿公顷）都变成草地或森林，也达不到世界平均水平。中国现有耕地面积 1.35 亿公顷，占国土面积 14%，要使中国人均耕地达到世界平均水平，必须将 42% 的国土开垦为耕地，这显然是不现实的。中国的人均资源禀赋达不到世界平均水平，并不是需要解决的问题。真正需要解决的是中国的人均资源禀赋如何满足人均资源需求的问题。

第四节　气候变化

在过去的几十年里，全球气候变化得越来越显著，已经成为不争的事实，由此出现的更多的极端天气、气候事件，对农业生产产生了严重影响。政府间气候变化专门委员会（IPCC）第五次评估报告（AR5）按全球气候模式（GCMs）所做的预测表明，21 世纪全球变暖将持续发生，有可能导致粮食核心生产区更频繁地出现极端天气、气候事件，尤其是洪水和干旱。

一　气候变化对粮食生产的正面影响

利用降尺度技术开发的最新气候变化模拟模型的预测结果表明，未来气候变化对粮食产量可能产生正负面两个方面的影响。在正面影响方面，温室气体排放量的增加将会导致气温升高、冻害减弱、降雨量增加、降雨天数增多，从而延长农作物潜在生长期并为粮食作物生长提供更多的水分，有利于农业生产。

二 气候变化影响对农业生产的制约作用

但是，气候变化也会给粮食生产带来负面影响。未来气候变化可能会导致农作物生长期逐步延长、白天气温（和相关蒸散量）的升高，会对小麦和玉米产量产生负面影响。此外，由于农作物病虫害的发生与危害程度同温度和湿度具有很强相关性，气候变暖可能会使传统病虫害危害更加严重。随着气候变暖，南方的农作物害虫可能会向北迁徙，形成新的病虫灾害危及农业生产，导致粮食减产减收。降水方式和降水量变化以及温度变化还会通过土壤含水量、径流量、土壤侵蚀和土壤有机质含量、营养物质循环、盐碱化以及生物多样性的变化影响农作物生长。另外，气候变化不仅会直接影响农作物产量，还会影响可利用的灌溉水资源量，从而增大灌溉用水压力。

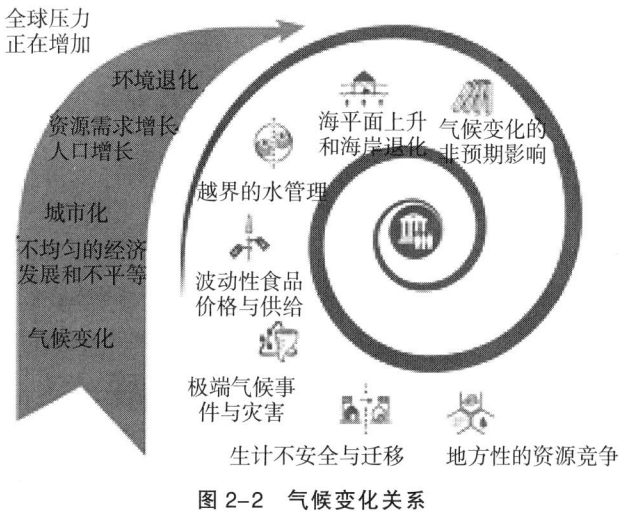

图 2-2 气候变化关系

资料来源：Rüttinger, Lukas et al., "A New Climate for Peace – Taking Action on Climate and Fragility Risks", *Adelphi, International Alert, The Wilson Center, EUISS*, 2015. https://www.adelphi.de/en/publication/new-climate-peace-%E2%80%93-taking-action-climate-and-fragility-risks。

此外，由于气候灾害发生的可能性增加，现有农田对自然灾害的总体抵抗力可能急剧下降，导致作物产量波动幅度更大。实际上，粮食主产区的农业生产已经遭受到了诸多气候灾害，包括以下几方面。

第一，春末夏初的干热风对小麦生长影响尤为明显。

第二，沙尘天气对沙区县农作物生长影响尤为严重（有时能见度仅为1公里）。

第三，初冬和初春霜冻、倒春寒天气和暴雪，可能会对小麦产量和质量产生较严重的负面影响。

第四，夏季强降雨会对农业生产产生严重的负面影响。

第五，水土流失灾害，也会对粮食主产区的耕地土壤肥力产生一定的负面影响。

总的来说，根据最近关于气候变化对粮食主产区农业生产力影响的研究，气候变化可能导致未来热风、干旱、严重和极端降雨天气的出现频率增加，因此而产生的暴风雨和洪水灾害的概率也大大增加。

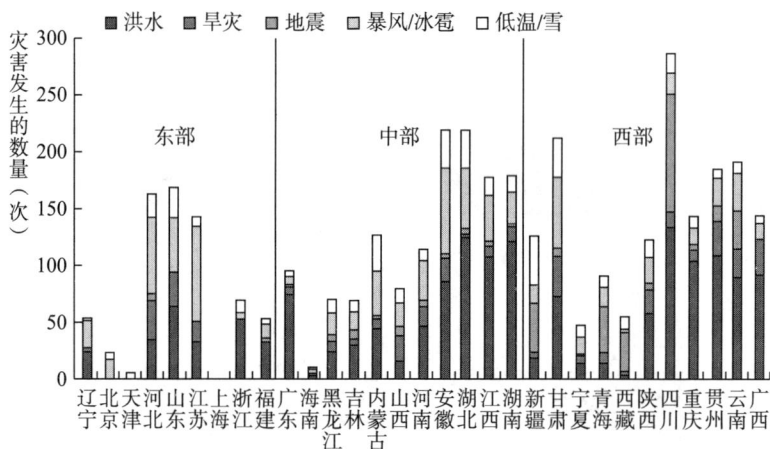

图 2-3　中国 31 个省（区、市）灾害发生数量（2008-2010 年）

资料来源：Yang Zhou, Yansui Liu, Wenxiang Wu, et al., "Integrated risk assessment of mutil-hazards in China", *Natural Hazards*, 2015, 78(1), pp.257-280.

第五节　农田防护林

一　近年的植树造林以及粮食主产区的生态安全

20 世纪 90 年代后期长江流域和黄河流域的重大洪灾被认为是由森林退

化、林业政策和策略转变而诱发的。因此，天然林保护和植树造林成为保障生态安全的迫切政策需求，中国从此开始了大规模的造林活动，速度远远超过世界上其他国家的再造林计划。在生态补偿政策的支持下，中国农区在21世纪初发起"六大林业重点工程"[①]后，造林面积激增，这些重点工程的重点是生态修复、水土流失治理和提高商品材产量（截至2015年，这些工程的实施为国内提供了大约40%的商品材）。虽然这些工程存在造林树种单一等问题，但仍然产生了巨大的环境效益。

在广大农户和各级政府管理部门的共同努力下，中国借助这些新造林和再造林工程促进了林区经济转型。例如，种植高附加价值的林产品，如蘑菇、水果、人参、药材、坚果等，也促进了私营企业的发展。但是，相较于生态林产生的环境价值，林区人民获得的生态补偿太少，这就带来了很多的隐患，如林地的过度商业化，尤其是在偏远地区。

在过去的几十年里，中国的森林覆盖率有显著增加。据统计，中国的森林覆盖率已经从1977~1981年的12%增加到了2014~2018年的22.96%，同期，全国森林总面积由1.34亿公顷增加到2.08亿公顷，森林蓄积量由102.6亿立方米增加到151.4亿立方米，分别增长了55.2%和47.6%。[②]在如此短的时间内取得了如此显著的造林成果，恐怕其他国家没有经历过。这些增长特别归因于2000年初开始的国家造林和天然林保护计划，即天然林保护工程（NFPP）和退耕还林工程（SLCP）。中国政府承诺，到2020年，全国森林覆盖率将提高到23%，到2035年达到26%，到21世纪中叶达到世界平均水平。[③]这说明植树造林已成为中国改善环境和应对气候变化的努力的重要组成部分。

[①] 六大林业重点工程具体为：①天然林保护工程（Natural Forest Protection Project）；②退耕还林还草工程（Green for Grain Project）；③"三北"和长江中下游地区等重点防护林体系建设工程；④重点地区以速生丰产用材林为主的林业产业建设工程；⑤野生动植物保护及自然保护区建设工程；⑥环北京地区防沙治沙工程。

[②] 林业部：《第二次全国森林资源清查成果》，1982年；国家林业和草原局：《第九次全国森林资源清查成果》，2019年。

[③] 焦玉海：《我国将启动大规模国土绿化行动》，《中国绿色时报》，2018年1月10日。

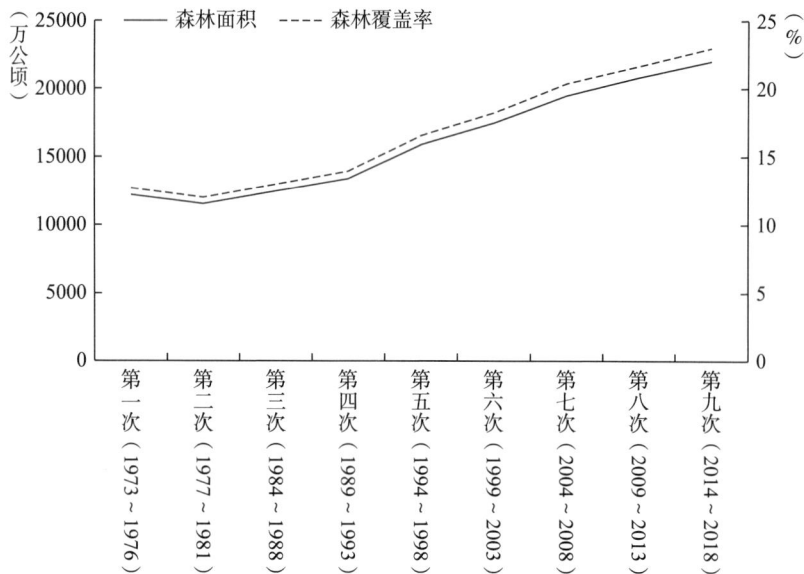

图 2-4　2004~2016 年中国森林面积占国土面积的百分比

注：针对森林资源调查中存在的不足，从 1984~1988 年开始，林业部门的森林资源清查采用的新的调查框架和调查方法。1984~1988 年的森林资源清查涉及了 1982~1983 年的资源状况，但为了保持 5 年一次的连续性，没有称其为 1982~1988 年森林资源清查，所以没有 1982~1983 年的数据。

资料来源：国家林业局：《历次全国森林资源清查数据》。

二　中国植树造林计划成功的主要原因

中国植树造林计划的成功有两大主要原因：林地和林权改革；生态补偿政策和免税政策（环境服务付费 PES）。

1. 林地和林权改革

在中国，林地分为国有和集体所有两大类，其中，集体林地面积（1.8 亿公顷）占全国林地总面积的 60%，它们绝大部分归村集体所有，但也有很少一部分归乡集体所有；其余 40% 的林地归中央、省、市/县政府所有。[①]

林权分为国有、集体所有和私有。2004 年以来实施的新一轮林权改革被认为是中国成功发展人工林的关键驱动力。对于林业部门而言，新一轮林权改革旨在减轻农村地区的贫困程度、完善森林保护并刺激当地林业投

---

① 全国绿化委员会办公室：《2017 年中国国土绿化状况公报》。

资。通过有效期长达 70 年的农村土地承包合同，林权改革赋予了个人更大的权利，包括土地流转、继承和抵押等。截至 2011 年，集体林地面积达1.73 亿公顷，其中，95% 的林地被承包给了农户，户均林地面积为 2.7~3.3公顷 [①] 。随着新一轮林权改革的完成，中国私有林的比例有所增加。

2. 生态补偿和免税政策

除了林地和林权改革，中国还实施了一系列的政策改革，鼓励农民更多地参与植树造林。其中影响力最大的政策是"生态补偿" [②] 和免税政策，所谓生态补偿就是向项目参与者提供现金或实物，并要求他们参与改善与森林有关的环境服务活动。此外，中央政府免除了林业税，以鼓励农户生产林产品；同时以财政转移支付的方式补偿地方政府，确保它们有经费开展原先由林业税费支撑的管理活动。

根据集体林权制度改革监测报告，由于农民可以更多样地使用其承包的林地，因此生态补偿措施显著增加了林农的人均纯收入。但是，关于生态补偿支付的社会经济影响评估研究表明，退耕还林、还草计划下的重新造林并没有像政府预期的那样将劳动力转移到非农业活动上。 [③] 尽管如此，目前与天然林禁伐令有关的重新造林、植树造林计划正在对全球生态安全产生了积极的影响，因为这些计划的实施，森林覆盖率增加了，碳封存量增多了，同时也保护了农田，改善了水供应，减少了水土流失。

三　影响林业生态安全效益的主要问题

相关遥感研究显示，森林覆盖率的显著增加主要是由于农田转化为人工林，特别是木材和水果等林产品生产所采用的单一树种的单一种植，使

---

① Fangyuan Hua et al., "Tree plantations displacing native forests: The nature and drivers of apparent forest recovery on former cropland is Southwestern China from 2000 to 2015", *Biological Conservation*, 2018（222）, pp. 113-124.

② 1998 年长江流域特大洪水造成了数千人死亡，数百万人无家可归，当时政府意识到维护上游森林对于防洪的重要性，因此提出向农民支付保护或恢复森林的补偿费用，此为"生态补偿"在中国的初体验。目前，中国的生态补偿支付，生态服务付费原则被纳入林业发展中，主要集中在非商业林。

③ Li Jie et. al., "Climate Change in China: Policy Evolution, Action taken and Options Ahead January 2011", *Journal of Natural Resources Policy Research*, 2001(1), pp.23-35.

中国林业的生物多样性和生态系统服务效益非常有限。① 在某些情况下,甚至会威胁野生动物的生存。更为棘手的是,中国大部分林业管理干部对单一作物种植可能造成的负面影响缺乏足够的认识,也不熟悉"近自然林业"对森林可持续经营的作用,极大地影响了鼓励以"近自然林业"方法恢复森林的政策的制定和实施。

尽管中国已经承诺将可持续森林管理纳入可持续发展战略之中,以促进多用途森林管理和增加再造林带来的多重环境和社会经济效益,但目前的森林管理实践在改善森林生态功能方面的进展缓慢,主要原因有以下两点。

第一,人工林的轮伐期(10~30年)很短,为便于采伐和更新,林木通常是单龄级的。造林后的再造林需要施用化肥和杀虫剂来控制病虫害。这种管理程序与可持续管理做法不相容,不利于生物多样性保护。

第二,根据天然林保护工程和生态公益林的分类,这些森林在通常情况下是不采取经营措施的。此外,由于天然林通常位于比较偏远的地区,森林经营还受基础设施不足,特别是森林道路和设备不足的制约。

然而,自2010年以来,原国家林业局采取了一系列措施和政策来克服上述限制因素,并加强可持续林业管理,具体包括以下几项。

2011年,国家林业局制订了2011~2015年我国林业发展的计划,该计划阐述了基本的可持续林业管理原则、主要目标和优先事项。

2013年,国家林业局制订了《推进生态文明建设规划纲要(2013—2020年)》,明确了中长期林业战略和重大行动,如生态保护红线,建立生态保护重点功能区。

2013年,国家林业局颁布了《全国木材战略储备生产基地建设计划(2013—2020年)》,该计划重在速生林的发展和管理,以缓解日益增长的林产品需求。

2014年,国家林业局印发《全国林业扶贫攻坚规划(2013—2020年)》,重点在六盘山、秦巴山、武陵山、乌蒙山、滇桂黔石漠化、滇西边境、大兴安岭南麓山、燕山—太行山、吕梁山、大别山、罗霄山、西藏、四省藏

---

① Fangyuan Hua et al., "Tree plantations displacing native forests: The nature and drivers of apparent forest recovery on former cropland is Southwestern China from 2000 to 2015", *Biological Conservation*, 2018(222), pp. 113-124.

区及新疆南疆三地州 14 个片区共 713 个县（市、区）开展林业扶贫攻坚。[①]

2016 年，国家颁布了《"十三五"发展规划纲要》，林业的重点是加强森林资源的生态利用，特别是水、污染防治、生态系统功能改善、生态恢复、生物多样性保护，应对气候变化以及生态和环境保护。

四　中国在农田防护林和林粮间作上的经验

世界上近一半的农业景观至少有 10% 被树木覆盖。这表明农场内的树木或农业景观中的树木有助于农业的可持续发展。国际上通常把将树木整合到农业系统中的模式称为"农林复合经营"模式[②]，但在中国，"农林复合经营"模式通常仅指"树木—作物"间作或轮作。在国际政策会议上，特别是《联合国气候变化框架公约》（UNFCCC）和《生物多样性公约》（CBD），已经认可将树木融入农业景观以促进可持续农业和可持续经济发展的潜力，并强调要增加对其投资。

林粮间作的农业实践在中国有着悠久的历史。例如，根据历史资料，在河南省平原地区，利用枣粮间作防治表层土壤水土流失的做法至少有一千多年的历史。20 世纪 50 年代末，大炼钢铁运动导致大量农田防护林被砍伐。这是 20 世纪 50 年代后期这些防护林被砍伐的地区建设农田防护林的重要原因之一。在人民公社时期，农田防护林规模不仅增速惊人，而且更加整齐划一，这种态势一直持续到家庭联产承包责任制推行之后。如果当时没有农田防护林的防护，农业生产将遭受严重威胁，由此产生了谚语："农田不防沙，种子难安家。"

目前在粮食主产区采用的农林复合经营模式包括以下几种方式。

农田林网（也称为"四旁植树"），主要包括在沟河路渠两边栽植树木形成的防风林、林带和河岸缓冲林等。

---

① 国家林业局计资司：《林业扶贫让困难地区同享生态文明建设成果》，《中国绿色时报》，2015 年 1 月 1 日。
② 根据世界农用林业中心（ICRAF）的说法，农林复合经营是一种土地多用途利用系统，通过空间和 / 或时间安排上将多年生木本植物和一年生作物和 / 或动物结合起来，可以最大限度地发挥互补作用或互惠互利，包括短期和长期的经济和生态效益，同时尽量减少对水分、养分、光和空间的竞争。

林粮间作，如桐粮间作、枣粮间作、果粮间作等。

果园种植。

沙地里的骨干林带（小型防护林）。

片林等，包括经济林或景观林。

因此，可以从地块植树和景观营造方面进行植树造林和退耕还林，即把树木种植融入农业景观中。在农场或村庄里，树木可以种在屋边、路边、公共娱乐区周边的户有和村有的林地上。在农场层面，人们普遍认为树木可能与作物产生直接竞争，但是实验表明，如果农场管理良好，树木的附加值会抵扣掉因此产生的损失。如果管理不到位则无法保证相同的成果。因此必须注意树木种植系统的类型和所选择的树种。

五　农田防护林和林粮间作的优势

在中国的粮食主产区中，农田防护林和林粮间作系统有可能解决四个相互关联的生态安全问题。

改善农业生产力的环境。长年田间科学研究证明，在河南省平原的农田周边种植树木有助于改善农田微气候、土壤肥力、水土保持、净化空气以及降低干热风、倒春寒、霜冻、沙暴等有害天气带来的风险。在田间和农田周边种植树木还具有固碳功能。植树造林具有良好的生态效益，根据林业和农业专家测算，在田间和农田周边种树可使粮食产量至少提高10%。此外，河南省粮食产量由1978年的2097万吨提高至2015年的6067万吨，粮食生产区农田防护林的生态保障功能也发挥了重要作用，这也得到了有关方面的认可。此外，林粮间作系统可以减少对农业化学品的依赖，生产更安全的农产品。该系统除了收获农产品，还可以通过销售木材产品获得额外收入。

从农田和景观层面适应气候变化。除了减少温室气体排放、隔离叶片和根系中的碳外，农田防护林和农林间作通过增加农业用地的用途多样化来抵御气候变化的影响，并增加其应对气候变化的弹性。降雨和温度的年际变化使气候不确定性和波动性增加，这将导致一年生作物的单一栽培系统难以抵御气候变化的风险。

增加生物多样性。农田防护林和林粮间作系统可以增加节肢动物、小型哺乳动物和鸟类等的种类，为增加生物多样性提供更多机会，特别是有利于蜜蜂传粉。一些害虫捕食者的数量增加或微气候的变化也可导致一些害虫（例如谷物蚜虫）的数量减少。而且，农场或景观层面上有树木并不会妨碍开展环境友好型病虫害控制所需的研究环境。

提高农村地区人民的生活质量，促进农村经济多样化。除了改善粮食生产外，在农田内及周边植树造林可通过出售木材、生产纸浆和造纸用圆木、木材燃料以及非木材产品，例如饲料、花、水果等产品来提高农民收入，从而推动林业行业发展。农田防护林和林粮间作系统还会带来其他社会经济效益，包括增加农村就业机会，使当地经济和产品多样化，以及产生与景观、美学、娱乐和其他生态系统服务相关的非市场效益。

2016年亚洲开发银行在河南省开展的技术援助项目（TA-8962）中的经济分析表明,2010年河南省粮食主产区林业平均收入达到918元/公顷。同时，利用经济模型对现有的林粮间作模式进行了分析，分析结果如表2-8所示。

表 2-8　河南省典型林粮间作模式的经济分析

单位：%

序号	复合模式	经济内部收益率
1	杨树农田防护林网模式	43
2	农桐间作模式	35
3	条（白蜡条）农间作模式	N/A
4	廊道绿化模式	N/A
5	核桃与油用牡丹间作模式	55
6	核桃林下养殖模式	55
7	核桃林下种植柴胡模式	55
8	杨树林下种植食用菌模式	40

注：N/A 代表数据暂缺。
资料来源：林万龙：《项目经济财务分析，亚洲开发银行 TA-8962 PRC，构建河南省国家粮食主产区生态保障体系项目》，附件8。

此外，农田防护林和林粮间作系统还可以促进联合国社会发展目标（SDGs）的实现。为了实现可持续发展预期目标，必须持续地提高和维护农业和林业用地的土地生产力。通过适当组合树木、作物和畜禽，农田防护林和林粮间作系统可以同时提供一系列商品、福利和服务，如营养安全的食品、可再生能源和清洁水，同时可以保护生物多样性、增加农业收入。

表 2-9　农林复合经营系统林木对农作物的正面和负面影响

正面影响	负面影响
● 改善小气候 ● 改善土壤肥力	● 遮阴 ● 资源竞争（营养物和水分）
● 保持水质 ● 补充地下水 ● 固碳和减缓温室气体排放 ● 生态修复 ● 植物修复	● 植化相克（化学干扰）
● 杂草和害虫治理 ● 提高生物多样性 ● 野生动物栖息地	● 为病原菌和害虫提供栖息场所 ● 引进物种的入侵行为

资料来源：Daizy Batish, Ravinder Kohli, Shibu Jose, H. P. Singh, *Ecological Basis of Agroforestry*, Boca Raton, FL, CRC Press, 2007.

六　粮食主产区农田防护林发展的制约因素

尽管历史证明农田防护林和林粮间作对作物生产力保护和发展有益处，但是，也存在影响粮食主产区维护和拓展农田防护林的问题和制约因素，并需要加以解决。河南亚洲银行技术援助项目（TA-8962）就农民和林业推广人员对农田防护林的评价进行了调查，这些问题已经得到了确认。

从农民的角度看，农田防护林保护、维护和发展的最主要障碍包括以下几点。

（1）农田防护林布局太密集，网格太窄，阻碍了农业机械化。

（2）农田防护林的树荫、根系对养分和土壤水分的竞争等，对作物生产力施加了负面影响。截至目前，有关农田防护林对作物生产力的负面影响的研究尚未引起足够的关注。

（3）所有权不明确、树木管理和采伐法规不完善，这些都是影响农民维持和发展农田防护林的障碍。与之相关的是，政策规定农民不得在基本农田上种树。

（4）林产品价格下降，导致农田防护林、片林和间作的经济效益下降。例如，十年前大直径杨木的价格为每立方米 1000 元以上，如今已经降至每立方米 500 元至 600 元。

（5）没有适宜的经济补偿措施，导致农民不愿意在农地上配置农田防护林。实际上，农民关心的是农业收入，大多数农民考虑的是，为实现生态安全而建立和维护的农田防护林，若其对农作物生产带来损失的话，这些损失应该由政府承担。因此，政府面临的真正挑战是，为了实现生态安全，提供的经济补偿水平是否足以吸引农民参与农田防护林的恢复、拓展和维护。

同时，该技术援助项目还对县级林业和农业推广人员进行了调研，他们认为农田防护林保护和发展方面的问题和障碍有以下几方面。

（1）缺乏行业间的政策框架，尤其是农田防护林在保护农田生态安全方面缺少相关政策框架。他们还进一步指出，行业间政策框架的缺乏源于当前体制中的某些不合理因素。目前，省级涉农部门之间的横向和纵向沟通有困难。若能建立起行业间的协调机制，则各部门可以共同克服影响粮食主产区的问题。

（2）预算拨款不足。一些县甚至不得不从银行贷款来维持现有的农田防护林。

（3）缺乏恰当的推广战略、能力和技术专长，特别是在生态安全方面，一些县长期缺乏生态安全培训和能力建设。对于林业推广而言，这种情况会导致农民与技术人员缺乏交流、对现代通信技术的了解不多，无法进行推广。因此，有关方面应提高认识、开展宣传和教育，以传播最新的可持续技术。

（4）缺乏应用研究工作来满足现实中所需的管理技术，农田防护林的短期或中期效益无法最大限度地提高。要对粮食主产区开展区域范围研究，分析其潜在的经济成本、效益和与农田防护林相关的风险以及林粮间作对环境的作用，结合当前不断变化的气候环境，为优化农田防护林提供科学依据。要将农田防护林作为经济案例研究，视其为生态安全、国家粮食安全和食品安全的重要资产。

上述问题和制约因素表明，尽管历史证明了农田防护林固有的环境和经济效益以及对作物生产力的影响，但在人民公社时期形成的农田防护林和其他林粮间作实践活动逐渐减少。此外，目前有关农业用地转换的规定，在农田内和农田外建立和维护农田防护林、在基本农田上开展林粮间作模式以改善粮食主产区生态安全和增加作物生产力等方面的认识仍有待完善。

如果要解决农民和推广人员提出的上述问题和障碍，想办法吸引他们更积极地参与粮食主产区的生态安全保护就显得至关重要了。其中所面临的主要挑战就是支持农民在基本农田和一般农田上采用种植农田防护林的方法，包括在某些特定地区的农田 [①] 里种植树木，为作物生长提供充分的环境保护，从而实现国家和省级在粮食安全和经济可持续发展方面的目标。

第六节　耕地

一　耕地的平均污染程度

从表 2-10 可以看出，中国耕地土壤的点位超标率为 19.4%，其中轻微、轻度、中度和重度污染点位超标率分别为 13.7%、2.8%、1.8% 和 1.1%。

全国土地土壤的点位超标率为 16.1%，其中轻微、轻度、中度和重度污染点位超标率分别为 11.2%、2.3%、1.5% 和 1.1%。除了重度污染点位超标率相同外，耕地的其他污染等级的土壤点位超标率都高于全国土地土壤点位超标率，这说明耕地的平均污染程度高于全国土地的平均污染程度。

表 2-10　中国土壤污染情况

土壤点位超标率	全国土地（%）	耕地（%）	差异（百分点）
	16.1	19.4	3.3
轻微	11.2	13.7	2.5
轻度	2.3	2.8	0.5
中度	1.5	1.8	0.3
重度	1.1	1.1	0

注：本次调查的土壤污染程度分为 5 级：污染物含量未超过评价标准为无污染；1~2 倍为轻微污染；2~3 倍为轻度污染；3~5 倍为中度污染；5 倍以上为重度污染。

资料来源：环境保护部和国土资源部发布的《全国土壤污染状况第三次调查公报》，2014 年 4 月。

---

① 特别是在沙质土、水土流失严重的一般农田上。

二 东北地区黑土层变薄

黑土是世界公认的肥沃土壤。截至 2015 年，中国东北地区的黑土区面积为 10300 万公顷，其中耕地约 3200 万公顷，对于保障国家粮食安全具有重要地位。监测数据表明，中国东北地区黑土区耕地的表土平均每年流失 0.3cm~1.0cm，一部分耕地的黑土层厚度已由开垦之初的 80cm~100cm 下降到目前的 40cm~50cm，部分地区甚至下降到 20cm~30cm；有机质含量已由开垦之初的 3%~6% 下降到目前的 2%~3%。[①]

吉林和黑龙江省的黑土层变薄情况尤为突出。吉林省有黑土耕地 520 万公顷，占全省耕地面积的 7 成以上。每年平均流失表层土壤 0.3cm~0.7cm，耕层有机质以每年 0.1% 的速度下降。耕地的犁底层深度已由 20 世纪 80 年代的 20cm 左右下降到 13cm。土壤持续供肥能力的下降，在一定程度上提高了作物病害的发生频率。[②] 黑龙江省有黑土耕地面积 1593 万公顷。由于利用不当，耕地黑土层的平均厚度由 1982 年第二次土壤普查时的 28.8cm 下降到 2012 年的 19.7cm，30 年里少了 9.1cm。耕地土壤有机质平均含量和耕层土壤全氮含量分别由 1982 年的 4.32% 和 2.15g/kg 降至 2012 年的 2.68% 和 1.84g/kg。耕层有效钾含量也急速下降。同期，黑龙江省的盐碱耕地面积由 23.33 万公顷增至 56.67 万公顷，增长了 143%。在化肥投入量逐年加大、农家肥投入量逐年减少和使用除草剂等因素的影响下，耕地土壤板结硬化程度也逐年加剧。

三 重金属污染

耕地的重金属污染指土壤中重金属含量过高造成土壤生态环境恶化的现象。中国目前尚未公布全国耕地土壤重金属污染数据，但是许多已完成土壤重金属污染监测和调查工作的区域，其相关数据和结果已出现在国内外学者发表的论文中。收集整理这些已发表的数据，构建耕地土壤重金属污染数据库，可用来估计中国耕地土壤重金属污染状况。[③]

---

① 金亮等：《治疗黑土地"贫血症"》，《经济日报》2015 年 7 月 28 日。
② 刘伟林：《黑土地的"绿色蝶变"》，《农民日报》2017 年 9 月 14 日。
③ 研究团队从检索到的近千篇文献中筛选出 138 篇，涉及 26 个省（区、市）、78 个地级市和 62 个县，可以大体反映中国耕地土壤重金属污染概况。

根据划定的土壤污染等级（见表 2-11），中国耕地属于清洁的土壤为 68.12%，尚清洁为 14.49%；轻污染为 15.22%；中污染和重污染分别为 1.45% 和 0.72%。

表 2-11 土壤污染程度分级

等级	污染指数	污染程度	污染水平
1	P ≤ 0.7	清洁	安全
2	0.7<P ≤ 1	尚清洁	安全，但处于警戒范围内
3	1<P ≤ 2	轻污染	土壤污染物超过标准，作物开始受污染
4	2<P ≤ 3	中污染	土壤、作物受到中度污染
5	P>3	重污染	土壤、作物受污染已相当严重

资料来源：宋伟、陈百明、刘琳：《中国耕地土壤重金属污染概况》，《水土保持研究》2013 年第 2 期。

8 种土壤重金属污染元素中，镉元素发生污染的概率最大，为 25.20%；镍元素和汞元素的污染概率其次，分别为 5.17% 和 3.31%；砷元素和铅元素发生污染的概率再次，分别为 0.92% 和 0.72%；锌、铬和铜元素引起污染的概率较小。

根据调查，除内蒙古自治区外，其余十二个粮食主产地区，或多或少都有土壤被严重污染的问题，个别主产区还有镉污染，以及土壤严重污染与镉污染叠加的问题。

简而言之，中国耕地不安全问题可以归纳为"三大"与"三低"。

"三大"是指中低产田比例较大，中低产田占耕地总面积的 70%；耕地质量退化面积较大，退化面积占耕地总面积的 40% 以上；污染耕地面积较大，全国耕地土壤点位超标率达到 19.4%。

"三低"是指有机质含量低，全国耕地土壤有机质含量为 2.08%，比 20 世纪 90 年代初低 0.07 个百分点；补充耕地等级低，每年占补平衡耕地超过 500 万亩，相差 2~3 个地力等级；基础地力低，基础地力贡献率为 50% 左右，比发达国家低 20~30 个百分点。

耕地不安全有如下特点。

难观察。大气污染和水污染通过感官就能察觉到，土壤污染必须通过土壤样品分析、农作物检测，甚至通过人畜健康评价才能确定。土壤污染从产生到发现危害通常需要较长时间。

易累积。土壤中污染物的迁移性、扩散性和稀释性都较弱，易在土壤中累积。

不均匀。土壤性质差异较大，土壤中污染物分布不均匀，空间变异性较大。

降解慢。土壤中的重金属，许多有机污染物的降解需要很长时间。

治理难。土壤污染不是切断污染源就能解决的。治理具有成本高、周期长、难度大的特点。

农用地《土壤污染风险管控标准》于 2018 年 7 月 10 日发布

2018 年 8 月 1 日，国内新的《土壤环境质量—农用地土壤污染风险管控标准（试行）》正式生效，该标准于 1995 年第一次发布，本次为第一次修订。本标准规定了农用地土壤中镉、汞、砷、铅、铬等的风险筛选值。在《土壤环境质量—建设用地土壤污染风险管控标准》中，它规定了保护人体健康的建设用地土壤污染风险筛选值和管制值，同时还考虑了长期暴露于有毒物质和致癌物质可能带来的后果。

1995 年首次制定的《土壤环境质量标准》在土壤环境保护中发挥了积极作用，但已经无法满足当前土壤环境管理和食品安全标准的要求。为了充分体现土地风险管理和控制的理念，新的"农用地土壤污染风险管控标准"和"建设用地土壤污染风险管控标准"已经以"土壤污染风险控制标准"的名义发布。

四　影响耕地安全的其他因素

1. 水土流失

水利部 2010~2012 年开展的第一次全国水利普查显示，黄土高原是我国水土流失最严重的地区，每年流失表土 1 厘米以上，全国每年因水土流失损失耕地约 100 万亩。

2. 耕层变薄

为了吸收养分，农作物的根系会使劲往土里扎，例如小麦，根系能扎 2 米。

现在耕地表层 10 厘米，最多 15 厘米，要水有水、要肥有肥，农作物的根系都长在上面，不再往下扎了。如果管理上没有要求，长此以往，一方面会造成作物性能退化，另一方面会使耕地 15 厘米以下的土层变硬，形成硬底层，造成土壤耕作层变薄，对耕地可持续利用造成负面影响。

3. 农膜过薄

原来的农用地膜厚度国家标准为 0.008±0.003 毫米。由于太薄，农用地膜极易破碎，把废弃的农膜收集起来的用工量很大，被农民丢弃在地里，造成白色污染。针对这一问题，国家已于 2018 年 5 月 1 日正式实施《聚乙烯吹塑农用地面覆盖薄膜标准》。该标准规定，地膜厚度不得小于 0.010 毫米，偏差不得高出 0.003 毫米、低于 0.002 毫米。但此项标准不适用于降解地膜。

4. 监管不力

由于市、县级环境监测机构没有配置土壤环境监测人员和监测仪器设备，耕地土壤监管的常规运行监测体系尚未形成。土壤环境监督执法、风险预警、应急体系建设滞后，大气、水、土壤全要素协同监管机制尚未建立。土壤污染防治涉及环保、发改、科技、工信、财政、国土、住建等部门，但部门协调工作机制尚未建立。

第三章　粮食安全相关政策

　　自1978年实施改革开放以来，中国经济得到了迅速的发展，但一度忽略了发展带来的长期环境影响。面对重大的生态挑战，中国正在大力推动建设生态文明。这一概念最初是在党的十七大上提出的，党的十八大将其纳入党章，这标志着生态文明建设在中国发展的战略地位上得到进一步提升。建设生态文明的核心目标是平衡人与自然的关系，包括平衡经济发展与人口、资源和环境的关系。生态文明概念的提出旨在创造"天人和谐"的发展方式，它既源于对我国面临的生态困境的反思，也是对西方工业化的批判性发展。

　　因此，自2000年代初以来，中国政府的决策非常重视制定全面的环境保护政策和相关方案。事实上，中国共产党已经接受了国家环境状况急需改善的现状，特别是在空气、水和土壤质量方面。在中国生态文明理念背景下，将优先考虑绿色发展，特别是减少污染、有效利用自然资源、粮食安全、减缓和适应气候变化，以解决与发展有关的问题。更具体地说，在生态文明的背景下，环境保护、农村可持续发展、粮食安全和气候变化已被牢牢置于中国农业政策发展议程的核心位置，包括2004年以来的每年中央一号文件、《中国应对气候变化国家方案》《中国生物多样性保护战略与行动计划》《中国落实2030年可持续发展议程国别方案》，以及20世纪90年代以来开展的16大类可持续发展项目。

第一节　中国粮食安全政策的总体评价

一　粮食安全目标的演进

1. 增加粮食总产量，满足居民温饱需求

1949~1984 年，中国粮食的主要问题是总量短缺，难以满足全体国民的温饱需求。该阶段粮食安全政策的主要目标是增加粮食总产量，扭转粮食供不应求的局面。其中，生产措施是：①集中人力、物力和财力兴修水利、扩大垦殖范围以增加耕地面积，整治农田以扩大种植面积和营造农田防护林；②集中科研力量开展杂交水稻、杂交玉米、矮秆小麦育种和栽培技术攻关；③要求各地追求单位面积粮食产量"上纲要，过黄河，跨长江"。管理措施是：①把全国 85% 以上的耕地纳入粮食生产计划；②对粮棉油等重要农副产品实行涵盖定产、定购和定销三个方面内容的统购统销政策；③对城镇居民的粮棉油等消费实行凭票证供应政策。④粮棉油等重要农副产品的收购、调运和销售全部由国营商业部门承担。

2. 健全农民种粮激励，提高农地粮食产出

1978 年至 1998 年，中国政府围绕粮食安全这个中心任务采取了一系列改革举措。①改集体生产经营为家庭生产经营，它以农户生产的粮食扣除数量固定的国家公粮和集体提留外全部归农户支配的方式，激励农民提高粮食产量；②粮食收购价格提高 20%，以农民增收幅度高于粮食增产幅度的方式，激励农民提高粮食产量；③超购加价政策，以农民超过计划征购部分加价 50% 的方式，激励农民提高粮食产量；④逐步缩小统购统销制度实施的范围和逐步降低统购统销制度实施的比例，使合同定购和市场收购并存的粮食购销"双轨制"中市场的作用越来越大；⑤实行保留定购数量、价格随行就市的"保量放价"政策。

3. 提高粮食供需平衡稳定性，增强粮食供给可持续性

1998 年以后，中国的粮食基本实现供需平衡。粮食安全的主要任务转向降低粮食供给风险和提高粮食生产能力与可持续性上。主要措施包括：

①健全农业基础设施。化解极端气候引发的粮食减产风险。②实行省长负责制。形成各级领导都履行稳定粮食生产责任的局面。③实行最低收购价政策。粮食供过于求时，对水稻小麦实行最低收购价政策，稳定农民的粮食收入预期。④依托农业技术创新，提高农业投入要素的利用效率。⑤依托化肥农药施用标准和倡导绿色生产，把农用化学品和灌溉用水投入控制在环境可降解和水土资源可持续利用范围内。

二　粮食安全政策的演变

在粮食供需由供不应求向供需均衡转变，粮价形成由政府调控为主向市场调控为主转变，粮食消费由满足生存需求向提高生活品质转变的过程中，中国的粮食安全政策发生了相应的演化。

1. 粮食补贴政策

中国最初实行的是粮食消费补贴政策，补贴对象是城镇居民。这项补贴随着粮票制度的取消和粮价由市场供求形成的改革而不再存在，也消除了粮食产量增加和粮食收购价格提高而销售价格不变给政府造成的沉重的财政压力。1985年中国实行粮食合同定购同供应平价化肥、柴油及发放预购定金"三挂钩"政策，是向农业生产者发放粮食补贴的起始点。之后，补贴内容逐渐增多，补贴方式逐渐改进。

2. 粮食流通政策

1953~1984年中国实行统购统销政策，粮食价格和粮食经营管理完全由政府运作，严禁个人或企业主体进行粮食贸易。1985~1997年，中国实行合同定购与市场购销并行的"双轨制"。此时国有粮食企业除了在粮食市场进行粮食买卖外，还要履行政府安排的宏观调控粮食市场的职责，国家为此向它们提供一定数量的财政资金。1998年粮食流通实行了政企分开、储备与经营分开、中央与地方责任分开、新老粮食财务挂账分开，完善粮食价格机制，即"四分开、一完善"改革，粮食流通和粮价形成向市场化过渡，直至全面放开粮食购销。

3. 粮食储备政策

新中国成立初期中国粮食购销实行市场体制。针对一些私商哄抬粮价、导致粮食市场出现各种乱象的情况，国家采取了利用储备粮平抑粮价波动的策略。为保障粮食有效供应，维护社会稳定，1953年和1954年国家建立了国有粮食储备制度，1965年建立了农村集体粮食储备制度。改革以后，农村集体粮食储备制度失效，国家专项粮食储备制度得到进一步强化，颁布和实施了《中央储备粮管理条例》。为切实解决农民"卖粮难"问题和维护粮食主产区粮农的合法权益，制定了粮食临时收储政策。

4. 粮食贸易政策

20世纪50年代至90年代中期，粮食国际贸易权由政府掌握，政府根据国内粮食供求状况制订年度进出口计划，并将目标分解到各个省（区、市）。粮食进出口贸易由中国粮油食品进出口总公司负责运营。粮食贸易政策总体上是限制进口、鼓励出口。20世纪90年代中期以后，国家逐步放松对粮食国际贸易的管控，降低了关税税率，对米、麦等农产品进口实行配额管理政策，对重点粮食出口实行退税政策，取消了米、麦的铁路运输建设基金。

三 现行的粮食安全政策

1. 粮食安全政策的主要目标

提高粮食综合生产能力，提高农民生产积极性，提高生态环境质量，维护95%的粮食自给率和可持续的粮食生产能力。提高粮食流通效率和效益，减少行政管制、审批等手续，为市场主体提供更多的活动空间，充分发挥市场在资源配置中的决定性作用。稳定粮食价格，维护粮农和消费者的利益。

2. 耕地保护政策

制定土地利用规划。根据土地规划制止农业用地非农化利用行为。实施耕地占补平衡制度。国家许可占用的农业用地严格按占用的耕地面积开垦出相应数量的耕地。达不到所占耕地的数量和质量，要向国家缴纳开垦费，用于开垦耕地。实施基本农田保护制度。各级地方政府主要负责人应对本行政区域内耕地保有量和基本农田保护面积、土地利用总体规划和年度计划执行情况负总责。所有农业生产经营者要按照《基本农田保护条例》的规定承担保护农田的相应责任。设立农地生态保护区。保护区内的耕地实行更为严格的保护和养护措施，保证土壤肥力与质量，以防受到污染。同时建立耕地保护激励机制，提高耕地保护区及粮食生产基地地方政府保护耕地的积极性。制定和实施耕地保护法律法规。1978~1985 年，国家针对建设项目占用耕地的现象出台了一系列耕地保护措施，但尚无明确的法律规定。1986 年国家颁布和实施《土地管理法》。1994 年颁布和实施《基本农田保护条例》。1998 年修订的《土地管理法》用专门章节列明了耕地保护的各项细节和措施。1997 年首次将破坏耕地罪等条文列入《刑法》。

3. 粮食科技政策

建立健全粮食科技研发体系。深化粮食科技体制改革，形成以维护粮食安全为目标，以公益性研究为主体，以应用基础研究为主要内容，以创新为引领，以市场为导向、产学研相结合的现代科研体系。建立健全粮食科技推广制度。在粮食主产区内建立科技研发、培训以及示范基地，每村选择一户粮食科技示范户，优化粮食科技成果转化的微观环境。提高农户利用先进适宜技术的便利性。编制适合大面积推广的粮食生产技术操作规程和实施农业科技下乡等政策，开展高产创建活动。

4. 粮食流通政策

全面放开粮食收购价格和粮食市场，使竞争更加公平、更加充分，粮食价格主要由市场形成。培育健康的粮食市场合作机制和建立粮食价格警示机制，把粮价控制在特定范围内，维护粮食供需平衡。健全粮食流通法律法规体系、粮食信息及预警体系和粮食市场监管体系，提高粮食行政执法水平，规范粮食流通秩序。

5. 粮食补贴政策

中国给粮食生产者的补贴包括两部分。一是生产要素补贴，包括对所有种粮农民根据其所有的耕地面积每年发放的资金补贴、农资综合补贴、良种补贴和农机具购置补贴，简称为"四补贴"。二是粮食产品补贴，即粮食最低收购价政策。它是指政府委托具有一定资质的粮食企业在粮食价格低于规定的市场最低价格时收购粮农的部分粮食。这些政策的实施对提高农民种粮积极性，增加农民收入，保障中国的粮食产量发挥了积极作用。

6.粮食储备政策

依据中国粮食产量和市场供求状况以及国际粮食市场动态，确定合理的储备规模，适宜的储备品种和储备地点。优化由中央、省级和地县三级主体组成的粮食储备体系。建立一个辐射全国、便于调度、利于吞吐的粮食储备网络。

7.粮食贸易政策

利用各个国家和地区的比较优势，降低粮食总供给成本和耕地利用强度。例如南方进口各种农作物和动物饲料，北方向外出口玉米、小麦等农产品。对大宗农产品实行配额管理制度。国家根据国内外主要粮食的供求状况制定它们的进出口数额。对超过配额范围的粮食进口和其他粮食品种征收高关税。

第二节　新时期粮食安全战略政策体系

党的十九届五中全会审议通过的《中共中央关于制定国民经济和社会发展第十四个五年规划和二〇三五年远景目标的建议》指出，解决好"三农"问题仍是"十四五"时期全党工作重中之重。粮食安全以及与之相关的粮农收入则是"三农"的核心问题，构建新时期粮食安全战略的政策体系，则是解决好这个核心问题的关键所在。

一　中国粮食产业面临新的形势与新要求

当前国际国内形势错综复杂，经济、科技、文化、安全等领域的格局都在发生深刻调整。认识和把握国内外发展的新变化，全方位多角度地分析和判定当前中国粮食产业由增产导向转向提质导向的新形势与新要求很有必要。

1.消费需求升级产生了新要求

随着生活水平的提高，居民对于绿色、有机、健康等优质食物的消费需求不断增加，由"吃得饱"向"吃得好""吃得健康"升级。相比之下，由于长期以来中国粮食产业单产增加主要依靠投入大量的化肥、农药等现代化工产品，居民的营养健康需求还难以满足。广大居民对粮食产品高品质的消费需求与中国粮食生产供给之间存在的错位或供需矛盾亟须破解。

2. 资源环境约束带来新压力

改革开放以来，中国农业发展取得了巨大成就，成为世界第一的粮食生产大国，实现了谷物基本自给、口粮绝对安全的粮食安全目标。经过持续几十年的快速发展，中国经济实力、科技实力、综合国力不断提升，现代农业发展稳步推进。但与此同时，中国耕地存在质量下降、土壤污染等问题。立足当前，展望未来，中国粮食产业将面临日趋增强的资源环境硬约束。

3. 错综复杂的国际市场环境提出了新挑战

受新冠肺炎疫情和地缘政治等非传统安全因素影响，世界经济与秩序不稳定因素明显增加，粮食安全问题再次成为世界瞩目的焦点。世界粮食市场环境日趋复杂，对中国提出了极大的挑战。

4. 技术创新带来了新动力

2019年中国农业全要素生产率的贡献率已达到59.2%。技术、制度和组织创新已经成为粮食增产提质的关键要素。从目前中国粮食产业科技创新的发展实践来看，中国需要充分发挥科技变革对粮食生产的支撑作用，加快信息技术、生物技术、降耗技术和装备技术的成果转化，提高科技采纳率和科技进步贡献率，加快推进粮食产业高质量发展。

5. 制度和组织创新提供了新活力

随着中国农业现代化进程的推进，中国粮食生产的产业组织不断发展，涌现出一批规模大、现代化水平高的粮食生产新型经营主体，如合作社、家庭农场等。多样化的产业组织形式，更有利于中国粮食产业的高质量和可持续发展。

6. 宏观政策变革提供了新机遇

中国粮食产业支持政策在中国粮食产业发展过程中起着至关重要的作用，但中国现行的粮食产业支持政策也存在对水、土等自然资源使用集约度不足，国家执行价格支持政策成本不断上涨等问题。在当前错综复杂的新环境下，加快粮食产业支持政策改革，构建中国新时期粮食安全战略政策体系迫在眉睫。

二 构建中国新时期粮食安全战略政策体系具体目标与思路

构建中国新时期粮食安全战略政策体系，需要立足基本国情和发展阶段，针对粮食产业的重点问题，科学确定发展方向，明确政策实施的目标任务。新形势下，要着力解决农业发展中存在的深层次矛盾和问题，重点从农产品结构、抗风险能力、农业现代化水平上发力。总体上看，未来中国粮食安全战略政策体系应聚焦以下三个目标：一是稳定粮食生产面积、产量水平，加快提高粮食质量；二是大幅度提高生产要素效率，缓解水土等资源压力；三是增强粮食产业竞争力，管控国外冲击，稳步提高种粮收益。依据不同的目标，制定对应的政策，最终形成新时期粮食安全战略政策体系。

1. 创设结构调整政策，优化现有相关支持政策

要适应确保国计民生要求，以保障国家粮食安全为底线，健全农业支持保护制度。以保障国内粮食生产能力为前提，确立粮食生产补贴的基本思路，短期内稳定粮食生产补贴水平，中长期逐步提高粮食生产补贴力度。首先要支持生产结构调整，以提质增效为基本方向。在保障产量有效供给的前提下，优化产品生产结构，以市场为导向，积极引导农户进行合适的种植决策。其次要改革和优化现有支持政策，同时发挥市场配置资源的作用。要保留并逐步降低两大口粮最低收购价水平，同时稳定或提高农机购置补贴、金融保险、资源环境保护等方面的支持力度，大幅度拓展"绿箱"政策空间，加快创设结构调整支持政策，将现有的地力补贴转化为对规模生产经营者的不挂钩直接收入补贴，在适当地区扩大试点休耕补贴政策。

2. 提高科研支持力度，加快培育新型主体

加强顶层设计，明确粮食产业科研战略布局。充分整合科研机构、人员、研究成果等资源，建设科研共享平台，避免各自为政，提高科研成果的转化成功率。加大中央和地方财政资金对粮食产业的科技研发支持力度，探索合理的利益分配机制。注重科研人员培养，鼓励支持各大院校、科研机构开设相关课程，探索人才交流机制，加强国际与国内、院校与院校之间的科研交流合作，注重科研单位和粮食企业的合作交流，注重目标导向，

提高科研成果的实用性。

3. 进行粮食储备机制改革，建立多层次粮食储备体系。

近年来中国粮食收储主体已呈现多元化发展趋势，但由于国家主要依据存粮数量对收储企业进行补贴，导致收储企业的利益关注点更偏向于仓内存粮数量，缺少对国家整体粮食流通效率的考量，粮食储备机制改革迫在眉睫。首先，以市场化为方向，确立合理的收购配额，以保障国家粮食安全为核心目标。其次，可以借鉴发达国家经验，将国内的相关粮食企业也纳入承担收储任务的主体之中，由国家给予一定补贴，建设由国家、专业收储企业、粮食企业等多主体共同形成的多层次粮食收储体系，并在全国范围内建设信息交流平台，依据互联网、大数据等信息工具以及高铁等新时代运输工具，提高粮食在全国范围内调配效率。最后，要进一步丰富粮食储备的内涵。一是综合考虑供需状况、仓储压力、生态要求等因素，稳产量，保产能，实现"储粮于地"；二是加快科技进步，提高粮食生产中的科技含量水平，稳固提高中国粮食的单产水平和资源利用效率，实现"储粮于技"；三是对农户进行宣传教育，增强农户自身的储备能力，降低因为储备过程中不当操作而导致的浪费数量，实现"储粮于民"。

4. 增强粮食产业竞争力，加强品牌建设支持力度

中国虽然是粮食生产、消费、贸易大国，但是在粮食国际市场上并不具备较高话语权，根本原因在于中国粮食产业在产品质量、种粮效益等方面的国际竞争力较低。为此，首先，应该加快打造粮食全产业链。坚持因地制宜、因企施策，推广全产业链经营、产业集聚、产业融合、产后服务带动等模式，在农户、合作社、企业、消费者之间搭建流畅的信息传递桥梁，引导资源在多环节中的有效配置，强化产业链条中的科技支撑，实现粮食产业高效、协调、健康、可持续发展。其次，要加强粮食产业品牌建设力度。一方面通过品牌效应带动，增强粮食产业链条的增值效果；另一方面以品牌产品为载体，增加中国粮食产品在国际市场上的知名度，提高中国粮食产业对国际粮食市场的影响力。

5. 积极利用海外市场，多元化布局进口来源地

面对新的全球环境，中国需要科学制定重要粮食品种进口国别布局规

划,科学确定重要粮食品种的国内保障水平,确保中国粮食供给安全。首先,要把握好粮食进口的节奏,遵循补充国内市场缺口,维持国内市场稳定的基本思路,避免非必需进口。其次,加强与其他国家的协商沟通,确保进口规模的有效控制,在未来的多边贸易谈判中,坚持不下调两大口粮关税保护水平的基本原则,在周边优先的前提下,多元化布局中国粮食短缺品种的进口来源地,降低贸易过程的不稳定因素。最后,要逐步推进放开国内市场。中国市场体量巨大,对于世界粮食市场的影响非同小可,为避免对国际国内市场的冲击过大,应该坚持逐步放开原则,在利用国际市场补充国内粮食供给的同时,加快提高国内粮食产业的竞争力。

三 全面推进绿色生产行动

1. 耕地质量保育行动

以实施国家耕地保护工程为抓手,中国应推进东北地区黑土保育和有机质提升,以及北方旱地耕层维护与地力培育、西北地区农田残膜回收、西南水旱轮作区地力培肥、黄淮海地区盐碱地综合改良工作。重点是保育黑土地,夯实东北大粮仓。以免耕、少耕和秸秆、根茬覆盖等保护性耕作方式,改善土壤的结构和肥力,增强土壤的蓄水、保水和抗旱、抗侵蚀能力,减少土壤的风蚀、水蚀;在雨量充沛的作物生长期间进行融打破犁底层、减少土壤板结和蓄纳雨水等效应于一体的深松。

2. 耕地轮作休耕行动

中国部分耕地存在地力透支、地下水超采、面源污染加重等问题。抓住国内粮食库存较多和国际市场粮价走低的时机实行轮作休耕,有助于养护耕地、平衡粮食供求关系和减轻财政压力。该行动可先在地下水漏斗区、重金属污染区、土层过薄区和生态严重退化区实施,再拓展到其他区。轮作休耕是"藏粮于地"的战略举措,为了不影响农户的短期收入,政府应提供休耕补贴,并引导农民拓宽收入来源。

3. 绿色生产经营行动

片面追求短期产量和收益而过量施用水肥,使耕地表层要水有水、要肥有肥,农作物根系就不再往下扎了。长此以往,这会造成作物性能退化和耕地 15 厘米以下土层变硬。扭转这种局面的策略是控制化肥投入，减少资源能源消耗和面源污染，提高食物品质和农业可持续性；以有机肥、新型肥替代化肥，减少化肥用量；以创建绿色防控示范县为抓手，推广免疫诱抗、防虫灯（板、网）、昆虫天敌、生物农药等农作物病虫害绿色防控产品和技术，把化学农药用量控制在允许范围内。发展节水和旱作农业，除了应用节水技术外，通过培育抗旱品种和发展旱作农业，减少作物需水量；通过农田覆盖减少无效蒸发，增强"土壤—作物"水分小循环和提高地温，改善作物生长条件；通过种植绿肥和秸秆还田改善土壤物理结构，增强土壤蓄水和保水能力；通过建立非充分灌溉制度，激活作物抗旱性能和提高水资源利用效率；把农业生产能力的提高建立在稳定农业灌溉用水总量的基础上。

4. 试行食品安全标准体系

消费者对食品安全越来越感兴趣，特别是对那些带着"天然""环保""有机"或"健康"标签的农产品。政府制定与消费者对食品安全期望相匹配的干预措施，不仅迫切需要制定可靠的食品安全监管制度，包括食品生产的安全标准和产品质量标准，也迫切需要能够执行质量和安全监督、检查和测试的系统，涵盖食品生产、加工、储存、运输和销售的整个过程。理想情况下，这种食品安全标准应该按照国际公认的生态标签和 / 或认证标准来制定，如 HACCP 安全协议、绿色农产品、有机农产品、农产品地理标志等。在中国国内环境下改进和推广食品安全标准的过程中，应考虑一些基本的政策建议，以增强公众健康和提高消费者的信心。包括：①提高属地（县）政府的管理责任和能力，对农产品的质量安全，包括产地和供应链进行监测、监督和审核；②确保标签清晰准确；③提高农业推广能力，提升农民对食品安全生产的能力；④提高生产者、加工者和销售者的意识和自律性，严格执行过失责任；⑤扩大对参与食品安全监督、监测和审计的官员和食品安全推广人员的培训，向消费者提供事实信息、教育和相关建议；⑥拓宽公众参与食品供应链监督、监测和审计的渠道；⑦投资食品安全研究，提高食品的微生物、化学和物理安全，以及食源性污染物和疾病的检验检测方法。在这个基础上试行食用农产品达标合格证制度。全面落实地方政府属地管理责任，提升基层政府对农业投入品、农产品质量安全和产地环境监测监管的能力，整体提升全国农产品质量安全水平。拓宽公众参与监管的渠道，增强生产经营者的自律意识，提升消费者对食用农产品安全的满意度。

第三节 生态文明与粮食安全

一 《全国农业可持续发展规划（2015—2030年）》

在生态文明的理念下，中国正在积极寻求资源管理、环境保护和可持续农业发展的平衡来实现粮食安全。《全国农业可持续发展规划（2015—2030年）》的印发为农业开展生态文明建设和改进农业发展政策和体制提供了框架。《全国农业可持续发展规划（2015—2030年）》强调了与中国粮食安全和食品安全相关的如下六大关联任务。

（1）优化发展布局，稳定提升农业产能。

（2）保护耕地资源，促进农田永续利用。包括防治耕地污染，建立农产品产地土壤分级管理和利用制度。

（3）节约高效用水，保障农业用水安全。确立水资源开发利用控制红线，到2020年和2030年全国农业灌溉用水量分别保持在3720亿立方米和3730亿立方米。

（4）治理环境污染，改善农业农村环境。全面加强农业面源污染防控，科学合理使用农业投入品，提高使用效率，减少农业内源性污染。到2020年实现农药和化肥施用量零增长。

（5）修复农业生态，提升生态功能。保护草原生态和恢复水生生态系统，保护生物多样性。

（6）增加森林覆盖率，增加木材供给、贡献于生态安全。

2017年和2018年的中央1号文件进一步详述了农业政策目标，这两个文件都确立了"要基于良好的生态基本条件、产量高、巨大的粮食转移能力等特征，推行粮食主产区的执行"的目标。这些粮食主产区的目标是保证中国的粮食安全，使其粮食产量占全国总产量的75%以上。

此外，《全国农业可持续发展规划（2015—2030年）》中提到的各大任务在这两个中央一号文件中都有更进一步的阐述。

粮食安全。中国政府提出将确保口粮的绝对安全（例如，水稻、玉米和小麦），重点发展优质稻米和强筋、弱筋小麦，继续调减非优势区籽粒玉米，增加优质食用大豆、薯类、杂粮杂豆等。此外，为确保粮食安全，2017年和2018年的中央一号文件都提出要进一步优化农业区域布局，即以主体功能区规划和优势农产品布局规划为依托，科学合理划定稻谷、小麦、玉米粮食生产功能区和大豆、棉花、油菜籽、糖料蔗、天然橡胶等重要农产品生产保护区。在此框架下，截至2020年，至少要新增5300万公顷的高产优质农田，推广环境友好的种植方式，以确保粮食产量的稳定，并能够应对气候变化引起的天气异常，尤其是洪水和干旱所带来的影响。

食品安全。2017年和2018年的中央一号文件都指出在农作物生产和畜禽养殖过程中农用化学品的施用量远远大于其他发达国家。农用化学品的过度施用不仅污染了土壤、地表水和地下水，而且还给人类健康带来了安全隐患。因此，两个中央一号文件要求建立可以保护水资源和土壤的绿色生产模式，提高自然资源利用效率，防止资源过度开采；同时要提高农产品质量和安全标准，推行良好农业规范（GAP）等可持续发展的做法。所以，政府要加强对农用化学品应用的监督，并严厉打击过度使用或使用非法药物的行为。同时文件还强调，未来将建立产品追溯系统。此外，政府还加强了对森林和湿地的保护和恢复，并开展新一轮退耕还林还草。

农业技术。政府继续高度重视农业研发和农产品加工创新技术的转移，利用电子商务进一步促进农产品营销。同时，持续推进培训以发展农村人力资源，并进一步推进精准扶贫各项政策措施的落实。此外，政府将建立农业技术资源共享平台，鼓励自主开发和创新，特别是以种子产业为重点。

体制改革。统筹推进农村各项改革，增加农民收入。深化粮食等重要农产品价格形成机制和收储制度改革。完善农业补贴制度，改进补贴方式。改革财政支农投入机制（包括建立风险补偿机制），深化农村集体产权制度改革。

农村地区经济发展。重点是向有困难的群众提供更多资金，在其家乡或附近地区提供非农就业岗位；推进第一、第二、第三产业在农村地区的融合发展。大力实施区域规模化节水灌溉行动；提供安全的饮用水、电力和更好的农村道路基础设施，以推进农村地区的产业融合，促进农产品批发市场的发展。

总而言之，粮食安全仍然是政府工作的重中之重，且中国农业政策的重点已逐渐由数量转向质量，这也正是所谓的农业供给侧结构性改革方案的核心。换句话说，政府鼓励农民提高产品质量或生产出能满足消费者更好、更安全和更多样化需求的农产品。政府鼓励农民扩大饲料作物的种植面积，如青贮玉米和苜蓿等优质牧草，大力培育现代饲草料产业体系。继续开展粮改饲、粮改豆补贴试点。

二 《国家应对气候变化规划（2014—2020 年）》

气候变化对粮食生产体系带来的不利影响尤为显著，并成为影响粮食安全的关键因素之一。气候变化可能会对粮食生产带来不同的影响。它有可能会引起粮食减产，也可能会产生大量的热能资源，使耕作边界有所扩大。然而，气温上升也可能会缩短农作物的生长周期，导致平均产量下降。此外，频繁的季节性干旱会给灌溉用水的供应带来压力。保护粮食安全，特别是保护粮食生产体系免受气候变化的不利影响，现已被视为 2015 年《巴黎气候协议》的基本优先事项。专家们估计，在中国，到 2030 年，即便采用了节水灌溉技术，但由气候变化导致的季节性干旱也可能会导致三种主要粮食作物稻米、小麦和玉米产量损失近 8%。在这三种谷物中，玉米单产可能遭受的影响最大，预计产量损失近五分之一，其次是小麦，产量损失约为 4%，水稻产量损失约为 1.5%。

为应对气候变化对粮食安全的不利影响，中国政府出台了综合战略——《国家应对气候变化规划（2014—2020 年）》，其涵盖了缓解和适应措施、科学研究和公众意识提升等措施，克服气候变化对中国可持续发展所带来的影响。简而言之，截至 2020 年，应对气候变化工作的目标包括：①稳定温室气体排放总量；②单位国内生产总值二氧化碳排放比 2005 年下降 40%~45%；③非化石能源占一次能源消费的比重提高到 15% 左右；④采用适应气候变化的种植方式；⑤森林面积比 2005

年增加 4000 万公顷。

专栏:《国家应对气候变化规划》中与粮食安全有关的内容

i. 加快推进农业现代化和生产模式的转变,包括采取措施尽量减少气候灾害带来的负面影响。

ii. 大力开展保护性耕作（包括推广秸秆还田,以刺激其微生物分解,提升土壤有机质）,大力推广节水灌溉和旱作农业,提高土壤水分,推广测土配方施肥技术(与 2020 年化肥和农药零增长行动相协同),以加强农业对气候变化的适应能力。

iii. 根据气候变化趋势调整作物品种布局和种植制度,加强农业基础设施建设;培养高光效、耐高温和耐旱作物品种;大力推广节水技术,提高用水效率;采用覆膜技术减少无效蒸腾和防止晚春霜冻等。

iv. 加快农田灌溉和水利基础设施建设,包括修复或建设水渠、排灌站和水井;治理水土流失。

v. 加强森林经营、抚育和低效林改造,调整林分结构,包括防护林和防风林建设,保护农田,努力增加碳汇。

vi. 加强极端天气气候事件预测预警系统,加强防洪减灾工作,提高抵抗气候变化风险的能力。

vii. 加强气候变化监测预测研究。

viii. 加强教育培训和舆论引导。

三 《中国生物多样性保护战略与行动计划（2011—2030 年）》

回顾 7000 多年的农业生产历史,中国农业成功地支持了不断增长的人口数量,同时又没有改变传统的、生物多样性友好的农业景观的稳定性,这种农业景观融合了各种优良的技术,如使用有机肥、传统农业技术,如稻鱼共生、作物轮作、林粮间作、保护传统农业景观,包括各种自然和半自然的元素。这些体系是为了保持农业景观中的土壤健康、复杂的结构和栖息地的多样化,这有利于维持物种的多样性和生态系统功能的稳定性。

改革开放的前 20 年,基于农田扩张和集约化水平提高的农业总产出的增长,使中国的土壤退化日益严重,生物栖息地丧失显著:90% 的天然草地和 40% 的湿地已显著恶化,原始森林面积多年来以每年约 5 万平方公里的速度减少。此外，农用化学品使用量的快速增加，造成了严重的土壤侵蚀和污染问题，以及随后的半自然栖息地迅速丧失和害虫天敌丧失、水污染和空气污染。这些变化对生物多样性和社会经济发展产生了显著的负面影响 [①] 。

为应对农业和环境上的诸多退化现象，中国政府出台了《中国生物多样性保护战略与行动计划（2011—2030 年）》，以期待解决三个主要的粮食安全问题：①部分生态系统功能不断退化；②物种濒危程度加剧；③遗传资源不断丧失和流失。为解决上述影响农业景观生物多样性保护的主要问题和挑战，该计划中提出八大战略任务：①完善生物多样性保护相关政策、法规和制度；②推动生物多样性保护纳入相关规划；③加强生物多样性保护能力建设；④强化生物多样性就地保护，合理开展迁地保护；⑤促进生物资源可持续开发利用；⑥推进生物遗传资源及相关传统知识惠益分享；⑦提高应对生物多样性新威胁和新挑战的能力；⑧提高公众参与意识，加强国际合作和交流。然而，农业集约化是生物多样性丧失和农业生态系统退化的主要驱动因素已经是无须争议的事实，但中国已经开始采取一系列举措来保护生物多样性，同时保护生态系统，恢复受损的农业生态系统。并把改善农村环境作为中国生态文明建设的一部分。

专栏：《中国生物多样性保护战略与行动计划（2011—2030 年)》中
与粮食安全有关的内容

i. 严格保护生态敏感或脆弱地区的系统功能，以支持社会经济发展，特别是粮食安全（严格划定生态红线区域）。

ii. 实施生态修复项目。

iii. 发展旨在加强环境保护、改善农村生态条件和建设"美丽村庄"的示范项目，改善农村环境。这些示范项目的内容包括调整农业种植结构、发展循环经济、处理农业非点源污染、提升农产品质量和安全等。

iv. 深入开展生态省、生态市、生态县、生态乡镇、生态村等生态示范区、国家园林城市（县城、城镇）以及国家生态园林城市建设工作。

[①] 原环保部于 2009 年时估计，由于环境破坏导致的经济损失达到了 GDP 的 4.5%~18%。

四　中国的 16 项环境可持续发展优先计划 [①]

除上述政策外，为了应对新出现的环境挑战，中国政府从 20 世纪 70 年代末开始至 21 世纪初还提出了 16 项主要的可持续发展计划，主要目标是减少长江流域和黄河流域的水土流失、泥沙沉积和洪水泛滥、保护东北部的森林、减轻华北地区干旱、沙漠化和沙尘暴、提高中东部地区的农业生产力等。同时，这些计划的实施也会带来很好的社会和经济效益，例如，减贫、农村经济发展和国家粮食安全。1978~2015 年期间在环境可持续性计划上的项目投资总额为 3785 亿美元（2015 年）。下框总结了这些项目的目标。

P1. "三北"防护林工程（1978—2050 年）。通过人工造林、封山育林和沙地治理来控制北方土地荒漠化

P2. 水土保持规划（1983—2017 年）。通过植被再造、植树和其他生物措施和工程措施控制水土流失，改善农民的生计和农业生产

P3. 长江中下游地区等五个防护林体系建设工程（1987—2020 年）。通过人工造林、封山育林、飞播造林和建立防护林等措施抑制长江流域、珠江流域、太行山区等地区的环境恶化

P4. 农业综合开发项目（1988—2020 年）。改善农村生活质量、保障粮食和食品安全

P5. 长江流域水土保持工程（1989 年至今）。减少泥沙沉降，改善长江水土健康状况，控制上游的水土流失，确保三峡大坝的健康运行

P6. 全国土地开发整理规划（1997—2020 年）。通过土地开发和整理，修建高标准农田，改善土地利用和管理

P7. 天然林保护工程（1998—2020 年）。通过封山育林、禁伐等措施，保护天然林，同时为林业企业职工提供非林就业机会

P8. 退耕还林工程（1999—2020 年）。防止水土流失，减少和减轻水旱灾害、增加碳储存，并通过退耕还林、荒山荒坡造林等措施提高森林覆盖率

P9. 速生丰产林建设工程（2001—2015 年）。以新的木材生产基地替代天然林和次生林的木材供给，从而不影响木材供需平衡

P10. 森林生态效益补偿基金（2001—2016 年）。通过次生林修复和天然林保护，保护生物多样性和生态系统，实现可持续的经济和社会发展

P11. 京津风沙源治理工程（2001—2022年）。通过植树造林、草原管理和节约用水，减少和减轻荒漠化和沙尘暴危害，改善京津地区的生态环境

P12. 野生动植物及自然保护区建设工程（2001—2050年）。通过扩大自然保护区的面积和提高保护水平，更好地保护关键物种、生物多样性和自然生态系统，促进可持续发展

P13. 土地退化防治伙伴关系（2002—2023年）。改善西部的土地和水资源管理，减少贫困，保护生物多样性和应对气候变化

P14. 石漠化治理工程（2008—2020年）。通过基本农田建设和水资源保护，特别是植被保护和恢复，遏制石漠化地区的土地退化，促进土地可持续利用，改善生态环境，增加农民收入，消除农村贫困

P15. 草原生态保护工程（2011—2020年）。通过退牧还草，提高草原植被盖度/生物质量，消除和减轻草地退化，促进牧区可持续发展，增加牧民收入

P16. 耕地质量提升规划（2015—2020年）。通过解决土壤酸化、盐渍化、养分不平衡、污染，浅表土肥力不佳等问题，提高粮食安全、农业生产和农业质量

需要指出，上述项目只有部分达到了农业可持续性和粮食安全的要求。所以，如何确保粮食主产区的生态安全，仍是一个亟待研究和加以解决的重要问题。

第四章　改善粮食主产区生态安全的农林业技术措施

第一节　农业生产过度依赖化肥的问题

2011 年，中国粮食产量首次跃上了 5.5 亿吨的新台阶，实现了半个世纪以来首次"八连增"，创造了粮食产量连续 5 年过 5 亿吨的新纪录，达到了 2020 年粮食产能规划水平。

与过量施肥伴生的就是盲目施肥、滥施肥，这无疑导致了化肥利用率低，中国化肥利用率只有 30%，远低于西方发达国家 40% 以上的水平。河南省农业农村厅一项调查表明，该省每年施用的 300 多万吨化肥中，只有 1/3 被农作物吸收。

与化肥过度施用一样，农药的滥用程度，也被专家认为到了临界点。

经济因素驱使农民更多地选择化学农药。虽然生物农药对人的副作用小，但是杀虫效果不如化学农药好，而且贵。农民不愿意为此投入，因此生物农药推广不开来。

第二节　安全施肥标准

首先，我们需要廓清中国谷物生产的化肥平均施用量。通过一系列分析，我们得出了谷物生产的化肥实际施用量超过了每公顷 225 公斤的安全水平的 30%~40%。这部分工作的任务是探讨减施这些化肥的途径。一些学者认为，现实中过量施用的化肥并没有增产效应，因此，减施这部分化肥并不会影响粮食产量，进而不会影响粮食安全。然而，这种观点显然失之偏颇。农户过量施用化肥毕竟是要花钱的，如果过量施用的化肥对粮食产量不起任何作用，他们是不可能年复一年地过量施用化肥的。所以，要使中国谷物生产的化肥施用量达到安全水平，必须采取一系列能够提高化肥利用率的精准施肥技术和有机肥替代技术，而绝不是简单地减量就可以奏效的。

一 推广缓控释肥

试验研究表明，缓控释肥可提高肥料利用率 10%~30%，平均提高氮肥利用率 22.8%。因此，推广缓控释肥是提高肥料利用率的重要保证，也是确保国家粮食安全的有效途径。

表 4-1 等量缓控释肥与普通速效肥料增产率及氮素利用率增加量对比

单位：%

地点	作物	增产率	氮素利用率增加量
黑龙江庆安	水稻	10.5	17.0
浙江萧山	水稻	16.0	16.2
河南驻马店	玉米	16.2	25.3
吉林公主岭	玉米	11.2	18.6
黑龙江呼兰	玉米	11.9	17.6
河南驻马店	小麦	12.0	26.2
河南遂平	小麦	13.9	28.5
湖北黄冈	棉花	26.2	36.6
湖北枝江	油菜	14.9	16.5
浙江仙居	柑橘	37.6	25.5
平均值		17.0	22.8

资料来源：李家康、林葆、梁国庆《中国的化肥结构和发展预测》，中国农业科学院土壤肥料研究所。

缓控释肥料具有提高肥料利用率、消除化肥污染和减少农户施肥用工等一系列优点。包括以下几点。

（1）在水中的溶解度小。营养元素在土壤中释放缓慢，可减少营养元素的损失。

（2）施肥可一次完成。缓控释肥养分释放慢，不会因养分释放过快导致土壤盐分过高而"烧苗"。施肥次数的减少可带来成本节约。

（3）可减少化肥用量。由此可减少化肥生产所需的煤、电、天然气等原料，减少生态环境污染等。

中国于20世纪60年代末研制出包膜长效碳酸氢铵，近些年缓释肥的开发应用研究取得实质性进展，研制出的控释肥已达到国外同类产品的质量标准和水平。2015年中国缓控释肥产量为330万吨，90%用于大田作物，5%用于花卉、草坪，5%用于出口。经过十年的发展，中国缓控释肥龙头企业领衔制定了控释肥料的国际标准，提升了中国缓控释肥的国际影响力。

同时需要看到，中国的缓控释肥还存在生产成本较高、产品的国际竞争力较弱等问题。为此，中国需继续进行缓控释肥生产技术的创新和农业推广体系的体制、机制改革，提高缓控释肥产品的国际竞争力，提高农民对缓控释肥产品的认知水平。

二　改进测土配方施肥

在中国，农作物产量的形成有40%~80%的养分来自土壤，但土壤并不是一个取之不尽、用之不竭的"养分库"。为保证土壤有足够的养分供应容量和强度，保持土壤养分的输出与输入平衡，要通过施肥来实现。所谓测土配方施肥是以土壤测试和肥料田间试验为基础，根据作物的养分需求和土壤供肥性能，有针对性地补充作物所需的营养元素，实现各种养分的供需平衡，满足作物的养分需要，达到提高肥料利用率和减少用量和节支目的。

针对过量施肥问题，2005年中央一号文件明确提出，要努力实行科学施肥，搞好"沃土工程"，推广测土配方施肥，增加土壤有机质。农业部在财政部的支持下，于2005年启动了测土配方施肥补贴项目。到2015年，累计投入资金78亿元，推动了科学施肥工作开展。具体包括以下几点。

（1）开展取土化验。十年来各地共采集土壤样品1798万个、分析数据

1.24 亿个，初步摸清了 1857 个项目县（场）14 亿亩 [①] 耕地土壤养分状况。

（2）开展肥效试验。各项目县每年安排 1~2 种主要作物的田间肥效试验和校正试验，累计试验数达到 33 万多个。基本掌握了水稻、小麦、玉米、马铃薯等主要作物需肥规律。

（3）推广测土配方施肥技术。十年来，为指导农民合理施肥，各地制定了区域性肥料配方施肥方案，共发放施肥建议卡 9.2 亿份、组织培训 49.4 万次、现场观摩 13.6 万次。

中国使用测土配方施肥技术产生的社会经济效果可总结如下。

（1）作物产量和农民收入"双增"。根据农户抽样调查，应用测土配方施肥技术，小麦、水稻、玉米亩均增产 3.7%、3.8% 和 5.9%、增收 30 元以上；蔬菜亩均增收 100 元以上。

（2）生产成本和资源消耗"双节"。采用测土配方施肥，每公顷可节约氮肥 19.81~34.65 千克（折纯），减少氮、磷流失 8%~30%。

（3）施肥结构和肥料产业结构"双优"。项目的实施不仅优化了施肥结构，而且初步摸清了氮磷钾肥的需求，引导肥料企业生产配方肥和进行肥料产业结构调整。

（4）施肥水平和化肥利用率"双提"。据抽样调查，测土配方施肥示范区约 70% 的农户采用了测土配方施肥技术，化肥利用率提高了 5 个百分点。

三　水肥一体化技术

水肥一体化技术是将灌溉与施肥融为一体的农业技术。它借助有压力的管道灌溉系统，将可溶性固体肥料或液体肥料配兑成肥液与灌溉水一起，均匀、准确地输送到作物根部土壤。它可以按照作物全生育期的水分和养分需求，把作物所需的水分、养分和微量元素定量、定时，按比例直接提供给作物，作物根系在吸收水分的同时吸收养分，使施入土壤的肥料得到更充分的吸收，进而在节水的同时产生提高肥料利用率和节省施肥用工的效果。

水肥一体化技术主要应用在蔬菜和水果生产中。粮食生产中的水肥一

---

① 约 9330 万公顷。

体化技术有固定式喷水带施肥模式和移动式喷灌施肥模式。固定式施肥模式适合地头有输水管道口的水浇地，喷洒半径较小。移动式施肥模式适合面积较大的田块，喷洒半径较大。中国现有 700 万亩玉米、200 万亩小麦和 100 万亩马铃薯采用水肥一体化技术，累计应用面积为 2500 万亩。监测数据表明，该技术可使氮、磷和钾肥分别减施 20%、10% 和 20%。

四 有机肥替代技术

据测算，每公顷耕地增施 4.5 吨~7.5 吨商品有机肥，可减少 15%~20% 的化肥用量。

由于农业用工价格的快速上升，有机肥的施用方式必须像化肥施用一样方便，方能被农户所接受。谷物生产比较利益较低，而且增施有机肥的谷物和未增施有机肥的谷物的品质差异不易被消费者识别，因而谷物生产目前还不具备大量施用袋装商品性有机肥的条件。蔬菜、水果生产比较利益较高，基本上具备施用袋装商品性有机肥的条件；施用有机肥的蔬菜、水果和施用化肥的蔬菜、水果的品质差异消费者是容易识别的，蔬菜和水果的检测体系要比谷物更为健全，所以在菜地、果园里以有机肥替代过量施用的化肥是有可能的。中国蔬菜、水果的化肥施用量很大，而且面积多达 3500 万公顷，对袋装商品性有机肥会有较大的需求。

一言以蔽之，缓控释肥料、测土配方施肥和水肥一体化三种技术叠加在一起，足以减施 35% 以上的化肥施用量，所以全面推广这些肥料和施肥技术可以基本上消除谷物的过量施肥问题；消除蔬菜过量施肥问题，除了采用更好的施肥技术外，还要采取有机肥替代化肥的措施。当然，谷物生产也应倡导施用有机肥。

五 构建规模化畜禽养殖和有机肥生产于一体的产业链

规模化畜禽养殖污染已经成为中国农业面源污染主要来源之一，而且畜禽养殖总规模和规模化养殖比例都有进一步扩大的趋势，所以环保部门十分重视规模化畜禽养殖场的粪便治理问题。略嫌不足的是，环保部门以末端治理的方式要求每个规模化畜禽养殖场配置畜禽粪便处置装置。养殖污染治理的规模经济显著大于畜禽养殖的规模经济，以畜禽养殖场为单位配置畜禽粪便处置装置，显然是不适宜的。这是现实中畜禽养殖场配置的畜禽粪便处置装置大多没有正常运行的主要原因。更为适宜的做法是在畜禽养殖大县的农区设置畜禽养殖生态产业园区，构建集农业生产、规模化畜禽养殖、有机肥生产、畜禽屠宰加工和基于屠宰加工剩余物的饲料生产于一体的生态产业体系。

规模化畜禽养殖企业集中起来，就可以为有机肥厂提供足够的原料；所有畜禽养殖场的畜禽排泄物都由有机肥厂处置，就解决了单个养殖企业治理畜禽粪便的规模不经济问题；处理过程中产生的沼气可成为养殖场所需的能源，生产的有机肥可供周边农田使用；在相互毗邻的若干个养殖大县里建设一个屠宰加工企业，除了生产主产品外，以屠宰和加工剩余物为原料生产饲料，供养殖场使用；这样就可以实现养殖业污染的零排放。

建设畜禽养殖生态产业园区的关键是制定生态产业园区规划和利益相关者协同机制，确保规模化畜禽养殖场、有机肥厂、畜禽屠宰厂、畜禽产品加工厂、饲料厂和农民组织合作共赢。

根据四川省规模化畜禽养殖粪污染综合利用示范项目的技术要求，按照 1 头猪一年产生 0.1 吨粪便，可生产 0.075 吨有机肥这两个参数计算，建设一个有机肥原料厂或一个有机肥厂分别需要养殖区内有 11 万头和 22 万头猪当量的生产能力。这与浙江萧山的畜禽养殖园区的规模非常接近。一个屠宰加工厂和饲料厂可能需要 3~5 个养殖园区提供支撑。

六 施肥对农产品品质的影响

有机肥的效应。原农业部组织的攻关组对 20 余种农作物的研究表明，施用有机肥能改善农产品品质，如小麦和玉米蛋白质增加 2%~3.5%，面筋增加 1.4%~3.6%，8 种必需氨基酸增加 0.3%~0.48%；大豆脂肪提高 0.56%，亚油酸和油酸分别增加 0.31% 和 0.92%；叶菜硝酸盐含量降低 33%~35.5%。

氮肥的效应。研究表明，甜瓜单施氮肥，果实甜度下降，硝酸盐含量增加。施氮肥过量，会影响果实色泽，延迟成熟并使成熟期参差不齐。

磷肥的效应。试验表明，芥菜型油菜极端缺磷时，含油量从 33% 降低到 23%。

钾肥的效应。施钾不仅能增加小麦千粒重，还能改善面粉的烘烤性状。

微肥的作用。适度增施锰肥，可提高农产品中维生素的含量。食物和饲料中的含锰量和含钼量是农产品的一种重要质量标准。

第三节　消除农药过量施用的措施

减少农药的过量使用有助于提高农产品的质量和安全性，保护农业生态环境，增加农民收入。中国从 20 世纪 90 年代末开始实施关于减少农药使用的政策。1997 年，中国颁布了《农药管理条例》和《农药管理条例实施办法》。根据国际经验，规范农药市场管理和使用标准是减少农药使用量最关键的措施。我们建议主要采用以下六项措施，以减少农药使用量，提高农药的使用效率。

一　改进施药技术

Hubbell 的研究表明，在保证防治效果的前提下，采用静电喷雾、循环喷雾等先进施药器械可以减少农药用量，减少幅度可以达到 50%~95%。

二　适度提高农药价格

农药价格与农药用量呈负相关，调整补贴农药生产和施用政策，消除农药价格扭曲，可产生抑制农药用量的效应。

三　发展绿色环保农药

发展绿色环保的农药制剂，开展低毒生物农药示范补助试点，补助农民因采用低毒生物农药而增加的用药支出，鼓励和带动低毒生物农药的推广应用，借助生物技术对病虫害进行防治，以减少化学农药用量。

四 加强宣传和培训

国内最新的研究已经证明，许多农民对农药过度使用并不敏感。此外，如果使用或管理不当，农药对使用者、使用者的家庭、贸易和环境带来危险。因此，显然需要提高农民对农药使用危险的认识，并在安全使用农药和熟练使用农药方面接受适当的、最新的培训。在许多发达国家，农业、园艺和林业上农药的使用需要相应的"能力证书"（英国）或"认证"（EPA-USA）。

农民的培训内容一般包括：法律法规、与杀虫剂使用有关的风险（特别是对环境的影响）；使用农药可能导致的风险；安全的工作实践（例如传粉媒介的保护）；应用参数；安全培训；农药洒出后的紧急处理措施；农药中毒后的紧急处理措施；遭遇火灾或其他事件的紧急行动；农药处置和储存规则；农药施用设备等。在中国的绿色农民培训计划下，沃尔玛（中国）等已开展了此类培训，但规模较为有限。

五 扩大粮食生产保险范围

进一步提高中央、省级财政对主要粮食作物保险的保费补贴比例，不断提高稻子、小麦、玉米三大粮食品种保险的覆盖面和风险保障水平；有条件的市县也应提供保费补贴，中央财政通过以奖代补等方式予以支持。

六 扩大农户经营规模

要抓住越来越多的农户不愿从事超小规模农业的有利时机，促进土地流转，逐步扩大农户的经营规模，以提高农药施用的精准性，进而减少农药施用量。

第四节 消除水资源过度耗用的措施

一 概述

地下水的库容量要比地表水的库容量大得多，它类似于一笔数额巨大的"存款"。对于这笔能为人类应对气候变化带来的风险发挥举足轻重作用的"存款",绝不能随意地将其挥霍殆尽。具体地说,就是枯水年抽取,平水年不变,丰水年补给,使其维持动态平衡。其实,地下水位下降是最近几十年出现的新问题。例如目前地下水开采最严重的华北平原,农民原来用地表水灌溉,由于地下水位很高,存在内涝和盐碱化问题。随着用水量的增大和地表水灌溉系统的损坏,农户开始抽取地下水。地下水位下降会带来两个问题:第一,抽水成本越来越高,可抽水量越来越少;第二,造成一系列严重后果,包括湿地消失、河流枯竭、地面沉降和海水入侵等。地面沉降会对建在地面和地下的基础设施造成破坏,例如输水管道破裂、甚至轨道高低不平造成火车脱轨;超采会引起海水入侵,使入侵区内的地下水变成无法用于灌溉或饮用的咸水。更为严重的是,一旦地下水抽完了,粮食产量就难以维持了。

为了保障地下水资源可持续利用,必须采取农业用水的科学调控、种植结构的优化调整、节水技术的广泛应用和节水制度的构建完善等一系列措施。

二 农业用水的科学调控

消除地下水资源过量使用,需要采取一系列措施。包括:①扩大低耗水粮食作物的播种面积,以降低粮食生产对水资源的需求;②扩大同区域内降水匹配更好的粮食作物的播种面积,以降低粮食生产对地下水资源的需求;③改进灌溉方式,以提高水资源利用效率;④加强区域内水利基础设施建设,把区域内的地表水充分利用起来;⑤加强区域间水利基础设施建设,通过跨区域调水,增加水资源供给;⑥严格实施地下水利用制度,把地下水抽取量控制在可持续利用的范围内。

改进灌溉方式。在中国粮食主产区,粗放的灌溉方式仍然占据较大比重,采用这种灌溉方式泡田时间较长,水分蒸发较多,灌溉用水效率较低,甚至会导致耕地板结或返碱。所以,推广节水灌溉技术、减少蒸腾技术、生物节水技术等,对于解决地下水超采问题具有重大的现实意义。

节水灌溉技术。有关研究表明,将大水淹灌转变为小畦低压管道输水灌溉，减少的输水损失相当于节水 30%，地面不平整的耕地采用喷灌技术，以提高灌水均匀度，可使深层渗漏水量减少 30%~50%。

减少蒸腾技术。中国北部粮食主产区的许多地方的水分蒸发量大于1100毫米，如果春季和夏季采用农田覆盖技术，减少的无效蒸发量可达到作物总耗水量的 28%~46%。农田覆盖技术包括地膜覆盖和秸秆覆盖等方式。它的实质是在农田表面设置一层微透气的地膜，抑制土地水分蒸发进入大气，从而强化土壤—作物小系统水分小循环，降低无效蒸发量。地膜上凝结的露珠可以阻隔长波通过，将因水分蒸发而带走的潜热保存下来，并向膜下输送，使地温升高，有利作物生长。采用这类技术，可比常规灌溉节水 25%~42%。

培肥土壤技术。具体措施包括：增施有机肥、种植绿肥、秸秆还田和合理施用化肥，以提高肥力水平，改善土壤物理结构，提高土壤蓄水、节水、保水和供水能力。通过平衡施肥提高土壤水分利用率，提高幅度可达28%~49%。

生物节水技术。所谓生物节水是指利用生物体自身的生理和基因潜力，进行高耐旱超级种的培育及产业化，提高植物水分利用效率，从而在同等水供应条件下获得更多的粮食产量。生物节水有遗传改良、群体适应和生理调控三个途径。遗传改良就是培育抗旱节水品种，这是生物节水的基本路径。群体适应是根据作物的需水特性和耗水规律优化配置水资源，达到节水不减产的目标。生理调控是按照适度水分亏缺可产生补偿效应的原理，建立非充分灌溉制度。研究表明，通过生物节水技术，优化调控光合速率和蒸腾速率，可提高作物的抗旱性和节水 30% 以上。

三　调整粮食作物结构

中国粮食主产区都是耕地资源丰富、水资源条件相对较好的地区。即使是位于北方的粮食主省，其降雨量也足以生产一季粮食。例如河南省和河北省，种植玉米几乎不需要灌溉，冬小麦在缺水的季节生长，不得不抽取地下水。为了缓解地下水超采的严峻趋势，必须实行"一季休耕、一季雨养"模式，将小麦、玉米一年两熟制改为一年一熟制，或将高耗水作物小麦改为低耗水作物马铃薯,以保持粮食产量水平,并减少地下水需求量,既达到逐步恢复提高地力的"藏粮于地"的目标,又解决化肥农药过量使用、地表沉降、海水入侵等一系列问题。

四 发展规模经营和合作经营

农业经营规模越小,农业收入的作用越有限,农户对农业的重视程度就越低。所以,农业经营达到一定规模是实现精准灌溉的必要条件。调查表明,大农场的用水效率显著高于小农场。中国的农业正在向适度经营规模的方向过渡,但尚有租赁期短和租金过高等问题需要解决。中国农村的一些地表水灌溉系统在实施了农户联产承包责任制之后逐渐衰败的现象表明,地表水灌溉体系的有效运转需要基于社区和跨社区的农户合作做支撑。近些年,中国的农业正在恢复合作经营,但真正做得好的并不多。现在最需要做的工作是认真研究成功的合作案例,并将它们凝练成可复制性强的经验加以推广。

五 建立水权交易市场

一些学者认为,过量抽取地下水的主要原因是水费太低或没有收取水费,可以采取提高水费的办法来解决地下水过量抽取问题。然而,以提高水费这种人为恶化粮食生产条件的做法来解决地下水过量抽取问题并不是最适宜的办法,也难以得到农户的支持。其实,农民抽取地下水是要花钱的,从图4-1可以看出,2005年,河北省平均每亩耕地的灌溉费用为55元,是全国平均水平的2倍多。为了降低灌溉支出,他们会尽可能地少抽取地下水,更不会故意浪费水。

更为适宜的做法是在明确界定农民用水权的基础上开展水权交易,让农民拥有更多的选择。具体地说,农民拥有的水权的收益既可以通过种粮得到,也可以通过让渡得到。农户的用水权多少用于种粮、多少用于交易,取决于粮食价格和水权价格的比较。政府和非政府组织的责任是按市场上的水权价格购买同过量使用的地下水相对应的水权,如此,水资源利用效率更高,进而出价更高的产业部门也以这种方式获得水权。这种由市场机制决定水资源使用权（水权）价格的做法，与由政府运用行政管理权限提高水资源价格的做法相比，由于它未对农民造成任何伤害，所以会得到农民的普遍支持。换言之，以政府阐述农户使用水资源必须足额付费的道理，并测算水资源价格的策略来解决地下水过量使用问题，看似最为简单，实际上缺乏可操作性。

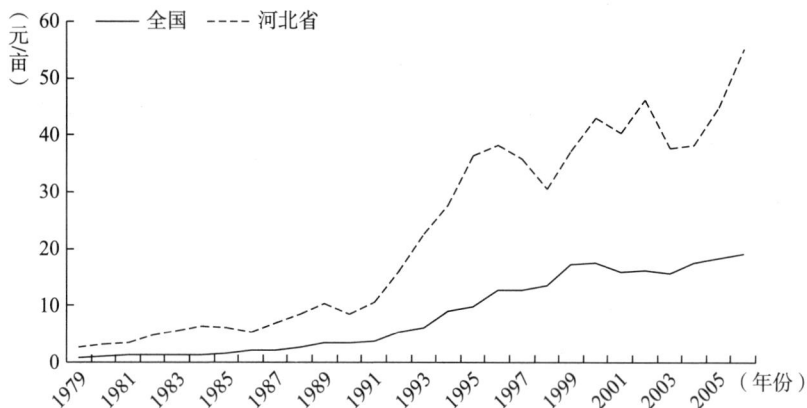

图4-1　河北省和全国小麦亩均灌溉费用的变化

最重要的是，中国已经基本具备了开展水权交易的条件。近些年，中国的地下水管理正在采用"一井一表、一户一卡"的计量模式，即每眼机井都安装一个智能水表，每个农户都按照其拥有的水权去水务局买水，得到一个IC卡，IC卡插入智能水表就开始抽水，并根据取水量扣除卡上的水量，卡上水量用完了就无法取水了。为推广这种模式，由国家投资改造机井，目前山东的42万眼机井和河南的38万眼机井都具备了采用该模式的条件。

地下水抽取需要用电，一度电可以抽取多少地下水，可以通过抽水试验获得，并由此确定不同地下水位的水电转换系数，然后以实名购电方式将对应于水权量的抽水电量卖给农户。只要用电量控制住了，地下水抽取量控制住了。农户IC卡上的剩余电量与水电转换系数相乘，就得到其可交易的水权量。农户愿意少抽取多少地下水，政府希望少抽多少地下水，都取决于水权交易价格。这样，解决过量抽取地下水的问题的关键——水权价格就会在重复博弈中形成，政府购买农户水权所需的财政资金就会通过水权交易获得确切的依据。采用这种方式解决地下水过度开采的另一个好处是政府不再需要建立水费收取系统。当然，这里还有生态安全和粮食安全的协调问题。

六　加强水资源管理

在水资源管理技术方面，主要包括以下四条建议。

加强水资源利用规划。在水资源规划中，要像划定 18 亿亩耕地红线那样划定地下水资源红线来保护粮食安全，不仅要有制止地下水位下降的措施，还要有逐步恢复地下水位的措施。通过严格的规划管理和用水定额管理，引导各地开展粮食作物种植结构调整，把制止地下水位下降的目标落到实处，通过一系列生态文明建设重大项目的实施，将地下水位恢复的目标落到实处。

完善水资源法律法规。加强调查研究，切实了解立法需求，增强立法的针对性和预见性；分析拟定法律制度的必要性、合理性和可行性；加强立法协调，维护法治统一；健全法律法规定期清理制度，切实解决法律规范之间的矛盾和冲突。健全执法队伍责任制，强化水资源保护的法律责任；增强依法行政观念，加强规划实施的监督管理，完善水事纠纷调解机制和应对突发性水事纠纷的机制。加强能力建设，加大执法力度。提高执法水平，提高现场执法能力和应对突发性水事纠纷的能力。

改进水资源管理政策。水资源状况是衡量一个国家可持续发展能力的重要指标。为了不断改善水资源状况，实现水资源可持续利用，必须探索有利于水资源合理开发、优化配置、高效利用、全面节约、有效保护和综合治理的体制和机制；建立水资源供给与高效利用体系和水生态系统安全保障体系；健全群众参与、专家咨询和政府决策相结合的机制，保障水资源管理决策的科学化、民主化。

开展宣传教育。以灵活多样、群众喜闻乐见的方式开展水资源利用教育和宣传活动，提高农民的水法规意识、水资源紧缺的忧患意识、节水意识和水环境保护意识，增强农民保护水资源的主动性，使之形成依法取用、有偿使用的理念，放弃私自兴建水工程等不当行为。

现实中，人们对空气污染的严重程度马上能感觉到，而对地下水位下降的严重程度很难察觉到,所以要在村庄安装表达水位的显示器,让村民们看到地下水位距离红线还有多远。以引导他们在发展节水农业、提高地下水涵养能力等方面开展合作,采取共同的行动。

第五节 改善森林管理的措施

一 造林管理要求

在退耕还林工程中建立的经典人工林模型存在的主要问题有:生态和结构稳定性缺乏;灵活性有限;无法应对自然和人为干扰,特别是气候变化的影响。这些问题的出现促使林业专家更积极地寻找其他可替代的森林管理办法。除了提供传统的木材之外,现在的林业已可以提供更多其他方面的价值,尤其是在环境保护、生态系统保护、生物多样性保护方面,而挖掘林业的娱乐和社会价值,也逐渐成为主要的政策目标。因此,除了木材生产带来的经济效益,许多发达国家还逐步考虑林业的生态和社会参数,以提高森林的多用途功能。

由于这些原因,新的森林管理战略已经超越了单纯的造林,还需要找到可带有"自然"和"生态"的造林方法。这些造林方法试图模仿森林管理中的自然过程,最大限度地减少干扰,例如非本地植物、昆虫、病原体、野生动物的入侵,气候变化的影响和/或无法避免的人为影响。Silva 教授在2012 年倡导的这种方法可以概括为"基于自然的人工造林"或"近自然森林管理"或"近自然造林(CNS)"。近自然森林管理(或接近自然的森林培育)的基础是将天然森林生态系统的结构特征和功能特征纳入可持续森林管理原则,即整合再造过程,以增强天然林的结构层次。

专栏:近自然造林原则

近自然造林(CNS)的概念起源于中欧和东欧,自 19 世纪后期以来,森林循环模式已得到成功应用,重点是可持续的木材生产。

20世纪80年代，出现了新的林业范例，即与以前的造林方法相比，其被视为"近自然"的造林体系，更强调森林生态系统价值的潜力，例如，生物多样性规模的扩大，更传统的林业产品。这种造林方法包括单一树种选择模型，例如德国的Dauernwald概念（Möller，1922），瑞士的Plenterwald模式（Biollet，1920）；组合选择模型，例如德国和瑞士的间伐模型或Femelschlag；不规则的防护林模型。这些方法的一个共同特点是：虽然被认为是人为的手段，却更符合不断变化的社会目标，同时解决了树龄结构单一的问题，有更明确的采伐系统、增强了树种的多样性以及不同的树龄结构。

近自然造林是指将森林视为执行多功能生态系统的管理方法。近自然造林（CNS）试图通过最少的人为干预来实现管理目标。换句话说，近自然造林被广泛认为是一种在小空间尺度上优化森林多功能的方法，其特别关注以下几点：

i. 通过保持永久性森林气候和避免砍伐森林，为自然再生创造最佳条件；

ii. 推广乡土树种或者已经适应当地气候环境的树种；

iii. 选用适应当地的树种，营造不均匀的混合林分（多样化垂直和水平森林结构），提高稳定性和风险多样化（恢复力）；

iv. 及时适度地疏伐；

v. 保护森林生物之间的自然平衡，包括害虫，以促进生物多样性，避免使用农药；

vi. 避免明显皆伐。

但是，近自然造林并不存在一种特定的方案。它需要结合多种造林原则，需要考虑不同的土壤条件，即土壤养分、结构、孔隙度、水分、地形、气候和树种等。

与近自然造林相比，传统的造林方法会导致林分不太稳固。一般是以短轮伐期为重点的造林方法，其弱点在于忽略了森林在生态、社会和文化方面的功能，缺乏综合性和灵活性。近自然造林能够实现不同的管理目标，因为它允许在过程中逐步调整管理实践，以应对不断变化的社会目标和愿望。

表4-2总结了传统造林，基于自然的造林和严格的自然保护方法之间的差异，说明了传统造林方法主要只侧重于短期轮伐，而忽视了森林的生态和社会价值。[①] 此外，传统造林方法通常会导致林分不太稳固。相比之下，基于自然的造林方法，其综合能力和灵活性可以实现不同的管理目标，包括木材生产，这就解释了为什么基于自然的造林被作为可持续森林管理方法，在很多的发达国家被采用。此外，由于其是以自然为基础的方法，具有灵活性，森林管理者可以在管理过程中不断地逐步调整，以应对不断变化的社会目标和愿望。

表4-2 不同的森林管理方法及其各自可实现的管理目标

管理方法	传统造林方式	基于自然造林方法	严格的自然保护方法
具体管理目标	专注木材生产和直接经济成果	灵活的木材生产、自然保护和娱乐功能	遵循自然结构和过程，严格的森林保护
木材生产	5	4	1
长期经济成果	3	5	1
短期经济成果	5	3	1
生产优质木材	4	4	1
生态系统完整性	1	4	5
生物多样性保护	1	3	5
美观	1	5	5
景观整合	2	4	5
公共娱乐空间	2	4	2
对气候变化适应力	1	4	5
灵活改变目标	1	5	1

注：评分为1~5，1为目标实现最低；5为目标实现最高。

资料来源：Jørgen Bo Larsen, *Close to Nature Forest Management: The Danish Approach to Sustainable Forestry*, University of Copenhagen, Denmark, Sustainable Forest Management - Current Research, 2012, https://www.intechopen.com/chapters/36975.

[①] Jørgen Bo Larsen, *Close to Nature Forest Management: The Danish Approach to Sustainable Forestry*, University of Copenhagen, Denmark, 2012, https://www.intechopen.com/chapters/36975.

二　提高人工林的适应能力

以下的六种管理原则和人工林实践是被人们普遍认识到的，可以提高森林的适应能力，并提高其对气候变化的适应能力的原则。以下排列不分优先顺序，因为这些原则取决于已有森林的类型、状态、过往管理历史和适应能力。

增加树种丰富度。有强有力的证据表明，混合林分比单一林分对与气候相关的干扰（例如干旱或风暴）更具抵抗力，并且一旦发生干扰，抵抗干扰的能力也更具弹性。

增加树龄丰富性，增加结构多样性，以提高对生物（例如害虫）和物理干扰（例如风、火）等因素的总体抵抗力。结构多样性可以通过不均匀的造林体系（单一树种选择）实现，营造不规则的林分结构。通常增加林分结构的多样性（例如林下种植）、增加树种丰富度，以创建结构多样化的混合林分。

增加树种内遗传变异。树种内遗传变异的增加主要包括利用当地已适应的物种或其他种源的树种丰富现有种群，例如，已适应温暖气候和／或较干燥气候的品种。

增加人工林在生物和物理等各方面压力的抵抗力。对树顶进行修枝，去除顶端优势，增加根部的土壤体积，尽量修剪成分枝状结构，以便树能长成大冠状。

去除已被暴风雨、林火或害虫等破坏或颇具风险的林分，将老化的林分砍伐并更换成更具抵抗力的林分，或多层次树龄的林分。

保持低平均蓄积量。高的蓄积量通常与损害易感性成相关性。可根据当地的风险情况，通过增加或减少疏伐来调整蓄积量。但是，降低蓄积量会影响碳封存量，弱化其在碳中和中的作用。

第六节　改善耕地生态安全的措施

一　建立耕地质量调查体系

耕地的生产力受它所在空间位置、气候、复种指数、投入等一系列因素的影响,根据耕地全年农作物产量的差别把耕地划分为15个质量等别[①] 的单个指标评价方式,具有很大的局限性。要掌握耕地质量的动态变化,必须构建耕地质量调查体系,定期开展耕地土壤详查,弄清耕地土壤质量变化,以及它们对农产品产量和质量的影响。同时,建立包括耕地地形、地块面积、土壤、基础设施等信息在内的数据库和数据分析方法体系的耕地质量综合评价体系,对耕地质量的变化做出评价,并提出应对策略建议。

专栏:中国在耕地质量调查方面的经验

1999~2014 年,国土资源部共完成土地地球化学调查面积15070 万公顷,其中耕地调查面积9240 万公顷,占全国耕地总面积的68%。已完成调查区域内:

重金属超标耕地面积232.5 万公顷;

轻微—轻度污染或超标耕地526.6 万公顷;

局部地区土壤有机质下降;

北方土壤有碱化趋势,南方土壤有酸化趋势。

2012 年,农业部启动了农产品产地土壤重金属污染调查,调查面积10820 万公顷。

农业部发布的《2016 年全国耕地质量监测报告》指出,这次调查的国家监测点已由357 个增加到850 个,涵盖43 个主要耕地土类,增加年度监测数据2 万余个。调查结果显示:全国有65.5%的监测点耕层厚度较浅,少于适宜作物生长的耕层厚度(20cm);有25.9%的监测点土壤容重大于适宜作物生长的标准,土壤孔隙少、孔隙度小,板结现象较为严重。全国耕地土壤有机质、全氮、有效磷和速效钾养分含量整体提升;中量元素和部分微量元素含量水平较低;区域性土壤酸化现象日益显现。

经过持续 15 年的调查和对 60 余万件土、水、生物等样品的

---

① 2016 年全国耕地质量等别(全国耕地分为15 个等别,1 等质量最好,15 等最差)的评价结果表明。全国耕地平均质量等别为9.96 等,与2014 年末的9.96 等持平。耕地等别按周年产量评价。

54种元素指标的高精度测试，获得了3000余万个数据，建立了全国和31个省（区、市）土地地球化学动态数据库，对中国耕地的地球化学总体状况形成了初步认识和基本判断。

二　制定耕地安全管护制度和标准

耕地是人类赖以生存和发展的基础，事关国家的粮食安全、农业稳定和可持续发展。耕地安全保护包括以下几个方面。

耕地数量保护。实行基本农田保护制度，严格控制把耕地转为非耕地；实行耕地占补平衡制度，促进土地开发和废弃地的复垦；规范耕地流转行为，防止"非粮化"、禁止"非农化"；从而严守18亿亩耕地红线。

耕地质量保护。采用耕地质量保护措施，防止耕地水土流失和耕地沙化、盐碱化、贫瘠化等问题；采取耕地修复措施，解决耕地污染和耕层变薄等问题。

耕地利用保护。制定和实施化学、农药用量和农膜标准，灌溉水质和地下水抽取量标准等，消除化肥、农药施用过量、农膜过薄、污水灌溉造成的耕地不安全和地下水枯竭造成的耕地不安全。

实行耕地保护目标责任制。耕地保护的目标、任务、措施和责任要落实到各级人民政府、行政管理部门、农业企业、农村社区领导人和农户身上，运用目标化、定量化、制度化管理方法和追责机制，规范这些责任主体的耕地保护行为。

要想从法律和政策体系层面采取措施，实现耕地安全保护的话，则要做到以下几点。

完善耕地保护法律体系。国家现有的有关土地管理、农村土地承包和环保的法律法规，都涉及保护和合理利用农地的条款，但各有侧重、操作性不强。国家应以这些法律中的有关条款为基础制定有关耕地的保护法，形成以耕地保护法为核心，与土地管理法、农村土地承包法、环境保护法有机衔接、相互补充的耕地保护法律体系。引导政府、企业和农户依法规范保护耕地。

制定耕地保护条例。以法规的力量强制各行政区按照 18 亿亩耕地红线和土地用途管控的要求，把 80% 以上的耕地划为基本农田，优先将优质耕地，特别是位于城镇郊区、交通沿线易被占用的优质耕地划为永久基本农田，以乡镇为基本单位划定基本农田保护区，使 18 亿亩耕地红线由数量红线拓展为质量红线。

完善耕地质量标准和政策体系。制定耕地质量等级和耕地土壤环境标准，开展耕地评价和耕地占补平衡验收工作；完善耕地土壤监测评估、风险管控和治理修复技术的规范；修订肥料、饲料、灌溉用水中有毒有害物质限量和农用污泥中污染物控制标准，制订可降解农用地膜标准，修订农用地膜、农药包装标准；分类研制一批耕地土壤标准样品。

加强农田防护林和林粮间作对生态安全的影响。历史已经证明，农田和农业景观层面的农田防护林和林粮间作有利于改善生态环境，从而有利于提高农业生产力，特别是有利于改善微气候，保护农田免受由气候变化引起的相关异常天气现象和水土流失带来的影响，加强土壤养分循环、碳封存、生物多样性，生产价值更高的产品，如木材、食品、饲料、药用植物、精油以及用于当地工业的材料。实际上，目前农田防护林存在严重退化的情况，如果不能修复，可能会导致生态系统服务发生灾难性变化。由于大多数农田防护林体系是在农场和 / 或农业景观层面开发的，由于目前农业、林业、环境保护等部门的跨部门协调存在障碍，无法得到很好的沟通。这就意味着跨部门政策和机构协调仍然是一个亟待改进的问题。

三 编制耕地污染防治行动计划

中华人民共和国成立后的前 50 年，中国经济发展总体呈粗放式发展，产业结构不尽合理，污染物排放较多，耕地作为污染物最终受体之一，受到严重影响。实施耕地污染防治行动是消除这些影响的重大举措。

编制行动计划。国务院 2016 年发布了《土壤污染防治行动计划》。该计划的目标是，到 2020 年，受污染耕地安全利用率达到 90% 左右，污染地块安全利用率达到 90% 以上；到 2030 年，受污染耕地安全利用率达到 95% 以上，污染地块安全利用率达到 95% 以上。我国 13 个粮食主产省份也分别制定了本省（区、市）的《土壤污染防治行动计划》。

分类管控、综合施策。耕地污染防治应以保障耕地安全、农产品安全和人居环境安全为出发点，以保护和改善耕地质量为核心，采取分类管控、综合施策的策略。根据污染程度将农地分为三类，分别实施优先保护、安全利用和严格管控等措施，对未污染的、已污染的土壤，分别提出保护、管控和修复等措施。

建立政府主导、企业担责、公众参与、社会监督的耕地污染防治体系。耕地是人类赖以生存的基础，耕地安全是人人都应该关注的事情。所以既要充分发挥法治建设、科技支撑、改革创新和市场引导的作用，又要动员全社会力量参与、齐抓共管、发挥企业和公众参与的作用。需要指出的是，近年来，随着国家不断加大对耕地土壤修复的扶持力度，土壤修复产业规模正逐年扩大，市场机制在推动耕地土壤修复产业发展中的作用也越来越大。

四 实施耕地修复改良工程

实施耕地修复改良工程，是扭转耕地退化趋势的重大举措。总体目标是"两提一改"。其中，"两提"是指通过建设高标准农田，提高耕地基础地力 0.5 个等级，土壤有机质含量 0.5 个百分点。"一改"是指通过改良酸化、盐渍化等障碍性土壤，改善土壤性状，改善耕地质量。

制定耕地修复改良实施方案。耕地修复改良可分为调查评估、可行性研究和方案设计、工程施工、工程验收等阶段。调查评估包括污染物识别，污染程度和范围确定，污染风险评估，修复目标值制定等；可行性研究和方案设计包括修复技术筛选、工艺参数确定、工程量估算、可行性论证、施工图设计、环境管理计划等；工程施工是按方案设计组织现场施工和工程建设等；工程验收是对修复工程效果进行监测评估。在典型地区组织开展土壤污染治理试点示范，逐步建立土壤污染治理修复技术体系，有计划、分步骤地推进土壤污染治理修复。

启动耕地土壤污染治理与修复试点项目。项目区应采取控制水土流失、增加有机质含量、肥力培育等一系列措施，目标是 2020 年使试点项目区的耕地力提高 0.5 个等级以上，土壤有机质含量提高 0.5 个百分点，耕作层的厚度达到要求。

推广综合技术体系。具体包括保护性耕作,深松和精准施肥,控制化肥、农药用量等措施,以控制和消除重金属和有机物污染对耕地的负面影响。

五 完善耕地修复技术体系

耕地修复可采用物理、化学和生物和农艺等措施,具体包括以下四种措施。

物理修复措施。它是指通过各种物理过程去除或分离土壤中污染物的技术。包括客土法、热脱附、土壤气相抽提、机械通风等。它的优点是修复效率高、速度快,缺点是成本偏高。

化学修复措施。它是利用化学药剂的吸附、沉淀和络合等作用,去除或降低土壤中污染物的生物有效性或毒性,降低耕地的污染风险。它的优点是修复效率较高、速度较快,缺点是添加的化学药剂有可能产生二次污染。

生物修复技术。包括植物修复技术、微生物修复技术和生物联合修复技术。它是利用生物特有的吸收或分解有毒有害物质的能力,降低或去除土壤中污染物,逐步恢复耕地生产安全农产品的功能。主要措施是调整种植结构和退耕还林还草等。它的优点是不破坏土壤有机质和土壤结构、成本低,缺点是修复周期长。

农艺调控措施。它是指通过免耕少耕、深松、科学管理水分、施用功能性肥料等措施调节土壤理化性状,减轻农用地的污染风险。

后两种方法的投入较低、操作简便、适宜用来修复大面积和中、低浓度重金属污染土壤。

六 实施轮作休耕制度

实行轮作休耕制度,不仅是应对土层变薄、耕作层变浅、土壤酸化、退化、重金属超标,面源污染加重等造成耕地质量下降的举措,也是保护耕地安全和保障长期粮食安全,加快现代农业转型,促进中国农业可持续发展的举措。所以轮作休耕制度不仅在适度发展区和保护发展区要被采用,而且优化发展区也要被采用。

轮作是寓养于用的耕作方式，既保养地力，又不太影响粮食产量。稻麦轮作实验表明，连续 5 季 75% 秸秆还田可显著提高土壤有机碳含量，提高土壤速效磷含量和土壤肥力，恢复和培育土壤微生物群落，构建养分健康循环通道，改善土壤通透性，有效阻止土壤次生潜育和土壤酸化，促进中国耕地永续利用。①

实施轮作休耕制度，减少耕种面积或复种指数，逐步恢复提高地力，是实施"藏粮于地"战略的基本举措。中国粮食生产能力已经稳定在 6 亿吨水平上，而且粮食储备充裕，世界粮食供需状况也很好，它们为中国实施轮作休耕制度提供了一系列有利条件。实施轮作休耕制度不仅可以降低耕地污染水平，恢复、提高地力和改善农业生态环境，提高中国农产品的国际竞争力，而且还将促进中国农业补贴政策从"黄箱"政策转为"绿箱"政策。②

休耕涉及降低耕地复种指数、减少短期耕地种植面积和长期耕地种植面积（如退耕还林、还草），会影响粮食产量，所以休耕要处理好近期粮食安全和长期粮食安全的关系，农民短期利益和长期利益的关系；休耕既要发挥政府的作用，制定适宜的耕地休耕补偿标准，确保农户利益不受损失；又要发挥市场机制的作用，引导农民拓宽就业渠道，优化种植结构；还要发挥法律法规和问责机制的作用。休耕的重点区是地下水漏斗区、重金属污染区和土层过薄区。

七　加强农田防护林的生态效应

根据以往的经验，农林复合经营可以带来各种不可估量的益处。但是，当前农田防护林存在严重退化的现状，而引导农民重新在农田中植树以改

---

① 徐蒋来等：《连续秸秆还田对稻麦轮作农田土壤养分及碳库的影响》，《土壤》2016 年第 1 期。
② "黄箱"政策是对生产和贸易产生扭曲的政策。主要包括：农产品价格补贴，农产品营销贷款补贴，耕地面积补贴，牲畜数量补贴，种子、肥料、灌溉等投入品补贴，部分有补贴的贷款项目等，是必须逐步削减的政策。
　　"绿箱"政策是对生产和贸易不产生扭曲或仅有很微小的扭曲的政策。主要包括：农业研发和环境保护；农业病虫害防治，如自然灾害预报服务、检疫和抗灾行动等；农业科技人员和农民培训，含培训教育设施建设；农业技术推广和咨询服务；农产品卫生、安全检验服务；农产品市场信息、营销咨询及促销服务；农业基础设施建设；农业生产结构调整性补贴等。

善农田防护林的主要障碍有两点：①农田防护林的作用尚未成为社会共识；②农田防护林的维护和发展尚未成为农民的自觉行动。

根据欧盟共同农业政策（2014—2020），农林复合经营系统具有的下述功能，能帮助欧洲在2020年实现智慧型、可持续和包容性增长农业发展战略目标：

- 促进生物质的生产；
- 通过增加渗透能力和减缓硝酸盐淋溶速度改善水质；
- 改善土壤质量和肥力；
- 有助于恢复因过量施用矿物肥料、农药和除草剂而导致退化的农田生产潜力；
- 通过枯枝落叶的永久覆盖防治水土流失；
- 通过森林防护降低水分蒸发以适应和减轻气候变化的影响；
- 固碳功能；
- 对生物多样性产生积极的影响。

中国粮食主产区的主体是农业而不是林业。农田防护林体系建设必须服从这个大局，把国家和农民要做的事情做好，而不是让国家和农民为林业部门保持和提升地位出资出力。为了满足国家粮食安全战略需求和农民收入，农田防护林体系规划必须遵循以下两个原则。

第一，农田防护林为粮食生产提供的保障最优化。农田防护林的主要功能是保障国家粮食安全，而不是林业产出最大化。林带林网为粮食生产提供的保障最优化，是指它的防护效益带来的边际产量和占地、胁地造成的边际损失达到平衡。

第二，农田防护林应做到占地、胁地最小化。从这个意义上讲，林带林网既要防止过疏，又要防止过密，不能以林带林网减产一条线、增产一大片为理由占用更多的农地。

基于上述两个原则，农田防护林有望提高粮食主产区的粮食生产力和生态安全。根据过去的成功经验，我们将农田防护林体系（防风林、防护林带）主要划分为以下四层。

第一层防护体系主要是山地森林，尤其是退耕地上的森林。

第二层防护体系主要包括道路林带,即高速公路、高速铁路、省道、市道、县道和乡道的道路林带建设。

第三层防护体系主要包括村庄林。目前大部分的村庄都有专门的地方用于种植经济林、用材林或者是用作休闲或景观作用的景观林。

第四层防护体系主要包括沿农田边界或机耕道两侧、沟渠边的防护林。进入 21 世纪后,国家对粮食安全越来越重视,粮食主产区的农地整理项目的规模越来越大,标准越来越高。项目内容包括平整土地、打井修渠、田间通路通电和路边、渠边、沟边种树等。

在过去几十年中,粮食主产区粮食产量的持续增长可以用以下三个原因来解释:①品种的改良;②肥料和粮食价格支持政策;③农田防护林(上文中提到的四层防护林体系)。在这些措施成功实施的基础上,粮食主产区未来的农田防护林体系发展应进一步遵守以下原则。

从小网格到大网格转变。尽量减少农田防护林由于根系或树荫给农业生产带来的不良后果,尤其不能影响农业机械下地作业。

从对称性到非对称性转变。过去,农田防护林通常是小网格型的,在实施过程中,存在妨碍灌溉和机械作业的现象,而且林带胁地还造成农作物产量损失,此外没有任何林木收入的农民也有不满。因此,建议尽可能将农田防护林优先配置在道路、沟渠两侧,尽量不配置在农田边上。

从单一树种到多树种转变。首先,用多树种代替单一树种,最好是乔灌草相结合,以增加生物多样性和改善景观。其次,选择树干较低、树冠较小的树种,以减少树木胁地带来的作物产量损失。最后,提高管理的灵活性,使农民的收入更多元化。

从自成体系到融入体系转变。为了避免树木对基础设施带来的负面影响,例如对灌溉设施、道路和沟渠维护等的负面影响。农区防护林配置要由自成体系调整为农地整治体系的组成部分,实现部门内工作自治到部门间工作互治的转变。

因此,在维持和进一步发展农田防护林、适当的林粮间作,特别是提高已退化和 / 或污染农田的土壤肥力等方面,政府必须有明确的政策和保障条件。创新治理体系时要考虑到农田防护林(以及林粮间作)的多功能性以及跨部门的协调需求。要鼓励农民的充分参与,这对于维护现有的农田防护林及其进一步发展至关重要,这种创新治理体系应包括财政激励措施(如环境服务付费或生态补偿),或通过贷款或赠款提供资金上的支持,以用于支付维护和发展农田防护林的成本,以实现其在生态安全方面的作用。还要进一步澄清和明确林权(树权)、农田防护林管护的规定,尤其是那些沿着道路、沟渠等基础设施栽种的树木。此外,制定政策时要充分考虑到农民的参与性,这是政策能被广大农民认同的先决条件。

最后,要提高粮食主产区农户在农田防护林和林粮间作的参与性,至少要考虑社会、经济、政策和机构等方面,具体包括以下几点。

经济上的理由。农民以及有关机构的推广人员必须了解农田防护林和林粮间作能带来的生态、经济和社会效益。这就要求农业、林业部门有计划地组织推广人员进行研讨,为农民提供培训或为农民示范,使其能了解和体验如何将"有利可图的"农田防护林和林粮间作与单一作物体系进行比较。然而,要证明农田防护林和林粮间作具有"多功能盈利能力"需要一定的时间。

帮助农民克服资金困难。这就需要由具体的贷款或赠款单位来支持,实施资金上的激励措施,此举可通过生态补偿手段实现,例如,至少在农田防护林和林粮间作项目的初始实施阶段对参与农户进行生态补偿。特别是公益性较强的农田防护林项目应给予参与农户更多的建设和管护补贴。但是,这种补贴只仅限于公益性强的部分,而不是农田防护林和林粮间作涉及的所有树木。例如,农民有责任在农田边缘种植树木,以保护自己的农田,更有效地利用他的土地来获得更多收入,或恢复已退化或污染的土壤。将所有树木定义为农田防护林并对所有树木采取完全相同的管理政策并不是最好的策略,因为它们的用途不一。然而,有关部门仍然需要探讨出为农田防护林建设、管护提供生态补偿的充分理由、范围和程序。

提供综合技术援助。缺乏知识和缺乏有效的农林部门联合推广,阻碍了农田防护林发展。这就是为什么当地技术人员的联合培训对于保护和发展农田防护林和林粮间作发展至关重要,技术人员的参与可以向农户更好地传播关于农林复合经营的信息,包括农田防护林和林粮间作能创造的经济效益等，不失为推广农田防护林和林粮间作的一种有效方式。

对林权（地权）的保障。该先决条件特别适用于那些可能参与在农场植树、林粮间作和管护，但又没有长期土地使用权的农民。在这种情况下，相关参与农户如果没有土地和／或树木的所有权，可能会成为农田防护林发展的障碍。此外，由于没有明确的地权或林权，将难以获得贷款或其他形式的财政支持，如生态补偿或补贴等。

林业法规。出于生态安全的原因鼓励农民投资在农场内和农场外植树，从长远角度来看，需要创建新的林业法规。现有农田防护林中的树木砍伐之前需要获得准许，也因此造成了一些冲突。类似的法规可能会阻碍非林地的植树和管护。例如，在一般农田中，如果农民更愿意种植树木来创造更多的价值，此类的行为可以被免除严格的树木采伐要求。

监测和评估。2016 年在河南省粮食主产区开展的调查表明，林业部门官员的观点恰好与农民相反，林业部门官员始终强调农田防护林对作物产量的积极影响，却将林带对周边区域带来的减产等问题最小化。此外，调查还表明，农业部门官员并未充分了解农田防护林和林粮间作的效益范围。想要克服农民对农田防护林的不情愿以及对农业工作人员的不信任，则需要建立起客观的监督和监测体系。此外，同样重要的还有信息系统的开发，以收集有关农田防护林和林粮间作对经济和环境影响等关键问题所必需的数据。这种监督和监测体系应与耕地质量监督体系相结合。

八　加强耕地质量监管

耕地中的各种营养物质越丰富，生产出的粮食质量越好。由于耕地质量是粮食质量最重要的基础，所以耕地质量监管必须一手抓耕地污染治理，一手抓耕地质量提升。耕地污染治理是几十年、上百年的阶段性工作，耕地质量提升是一直要做的持久性工作。当然，中国近阶段耕地质量监管的重点是被污染的耕地。

耕地污染的风险包括影响农产品质量，危害人体健康，威胁生态安全；影响土壤的正常功能和植物、动物（如蚯蚓）和微生物（如根瘤菌）的生长和繁衍，以及土壤养分转化和肥力保持。土壤中污染物的转化和迁移，可能会对地表水、地下水甚至饮用水源造成污染。所以,国家要建立覆盖完整的耕地质量监管体系,将耕地质量终身追究责任制落到实处,将严格管理和控制农业生产中乱用和滥用化学品的行为,防止新的耕地污染的现象。

加强耕地质量监管,包括以下几点。

耕地污染风险监管。它采用概率方法评估耕地造成危害风险的可能性。其造成的生活风险是指粮食等农产品危害人畜健康的可能性,生态风险是指其危害生态系统或其中元素的可能性。

耕地利用监管。根据耕地质量实施耕地分类管理,分别采取优先保护、安全利用、严格管控等监管措施,保障农业生产环境安全;制定被污染耕地安全利用方案,以农艺调控、作物调整等措施消除农产品不达标风险;重度污染耕地可以种植其他农产品或退耕还林还草,不能种植食用农产品,以保障耕地安全利用,保障粮食和农产品安全。

耕地修复过程监管。耕地修复效果的显现具有较长的滞后期,它既有渐进又有突变,要弄清这个过程的动态变化,必须构建耕地修复监测网络,做好耕地修复过程的监管。这个监管还会对发育耕地修复市场发挥正面影响。

耕地质量综合监管。耕地安全不仅决定于耕地土壤安全,还决定于对它施加影响的水环境和大气环境,所以,要构建包括耕地土壤环境监管、耕地水环境监管和耕地大气环境监管的综合监管体系。

第五章　粮食主产区的生态安全战略

第一节　改善中国粮食主产区生态安全的基础

在粮食产量最大化政策目标的影响下，现行粮食生产体系的可持续性趋于下降的问题已经显现。尤其是，未来面临的挑战已经越来越明显：过度使用化肥和农药造成了土壤、地表水和地下水污染加重，土壤有机质减少和土壤健康情况恶化，灌溉用的地下水减少，农作物病虫害发生率增加，农田防护林保护功能退化，使气候变化引起的灾害对农业生产力的不利影响的风险越来越大。

环境污染问题是目前中国面临的最严重的问题之一，特别是土壤污染和水污染，已经影响到食品安全，从而威胁到人们的身体健康。化肥和杀虫剂的过量使用导致了严重的土壤污染，地下水的过量抽取导致可用水资源逐渐减少，人们对食品安全的关注度越来越高。因此，必须尽快解决诸如化肥与杀虫剂的残留以及重金属污染等影响食品安全的问题，以减少其对人类健康的威胁。

应对粮食主产区环境恶化的问题，改善生态安全，需要针对现实中的实际问题采取不同的措施，特别是要减少高耗水作物的种植面积，通过推行节水措施提高灌溉效率，减少化肥和杀虫剂的使用并尽可能地采用有机耕作实践，包括利用成熟的旱作技术并支持创新，如新的有机肥发酵技术，推广有机肥的应用等。

要改善粮食主产区的生态安全，必须积极应对那些影响粮食主产区粮食可持续生产的挑战：化肥或其他农用化学品过量使用所带来的对土壤和地下水造成长期负面影响的农业非点源污染，地下水过度开采造成的可用于灌溉的水量的持续减少，气候变化，特别是降水分布的变化，造成的土壤含水量、径流、养分循环、盐碱化、生物多样性、土壤有机质的变化和极端气候事件频率的增加；由于政策支持力度下降，未能妥善解决防护林胁地对作物产量所造成的负面影响的合理分担问题；农民普遍不愿继续管护农田防护林，造成的农田防护林的防护效应下降的问题。

我们可以预计到，如果粮食主产区的生态安全通过综合施策、跨部门合作等方式得到改善，将有助于实现多个可持续性发展目标。生态安全是解决与贫穷、饥饿、环境退化、气候变化等有关的既复杂又相互关联的各项挑战的整体解决方案的基础。然而，生态安全需要在政策、机构、农村组织及合作上创新，以达到《2030 年可持续发展议程》中所预期的食品生产、加工、营销和消费的要求。《2030 年可持续发展议程》是实现环境、社会和经济三个方面可持续综合发展的国家框架，它特别呼吁粮食和农业部门要在改善生态安全方面给予更好的政策、体制和技术考量，它同时呼吁，所有人都是这一变革过程的关键因素。

一　改善粮食主产区生态安全的挑战和机遇

改善粮食主产区的生态安全，应考虑以下挑战。

农民缺乏生态安全意识，特别是现今的高投入农业，对生态安全存在的潜在危害，农民缺乏相应的意识。

农业行业缺乏可持续性实践的经济支持。农业可通过综合农业体系创新和采用可持续性的粮食生产体系，如生态农业的相关做法，应对经济、社会和环境挑战，但目前尚缺乏政策支持。

粮食生产缺乏有利的政策环境。引导农民开展符合生态安全要求的农业实践需要积极的激励措施，帮助农民在生产系统适应生态安全要求的同时规避相应风险，实现其全部效益，需要一定的时间，而且目前缺乏采取需要一定时间方能见效的策略的政策环境。

政府部门缺乏政策协调和管理协调。生态安全需要行业、学界和行动者之间更多的互动，以实现其多重目标。行业政策需要进行跨部门（从地方到区域、再到国家）的整合，以实现其一致性。特别是，生态安全需要协调农场和农业景观层面的行动和治理方案。但到目前为止，政策和体制框架始终只针对各自行业的治理机制、监管体系和问责机制。

研究、教育和推广体系无法满足生态安全的需要。粮食主产区的生态安全需要一个能最大限度地发挥生产要素（例如土壤、水、树木、生物多样性、气候、人类行为等）协同作用的农业体系，以提高资源利用效率和风险抵抗力。管理这些要素取决于当地条件和农民的知识。然而，截至目前，研究、培训和推广体系主要侧重于单一部门的学科发展和方法应用，主要侧重于单一作物产量提高和自上而下的技术转让模式。为了提高农业生态安全水平，农业研究、培训和推广应重新定位于综合的知识创造方式，以及基于生态原则，最大限度地发挥生物和技术组成配制的作用。

改善粮食主产区生态安全，应把握以下机遇。

科学家们普遍认识到，基于高投入和资源密集型的农业实践目前已达到极限。联合国粮农组织 2017 年的报告指出，"高投入、资源密集型的农业，在过去几十年中一直有助于提高作物产量和粮食安全，但同时也造成了大量的土地枯竭、水资源短缺，森林砍伐和温室气体高排放，不再能够提供可持续的农业生产。因此，我们需要创新农业体系，例如在保护资源和环境的同时提高农业生产力的生态农业实践" [①]。

在政策和实践中确实存在改善粮食主产区生态安全的解决方案，包括保护性农业、气候智能型农业、有机农业，特别是生态农业，它们代表的是创新的、知识密集的、环境友好的、对社会负责的农业方式，并且依赖于技术型劳动。它们至少有一个共同点，即用有机投入物来替代化学品投入、多样化的作物轮作、改善土壤养分、提高水的利用效率、农林复合经营、少耕以减少水土流失、增加土壤容量以保持水分、增加固碳量以提高农业

[①] 联合国粮农组织：《粮食和农业的未来：趋势和挑战》，http://www.fao.org/3/a-i6583e.pdf，2017。

生产力。

此外，随着信息和通信技术的进展，城乡之间获取信息的数量差异和时间差异已经基本消除。整个粮食主产区的农民都可以迅速获得提高生态安全所需的科学知识。毫无疑问，信息和通信技术的这一新发展为各地的知识交流以及农民之间的经验交流提供了新的机会。

在传统农业基础上发展的新的农业实践，包括保护性农业、生态农业、气候智能型农业，林粮间作和有机农业等也可以应对和减缓气候变化带来的影响。农林复合经营模式，例如，农、林、牧经营模式实现了主体的多样化，可以提高资源利用效率和对气候变化的适应能力。同时，将管护和开发农田防护林作为生态农业实践的一个组成部分，以提高植被和土壤固碳能力，同时提供更多的额外收益。

公众对食物多样化和健康的需求在不断提高。中国人民和世界上其他国家的人民一样，也存在由于营养不良和肥胖而对健康食品和多样化饮食增加的需求。综合生态农业实践可以满足这些需求，同时改善土壤健康状况，减少环境退化和降低灌溉需求。中国各个地区的有机农产品市场正逐步形成，它会从农业需求侧促进农业生产系统的协同发展。

二　推广粮食主产区生态安全的公共政策

尽管生态安全方法因具有提高作物生产力、实现食品安全、缓解和适应气候变化以及增加农民收入等优点而越来越得到科学家和消费者的支持，但大多数政府却仍侧重于高投入农业，依赖于农业化学品投入、未能在食物营养和环境可持续发展的基础上推进粮食安全的实现。因此，我们迫切需要制定经济和社会等方面的相关政策，使高投入农业能够向生态安全农业过渡。制定此类政策需要采取跨部门的协作，需要从采用单一的、只关注农产品的方法发展到采用农业整体景观的方法。

2014~2015年，联合国粮农组织举办了一系列关于粮食安全与营养的农业生态学的区域性国际专题讨论会，并提出满足农业生态安全是减少对化石燃料依赖、解决传统高投入农业对社会和环境带来的负面影响的关键方法。为了推广粮食主产区的生态安全，提出以下五项政策建议。

满足生态安全要求的农业政策应具有包容性和跨部门性，应由社会活动家、科学家、教育工作者和其他人合作制定。

要发挥生态安全的全部潜力不仅需要有与作物生产有关的政策，还需要有与脱贫、健康（食品安全）、教育和环境保护等相关的激励政策。

满足生态安全要求的农业实践主要是基于特定环境和适应当地复杂动态生态和人类系统的知识；需要促进农民、推广人员、科学家和地方决策者之间共同创造知识。

生态安全政策应充分认识到生态农业实践对适应和减缓气候变化的潜力。事实上，生态农业系统可以通过丰富生物多样性、增加土壤有机物含量、增加土壤碳储存，在减缓气候变化影响等方面发挥重要作用。

生态农业实践要想取得成功，需要建立起生产者与消费者之间直接联系的价值链，完善农业生态产品的市场准入是至关重要的；要建立起面向农业生态产品的公共采购政策；开展关于生态农产品营养价值相关的促销活动。

第二节　生态安全战略的主要特点

一　生态安全战略的功能

改善粮食主产区生态安全具有以下三大战略功能。

改善生态安全的战略行动能够确保甚至提高作物生产能力，从而提高粮食主产区在国家粮食安全中的地位。

改善生态安全的战略行动能够消除影响作物生产力和食品安全的负面因素，并控制会产生负外部性的因素，如土壤和水污染，地下水供应量减少等。

改善生态安全的战略行动能够改善农民的生计状况，实现未来粮食主产区经济的可持续发展。

二　改善粮食主产区生态安全的战略行动路线

要想解决影响粮食主产区农业可持续发展的负面因素，需要综合实施四大战略行动，并辅以一系列政策和治理措施。单靠任何一组行动措施均不能实现提高中国粮食主产区生态安全的最终目标。这些战略行动包括以下几点。

首先，建立农业非点源污染的控制体系。减少化肥和农药用量，减轻农业面源污染，需要采取五类行动措施：逐步废除现行的化肥补贴政策，出台环境友好型肥料和农药的优惠补贴政策；通过发布定额，严控合成肥料和农药使用量；发展新型发酵技术，促进有机肥料供应和应用系统的改造，为有机肥施用提供便利；通过测土配方施肥的方法，了解耕地土壤养分和农作物的营养需求，注重氮磷钾肥、微量元素和有机肥对土壤肥力水平的互补性，减少化肥用量；建立农作物病虫害生物防控系统，推广机械化农药喷洒技术，提高农药喷洒的均匀性和精准性，减少合成农药的用量。

其次，发展水资源保障体系，实现以下四大目标：通过推广应用节水技术，提高水库、沟渠和灌溉基础设施的利用效率；发放可交易水券，确保农户不因减少用水量而减少收入；根据不同季节的土壤湿润程度和水资源可利用度，调整种植模式；推广旱作技术，包括免耕和覆膜技术，减少土壤水分蒸发以及表层土壤水土流失，增加土壤中的有益昆虫和微生物。

再次，根据当地的条件，修复和拓展包括四个层次的农田防护林体系：第一层防护体系是指粮食主产区周边山上的森林，包括划为自然保护区的特殊用途林、水土保持林等防护林、景观林和用材林等；第二层防护体系是指高速公路、高速铁路、省道、市道、县道和水系沿线营造的林带（防风林、防护林和河流缓冲林）；第三层防护体系是指村庄周围的经济林、用材林、景观林等；第四层防护体系是指在开展高标准农田建设时营造的农田防护林，栽植在乡道、村道和沟渠沿线的树木，以及为了修复已退化或重污染的农田而采用的林粮间作模式中的树木等。

最后，在农业领域发展生态农业。从传统的高投入农业过渡到尊重生态安全标准的可持续农业，其过程将是复杂的，需要调整农业规划、技术体系、管理方式和市场营销等。推广生态农业做法主要有三大目的：加强农业生物多样性，建立各组成部分之间有益的生物相互作用和协同关系，以加强生态服务，而不是只关注单一作物物种；将长期可持续性的概念纳入整个农业生态系统的设计和管理中；重视农业系统的总体健康状况，而不只是特定种植系统的产出。以下原则可作为在农业领域引入变化的一般性准则。

强调土壤、水、能源和生物资源的综合保护。

优化土壤养分和能源利用，为植物生长提供最有利的土壤条件。 优化土壤养分需要：①加强生物质的循环利用，提高有机质含量；②尽量减少能源、水、养分和遗传资源的损失；③定期使用大量不同类型的有机肥（如动物粪便、堆肥、落叶、植物覆盖、轮作植物的残留物等）；④避免或尽量减少使用不必要的农用化学品，以免对环境和人体健康造成不良影响。

提高集水效率。

采用少耕或免耕技术，减少土壤板结。

物种和遗传资源多样化（农场和景观层面）。通过加强生态化管理，实现农业系统的自身免疫能力提高，预防病虫害，而不是通过使用合成除草剂等化学投入品"控制"它们。

尊重农民在农业生态系统设计和管理方面的知识和经验。

第三节　生态安全战略的执行安排

一　政策支持要求

上述四条改善粮食主产区生态安全的战略行动路线的成功实施，需要三类生态保障政策的支持，包括强制性政策、激励性政策和协调性政策。

强制性政策。应包括制定出台新的农业法律法规，需要综合考虑保护土壤肥力、治理水土流失、提高灌溉效率、严格控制合成肥料和农药用量、防止土壤和水体污染和富营养化，通过农田防护林建设和维护以强化农田保护，以及通过生态和财政等激励措施来鼓励林粮间作。

激励性政策。主要包括三类：第一，出台相关规定奖励化肥用量低于定额的农户；第二，发放定额水券，鼓励农户减少自己耕作时的用水量；第三，出台生态补偿措施，鼓励农户保护生态环境并进行农田防护林建设与维护。

协调性政策。提高粮食主产区的生态保障水平，不仅需要制定强制性和激励性政策，还需要对经济、技术和资源管理政策进行协调。在这一方面，本战略期望所有产品补贴均将按照生态要求进行调整，制定环保肥料和农药使用补贴政策，替代现行的补贴化肥的政策；推广节水灌溉技术，减轻地下水压力；鼓励农田防护林建设和管护，改善可持续绿色农业发展条件。在农田防护林建设中，应根据当地条件和保护规定，将防护林配置调整为非对称性。非对称性设计应包括选择不同种类、特征和树龄的树木，并减轻林木对作物生产的负面效应。

二 部门间协调要求

从机构角度来看，粮食主产区生态安全战略的成功实施还需要政府相关部门进行跨行业和跨机构协作，各负其责，实施生态安全改善发展战略，实现提高粮食安全和减轻贫困的目的。但是，到目前为止，这些政府部门机构间的合作局面有待形成。关键部门要跳出本位思想，承诺政策合作和协调，实现横向的部门间协作，以及县乡部门及其他机构间（如非政府组织、农民协会等）的纵向协作。粮食主产区的现行生态安全改善政策仍然存在不足，原因是各个行业倾向于执行本行业计划，而不是采用更加全面的措施，改善横向和纵向协作，以提高总体生态安全水平。

因此，发展生态安全战略体系的一个重要先决条件是提高部门之间的协同合作，需要满足以下四个要求：第一，要增强协同意识，激发协同需求，实现资源配置优势互补和规避劣势；第二，要对跨部门协作进行管理，确保参与者的权利、责任、利益的对称；第三，加快信息交流，使信息交流更有效、更综合，提高相关服务的公开性、透明性和实用性；第四，建立不协同行为的惩罚机制，降低协同风险。

三 监测和评估要求

按照上述四个要求建立跨部门生态安全监测评估体系。该体系目的是监测和评估地下水位变化的影响、农业面源污染和土壤质量，以及四层防护林体系的保护效率和效能。监测和评估组织应由有关部门、农民和外部监测评估专家三方面人员组成。监测评估方法要简单、便宜、有效。监测评估指标应具有简单、准确、稳定的特点，可以通过遥感数据分析、固定样本调查和随机抽样等方法进行直接监测。最后，监测与评估系统应与信息公开制度相结合。

具体而言，为了改善生态安全水平，需要加强以下五个层面的协同合作：

- 政府行业间部门合作；
- 政府行业部门与地方政府机构合作；
- 政府与村社合作；
- 农民间合作；
- 第三方监测与评估机构与利益相关者的合作。

四　生态补偿要求

中国自 2000 年初开始正式开展生态补偿项目试点工作，主要实施了生态保护项目（如天然林保护工程）、生态恢复项目（如京津防沙治沙工程）和生态建设项目（退耕还林 ①、还草工程）。这些项目都具有以下四个特点。

国家是生态补偿的主要推动者，也是生态补偿资金的主要出资者；政府虽然认识到应该动员市场主体参与，从而减轻政府财政压力，但是，到目前为止，市场机制仍处于初期阶段。

经协商自愿参与国家生态补偿项目的参与者一方面按规定获得生态补偿，另一方面按强制性要求履行义务，如规定的造林或管护任务。

现有生态补偿转移支付既有纵向的（中央政府向各省支付），也有横向的（受益的省、市、县向承担义务的省、市、县支付）。

生态补偿制度主要根据各地实际情况设计，因此生态补偿资金分配和使用方式具有多样化的特征。

生态补偿是对生态保护和建设参与者的投入或支付的成本的补偿。所

---

① 退耕还林是一个环境政策和工具的纲要，它通过包括一系列有条件转移的财政改革和更广泛的政策促进非农收入增长，鼓励生态恢复，为中国的"生态文明"理念做贡献。截至 2015 年，投资总额达 690 亿美元。

以，生态补偿应该瞄准那些为改善环境做出贡献的行动者，排除不威胁环境的那些人。不补偿那些不威胁环境的人并非不公平，因为他们的生计并没有因为保护环境而受到影响，也没有产生保护成本。所以，生态补偿要从区域识别转为对贡献者和其贡献的识别上，而不宜停留在区域识别阶段。

五　粮食主产区开展生态补偿的意义

生态补偿既要有实现特定环境项目的目标，又要有改善人民福祉的目标。换言之，生态补偿除了确立环境保护目标外，还要包含减贫目标。就此而言，试图引导人们参与采取保护环境行动（如改善生态安全）的生态补偿项目，可以使用不同的激励方案，包括现金和实物奖励。

在中国，生态补偿计划应该具有三个方面的主要功能：①鼓励生态保护；②促进正外部性内部化，促进社会公平；③促进区域合作和协调发展。在这一背景下，生态补偿基本上包含三个利益相关方：农民、相关部门和环境保护组织。这三个利益相关方也解释了生态补偿措施可能具有多样化特征的原因。

粮食主产区具有生产物质产品和生态产品的双重功能。我们要抓住国家加大生态补偿力度的有利条件设计生态补偿方案，将粮食主产区纳入生态补偿范围。设计生态补偿方案时必须把握好以下四点：

第一，生态服务补偿不宜扭曲为生产损失赔偿；

第二，生态补偿应与生态服务价值增量挂钩；

第三，生态补偿应以生态保护和建设的成本或机会成本为依据；

第四，生态补偿不宜同生产损失挂钩。生产损失只是生态建设的一部分机会成本，以生产损失作为生态补偿的依据，会大大低估生态补偿的标准。

粮食主产区生态补偿主要采用"谁受益谁补偿、谁破坏谁赔偿"原则。此外，生态补偿制度应确保权利和义务对称，受益和损失计量精准，要与生态服务价值增量挂钩，公开运作并接受监管，最重要的是要有科学的生态保护和建设绩效评估制度。为了消除意外的通货膨胀对生态补偿金的影响，生态补偿应该以粮食等实物产品作为计量单位，补偿金额根据粮食数量和粮食实际价格计算。

六　在粮食主产区推广生态补偿措施

为了促进粮食主产区的生态安全，生态补偿金应主要用于建设农田防护林。在其四层保护体系中，应侧重于：①第一层防护体系即粮食主产区宜林荒山荒坡上的再造林；②第四层防护体系，即在高标准农田建设的同时，在乡道、村道、沟渠等沿线种植的农田防护林带。它们既可以并行使用，也可以与标准法规，财政手段、禁令、基础设施开发和／或教育项目一起使用或补充使用。

在粮食主产区宜林荒山荒坡的再造林，其生态补偿标准应符合退耕还林工程制定的补偿标准，即根据机会成本，或农户可以从用于生态保障林业建设项目的农田获得的最大收益计算生态补偿费。

建设高标准农田时在乡村道路沿线营造的农田防护林，应根据以下两个方面制定单独的生态补偿措施：①按农田种植树木数量及其造林、经营和管护成本支付造林补偿费；②由林业部门按照农田防护林边界效应所带来的生产损失计算生产损失补偿费。

上述两种措施都旨在解决管护或扩大再造林和农田防护林带来的环境正或负的外部性问题（以现金或实物形式），这些活动会增强或保护特定的生态系统服务。它们通常是并行使用或与标准、法规、财政工具、禁令、和／或中央或省级政府推进的关于支持粮食主产区生态安全的教育项目等互补配套使用。

在组织此类生态补偿计划时，财政，林业，农业部门和农民代表必须共同商讨生态补偿项目的目的、补偿标准等。此外，在核实和公示后，生态补偿金必须直接支付给对应的农户。此外，受益农民必须参与监测，以评估生态补偿金发放的效率和有效性。

第二层防护体系林业投资项目，由于大型基础设施沿线营造防护林带所用土地已经得到相关机构的补偿，因此，不应采取生态补偿措施。但是，在主要基础设施沿线建设防护林带，应该与交通或农村基础设施主管部门全面协作实施。第三层防护体系林业投资项目（村庄绿化），应首先选择按照开发成本给予奖励，而非生态补偿。

专栏：瑞士草原生物多样性保护转移支付

增加农业景观中的生物多样性是瑞士联邦宪法的目标之一，也是多功能农业的任务之一。瑞士有40%的农业草原。由于面积大，对生物多样性的影响很大，草原管理对整个国家的物种丰富至关重要。1993年，为了扭转物种衰退趋势，瑞士政府引入了农业环境计划。在该计划中，农民需要根据生态补偿区（ECA）规定，管理7%的已利用农业区（UAA）。作为回报，农民将按每年每亩收到基本款项。最近，瑞士议会开发了新的直接支付体系，该体系从2014年开始，将社会目标进行分配，并根据Tinbergen原则进行支付。根据该原则，每个目标必须遵循至少一种工具。例如，确保食品供应的支付将按每公顷计算，具体取决于生产能力，生物多样性支付仅给予那些种植有大量作物的土地。目前仍然发挥重要作用的以动物品种数量为基础的计算正在退出历史舞台。尽管新体系既没有改变转移到农民的资金数量，也没有迅速改变瑞士的农业结构，但有人认为，该系统变革可能具有历史意义，因为它使农业的社会转移更容易进行批判性分析和评估，因为它首次表明了Tinbergen原则在多功能性政策设计中的应用。

七 生态补偿最佳实践

我们可以从国际的生态服务付费项目上获得很多经验，包括退耕还林计划的生态补偿。它们都指出了制度和激励机制之间至关重要且不可分割的联系。要使生态补偿措施取得成功，应遵循以下关键规则。

加强农民对生态补偿项目的所有权。要做到这点，需要将社会保护与生态保护联系起来，增加农民对环境管理和保护的承诺。从这方面来看，生态补偿项目对地方环境和当地经济形势等异质性敏感。此外，在设计生态补偿时，考虑地方经济发展和环境恢复需求时要特别关注防返贫工作。

要重点关注条件最不利的社区，特别是那些受环境退化影响的社区，以及在城郊建立非农替代生计选择，这些应该都是加强农民参与的关键。[①]

扩大规模的生态补偿项目需要高度重视规划、管理、示范和试点。在这方面，对于大规模的生态补偿项目，鼓励农民或受益人抱团参加。

政策支持和最终拥有可持续融资手段都是决定性的，因为它们将确定生态补偿项目能否达到足够规模。这需要政府有一个明确和长期的战略，使生态补偿项目有足够的资金。这方面应特别注意建立独立的信托基金和多样化的融资工具组合。

生态补偿项目的开发应以独立的监测与评估系统为支撑，重点关注当地经济发展对环境质量和减贫的影响。从长远来看，也为了避免和最大限度降低与参与农民群体之间的冲突，这种监测与评价系统是提高生态补偿项目自适应能力的必要工具。

加强能力建设，在生态补偿项目的建模、规划、实施和监控方面取得科学进展，更好地理解行为变化的条件；作为推广的一部分，应特别注意"培训者培训"，以提高从业人员的能力。

八　有效实施粮食主产区生态补偿的体制和工具

根据上述建议，要在生态补偿支持下开发和维护农田防护林应至少满足以下基本要求。

明确地识别潜在的受益人和能力，清楚地掌握当地的社会经济情况和环境条件。

明确生态补偿付费的支付形式。生态补偿支付可以通过现金支付、实物奖励或混合形式。实物奖励形式包括社区层面的投资，表明生态系统服务的改善需要群体行动，其影响超出个人家庭；混合形式可以包括对社区

---

① Duan et al., "The effects of the SLCP on poverty alleviation in the Wulin Mountainous Areas", *Small Scale Forestry*, 2015 14 (3), pp. 331–350; Li et al., "Assessing the decadal impact of China SLCP on household income", *Forest Policy and Economics*, 2015 61, pp.95–103; Wang et al., "Impacts of regional payments for ecosystem service program on livelihoods of different rural households", *Journal of Cleaner Production*, 2017 164, pp.1058–1067.

基础设施和教育的投资，也可以与现金支付结合。现金则可通过已成立的金融机构向受益人直接更快速地支付。

清晰有效的制度设置和管理/监督系统[1]。当在大规模运作时，特别要做好不同政府部门（例如林业部门、农业部门和环境部门）之间的协调。

具有当地技术和管理能力。这将需要各级（包括村级）能力建设和培训活动的匹配，以及能力建设和推广人员的培训，有时需要重新部署。

明确地权和林权，这是管理者实施生态补偿支付的基本因素。

明确识别当地的保护需求，只有在恢复土壤肥力、减少与天气灾害有关的不利影响、稳定（或增加）粮食产量、提高农民收入等的情况下，才需要建立农田防护林或林粮间作。

提高保护效率，农田防护林的设计、设置和组成应最大限度地提高其保护效率和效益，特别是在提高粮食产量和农民收入方面。

不会对周围的农田和农民造成损害。

第四节　2030 年可持续发展议程中的粮食安全概念

一　《变革我们的世界：2030 年可持续发展议程》

遵循生态文明理念，2015 年 9 月，中国在联合国可持续发展峰会上批准了《变革我们的世界：2030 年可持续发展议程》。[2] 旨在为国内和国际合作提供指导，是应对各种全球挑战的具体行动，为加快经济和生态转型提供动力。事实上，2016 年十二届全国人大批准的"十三五"规划中就提出要坚定地致力于积极实施和整合议程中提及的 17 个社会发展目标（SDGs）和 169 个具体指标，从而实现该议程与中国在生态文明概念背景下制定的中长期发展战略之间形成协调效应。各省、自治区、直辖市的发

---

[1] 胡振通：《中国的草地生态补偿：哪些可被监测？哪些不可监测？》，第五届生态补偿国际会议，中国农村学习研究所，清华大学，2016。
[2] 《变革我们的世界：2030 年可持续发展议程》，外交部官网，https://sustainabledevelopment.un.org/post2015/transformingourworld。

展计划 ① 或将进一步补充全国性的承诺目标。

表 5-1 《变革我们的世界：2030 年可持续发展议程》中与中国粮食主产区生态
安全有关的内容

可持续发展目标	与粮食安全有关的目标
目标 1：在全世界消除一切形式的贫困 目标 2：消除饥饿，实现粮食安全，改善营养状况和促进可持续农业	农业政策的制定要关注减贫、增加对农业研究、推广服务和技术的投资，这对提高农业生产力至关重要
目标 3：确保健康的生活方式，促进各年龄段人群的福祉	减少危险化学品、大气污染、土壤和水污染造成的健康危害
目标 6：为所有人提供水和环境卫生并对其进行可持续管理	提高灌溉效率、减少农业非点源污染、提高水质，保护水生态系统
目标 8：促进持久、包容性和可持续经济增长，促进充分的生产性就业和人人获得体面工作	有效提高金融和保险服务的可得性，提高资源利用效率
目标 9：建造具备抵御灾害能力的基础设施，促进具有包容性的可持续工业化，推动创新	保证农民、中小微企业等及时获得价格合理、便捷安全的金融服务，为改善生态安全、抵御自然灾害（干旱，洪水）等发放补贴
目标 11：建设包容、安全、有抵御灾害能力和可持续的城市和人类住区	积极推动城乡绿化建设
目标 12：采用可持续的消费和生产模式	有效利用自然资源（土壤、水、生物多样性），对农业化学品进行无害化管理，发展气候智慧型农业以及减少对环境造成的破坏活动
目标 15：保护、恢复和促进可持续利用陆地生态系统，可持续地管理森林，防治荒漠化，制止和扭转土地退化，遏制生物多样性的丧失趋势	可持续地利用现有土壤和水资源，提升森林经营与管理的可持续性，预防土地沙化，不断拓展沙化土地治理范围，防治荒漠化，防止生物多样性丧失
目标 16：创建和平、包容的社会以促进可持续发展，让所有人都能诉诸司法，在各级建立有效、负责和包容的机构	跨部门机构的有效融合，加强横向和纵向的机构合作，特别是地方政府各部门之间的合作（例如，农业部门、林业部门、环保部门、以及其他与基础设施建设有关的部门）

由于农业的多维度特性，《变革我们的世界：2030 年可持续发展议程》中大部分的可持续发展目标都与其有直接或间接的关系。实际上，这些发展目标覆盖了整个可持续农业政策领域（见表 5-1），该议程的目标旨在成为所有发达国家和最不发达国家政府的可持续农业发展指南。议程中的某些目标主要是社会经济类的（目标 1、4、5、8~11、16、17），其他目标则集中在生

---

① 《中国落实 2030 年可持续发展议程国别方案》，外交部官网，http://www.fmprc.gov.cn/mfa_eng/zxxx_662805/W020161014332600482185.pdf。

物物理系统类，其中可持续农业对于粮食安全发挥着明显的作用。尽管存在区别，但这两类目标把人类管理粮食生产和农业生态系统服务的能力相互关联在一起，即为了实现以社会经济为重点的目标，需要考虑生态系统的动态行为，同时为实现以生态系统为重点的目标，也要考虑社会经济方面。

将消除贫困和饥饿作为首要关键目标，中国对落实该议程的承诺反映了中国对可持续农业和粮食安全的重视。此外，中国也将营养、贫困、生态安全、学习、创新和可持续性等列为关键目标，支持农业在可持续经济发展中发挥关键作用。上述几个主要涉猎领域也表明，可持续农业需要"以农民为中心"和"以知识为基础"，使得包括农民、农业实体企业等在内的所有主体都能发挥全部的潜力，让粮食安全和可持续发展成为现实。显然，农业发展背景下的环境可持续性（或生态安全）不仅取决于政策或制度的制定，也取决于农民或森林经营者等土地使用者的行为和习惯。因此，该议程在各种政策领域和体制框架中提出了真正的挑战。

中国政府从 2016 年开始实施对《变革我们的世界：2030 年可持续发展议程》的实践，并于 2017 年 8 月公布了《中国落实 2030 年可持续发展议程进展报告》。该报告强调了中国可持续农业发展优先领域，也强调了这些目标与粮食主产区生态安全的关系，例如，政策和体制机制、结构性调整、创新、健康土壤和清洁水（关键的自然资源）的可得性、气候变化和农业生产力。这些政策和体制应被视为中国粮食主产区生产力增长和可持续性的关键驱动因素。进一步来讲，它总结了引导粮食主产区的农民有效参与生态安全改善活动的四项激励政策。

经济赋权政策。给予机构大量的信任（例如，在安全、物权、公平方面的信任），这些措施对于吸引农民的参与和投资是很重要的。

投资激励政策。吸引公共部门和私营部门的投资，确保自然资源，尤其是土壤和水资源的可持续利用；加强创新，尤其是在保障生态安全的手段、市场准入、资本和知识层面的创新。

能力建设政策。特别是提高推广服务效率，促进生态安全措施的采用和创新，提高农民接受创新的技能，提高资源利用效率。

参与激励政策。旨在促进农业行业结构改革、资源可持续利用、创新和风险控制等，包括：①保障生态安全的法规和财政补贴、补偿政策；②鼓励农民为生态安全需求做贡献的激励政策；③提高农业环境措施的效率和有效性的技术和资源政策。

二　粮食安全与《中国落实 2030 年可持续发展议程国别方案》

生态安全是确保粮食安全的核心，也对发展可持续农业至关重要。因此，《中国落实 2030 年可持续发展议程国别方案》是实现国内与贫困、饥饿、气候变化、可持续利用陆地生态系统等相关的可持续发展目标的关键。生态安全[①]对人类社会的可持续发展至关重要，包括大气安全、土地安全、水安全、资源安全、生物安全、环境安全、粮食安全和社会秩序等。因此，它是维持人类社会与其活动相关的生态系统之间不断发展的关系中的动态平衡。换句话说，生态安全是指解决威胁人类生存、健康、粮食安全和食品安全、社会保障和社会秩序问题的能力。在实践中，生态安全的评估确实揭示了土地退化、森林砍伐、荒漠化、水和空气污染、能源短缺、温室气体排放和全球气候变化带来的各种挑战。因此，任何生态安全战略的目标都是提出、制定和实施适当的生态政策和治理框架，旨在防止这些问题给农业生产力、粮食安全、食品安全和生计带来负面影响，并在需要的地方随时随地修复已经受损的生态系统。

过去几十年里，粮食主产区的农业发展伴随着大量物理、生物和化学产品的投入，包括灌溉设备、拖拉机、化肥和农药、高产品种、速生品种等，因此，在过去几十年中，农作物生产力翻了一番甚至增长了三倍。虽然这种高投入的农业是增加粮食产量的一种非常有效的方法，但是，这种做法也给中国农业发展带来了诸多弊端，例如资金投入多、耗水量大、能耗高、地下水位下降快，化肥农药过量使用带来的农业非点源污染、土壤表层退化、土壤有机质含量降低、害虫的抗药性提高、本土生态资源的退化，以及 20 世纪集体化时期建成的农田防护林的大量退化问题。

---

① 生态安全是能源和水资源短缺、全球气候变化和人类安全等生态问题之间所有联系的总和。在大多数情况下，它不会指明新的威胁，更多是指明已有的环境问题，然后通过制定恰当的环境政策来应对，以达到更好的保护作用。

表 5-2 总结了《变革我们的世界：2030 年可持续发展议程》中与粮食主产区可持续发展和粮食生态安全有关的政策目标。

表 5-2　可持续发展目标和粮食生态安全目标的关系

可持续发展目标 ＼ 粮食生态安全目标	提高农作物生产力	减少农业非点源污染	提高灌溉效率	提高土壤蓄水能力	强化农田防护林的保护作用	增强碳储存、减少碳排放	降低气候异常对农业的影响	提供原料	增强土壤肥力和养分循环	规范病虫害防治方式	提升农村生态景观	健全结构提升政策体系	完善激励政策和补偿机制	修订不适当的部门政策	促进跨部门协作和合作	提高推广的有效性和效率
在全世界消除一切形式的贫困	×		×		×		×	×	×	×			×	×	×	×
消除饥饿，实现粮食安全，改善营养状况和促进可持续农业	×	×	×						×						×	×
确保健康的生活方式，促进各年龄段人群的福祉	×					×	×		×	×	×					
确保包容和公平的优质教育，让全民终身享有学习机会																×
实现性别平等，增强所有妇女和女童的权能																
为所有人提供水和环境卫生并对其进行可持续管理		×	×	×	×											
确保人人获得负担得起的、可靠的和可持续的现代能源						×		×								
促进持久、包容和可持续经济增长，充分就业和体面就业	×	×	×				×	×								
健全抵御灾害的基础设施，促进包容、可持续工业化和创新								×						×	×	×
减少国家内部和国家之间的不平等																
包容、安全、有抵御灾害能力和可持续的城市和人类住区	×	×		×	×	×										
采取可持续的消费和生产模式	×	×	×	×		×	×	×	×	×			×			
采取紧急行动应对气候变化及其影响						×	×	×		×						

续表

可持续发展目标 ＼ 粮食生态安全目标	提高农作物生产力	减少农业非点源污染	提高灌溉效率	提高土壤蓄水能力	强化农田防护林的保护作用	增强碳储存、减少碳排放	降低气候异常对农业的影响	提供原料	增强土壤肥力和养分循环	规范病虫害防治方式	提升农村生态景观	健全结构提升政策体系	完善激励政策和补偿机制	修订不适当的部门政策	促进跨部门协作和合作	提高推广的有效性和效率
保护和可持续利用海洋和海洋资源以促进可持续发展																
健全陆地生态系统可持续管理，防治荒漠化和生物多样性丧失	×	×	×	×	×	×	×		×			×	×	×		×
创建和平、包容的社会														×		×
加强执行手段，重振可持续发展全球伙伴关系							×								×	

资料来源：作者自制。

第五节　粮食主产区中生态安全行动计划的本质

制定将粮食主产区农田防护林（或四层防护林）整合起来的行动计划，其背后的必要性在于树木，尤其是农田防护林所起到的保护作用，其在历史上也提供了生态安全环境，提高了农业生产力。但是近年来，由于缺乏生态补偿激励，农民没有意愿管护农田防护林，或在其农田内外种植树木。实际上，如果不能扭转农田防护林的退化趋势，将会对生态系统带来灾难性变化。

该行动计划的提出旨在引入具体和完善的生态补偿付费机制，以维持和扩大现有农田防护林，改善粮食主产区生态安全。该行动计划的前提条件包括以下几个方面。

第一个前提条件是，将农民和农民社区作为改善国家粮食生产核心区生态安全的主要行动者。无论从区域还是当地层面，农民必须是生态安全各项具体行动解决方案的中心。

第二个前提条件是，建立一个激励机制（或生态补偿机制），鼓励农民参与改善生态安全和粮食生产的活动。

第三个前提条件是，明确农田防护林林地／林木所有权，并考虑实现这些林业生态安全目标的特殊管理要求。

第四个前提条件是，参与国家粮食生产核心区农业和林业开发的省级机构能够更密切地合作，能够更多地共享信息和资源。

第五个前提条件是，建立包括行业机构、农民和外部独立监测和评估专家三个有关方面参与的生态安全监测与评估体系。应将三方参与的生态安全监测与评估体系作为一个重要的管理工具，追踪项目进展状况，尤其是要追踪与生态安全战略目标的相关性和完成情况，拟实施开发活动的效率、有效性和可持续性，生态补偿措施的效率和有效性。

第六个前提条件是，以改善生态安全为目的（农田防护林建设和其他复合农林业／间作实践活动）的林业投资项目的设计与实施应符合并适应当地条件，尤其是要适应国家粮食生产核心区各个立地类型区当前的生态和社会经济条件。

第七个前提条件是，开展区域及定点跨学科应用研究，改善林业投资项目的设计方案。在选择和设计应用研究项目时，应优先考虑：①缓解树根、遮阴或树干对粮食生产造成的负面影响；②生态安全林业投资项目建设的直接和间接经济成本、环境效益与风险的量化分析。

第八个前提条件是，采用现代信息和通信技术工具开展推广活动，有利于加强推广专业人员和农民之间的联系以及农民相互间的联系，有助于加强农民的协调性和参与度，从而提高生态修复实践活动的应用范围。

一　六大行动预期目标

该行动计划中各项实施活动将围绕六个行动预期目标来设计，这六个目标如果处理得当，生态安全林业投资项目将会得到更大范围的推广并得到有效维护。具体包括以下六个目标。

增强利益相关者的生态意识。该目标的主要宗旨是扭转当前农田防护林的退化趋势。造成这种恶化状况的重要原因是缺乏激励措施，农民不愿意对其进行管护。因此，通过外向发展战略和培训活动，提高农民和决策者对农田防护林结构及其生态效益的认识，促使那些参与粮食主产区农业发展的农民和农民社区积极参与林业相关活动。

创造有利的政策和体制环境。该目标的保障手段包括：①改善机构间横向和纵向合作以保证行业政策的一致性和协同性；②修订完善不利的、可能会阻碍农民参与林业相关投资的林业和农业法规和法律；③明晰土地和树木权属；④建立联合监测和评价系统（M&E）来评估将与林业有关的投资融入粮食主产区发展之中的表现、成果、影响和经验教训；⑤在各种空间尺度上改进与林业发展有关的预算拨款。

提供激励措施。该目标旨在创造一个清晰的政策环境，根据农田防护林纳入农业发展中产生的收入和损失情况制定激励性生态补偿措施，提高农民参与度。当前，农民只希望从这些防护林中获得最佳生态服务，而不愿对其获得的生态保护支付费用，或者不愿意自己的责任田受到防护林干扰而影响其农业收入。因此，该目标主要通过委托研究机构对适应粮食主产区情况的生态补偿方案的设计进行系统研究，然后通过相关参与方的研讨会，共同确定林业投资项目，特别是确定农田防护林营造、改造和管理的生态补偿内容、范围和实施模式。

提升沟通技巧。没有一个功能良好的公共或私有林业推广体系，国家粮食生产核心区生态安全改善的林业项目便不可能成功。但是，目前中国对常规农业耕作和林业推广方法过度依赖，对生态安全和可持续农业发展方法重视不足，使政策制定者和农民对生态安全问题的兴趣下降。目前的推广和研究工作主要集中在短期的单一种植系统，对树种在改善生态安全和可持续农业方面的潜在作用重视不足。以提高农田防护林体系生产力和盈利能力为目的的适应性行动研究投资不足，从而导致这种状况更加恶化。此外，生态安全体系改善的理论与技术尚未纳入农业或林业院校课程体系。这样做的目的是提高机构能力，以便将林业投资项目纳入农业发展之中。这一目标意味着通过对推广专业人员和农民社区进行教育，加强农业和林业学科的联系，传播改良技术知识，以强化生态安全目标，让林业生态安全成为每个机构和农民社区的工作。在这一目标下拟订的活动有两个目标：

①制定与林业有关的信息通信技术推广战略，支持将与林业相关的投资纳入农业发展之中；②在机构和个人层面上开展能力建设和培训计划，使推广专业人员有效利用现代通信技术工具向农民提供技术、教育、财务和营销方面的援助。

提升农民在林业生态安全方面的知识水平。中国在利用和推广农田防护林和其他形式的农林技术上已经有几个世纪的经验，并将其作为一种改进的土地管理方式，旨在提高作物生产力和控制环境恶化。但是，随着时间的推移，农田防护林已经严重恶化，生态农业实践已经被农民放弃，转而改用农业单一种植耕作实践。因此，开展参与性应用研究，充分认识林业投资项目的预期效益，同时解决妨碍农民参与林业投资项目建设和管理的主要环境、经济和社会制约因素或问题，这些对于国家粮食生产核心区生态安全建设是至关重要的。该目标旨在连接农民、从业人员、科学家和技术顾问，进行机构间、多学科的应用研究，以提高生态安全中各种形式的林业相关投资的生态和经济效率。因此，需要提供林业投资项目对生态安全的实际影响信息，并展示农田防护林与生态安全、农作物生产力和经济增长之间的正相关联系。

适应当地环境的林业投资。该计划的主要目标是通过规划与各类林业相关（特别是农田防护林）的投资项目，改善优先选定的粮食主产区的生态安全。该目标的主要宗旨是针对现有生态安全问题和挑战，为上述林业相关活动制定一个详细的、综合的重点投资方案，以便在县、乡镇和村级层面上为农业生产创造健康的环境。该投资方案应包括以下内容：①根据生态和气候变化，或与天气相关的灾害等确定优先干预区域；②评估确定上述林业相关活动的相应规模及其投资和维护成本；③根据当地生态、社会经济和市场条件设计上述林业活动。此类支持活动应特别包括提高意识和加强宣传活动，基于使用信息通信技术的推广活动，制定针对当地的生态补偿方案，以及提高推广人员能力的培训方案。

我们预计，如果能在县级以综合方式实现上述六大目标的话，将有助于制定连贯、互动和积极主动的生态安全公共战略，以支持林业相关投资的发展，特别是农田防护林的发展，能实现改善中国粮食主产区的生态安全的目标。

第六章 实施生态安全战略，改善中国粮食安全

目前，新冠肺炎疫情及其对经济的严重冲击还在持续，气候变化和全球环境危机的重要性或紧迫性也没有由此而降低。随着新冠肺炎疫情防控形势趋好，我们选择什么样的路径来应对气候变化和全球环境危机是至关重要的。

影响了整个世界的新冠肺炎疫情，进一步证明了建立有弹性的食物体系的生态安全的必要性。截至目前，通过过度使用化学品、水资源的单一化种植体系和陆地（和海洋）上的集约化畜禽养殖体系生产的食物对土壤、水和其他自然资源造成的破坏超过了它们的再生速度。这些农业活动排放的温室气体占人为温室气体排放量的1/4，其中一半是牲畜排放的。当今世界有很多人遭受着水循环破坏、土壤和水污染、生态系统恶化、生物多样性急剧减少、荒漠化和不卫生的城市集中区带来的影响。随着气候变化和人口增长，影响当今食物系统的问题可能会使社会遭受更大的健康和金融方面的冲击。

此外，对粮食安全至关重要的部门并不是独立运作的。几十年来，同食物供给相关的农业、水利、环境、林业、卫生、气象、贸易和运输等部门都按自己的想法和战略运作，部门之间的协调运作很少。整合这些不同的部门，可使中国从新冠肺炎疫情中走出来变得更为强大。

本章提出的综合思维的系统观，可为我们解决以下复杂问题提供支撑，即如何确保食物体系的丰富收成，可满足2050年时中国人的营养食品需求和维持自然栖息地与健康生态系统？如何使灌溉用水在生态上更健康？如

何减少农业活动产生的氮磷钾污染？如何借助于树木和森林构建能使农业生产受益的农业景观？如何使农民获得适应和应对气候变化的能力？如何通过食物体系来消除同饮食有关的疾病？如何使食物体系来改善农民的生计？如何编制和实施食物体系转型的综合计划？

因此，新冠肺炎疫情后的经济恢复，为我们重新思考现有的食物体系和生产、分配、消费食物的方式，增强食物生产体系抵御未来可能由气候变化引发的冲击的能力，建设一个更健康的世界，并确保环境可持续性和所有人的健康营养，提供了一个独特的机会。

2008 年亚洲开发银行发布的《2008—2020 年长期战略框架》（亚洲开发银行 2020 年战略），明确了该机构 2020 年的目标。虽然亚洲开发银行 2020 年的战略侧重于三个关键战略议程——包容性经济发展、环境可持续增长和区域一体化，但该战略也涵盖了亚太国家面临的广泛的可持续发展问题和挑战。该战略框架特别强调，消除贫穷仍然是亚太国家的一项主要挑战，它们经济的快速增长正在给环境带来巨大的压力，特别是影响范围大的空气污染、土壤污染和水污染，以及自然资源基础破坏和气候变化。毫无疑问，这些巨大的压力正在破坏各国政府提高农业生产力和粮食安全的努力。

关于中国，亚洲开发银行董事会于 2016 年 2 月批准了 2016~2020 年的国家伙伴关系战略（CPS）。CPS 旨在支持中国政府的改革议程，特别是解决气候变化与环境问题、知识合作以及制度和治理改革。该战略认为，中国农业部门面临的气候变化和环境挑战大多非常严峻，迫切需要做出转型的回应。虽然中国水土污染和生态系统退化的损失很难评估，但大多人认为这些损失占国内生产总值（GDP）的 6%~9%。根据一项研究，2010 年，空气、土壤和水污染以及生态系统退化不仅损害了农业生产力和其他基于资源的产业，还造成 120 万人过早死亡。[①] 此外，中国还面临巨大且日益加剧的气候变化风险。2100 年的气候变化预测表明，中国北部和西部的气温预计上升 4.5 摄氏度，东南部将上升 3 摄氏度。东北部的降水量可能增加 20%，东南部的降水量增加很少甚至没有增加，它们的可变性是关键问题。

---

① Horton R., "Global Burden of Disease Study", *The Lancet*, 2012（380）.

而在 1.2 亿公顷农业用地中，因遭受风暴、干旱、洪水和山体滑坡等气候灾害影响的作物平均歉收面积估计为 3917 万公顷。[①]

第一节　中国粮食安全的挑战

一　粮食安全的概念

粮食安全的概念是 1972~1974 年发生世界粮食危机时首次被提出的。1974 年，联合国粮食和农业组织（FAO）在《世界粮食安全国际承诺书》中指出，粮食安全应被视为人类的一项基本生存权利。这个定义是基于这样一个事实，即在维持粮食消费的稳定增长和抵消生产和价格波动时，都要考虑让人们在任何时候都能有充足、营养丰富、多样化、平衡和合意的粮食供应。40 多年来，粮食安全的含义逐渐由数量型向质量型转变，即从粮食数量安全向粮食质量安全、资源安全和生态安全转变。

从全球角度看，2050 年全球人口预计增加到 91 亿左右，农业将面临多重挑战。在那时，世界必须用更少的劳动力生产更多的粮食来养活日益增长的人口，为潜在的巨大的生物能源市场提供更多的原料，并采用更高效、更可持续、更适应气候变化的生产方式来促进全面发展。要养活 91 亿人口，2050 年的粮食总产量应比 2005 年与 2007 年的总产量提高 70% 左右。联合国粮农组织提出，应对上述粮食安全挑战需要采取以下措施：第一，向同农业生产力增长密切相关的部门投资，如建设道路、电力、仓储和灌溉系统等农村基础设施；第二，向改善农民发展环境的机构投资，如建立技术研发、推广服务、土地产权制度，兽医和食品质量安全控制系统和保险；第三，向对人类福祉产生积极影响的社会部门投资，如建立食品质量安全网、兴办社会事业和为最贫困者提供扶持。[②]

---

① FAO:《2050 年或存在粮食不安全问题》http://www.savetheplanet.org.cn/gb/org/fao/3985.html.
② FAO, *Global agriculture towards 2050*, http://www.fao.org/fileadmin/templates/wsfs/docs/Issues_papers/HLEF2050_Global_Agriculture.pdf, 2009。

二 中国粮食产量 40 年的连续增长

几千年来，中国农业以传统农业为主，主要以农产品的数量满足人们对粮食的需求。传统农业主要从以下四个方面取得进步：第一，农田改良，特别是利用人畜粪便作为肥料和种植绿肥作物；第二，农业技术改进，如实行轮作、选种和培育新品种；第三，农具改进，特别是改进整地工具（如使用曲辕犁）和灌溉工具（如役畜驱动的水车）；第四，顺应当地条件，特别是农耕季节。尽管有这些改进，但这个时期的农业生产力仍受到洪水、干旱、霜冻等自然灾害或战争的影响。

在中国历史上，有限的耕作空间一直是粮食安全面临的重大挑战，这也使中国长期存在粮食短缺和饥荒。由于人口众多，耕地资源有限，中国粮食经常处于短缺状态。为了控制消费和激励生产，中国政府在城市实行了粮票制度（1955~1993 年），在农村实行了激励农民的土地承包改革（1981 年）。截至 2018 年，中国用世界上 8% 的农业用地养活了世界上 21% 的人口，人均耕地面积约为 0.09 公顷，仅为世界平均水平的 40%。[1] 此外，小农拥有的农田大多是分散的小地块，其中 60% 的地块低于 0.1 公顷。[2]

尽管存在这些不利条件，中国目前已经基本解决了粮食供给不足的问题。1996 年，中国政府发布了一份关于粮食生产问题的白皮书，确立了包括水稻、小麦和玉米在内的主要粮食作物自给率达到 95% 以上的目标。为了进一步加强粮食安全，2008 年中央一号文件提出要实施"粮食战略规划"和创建一批基础条件好、生产水平高、商品粮数量大的粮食核心产区的具体措施。党的十五届三中全会通过的《中共中央关于农业和农村工作若干重大问题的决定》明确指出，粮食主产区不仅要在粮食生产方面发挥重要作用，而且要在增强国家粮食安全方面发挥关键作用，因此，建立了河北、辽宁、吉林、黑龙江、江苏、安徽、江西、山东、河南、湖北、湖南、四川、

---

[1] Ge D. et al., "Farmland transition in its influences in grain production in China", *Land Use Policy*, 2018(70), pp.94–105.

[2] Xiao Y. et al., "Optimal farmland conversion under double restraints of economic growth and resources protection", *J. Cleaner Production*. 2017 (142), pp.524–537.

内蒙古自治区 13 个省（自治区）的粮食主产区。

中国在粮食安全方面的改革取得了非常显著的成果。这些成果的取得同家庭联产承包责任制、农业激励、技术改进和农田防护林建设的成功实施密切相关。2017 年，中国粮食产量从 1982 年的 3.54 亿吨增加到 6.18 亿吨，增长了 74%，超过同期人口增长率约 34 个百分点。① 小麦、水稻和玉米三种主要粮食作物的自给率超过 95%，消费的大豆约 80% 是进口的，牛奶和糖料的进口也较多。中国农业是农村就业的重要引擎，为 3.2 亿农民的就业和收入做出了贡献。从同期全球比较来看，中国粮食产量占世界粮食总产量（28.18 亿吨）的比重稳定在 29% 左右。② 这表明，中国已经成功地保证了稳定的粮食自给，并确保了近乎绝对的粮食安全，以满足其人口的巨大粮食需求。③ 事实上，目前的粮食生产似乎处于结构性供过于求的状态。④ 今后，随着良种的发展，灌溉效率的提升，地膜覆盖面积的扩大，农业机械化水平的提高，土地流转和新型农业经营主体出现带来规模经济的增加，中国粮食安全在数量上是有保障的。⑤

三　中国粮食安全面临的挑战

中国由于过去几十年管理松懈，以及片面追求国内生产总值的增长而过度开采国家的自然资源，破坏了环境条件。特别是在粮食主产区和平原农区，这种发展模式导致的一系列严重的生态和环境问题对粮食安全造成了挑战。它们包括以下几个方面。

土壤非点源化学污染。它是由过量施用化学肥料和杀虫剂导致的农地

---

① 中华人民共和国农业部：《中国农业年鉴》，中国农业出版社；Carter C.A. et al., "Advances in Chinese agriculture and its global implications", *Economic Perspectives and Policy*, 2012, 34(1), pp.1–36.

② World Bank, *World Bank Open Data*, available online: https://data.worldbank.org.cn.

③ Huang J. et al., "Understanding recent challenges and new food policy in China", *Global Food Security*, 2017（12）, pp.119–126.

④ Wang D.et al., "The implications on food security in China based on the reform of the agricultural supply side structure", *Economist*, 2017.

⑤ Zhun Xu et al., "A Decade of Consecutive Growth or Stagnation? University of Oregon", *Monthly Review*, 2014（66）.

污染扩散的有害状态。[①] 这类污染至少造成 3 种后果：质量平衡（调节功能）受损；作物生长（生产功能）有缺陷；人和动物食用受污染的产品和饮用被污染的地下水而有健康风险。事实上，40 多年来，中国化肥施用量从 1980 年的 1269.4 万吨增加到 2016 年的 5984.1 万吨，增长了 3.7 倍。其中复合肥施用量增长最快，达 80.1 倍。同期杀虫剂施用量从不足 100 万吨增至 370 万吨，2017 年中国每公顷粮田的杀虫剂平均施用量为 11.6 公斤，比发达国家每公顷粮田的杀虫剂平均施用量高出约 50%。

土壤点源污染。它们主要来自工矿区周边的倾倒区和废水池，以及交通基础设施和城市中心的大气沉降、重金属及其他有害物质。在重金属中，镉（Cd）污染发生的概率最高（25.3%），其次是镍（Ni）、汞（Hg）、砷（As）和铅（Pb）污染。

农地土壤板结引发的地表水径流造成的土壤侵蚀。它主要是由化肥替代有机肥和过量施用化肥造成的。

农田表土侵蚀率加快。特别是东北地区肥沃的黑土层侵蚀和西南喀斯特地区石漠化的加剧。当前的监测数据显示，黑土区耕地表土层每年流失 0.3 厘米~1.0 厘米，部分耕地黑土层厚度由 80 厘米~100 厘米减少到 40 厘米~50 厘米甚至 20 厘米~30 厘米。随着黑土层变薄，土壤有机质含量由原来的 3%~6% 下降到当前的 2%~3%。

地表和地下水资源减少。由于灌溉效率低下，用于灌溉的地表水和地下水资源减少，导致一些地区缺水。[②] 用于灌溉的地下水的水位下降的主要原因是灌溉面积扩大（中国的有效灌溉面积从 1949 年的 1590 万公顷增加到 1978 年的 4496 万公顷和 2016 年的 6710 万公顷）和农民偏爱用地下水灌溉。实行家庭联产承包责任制以后，安排农户之间的灌溉次序和组织灌区设施维护的集体行动的难度都变大了，农民之间的用水矛盾也增多了。

[①] 农地的非点源污染主要是化肥的过量和低效使用造成的。中国化肥用量在过去 30 年中增加了 3 倍，平均利用效率为 32%，而世界的平均利用效率为 55%。现代农业实践通常需要高水平的肥料和农药，由此造成的营养和化学元素盈余通过各种扩散过程转移到土壤和水体中。水体中营养素浓度过高引起的富营养化和动植物物种的损失，会产生不利影响。

[②] 中国人均可用水量只有 2050 立方米，是世界人均水平的 25%。农村作物灌溉用水占中国需水总量的 60%，农业用水效率为 30%~40%，而发达国家的农业用水效率为 70%~80%。

在自己地里打井和改用地下水灌溉，确实是解决这些问题的途径之一。改革开放以来打井和抽水装备越来越先进、电力可用性越来越好、输水管越来越轻便，极大地降低了农民用地下水灌溉的成本，这也是农民偏爱井灌的重要原因。

农膜太薄、易碎导致的农田白色污染。现实中使用的农膜太薄且易碎，极大地增加了农民收集废弃农膜的劳动量。散落在农地表面的废弃农膜又随着犁地进入土壤，造成了农田的白色污染。截至目前，尚不清楚这些进入土壤且越来越多的塑料残留物会对陆地环境造成哪些负面影响。

耕地被城市、工业和基础设施占用而减少。1984年以来，中国的城市化、工业化进程明显加快，基础设施建设力度不断加大，这些建设占用了相当一部分耕地。这些活动占用的大多是优质耕地，它们对农业用地造成的冲击性影响要显著大于其占用的耕地面积的影响。

农田防护林的生态效益下降。农田防护林和农林间作在中国有悠久的历史。农田防护林在实践中确实对作物生产力施加了许多积极的影响。它们提供的内部服务包括改善小气候、提高土壤肥力、保持水质和恢复地下水位、封存碳和减少温室气体排放，以及获得木材和相关的特殊产品等额外收入。尽管防护林对作物生产力有上述好处，但也存在影响农民在农业景观中维持和扩展它们的一系列制约因素和障碍。它们包括林带或林木配置过密、胁地（树冠遮阴）、树木产权不明确、管理规定不健全、木材价格下降和木材替代品增多对农业生产的影响。最主要的问题是，缺乏足够的财政支持来补偿农民营造和维护防护林的成本。为了增加耕地面积而去除防护林或使其退化，可能会产生土壤退化等负面影响，增加山洪暴发的可能性，并大大降低地下水补给的可能性。①

森林生态系统退化。它与生物多样性普遍丧失有关。1998年以前，过度采伐和忽视森林管理导致天然林面积大幅度减少，径流量增加、洪涝风险和河道侵蚀增加，降雨量和湿度、地表和地下水资源、动植物的生物多

---

① David Ellison, "Background Study prepared for the 13th session of the United Nations Forum on Forests *UNFF–Forests and Water*, 2018.

样性和耕地生态保护减少。中国森林覆盖率在过去 40 多年里显著增加，六大林业重点工程的实施[①]，缓解了环境退化，满足了中国对林产品的巨大需求。根据国家森林资源清查，中国森林覆盖率从 1981 年的 14% 增加到 2015 年的 22.16%，全国森林总面积达到 2.083 亿公顷，其中天然林面积达 1.218 亿公顷。然而，最近的遥感研究表明，森林覆盖率的显著增加主要因为农地转为了林地，这些人工林主要采用单一种植单一树种的方式，主要用来生产木材、纤维和水果，而不是增加生物多样性和生态系统服务效益。此外，中国的许多地区不太关注天然林的可持续管理，缺乏相应的措施。消除人工林经营中的缺陷，采用天然更新的方式恢复森林和生物多样性，改善农业景观，仍然是政府迫切需要解决的问题。

当前的种植模式在应对气候变化影响时具有脆弱性。2018 年 10 月 IPCC 发布的一份报告指出，除非全球气温上升保持在 1.5 摄氏度以下，否则人类和自然生态系统的运行状况将面临巨大困难。因此，气候变化是影响中国粮食安全的关键因素之一。气候变化可能导致作物生长期的逐渐延长，气温的升高进而使蒸散量增大可能会对粮食生产产生不利影响，特别是对小麦和玉米产量有影响。此外，气候变暖有可能增加常见病虫害的风险，并导致南方作物害虫北移，产生新的病虫害，从而使粮食减产。新的研究表明，气温每升高 1 摄氏度，三种最重要的粮食作物——小麦、水稻和玉米，因虫害造成的产量损失可能增加 10%~25%。气候变化不仅会影响作物产量，还会影响灌溉用水的可用性，进而增加灌溉用水的压力。正如过去几十年经历的那样，由于同气候有关的灾害发生的可能性增加，现有农田对自然灾害的总体抵抗力可能急剧下降，从而作物产量在不久的将来会出现更大的波动。

这些问题会造成农业用地的生态系统功能迅速退化，对农业生产力、粮食数量安全和粮食质量安全造成严重后果。如果说中国现在正在为过去几十年依靠化肥农药集约投入和灌溉实现的农业生产的巨大增长付出沉重

---

① 即退耕还林工程、天然林保护工程、防护林体系建设工程（三北防护林工程）、工业人工林工程、野生动植物保育和自然保护区保护工程、环北京荒漠化防治工程。

的代价，那么当前的生态系统退化和环境污染正在威胁中国的经济增长、社会发展和粮食安全。[①] 在最坏的情况下，农用化学品的过量投入对土壤和水的化学和物理影响要么是不可逆转的，要么只能以非常高的代价逆转。因此，强烈建议中国政府在农业景观保护中坚持预防性原则，这是十分必要的。鉴于这一现状，为了确保农业土壤能够继续发挥其维持生命的功能，绝对需要一种考虑到所有自然资源，特别是土壤和水的功能的可持续和综合的土地管理办法。

上面提及的问题并不是中国才有的问题。世界上约有1/4的耕地退化，[②] 这种退化同环境退化结合在一起，如森林生态系统退化、土地污染、土壤养分退化和土壤盐碱化，会造成粮食生产的自然资源需求和环境提供和补充这些资源的能力之间的差距越来越大。例如，南亚大约43%的农地已经退化，3100万公顷的农地已经高度退化。由于无管制的开采和工农业之间、商用与民用之间、城乡居民之间对稀缺的水资源竞争的加剧，地下水的含水层迅速枯竭，灌溉用水可得性的威胁越来越大。总之，这些问题造成了土地和水资源的破坏和严重的生产和收入损失 [③]，进一步威胁到粮食安全、经济持续增长和减贫的前景。因此，维护自然资本也必须是所有亚洲国家的一个重要目标。[④]

四　中国粮食安全政策背景

21世纪初以来，中国政府非常重视制定综合环境保护政策和相关规划。特别是在空气、水和土壤质量方面，中国政府采取了一系列旨在改善中国环境状况的行动。更具体地说，在建设生态文明的背景下 [⑤]，环境保护、粮

---

① Honggi Zhang and Erqi Xu，"An evaluation of the ecological and environmental security on China's terrestrial ecosystems"，*Science Report*，2017（7），pp.811.

② FAO: The State of Food and Agriculture 2014，Innovation in Family Farming, Rome, 2014.

③ M. Khor.，*Land degradation causes $10 billion loss to South Asia Annually*，2013，http://www.twnside. org.sg/title/land-ch.htm.

④ ADB，*Environment Operational Directions 2013—2020: Promoting Transitions to Green Growth in Asia and the Pacific*. Manila，2013.

⑤ UNEP，*Green is Gold: The Strategy and Actions of China's Ecological Civilization*，2016.

食安全、自然资源可持续利用、减少污染、农村可持续发展、减缓和适应气候变化已被牢牢地放在中国农业政策发展议程的核心位置。从 20 世纪 90 年代末到 21 世纪初，中国制定的《中国 2030 年可持续发展议程国家实施方案》、《国家可持续农业发展规划（2015—2020 年）》（以及相关的中央一号文件）、《国家气候变化规划（2014—2020 年）》、《中国生物多样性保护战略与行动计划（2011—2030 年）》等 16 个相关的可持续发展规划践行了这一承诺。

此外，2018 年 9 月，国务院发布了《乡村振兴战略规划（2018—2022 年）》。这项新的政策文件概述了为实现农村产业兴旺、生态宜居、乡风文明、治理有效、生活富裕的目标而要完成的主要任务。这一新战略体现了中国在农村地区实现乡村振兴三个目标的路线图：2020 年，建立乡村振兴的体制和治理框架；2035 年，完成农村和农业现代化；2050 年，实现城乡生活水平均等化，完成乡村振兴战略。

这一战略特别强调，解决与农业、农村和农民有关的问题是中国的根本，因为这些问题直接关系到国家稳定、粮食安全和人民福祉，因此必须优先发展农业和农村地区。在农业转型方面，该战略提供了更清晰的路径，旨在巩固和完善农村基本经营制度。提倡农村土地制度改革，完善农村承包地所有权、承包权、经营权分离制度。在这方面，它确认农村土地承包做法将保持稳定和长期不变，在现有合同到期后再延长 30 年。这一战略还强调，中国应该始终保障自己的粮食安全。从这个意义上讲，中国农业必须建立产业、生产和商业运作体系，形成一个坚持绿色发展的现代农业，特别是生态农业。同时，要完善支持农业和保护农业的治理体系，突出山、水、林、田、湖、草的综合保护。该战略还强调环境可持续发展的重要性，特别是消除非点源污染的负面影响，可持续地利用地表和地下水资源以及综合利用农村废弃物，提高农产品的安全和质量。因此，该战略要求地方政府加强农民的生态环境保护意识，使他们深刻认识到，生态环境良好的农业景观不仅有利于农民的生产和生活，而且有利于国家粮食安全。

第二节　转变视角：将生态安全理念引入中国粮食安全

一　中国生态安全：一个新的概念

生态安全是指生态系统的完整性和健康性[①]。景观的可持续性可以通过结构的稳定性等指标来衡量。该系统还可以衡量的是生态系统对压力的恢复力。生态安全是人类生存和发展的前提。生态安全的维护需要采取两项措施，一是通过保护消除生态风险，二是通过发展降低生态系统的生态脆弱性。由于不同生态系统生态安全的变异程度不同，生态安全水平存在差异。此外，生态安全的程度是动态的，它会随着社会发展和生态需求的提高而发生变化。也就是说，人类可以通过保护和发展调节生态安全。然而，生态安全的维护是有代价的，消除那些来自人类活动的生态安全威胁，需要大量的投资。

在中国，由于影响粮食安全的生态和环境问题的严重性，将自然资源问题和社会生态结合在一起的必要性变得越来越重要，因为在生态文明的概念范围内，传统的国家安全观已逐渐扩展到环境和人类安全问题方面。纵观影响中国安全的六大生态安全压力——粮食安全、生态系统退化、能源、水、城市化和气候变化，可以发现，当前的政策需要完善。事实上，中国的生态系统仍面临着自然资源退化、粮食供应紧张、能源需求快速增长，以及水质和水量的冲突等问题；对快速城市化进程中的环境和社会问题，以及气候变化影响的日益加剧，缺乏充分的关注等问题。为了解决这些安全问题，中国的政策制定者必须减少对技术解决方案的依赖，而应该进行适应性管理改革，通过跨学科问题的解决、制度能力的提高和政策与实施差距的消除来解决生态安全问题。

二　生态安全与粮食安全具有明显的协同效应

现在，粮食主产区以谷物为中心的投入密集型的生产系统的可持续性

[①] 国际应用系统分析研究所于1989年将生态安全定义为人类生活、健康、福祉、基本权利、生计保障来源、必要资源、社会秩序和人类适应环境能力的变化。它包括自然生态安全、经济安全和社会安全。生态安全与生态风险负相关，与生态健康正相关。

已经出现了问题。特别是，未来的挑战已经显现，例如要素生产率下降；土壤肥力退化和污染，以及过度使用化肥和杀虫剂造成的地下水和地表水污染；可用于灌溉的地下水减少；土壤有机质下降；土壤板结、投入品成本增加和农场利润的相对下降、农田防护林保护功能退化；气候异常对农业生产力不利影响的风险增加，气候变化导致的病虫害发生率增加等。

在当前气候变化的情境下，中国农业确实面临着三重挑战。为了满足粮食安全的需要，中国必须提高农业生产力，特别要缩小实际产量和可获得产量之间的差距，同时要适应气候变化，减少其对环境的影响。鉴于极端天气风险的增加，这不能仅以牺牲生产弹性为代价。需要同时提高生产力、可持续性和应对气候变化的能力。这将需要大量投资，以及改善跨部门的协作方式。

加强生态安全，保障粮食安全，需要克服影响当前农业生产可持续性的主要挑战，特别是减少影响作物生产方面的挑战。从这个意义上说，生态安全的保障取决于减少过度使用合成肥料、杀虫剂和其他农用化学品对农业土壤和地下水造成的持续和持久的非点源污染[1]；减少过度开采可利用的地下水资源造成的灌溉用水可得性的不断减少；减少气候变化带来的不利影响，特别是降水模式变化导致的土壤含水量、径流和侵蚀、养分循环、盐碱化、生物多样性和土壤有机质的变化，以及减少极端气候事件频发而带来的影响，此外，还应减少一系列导致农田防护林防护效益不断退化的制约因素带来的影响，包括农田防护林的胁地影响，使农民愿意保存农田防护林，这也需要得到政府的财政支持。

上述问题的解决，需要运用综合措施改善农业景观层面的生态安全，辅之协调一致的跨部门政策处理好粮食生产系统的经济、环境和社会层面的问题，这将有助于实现多种可持续性发展目标。在这方面，生态安全是解决复杂的相互关联和多部门挑战的基础，特别是《中国落实2030年可持续发展议程国别方案》这个实现环境、社会和经济三个层面的综合可持续

---

[1] 合成肥料是甲烷气体排放及土地和水污染的主要来源，减少合成肥料的用量将降低土壤和水污染的风险以及减少与不当使用有关的特定健康问题。

发展的国家框架提出的解决与贫困、饥饿、环境退化和气候变化有关的复杂挑战的基础。此外，生态安全需要在政策推广、农村机构和伙伴关系以及粮食生产、加工、营销和消费方面进行创新。《中国落实2030年可持续发展议程国别方案》特别呼吁，在改善粮食和农业部门的生态安全方面，要有更好的政策、体制和技术。它还呼吁所有人都应成为变革的重要推动者。

三 中国生态安全面临的七大挑战

中国的农业文化可以追溯到5000年前。但是，这种文化过去与自然和谐相处，而现在一切都依赖化学品和过度使用水资源。1979年以前，农家肥被用作农业生产中的主要肥料，水污染非常罕见。《土壤污染防治法》旨在对化肥和农药的使用进行立法规范，防止土壤污染。虽然，这部法律早就实施了，但目前还没有迹象表明现行法律确实对生态安全产生了积极影响。实际上，正是经济因素和投入补贴政策促使农民使用更多的化肥和农药。至于农药，如果生物农药对人体的影响较小，它们对害虫防治就没有那么有效，而且价格更贵。农民大多不愿意支付更高的费用购买药效较低的生物农药，其后果是生物农药替代品市场目前尚未发育起来。

针对未来粮食安全面临的七大挑战，即化肥农药过量施用引起农村面源污染的挑战，地下水资源过度利用引起地下水位下降的挑战，耕地土壤污染、土层变薄和被占用对粮食总产量和质量的挑战，林带林网破碎化引起农田防护林防护功能下降的挑战，农业劳动力成本快速上升引起农业竞争力下降的挑战，农村青壮年劳动力进城就业引起农业劳动力老龄化的挑战，气候变化引起极端气候发生概率增加的挑战，中国采取了以下措施：减少粮食系统对生态系统，特别是土地、土壤、水和生物多样性的负面影响，提高它们应对自然灾害和紧急情况的能力；建立"有利于自然"的粮食系统，维持乃至增加农业生态系统以及粮食安全所依赖的自然资源和生态系统服务；完善综合粮食安全治理系统，特别是将环境保护纳入景观或流域一级粮食安全政策的主流，促进和维护复杂的多功能农业景观，增加农业生产和生态系统服务；制定部门政策协调流程，提高决策者跨多个部门（纵向、横向和暂时）工作的能力，支持基于化学品投入的集约型农业向更具弹性的生态型农业转型，以应对未来危机；支持积极的激励措施——从监管到基于市场和规范的激励措施，以引导农民为发展可持续、自然积极的食品体系做出生产选择。通过培训、程序、激励、监测和评估改善推广管理，特别是通过使用数字工具改善与农民的互动（例如及时、适当地向农民提供正确的信息），提高农业推广系统治理的效率。

第三节　实施生态安全战略提高中国粮食安全水平

粮食安全的脆弱性始于单个农场，扩展到粮食主产区则体现为益鸟益虫栖息地消失、农地物种多样性减少，土壤板结和地边防护林退化。由于可持续粮食安全所需的许多资源已经捉襟见肘，随着前所未有的城市化和工业化，农田污染，水资源减少和自然栖息地破坏，中国的粮食安全遇到了巨大挑战，而多重压力同气候变化相叠加也使克服这些挑战变得更加困难。它们不仅会对农业生产力产生重大影响，进而对粮食安全产生重大影响，而且还会对数百万农民的社会经济状况产生重大影响。

如上所述，增强中国农场和农业景观层面的生态安全的主要措施是践行生态农业，减少非点源污染，恢复退化的和重污染的土壤的肥力；建立更有效的灌溉系统和改善地下水管理，保护土壤水分、有机质和养分；推广抗旱品种和在农场、景观层面重新引进树木，提高粮食安全体系的复原力；重点改善农民的社会经济条件。然而，中国同其他发达和发展中国家一样，农民无法独自应对巨大的风险，这些风险很可能在不久的将来影响到粮食安全，因此，他们需要得到政府的支持。

在中国粮食安全的背景下，从农田和景观层面解决影响可持续农业的生态安全负面因素，需要综合实施四条战略行动路线。没有哪一组行动能够单独达到改善农场和景观层面生态安全的最终目标。

一　建立农业景观和农场层面的生态保护体系

该体系的目标不仅要从景观层面控制土地退化和侵蚀，还要加强农业生态系统的功能和农业生产，维护和提高现有生物多样性的效益，改善农民生活条件，为复兴农业景观及增强其旅游吸引力提供重大支持。生态安全防护体系建设的第一阶段始于 20 世纪 70 年代，先后启动了"十大"防护林体系，主要包括三北防护林体系、七大江河防护林体系、沿海防护林体系和旨在控制土地侵蚀和荒漠化的农田防护林体系。该体系建设的第二阶段始于 1990 年代末，包括天然林保护工程、退耕还林工程、退牧还草工程和湿地保护与恢复工程等。这些生态保护工程目前仍在实施中，预计将实施 20~40 年。

这个可持续的土地管理体系的基本组成部分之一是有益于生态安全的生态保护结构，如农田防护林、保护自然栖息地和生物多样性的生态位缓冲带、生态廊道和湿地，以及为授粉的昆虫提供筑巢机会等。为了提供一个有利于农业生产力的生态安全的环境，中国在历史上就采用了把树木融入农业景观的做法，特别是设计有利于作物产量的微气候，保护农田免受气候异常造成的干热风和干旱的影响，控制水土流失，增强土壤养分循环，固碳和保护生物多样性，生产木材、食物、饲料、药用植物、精油和地方产业所需的材料等。把树木和自然栖息地保育融入农业景观也是在所有尺度上建立气候变化复原力以及加强碳封存的重要举措。世界银行最近的一项研究甚至提出，在一系列生态农业实践中，农业景观中的树木具有最高的固碳潜力。

构建这些生态保护结构时，应注意乔木、灌木与作物系统相结合，以尽量减少树木对作物生产力可能产生的负面影响，同时不影响农业机械作业。由于大多数生态保护结构是在农场和／或农业景观层面发展的，所以部门之间的政策和制度协调仍然是一个重要的改进事项。其他需要考虑的部门协调问题包括以下几点。

明确土地和林木的产权和管理义务，特别是在景观和农场层面上营造农田防护林，产权和管理义务不清会限制它们发展和降低维护防护林农民的参与度。

采取适当的财政补偿（中国的生态补偿政策），进一步提高农民在建设和维护这些生态保护结构中的参与度。

采用近自然的森林管理方法，提高根据再造林规划建造的人工林的生态和结构稳定性，提高其应对自然和人为干扰，特别是气候变化带来的影响的灵活性和能力。

二　建立农业非点源污染控制体系

提高农田土壤肥力的同时要减少化肥和农药的使用，从而减少农业非点源污染。提高农田肥力和生产安全食品需要采取以下四类措施。

严格控制合成肥料和农药的施用量。按照现有的测土配方施肥，发放用肥配额和推广缓控释肥、有机肥等。然而，增加有机肥的供给和用量需要建立生态产业链，要在大型畜禽养殖公司产生的原料的基础上运作。

根据农田污染或退化的严重程度，采取物理、化学、生物或农艺措施，恢复被污染和已经退化的农田的肥力。

加强生态友好型农药和应用技术的使用。开展生态友好型农药的使用，需要增加低毒生物农药研发试点，为农民加快使用和安全使用生态友好型农药进行培训和提供补贴。

提高地膜标准和完善相关的质量控制机制，减少白色污染。加大研发力度，开发轻型可生物降解的地膜和农耕作业中经常使用的多功能残膜收集和回收设备。

三　开展点源污染治理

乡镇工业层面的点源污染治理和改造需要采用两项主要措施：关停小水泥厂、小皮革厂、土法炼焦厂等15类污染最严重的小企业；建立县级点源污染综合控制体系，对分散在县内的企业的污染风险、污染程度和需要采取的补救措施进行评估。这个点源污染控制系统的目标是创建一个无污染的县级工业区。根据土壤污染防治行动计划，这两项措施目前已在实施中。

四　建立水资源保护体系

该体系旨在减少地下水用量和推广节水灌溉技术的水资源保护制度包括以下四项措施。

推广低压管道、喷灌和滴灌（替代漫灌）的灌溉方式，使渗入农田的水不受田面高低不平的影响，并减少水渗漏，灌溉均匀性的提高可以减少30%~50%的用水量。

实行用水定额制度和发放可交易的水票。发展水权交易市场，鼓励农民将自己的用水量降低到粮食生产所需的水平上，并将余下的水票卖出去获取收益。近年来，中国地下水管理采取了"一井一表、一户一卡"的计量模式，政府在每口井旁安装一个智能水表，使农民可以对用多少水权购买灌溉用水和通过水权让渡获得水权收益做出选择。

调整种植模式（如"一季休耕一季雨养"模式和改"小麦、玉米一年两收为一年一收"）和粮食作物结构，适应季节特点，提升土壤水分和水资源可用性（如增加低耗水作物和/或采用旱作耕作方式）。

进一步推广农田覆盖技术，包括地膜覆盖和秸秆覆盖。

五　采取生态耕作实践

按照生态安全的标准和生态农业的实践改造传统的高投入农业，以保障农田安全，是一个巨大的挑战。向更可持续的农业系统转型，需要改变现有的耕作方式，农场层面的日常管理、计划和营销。促进生态耕作有三个目标：加强农业生物多样性系统各组分之间的有益生物相互作用和协同作用，以加强生态服务，而不是只注重作物系统；将长期可持续性的概念纳入农业生态系统的总体设计和管理；高度重视农业系统的整体健康，而不是特定种植制度的成果。

六　构建农田生态景观体系

一些管理规则正在管理生态农业实践。它们的基本目的是提供最有利的土壤和小气候条件，特别是通过管理有机质和增强土壤生物活性。

从单作制转向复种制，目的是为作物提供最有利的土壤和小气候条件，特别是通过定期使用大量不同类型的有机材料来管理有机质和增强土壤生物活性。

定期使用大量不同类型的有机材料——动物粪便、堆肥、树叶、覆盖作物和能在地里留下大量作物残留物的轮作作物。

鼓励执行作物轮作和休耕制度和全面的农田管理实践，以提高作物产量的稳定性，如林粮间作、防风林、防护林、河流缓冲带、昆虫带、生物篱笆、林地等。

经常用生物或作物秸秆覆盖土壤，采用覆盖作物和草皮作物轮作，减耕、小耕或免耕。

持续支持作物品种的遗传改良。

第四节　构建中国农业景观生态安全的支持政策和制度

改善中国粮食主产区农业景观的生态安全的治理需要四个先决条件，即建立有利的政策环境，包括强制性、激励性和协调性政策；加强部门间协调机制；建立部门间监测和评价机制，评估生态安全措施的执行情况；修改授权，提高农业推广效率。

一　建立有利的政策环境

向农区特别是粮食主产区农业景观的生态安全投资，确保高度集约的农业系统过渡到可持续农业系统，克服气候变化对粮食安全的威胁，减少污染和化石能源的用量。上述目标的实现需要一个有利的治理框架。要在上述四个治理先决条件基础上补充三类政策。

加强农业景观层面的生态安全和农场层面的耕地保护的强制性政策、法律和法规。它们的目标是保护耕地，保育土壤肥力，控制水土流失，提高灌溉效率，严格控制合成肥料和农药用量，以保护水土免遭污染和富营养化。在这方面应考虑四类综合政策行动：改革现行的农业投入补贴政策体系，使投入补贴适合生态需求，对使用环境友好型化肥和农药实行优惠补贴；加强法律法规，制定并实施化肥农药施用定额，严格控制合成肥料和农药的使用，推广使用含微肥的强化有机肥；加强法律法规建设，加强水资源节约和节水技术的引进；农区特别是在粮食主产区建立农作物病虫害生物防治体系，推广机械化喷药技术，减少合成农药的施用量。

虽然《土地管理法》《农村土地承包法》和新修订的《环境保护法》都有保护和合理利用耕地的规定，但这些规定的可操作性有待完善。因此，建议政府根据这些法律的有关规定和生态安全要求，制定专门的耕地保护法律。这部新法律的目标是建立一个以耕地生态安全为核心，与现行耕地法规相衔接的法律体系。这部新法律应该成为各级政府、企业和农民规范保护耕地的指导。该法律应着眼于：建立面积为 1.2 亿公顷的永久性基本农田保护区；制定化肥、饲料、灌溉用水中危险和有害物质新标准，生物降解农用塑料薄膜新标准和修订农药包装标准；推广保护性耕作或免耕，防止水土流失、荒漠化、盐渍化、土壤板结和耕地裸露等；实施土地恢复措施，解决农田污染和表土变薄等问题；制定农用化学品使用标准和灌溉水质标准等；制定旨在提高农田防护林和农林复合经营的生态安全效益的新规定。如果对目前的农田防护林退化不加以扭转，它们历史上所提供的生态系统服务可能会荡然无存。由于目前农业、林业、自然保育和环境保护部门都自成体系，部门间政策和体制协调仍然是一个关键的改进事项。

鼓励农民改善农业景观的生态安全和保护耕地，需要三类激励政策：一是对化肥施用量低于用肥定额的农民发放奖金；二是发放可交易的水票，鼓励农民将超过粮食生产所需用水量的水票卖掉；三是采取生态补偿措施，鼓励农民保护生态环境，引导他们改善和维护农田生态景观。

二　完善生态补偿政策

在制定新的激励政策框架时，要特别注意生态补偿政策。生态补偿是将"生态文明"付诸实践的八种机制之一，包括环境财政改革，例如根据受益者和污染者付费原则和财政转移调整税收、补贴和价格，使生产经营者改变行为和方案，响应重要功能地区的需求。中国多年来一直在实施生态补偿，作为补偿生态系统服务的市场信号。[1] 更具体地说，推进中国农

---

[1] 截至 2015 年，以粮食补贴、有条件转移支付、实物奖励（如社区层面的投资）和混合奖励等形式进行的生态补偿投资总量为 690 亿美元。

业景观的生态安全需要采取以下生态补偿措施。

完全遵守旨在减少农用化学品投入的用量定额标准。

根据当地气候和土壤条件,控制和减少灌溉用水,确保粮食可持续生产。

促进有机肥和生物农药的使用,逐步提高土壤肥力。

改善农田生态景观,包括粮食主产区周边荒山荒坡的再造林、农林复合经营和平原农业景观的绿化,要特别重视在适宜地区建立和维护农田防护林。

设立旨在以可持续方式改善生态农业系统的研发项目,保障可持续的粮食生产。

提高跨部门效率的协调政策。加强农业景观中的生态安全的多功能作用,需要得到经济、金融、农业、林业、土地资源管理和气候变化政策的支持。仅靠农业部门一己之力通常不足以履行这一职能。经验表明,各部门政策的施行效率是通过部门间的相互协调而提高的,要满足生态安全要求,需要在各个部门和有关农民之间建立具体的国家治理和协调机制,加强农业景观生态安全所需的政策、生态农业实践和补救行动应以综合方式实施。[①]因此,加强部门间协调是完善农业景观生态安全战略的重要前提。这就需要有四个配套措施:一是增强合作意识,激发协作需求,强调优势互补,消除部门独自配置资源的诸多缺陷;二是规范部门间协调,确保参与者权利、责任和利益的对称;三是加快信息交流,提高信息交流的效率和综合性,使各自的管理更加公开、透明、高效、有用;四是通过建立退出机制和惩罚不合作行为来降低合作风险。

三 健全生态安全措施绩效监测评估机制

健全评估生态安全措施绩效的部门间监测和评估机制。透明的、独立的第三方监测和评价机制是部门间重要的协调工具。它的目标是评估和展示旨在加强农业景观和农田层面的生态安全而采取的政策、制度和技术措

---

① 例如,通过更好的政策协调会促进农田生态景观的开发、管理和维护,特别是但不限于农业和林业部门之间的协调,改善发展生态农业的条件,包括在适当情况下建设农田防护林的条件。

施的影响。对这个框架的主要建议是在监测和评价系统中嵌入环境影响评估研究，以确保政策、制度和技术措施的实施以及它们对农业社区的好处的长期可持续性。设计这种监测和评价系统时，应特别注意监测和评估生态补偿措施对生态安全和减贫的影响。监测和评估应该由相关部门、农民及外部监测和评估专家分别开展，并相互验证。

修改农业推广任务。旨在维持甚至提高粮食数量和质量安全的生态安全是中国农业面临的重大挑战。在这方面，农民需要获得新的、充分的知识和信息，以便了解当前影响粮食数量和质量安全的生态安全问题。要实现生态安全的目标，必须发展与生态安全有关的推广服务，包括农民为提高其农场和景观层面的生态安全、提高农业生产的质量及改善生活和生计所需而获得的知识、信息、技术和食品安全标准的关键途径。因此，必须及时地向农民提供有关生态安全的知识和信息。

如今，信息和通信技术（ICT），[1] 特别是移动智能电话技术的采用提高了人们对其传播创新的可持续农业技术的期望，也提高了农民通过它获取其他相关知识和信息的意识。[2] 因此，除了传统的推广方法外，基于电信和计算机网络，农民和其他利益相关者进行交流的手段也逐渐出现。现在世界上很多国家在农业推广中采用了信息和通信技术。然而，如果传播有关农业实践的信息可以使农民学到新的做法的重要性能得到充分认同，那么在农民、研究人员、推广机构和决策者之间建立交流的内在价值就不会不那么为人所知。

尽管中国农林领域在引入基于信息和通信技术的服务方面已经取得了一些进展，但在进一步开发、部署和利用基于信息和通信技术的信息传播模式方面仍然存在许多障碍。[3] 为了确定最有效的信息和通信技术工具和

---

① 信息和通信技术是一个总称，包括任何通信设备或应用，如手机、无线电、电视、计算机和网络硬件、软件、卫星地球观测系统等，以及与其相关的各种服务和应用，例如视频会议、远程学习和网络研讨会。

② Karen Vignare ,"Options and Strategies for Information and Communication within Agricultural Extension and Advisory Services", *USDA/Feed the Future*, 2013.

③ Yun Zhang et al., "in Agricultural information dissemination using ICTs: A review and analysis of information dissemination", *China-INFORMATION PROCESSING IN AGRICULTURE 3*, 2016, pp.17–29.

基础设施，使其提高粮食安全的生态安全，应考虑以下五个战略要点。

建立适当的信息和通信技术治理结构。各级政府要加大对信息和通信技术在农业景观生态安全方面的推广力度，尤其是提高农业主题、部门学科和商品之间的一体化和一致性，给予农民专门的支持，使信息和通信技术的采用有利于生态安全。

大学和研究中心要对影响农村地区采用信息和通信技术的关键问题进行研究。农业大学和相关的研究中心的传统作用是创造、储存和传播知识，现在应该在促进生态安全的信息和通信技术方面发挥更重要和更广泛的作用。

开发人类管理、分享、交流和使用科学技术知识以及采用与生态安全有关的措施的技能和能力。目前知道这一点的推广人员很少，所以推广人员要接受如何把信息和通信技术作为一种推广工具和方法的培训。

加大在推广中对信息和通信技术的投资。倘若没有扩展预算，很可能一事无成，但推广预算应该做相应的审查。关于推广，这些预算应侧重于代表农民向网络公司购买一揽子服务和技术支持，使农民能够免费地获得这些信息，而不应侧重于购买信息和通信技术设备。农民必须知道信息和通信技术的潜力，推广服务部门有责任把这个信息传递给农民。先让农民知道信息和通信技术工具在生态安全推广中的作用，然后培训他们如何有效利用信息和通信技术。

为信息和通信技术的推广建立适当的体制基础设施。要使信息和通信技术成为促进生态安全的推广工具，必须有一个适当的推广基础设施。截至目前，由于尚未把计算机、笔记本电脑和移动电话等基本的信息和通信技术设备作为推广工具，或并非总是以适当的形式供推广人员和农民使用。所以，在基于信息和通信技术的推广组织工作中，要通过适当的政策、战略、资源配置、能力开发、组织结构和程序，把信息整合在通信管理中。

四 结论

中国史无前例的经济增长使数亿人摆脱了贫困，然而，这给粮食数量安全和粮食质量安全所依赖的生态系统——土地、土壤、水、生物多样性带来了沉重的压力。不可持续的生产和消费模式的影响面的扩大导致了大气和土壤恶化，以及水污染、水资源短缺和废弃物的产生。所有这些都威胁着粮食安全、环境以及人类健康。农业所需的化学品、自然资源的增多和农业集约度的增强，正在造成环境退化和生物多样性丧失。中国正在实施生态文明和乡村振兴战略，正朝着绿色增长的方向发展，用于生态系统修复、再造林或可再生能源等方面的投资有所增加，但粮食需求的爆炸式增长有可能对过去的粮食安全造成威胁。气候变化的不利影响和自然灾害风险的增大可能会加剧这种威胁，对人类和金融造成毁灭性的损失。现在预计极端气候事件将成为新常态。

目前新冠肺炎疫情造成了农民生计和收入方面的损失，威胁到粮食、健康和营养安全，特别是不富裕人口的粮食、健康和营养安全，但它也为更好地把人类粮食系统与生态系统结合起来，实现健康和粮食安全的可持续性，提高复原力，带来了一些动力和启示。

本书梳理了中国粮食安全面临的挑战，揭示了农业生态系统退化的驱动因素，提出了建立农业非点源污染控制体系、水资源保障体系、生态防护体系、生态农业体系、政策支持体系、部门间协调机制、跨部门生态安全监测评估体系和粮食主产区生态补偿体系等应对这些挑战的八条行动路线，以及抓住推广生态农业实践、智能农业实践、优质农产品生产实践等机遇和开展农业政策体系、农田防护林体系、部门协同体系等创新，使中国粮食系统更包容、更高效、更可持续、更健康和应对未来冲击更具弹性。

本书就应对中国未来粮食安全的七个主要挑战做出了以下回应。

大幅减轻粮食生产对生态系统——土地、土壤、水和生物多样性的重大影响和减少温室气体排放，增强其适应气候变化和应对自然灾害的适应力。

努力建立对自然有益的粮食生产系统，维护乃至提升粮食安全所依赖的农业生态系统、自然资源和生态系统服务。

从"生态—农业—粮食系统"的角度，构建一个包括粮食生产、自然资源保护和生态系统服务的综合方法，并把它作为粮食安全政策和制度的组成部分。

完善粮食安全综合治理体系，特别是景观和流域层面的环境保护要成为粮食安全政策的主要内容，以改善和维护复杂的多功能农业景观，进而增加农业生产和生态系统服务。

制定部门政策协调制度，提高决策者协调多部门工作的能力，促进基于化学品投入的集约农业向更有弹性的"生态—农业—粮食系统"转型，并应对未来的危机。

建议政府改进管理方法。将行政管制调整为基于市场和规范的激励，引导农民做出有利于可持续的、对自然有益的粮食系统形成的生产选择。

提高农业推广系统的治理效率。从培训、激励、监测和评估入手提高推广管理效率，特别是运用数字工具增强与农民的互动，例如，以适当的方法及时地为农民提供正确的信息。

农学家、环保主义者、社会学家、经济学家和卫生专家逐渐形成的共识是，关于生态安全战略的任何策略都不能孤立地采用，因为它们是相互关联的。中国必须以可持续的方式提高粮食安全，以免已经稀缺的自然资源（土壤、土地和水）和已经脆弱的生态系统进一步耗竭和退化，同时为农民提供稳定的收入，并以合理的价格向所有消费者提供粮食。气候变化的背景下的生态安全战略还包括两个附加的且互补的战略目标：①持续开展多部门的协同的新技术研发和创新，并根据未来的挑战完善"生态—农业—粮食系统"和提高农业全要素生产率；②通过反复培训和岗位培训计划，增强农民关于"生态—农业—粮食系统"基本的农艺、生态和经济知识，帮助农民适应与气候变化有关的更大不确定性。

发展"生态—农业—粮食系统"的技术并将其规模化需要大量的财政投资。生态安全战略目标的实现可能有难度，但中国政府应该把生态安全战略作为中国粮食安全的核心和不可或缺的目标。

附件1　全球主要国家农药使用量变化

· **欧洲主要国家**

1. 法国：2002 年前杀菌剂年用量为 4 万~6 万吨，2011 年减至 2.5 万吨；2000 年前除草剂年用量为 3 万~4 万吨，2010 年为 2.2 万吨；20 世纪 90 年代杀虫剂年用量约为 1 万吨，2000 年后年用量为 2000~3000 吨；受气候变化影响，2013 年三类农药年用量分别增到 3 万吨、约 3 万吨和 3318 吨。

2. 西班牙：2010 年以前，杀菌剂、杀虫剂和除草剂年用量均在 1.0 万~1.5 万吨。2013 年杀菌剂年用量为 3.2 万吨，增加 1 倍多；除草剂年用量约为 1.5 万吨，增长 50%；杀虫剂年用量为 0.7 万吨，下降 50%。

3. 英国：2005 年前除草剂年用量为 2.0 万~2.5 万吨，近年来因使用更高活性的除草剂，2011~2013 年除草剂年用量约 7500 吨。杀菌剂用量年度间变化不大，年均用量为 5000~6000 吨；2000 年前后杀虫剂用量在 1500 吨左右，2011 年后年用量在 600~700 吨。

4. 德国：农药使用以除草剂为主，年用量为 1.5 万~2.0 万吨；其次是杀菌剂，年用量约为 1 万吨；杀虫剂年用量约为 1000 吨。农药用量年度间变化不大，近年来除草剂用量有所增加。

5. 意大利：2008 年杀菌剂年用量 5 万吨，2013 年年用量为 3.2 万吨，下降 36%；杀虫剂和除草剂用量年度间变化不大，杀虫剂年用量为 1 万~1.2 万吨，除草剂年用量在 0.7 万~1 万吨。

6. 荷兰：由于大量减少土壤消毒剂用量，20 世纪 90 年代中期与 80 年代中期相比，单位面积农药用量减少 50%。近年来杀菌剂、除草剂和杀虫剂的年用量分别为约 4000 吨、约 3000 吨和 266.9 吨。每公顷农药用量由 2008 年前的 5 千克下降到 2013 年约 4 千克。

· 亚洲主要国家

1. 韩国：从 1996 年开始控制农药使用，2001 年农药用量开始下降。杀虫剂、杀菌剂和除草剂的年用量由 2001 年的 9880 吨、9332 吨和 6380 吨分别降到 2013 年的 6403 吨、6324 吨和 4479 吨。平均每公顷农药用量由 20 世纪 70 年代至 90 年代的 13 千克减至 2013 年的 9.6 千克。

2. 日本：农药用量从 20 世纪 90 年代开始下降。2000 年农药用量约 8 万吨，2013 年降至 5.2 万吨，下降 35%。同期杀菌剂年用量由 4 万吨降至 2.3 万吨，下降 42.5%；杀虫剂年用量由 2.7 万吨降至 1.7 万吨，下降 37%；除草剂用量稳定在 1.1 万吨左右。

· 美洲主要国家

1. 美国：农药年用量约 30 万吨，其中农业用途约占 80%。除草剂年用量约 20 万吨；2000 年前杀虫剂年用量约 10 万吨，近几年减至约 7.5 万吨；杀菌剂年用量稳定在 2 万吨左右。

2. 巴西：1990 年农药用量约为 5 万吨，2013 年为 35 万吨，增长了 600%。1990 年除草剂年用量 2.2 万吨，2013 年 24 万吨，增长 9 倍多；1990 年杀虫剂用量 1.8 万吨，2013 年为 7 万吨，增长近 3 倍；1990 年杀菌剂用量 0.8 万吨，2013 年约为 4.4 万吨，增长 4.5 倍。

3. 墨西哥：2006 年前杀菌剂年用量为 2 万~3 万吨，2007~2011 年为 5 万~5.5 万吨，近几年稳定在 4 万吨左右；2005 年以来除草剂年用量一直稳定在 3 万~3.5 万吨；2005 年前杀虫剂年用量约 1.5 万吨，2005~2010 年为 2 万~2.5 万吨，近几年年用量为 3 万~4 万吨。

4. 加拿大：2006 年前除草剂年用量约 3 万吨，2012 年增长到 5.8 万吨，增长 93%；2006 年前杀菌剂年用量约 3500 吨，2012 年增长到 7546 吨，增加了 1 倍多；杀虫剂年用量稳定在 3000 吨左右。

以上资料表明，第一，一个国家的农药施用量具有先增长后下降（呈"倒 U 形"曲线）的特征。这是现实中巴西等发展中国家农药施用量趋于上升，英国等发达国家农药施用量趋于下降的主要原因。这种变化同经济发展水平有关，更是对农药生产、销售、使用等实施严格的法律法规、标准和准入制度，以及施药技术进步的结果。第二，受气候变化等因素的影响，不同时期的病虫害的状况会有所不同，所以农药施用量的长期下降趋势和短期向上波动是交织在一起的，例如法国和德国。第三，不同国家的农业病虫害状况有所不同，所以经济发展水平相近国家的农业施药量仍会有较大的差异，例如荷兰和韩国。

附件 2 瑞士农业政策中的农民直接补贴 *

瑞士联邦政府的专属职责仅限于国防、国际贸易和农业，其他职权都下放到州。瑞士的 26 个州在其他政策领域拥有实质性权力，但在农业政策范围内主要是实施者。联邦政府在农业方面规定了预算、支付率和大部分政策的细节。

农业政策的生物地理适应性。瑞士的农场分布在多雨的平原地带、连绵起伏的丘陵以及高山牧场。瑞士据此将它们划分为三个生物地理区，三个生物地理区的农业政策有所不同。

农民的直接补贴。瑞士农民得到的直接补贴有两类：一类是市场价格支持，它按种植面积补贴，以确保粮食供给。市场价格支持占农业补贴总额的比重随着时间推移已由原来的 80% 减少到近些年的约 50%，尽管瑞士国内农产品平均价格高出世界平均价格 60%（2013~2015 年）。

瑞士还在生态条件不好的农场（需符合环境等各方面要求）自动采用更严格的耕作方法（如生态农业实践）以及确立动物福利目标，并提供直接补贴。这类补贴占农业补贴比重的比重由 20 世纪 80 年代的约 20% 增加到近些年的约 50%。

质量与数量同等重要。瑞士最引人注目的农业政策是要求农场把 7% 的农田用于维护生物多样性。许多瑞士人怀疑该要求的功效，因为农民不太

---

* 该附录总结的是 2014~2017 年瑞士农业政策框架中的瑞士农民直接支付体系。这个直接支付体系的执行期延长至 2021 年底（农业政策 2018~2021）。2020 年 2 月 12 日瑞士政府宣布，2022 年以后的瑞士农业政策的核心是促进持续性更强、价值量更大的农业的发展。这项新的农业政策预计在 2022 年初提交给瑞士议会。

可能把 7% 的土地配置在最需要维护生物多样性的地方。

2016 年，经合组织在它的农业政策监测和评估中把瑞士列为生产者支持估算（PSE）最高的国家。在瑞士最新的农业政策（始于 2014 年）中有 8 类补贴项目可供瑞士农民申请 ① 。它们是：食品安全补贴；耕地景观保护补贴；生物多样性保护补贴；农业景观质量补贴；生产系统补贴；特种农作物补贴；资源有效利用补贴；转型补贴。

瑞士农民要想获得补贴，首先要提供"生态绩效证明"（PEP）。"生态绩效证明"的要求是：

①作物轮作。轮作至少有四种作物，包括每种作物的限值；

②水土保持。土壤必须在 8 月 31 日前覆盖，并有减少土壤侵蚀的措施；

③生物多样性促进。需把 7% 的农田划为生物多样性栖息地（有 15 个合意栖息地的定义）；

④动物福利。保留相关的兽医记录，并证明有"良好的疾病管理"；

⑤农药使用。农场要有专门的综合农药管理计划、喷雾器测试和资格证书，以及河道和道路旁的缓冲带；

⑥营养平衡。氮和磷必须在农场层面保持平衡（±10%），需进行年度土壤分析。

A. 农用品安全补贴

基本补贴率	瑞士法郎 /（公顷·年）
用于粮食生产的耕地	900
开放的农田和多年生作物	400
草地	450

非粮农作物不在补贴之列。

基本补贴以农场达到补贴要求的面积。

生态差的地区耕作的额外补贴如下。

地带	瑞士法郎 /（公顷·年）
平原	0

---

① 本文没有介绍畜牧养殖和动物福利补贴。

地带	瑞士法郎/（公顷·年）
丘陵	240
阿尔卑斯山Ⅰ区	300
阿尔卑斯山Ⅱ区	320
阿尔卑斯山Ⅲ区	340
阿尔卑斯山Ⅳ区	360

B. 耕地景观保护补贴

耕地景观保护补贴按地带分配如下。

区域	瑞士法郎/（公顷·年）
平原	0
丘陵	100
阿尔卑斯山Ⅰ-Ⅳ区	230~390

C. 生物多样性保护补贴

大面积草地保护补贴如下。

区域	质量Ⅰ等	质量Ⅱ等
平原［瑞士法郎/（公顷·年）］	1080	1920
丘陵［瑞士法郎/（公顷·年）］	860	1840
阿尔卑斯山Ⅰ-Ⅱ区［瑞士法郎/（公顷·年）］	500	1700
阿尔卑斯山Ⅲ-Ⅳ区［瑞士法郎/（公顷·年）］	450	1100

注：质量Ⅰ等：用于生产饲料的草地必须每年割草一次，饲草割后必须清理；质量Ⅱ等：反映土壤营养不良和植被物种丰富的指示性植物要经常得到满足。

枯枝落叶区与凋落物区保护补贴如下。

区域	质量Ⅰ等	质量Ⅱ等
平原［瑞士法郎/（公顷·年）］	1440	2060
丘陵［瑞士法郎/（公顷·年）］	1220	1980
阿尔卑斯山Ⅰ-Ⅱ区［瑞士法郎/（公顷·年）］	860	1840
阿尔卑斯山Ⅲ-Ⅳ区［瑞士法郎/（公顷·年）］	680	1770

注：质量Ⅰ等和质量Ⅱ等的要求同上。

区域	质量 I 等	质量 II 等
平原、丘陵和阿尔卑斯山 I–II 区 [瑞士法郎 /（公顷·年）]	450	1200
阿尔卑斯山 III–IV 区 [瑞士法郎 /（公顷·年）]	450	1000

注：质量 I 等和 II 等：若使用粪肥或堆肥，每公顷土地施肥量不超过 30 公斤氮。

大面积牧场保护补贴如下。

区域	质量 I 等	质量 II 等
所有地区 [瑞士法郎 /（公顷·年）]	450	700

注：质量 I 等和质量 II 等的要求同上。

树木繁茂的牧场保护补贴如下。

区域	质量 I 等	质量 II 等
所有地区 [瑞士法郎 /（公顷·年）]	450	700

注：质量 I 等：农家肥、堆肥和非氮肥的使用必须经得林业推广服务站的同意。只有草地有权获得补贴；质量 II 等：与大面积牧场的规定相同。

树篱、林地和树木繁茂的河岸区域保护补贴如下。

区域	质量 I 等	质量 II 等
所有地区 [瑞士法郎 /（公顷·年）]	2160	2840

注：质量 I 等：树篱、林地和河岸两侧必须保留一条宽 3 米至 6 米的草或枯枝落叶区。草地或枯枝落叶地带至少每三年割草一次。木本植物覆盖区必须每 8 年管理一次。质量 II 等：树篱、林地和树木繁茂的河岸的植被要由本地木本植物组成。每 10 米至少有 5 种不同的木本植物。

花卉休耕地保护补贴如下。

区域	质量 I 等	质量 II 等
平原和丘陵 [瑞士法郎 /（公顷·年）]	3800	0

注：质量 I 等：播种前，休耕地必须使用或种植多年生作物。花卉休耕地至少保持 2 年，最多不超过 8 年。补贴年度次年的 2 月 15 日前不允许耕作。休耕期后，同一个地块只能在耕种后的第四个生长季重新分配。休耕年前的 10 月 1 日至 3 月 15 日期间可割草，但只能割一半。休耕第一年允许彻底割草，以防杂草入侵。

轮作休耕保护补贴如下。

区域	质量 I 等	质量 II 等
平原和丘陵 [瑞士法郎 /（公顷·年）]	3300	0

注：质量 I 等：播种前，地表必须被使用或种植多年生作物。休耕后，同一个地块可以在耕

作后的第四个生长季重新配置多年生作物。该地必须在 9 月 1 日至 4 月 30 日播种。一年的休耕时间必须维持在下一个年补贴年度的 2 月 15 日。两年或三年轮休地必须维持到第二个或第三个补贴年的 9 月 15 日。轮作休耕区只能在 10 月 1 日至 3 月 15 日终止。

沿河草原保护补贴如下。

区域	质量 I 等	质量 II 等
所有区域［瑞士法郎/（公顷·年）］	450	0

注：质量 I 等：地表必须每年至少割草一次。9 月 1 日至 11 月 30 日期间可以放牧。沿河草地的宽度不应超过 12 米。

树丛保护补贴如下。

1 株树的补贴最多为 5 瑞士法郎。树木种植间距必须达到 10 米。树木周围半径 3 米内不允许施肥。

花条授粉保护补贴如下。

区域	质量 I 等	质量 II 等
平原和丘陵［瑞士法郎/（公顷·年）］	2500	0

D. 景观质量改善补贴

每项措施的补贴根据它的成本和价值确定，每项措施的补贴由州政府确定。联邦政府每年对每个项目最多支持 90% 的金额：每公顷利用面积 360 瑞士法郎；每单位常规费用为 240 瑞士法郎。

州可用的补贴每年每公顷最多为 120 瑞士法郎，每单位常规费用最多为 80 瑞士法郎。

E. 生产系统补贴

生物农业补贴如下。

所有作物	瑞士法郎/（公顷·年）
特定作物	1600
大田作物和多年生作物	1200
赋予补贴权的其他作物	200

注：(1) 生物农业适用的相关法律；(2) 有机认证机构认可的控制。

推广种植的补贴如下。

所有作物	瑞士法郎 /（公顷·年）
推广种植的补贴	400

F. 资源高效利用补贴

技术推广补贴如下。

所有作物	瑞士法郎 /（公顷·年）
与技术推广有关的补贴	30

保护农业土壤的农业技术补贴如下。

所有作物	瑞士法郎 /（公顷·年）
直接播种	250
线条播种	200
膜下播种	250
不用除草剂的附加补贴	200

减施农药补贴如下。

所有作物	瑞士法郎 /（公顷·年）
果树—减少除草剂	
局部	200
总体	600
果树—减少杀菌剂	200
甜菜—减少除草剂	—
机械除草	200~400
不用除草剂	800
不用杀菌剂和杀虫剂	400

G. 特殊作物和可补充粮食作物的补贴

特殊作物补贴如下。

所有作物	瑞士法郎 /（公顷·年）
油菜籽、向日葵、油南瓜、亚麻籽	700
土豆和玉米的种子	700
饲料和豆科种子	1000

所有作物	瑞士法郎／（公顷·年）
饲用豆类、豌豆和羽扇豆	1000
（制糖的）甜菜	2100

粮食作物的补充补贴。补充补贴金额在每年年底根据配置的谷物资源和面积确定。

H. 转型补贴

转型补贴可用的资源与直接补贴的预算项目相对应，即减去所有类型补贴的支出（耕地景观补贴、供应安全补贴、生物多样性补贴、景观质量补贴、生产系统补贴和资源有效利用补贴）和资源有效利用和水保护项目的支出。

I. 政府对农民直接补贴总量

2017年，政府的直接补贴金额为 28.06 亿瑞士法郎，耕地平均补贴为每公顷 2745 瑞士法郎，共有 102.2 万公顷耕地，其中 27 万公顷大田作物和多年生作物，2.1 万公顷为葡萄园和果树等永久作物，73.1 万公顷草地。2014年以来，大田作物和多年生作物面积增加了 3000 公顷。

2017年与生物多样性、景观质量、生产系统和资源效率有关项目的直接补贴金额又略有增加。平原的生物多样性促进区面积 7.7 万公顷，超过 6.5 万公顷的目标值。农民开发的生物多样性促进区面积中有 40% 成为高质量区域，它们的 75% 实现了网络化。

2018年以来，瑞士根据农药行动计划制定了新的激励计划，以便在甜菜、水果和葡萄种植中部分或完全不使用杀虫剂。2019年将为其他主要作物制定类似的激励计划。

表 1　政府向农民直接补贴汇总

单位：百万瑞士法郎

年份	2015	2016	2017	2018
食物安全补贴	1094	1091	1086	1092
生产系统补贴	450	458	467	468
耕地景观保护补贴	504	507	523	535

续表

年份	2015	2016	2017	2018
生物多样性补贴	387	400	414	410
景观质量补贴	125	142	145	150
资源高效使用补贴	17	25	28	59
保护水资源和资源可持续利用补贴	26	12	18	—
转型补贴	178	162	129	98
减少 / 预计补贴	-2	-4	-4	—
总计	2779	2792	2806	2812

注：2018 年的数据引自 2018 年的相关预算。

基于与农民讨论有关环境保护的直接补贴问题，得到如下初步结论。

农民能在多大程度上成为提供公共物品的农民，或把生物多样性或其他公共物品作为农场业务的优先事项，关键在于环境补贴的力度。然而，瑞士宪法把粮食安全作为农业政策三个目标之一。它的三个收入支持项目一个以"保障粮食供应补贴"为标题，另两个以"转型补贴"和"农地补贴"为标题。联邦农业局强加这个限制，是因为一些农民不生产任何食物。直接补贴项目从技术上讲是自愿的，但从经济上讲大多数农民几乎没有选择。结果正如联邦农业局的一位官员所说，农民尚未接受其充当公共物品提供者的角色，而农民们则抱怨他们不想成为瑞士的园丁。

附件 3   缓控释肥的减施原理

缓控释肥原理

广义上讲，缓控释肥是指肥料养分释放速度较慢，释放期较长的肥料。狭义上讲，缓释肥 (SRFs) 是指施入土壤后有效养分释放速度慢于普通化肥的肥料，多为单体肥（氮肥）；它释放时受土壤 pH 值、土壤水分含量、土壤类型、微生物活动及灌溉水量等许多外界因素的影响，可控性较弱。控释肥（CRFs）多为复合肥或再加上微量元素的全营养肥，它是按预先设定的肥料养分释放模式，使肥料养分释放与作物养分吸收基本同步，可控性较强的肥料。具体标准是：在 25℃下，肥料养分在 24 小时内的释放率不超过 15%；28 天内养分释放率不超过 75%；在规定时间内养分释放率不低于75%；专用控释肥的养分释放曲线与相应作物的养分吸收曲线相吻合（欧洲标准化委员会，Committee European Normalization，CEN）。

针对化肥养分释放速度与植物养分吸收速度不协调的问题，有关专家在 20 世纪初就提出了缓释肥概念，1955 年缓释肥开始用于农业生产。20 世纪 60 年代缓释肥研发有明显进展，20 世纪 80 年代控释氮肥研发取得突飞猛进，20 世纪 90 年代缓释肥趋于成熟。

控释肥养分释放的控制是通过高分子树脂包膜来完成的。膜的表面充满孔隙，肥料施入土壤后，土壤水分从膜孔进入溶解养分，被溶解的养分再通过膜孔释放出来；温度升高时植物生长加快，养分需求量加大，肥料释放速度随之加快；温度降低时，植物生长缓慢或休眠，肥料释放速度随之变慢或停止释放。作物吸收养分多时，肥料颗粒膜外侧养分浓度下降，膜内外养分浓度差异增大，肥料释放速度加快，从而使养分释放曲线与作物养分与作物需肥曲线相一致，从而提高了肥料养分的利用率。

有机肥生产原理

有机肥替代化肥的主要模式包括：①畜禽粪污、秸秆等废弃物经过堆肥（沤肥）环节将其转换为无毒无害的有机肥；②畜禽粪污等废弃物经过肥（沤肥）环节转换为无毒无害的有机肥；③人畜粪便、秸秆经过沼气池转换成无毒无害的沼渣沼液。

后 记

在温饱问题尚未解决之前，粮食安全是生态安全的基础。温饱问题得不到解决，生态安全是无法得到保障的。越过温饱阶段之后，生态安全成为粮食安全的基础。没有生态安全，就不会有可持续的粮食安全。对于中国而言，粮食主产区的生态安全显得更为重要。基于这种认识，笔者开展了相关研究并撰写了《中国粮食主产区生态安全研究》一书。

本书不仅主要针对中国所有参与制定粮食安全政策的人员，如国家和省级的决策者、主要政策顾问、公务员及农学家，也面向发达国家和发展中国家的所有同行。本书旨在支持人们进一步认识到在当前气候变化的环境中，需要解决影响农业生态系统的生态安全问题，从而实现安全食品的可持续生产，以及从旨在改善生态安全以实现粮食安全的技术、政策和体制措施中获得收益。

这项研究始于2015年年末。2015年11月退休后，经苑鹏教授推荐，我加入了河南省林业厅主持的"河南省粮食生产核心区生态保障体系战略研究"课题组。2018年这项课题完成后，课题资助方亚洲开发银行项目官员苏珊娜（Suzanne Robertson）女士建议我和克劳德先生（Claude René Heimo，世界银行退休人员和日内瓦社会经济中心顾问）进一步拓展研究内容，特别是将对其他发展中国家有借鉴意义的中国经验总结出来，成为一项知识产品（Knowledge Product）。根据亚洲开发银行的建议，我向中国社会科学院外事局提出了开展《中国粮食主产区生态安全研究》的申请并得到了批准，亚洲开发银行提供了经费资助。研究报告的中文稿由我撰写，英文翻译工作由中国农业大学博士研究生周丽君承担，克劳德先生以讲好中国故事的目标，按照欧美人的阅读习惯对报告的第一版及其英文译本进行了微调。这本书实际上是克劳德先生和我共同完成的研究成果。

在《中国粮食主产区生态安全研究》出版之际，我要向为本书出版作出贡献的人士和机构表示感谢。首先，衷心感谢克劳德先生一丝不苟的工作和无私奉献的精神，感谢周丽君博士的辛勤工作。其次，感谢魏后凯研究员、杜志雄研究员对本书的推荐，感谢中国社会科学院农村发展研究所学术委员会和中国社会科学院老干部局对本书的认同，使本书有机会获得中国社会科学院退休学者研究基金的出版资助。再次，感谢责任编辑徐崇阳同志为本书出版所做的具体工作。

虽然我做了努力，但书中一定还有许多不尽如人意的地方。敬请大家不吝指正。

李周

2021 年 10 月 5 日

Preamble

This book is aimed primarily at all those involved in making sustainable agricultural policies at China's national and provincial levels, such as decision-makers, civil servants, and key policy advisers. Their function is to support increased recognition of the need to address issues affecting agriculture ecosystems, and by consequence, the sustainable production of food products, and notably the benefits that could be derived from improving ecological security in core grain growing areas of China, and raise the ecological security awareness of, or educate, those that are involved in food production, notably farmers and farming communities.

During the past Four decades, China experienced fast economic growth with huge environmental costs over a long period. The gross domestic product (GDP) growth by over management and irrational development has heavily exploited natural resources and damaged environment conditions. This results in a series of serious ecological and environmental problems, such as water scarcity and soil contamination, air pollution, soil erosion, ecosystem degradation, and loss of biodiversity. The ecosystem degradation and environmental pollution threaten and undermine the country's economic and social growth, as well as domestic survival and development [1].

To address the dilemma between economic growth and resource/environmental constraints, the government has in 2014 [2] proposed a policy of pursuing green development and building an *Eco-civilization*, which involves the management of the

---

[1] Hongii Zhang and Erqi Xu, "An evaluation of the ecological and environmental security on China's terrestrial ecosystems", Institute of Geographic Sciences and Natural Resources Research, Chinese Academy of Sciences; *Sci Rep*, April 2017, https://www.ncbi.nlm.nih.gov/pmc/articles/PMC5429794.

[2] See:*The 4th plenary session of the 18th National Congress of the Communist Party of the PRC.*

relationship between humans an nature in a comprehensive, scientific and systematic manner in line with *the 2030 Agenda for Sustainable Development*. The essence of the construction of an Eco-civilization is building a resource-saving and environment-friendly society based on the environmental carrying capacity of natural resources, the law of nature and sustainable development [1] . With regard to promoting Ecological Civilization, a number of policy measures were put forward by the Government. They include *inter-alia*: low carbon development, establishing natural resource property rights, enshrining in law national land use planning, strictly controlling environmental pollutants emissions and finally developing ecological compensation for the control of soil, water and air pollution on a sound legal foundation. There is a strong conviction among Chinese policymakers that, with those new policy measures, China has now entered a transition period towards "Green Development".

Due to the successes of Household Responsibility System (HRS) policies, agricultural incentives, technological improvements and implementation of farmland protection forests, agriculture production in its core grain growing (CGG) areas vastly increased to reach 618 million tons of grains in 2017. However, agriculture in CGG areas of China is nowadays a victim of its past success and challenges for the future have surfaced prominently, such as factor productivity; soils, groundwater and surface water pollution due to the excessive use of chemical fertilizers and pesticides; decline in soil organic matter and soil health; decreasing availability of groundwater for irrigation; increased incidence of crops' pests and diseases, degradation of the protective functions of farmland protection forests; and the increasing risk of adverse impacts on agricultural productivity from climatic anomalies due to climate change. Ecosystem degradation and environmental pollution, as opposed to sustainability is, therefore, one of most important issues facing today's sustainable agriculture development in core grain growing areas of China.

As a result, adapting agriculture in CGG areas to the above issues to maintain agricultural productivity at today's level will not only require adjusting farming practices, such as regulating the use of chemical fertilizers and pesticides to decrease agricultural NPS pollution, improving irrigation efficiency, adjusting the farming season

---

[1] See: *President Hu Jintao's speech at the seminar on Studying and Carrying Out the Achievement of the CPC's 17th National Congress.*

and selecting new varieties of drought and insect resistant crop and adopting the climate-smart agriculture concept, but also, more importantly, at developing complementary policy and institutional measures that would altogether, contribute to enhancing ecological security in core grain growing areas of China. Under this book, ecological security refers to the capacity for addressing situations that are threatening human survival, health, basic rights, food security and safety, social security, and resources required for social order, as well as the ability to adapt to climate change, including natural, economic and social development. According to this definition, ecological security depends upon the growth of population, economic development, climate related negative impacts, and all the connections that are relating to the ecological system, such as, land degradation, deforestation, desertification, water and air pollution, energy shortage, greenhouse gas, global climate change and human security. [1]

In particular, scaling up ecological security in CGG areas requires overcoming key challenges affecting the sustainability of current agriculture production, notably those affecting crop production in CGG areas, in particular overcoming the negative impacts of the following issues:

i. The continuous and persistent pollution of agricultural soils and groundwater due to an over application of synthetic agro-chemicals inputs;

ii. The continuous decrease of availability of water for irrigation due to an over exploitation of available groundwater resources for irrigation;

iii. The forthcoming negative impacts of climate change, notably due to both changes in precipitation pattern and the probable increasing frequencies of extreme climate events;

iv. The deterioration of the protection benefits of farmland protection forests; and

v. The low ecological protection effects of forestry plantation surrounding CGG areas in absence of close-to-nature forest management principles.

From a sustainable development point of view, meeting ecological security requirements in CGG areas of China (and by implication to the whole China agricultural sector) will embrace the spirit of the China Agenda 2030 by directly contributing towards a number of Social Development Goals (SDGs), notably: eradication of poverty

---

[1] According to the definition given by the International Institute for Applied Systems Analysis (IIASA) in 1989.

(SDG 1) and hunger (SDG 2), ensuring quality education (SDG 4), achieving gender equality (SDG 5), increasing water-use efficiency (SDG 6), promoting decent jobs (SDG 8), ensuring sustainable production and consumption (SDG 12), building climate resilience (SDG 13) and halting the loss of biodiversity (SDG 15).

This book is divided into six parts presenting a set of principles emphasizing the need to consider an innovative Ecological Security Strategy designed to improve ecological security in CGG areas rather than prescribed methods. It begins with the description of the concept, situation and challenges facing food security in China (Part I) and then, clarifies what current ecological security issues imply for China's food security (Part II). Those two sections are then followed by a brief description of China's agriculture and environmental policies addressing food security issues (Part III) and the resultant concrete agricultural and forestry technical measures that China should pursue to improve ecological security in CGG areas of China(Part IV). The book then concludes with a brief elaboration of policy and institutional elements that should be considered in devising an Ecological Security Strategy for the CGG areas of China(Part V). Finally, the book concludes by discussing the importance and general significance of investing in ecological security to improve food security in China and other countries (Part VI).

I   Issues Affecting Food Security in China

1. The Food Security Concept and Situation in China

1.1   Global food security situation

The Food and Agriculture Organization of the United Nations (FAO) defines food security as a condition when all people, at all times, have physical and economic access to sufficient, safe and nutritious food to meet their dietary needs and food preferences for an active and healthy life (FAO, 1996). The attainment of food security involves satisfying the following four basic dimensions simultaneously: "availability", "physical access", "economic access" and "utilization". A fifth dimension, "stability", is often added to emphasize the importance of the stability of the four dimensions over time. While each dimension is necessary for overall food security, they likely have different weightings in rural settings as compared with urban settings and also across economies with different incomes and net food trade balances.

Food security was first proposed at the time of the 1972-1974 world food crisis. In 1974 when the Food and Agriculture Organization of the United Nations (FAO) pointed out in the *International Undertaking on World Food Security* that food security should be considered as a basic survival rights to human beings. This definition is based on the fact that the availability, at all times, of adequate, nourishing, diverse, balanced and moderate world food supplies of basic foodstuffs should be considered when sustaining a steady expansion of food consumption and off-setting fluctuations in production and prices. During the past over 40 years, the meaning of food security has gradually evolved from a quantity-based towards a quality-based concept (i.e., from food security to food safety, resource security and ecological security).

Today, China feeds 21 percent of the world's population on 8 percent of the world's agriculture lands, which works out at about an average farmland availability of 0.09 ha per person. This strong contrast between a large population and limited availability of arable land resources creates significant challenges for China's food security. China's limited space for farming has been a problem throughout its history, leading to chronic food shortage and famine. As a matter of fact, in the past centuries, China experienced numerous food shortages, then corrected by implementing a quota system and a land contract reform.

Since the initiation of the reform period in 1984, self-sufficiency in grains, mainly due to system and technological innovations, has long been the hallmark of Chinese agricultural policies. From 1996 onwards, the explicit aim of China's food security was to produce 95 percent of its grain domestically. Since the popularization of the household contract responsibility system in the initial stage of the "Reform and Opening Up" policy, the central government initiated a series of strategic reforms, which played a critical role in improving China's grain production capacity. For instance, the State Council Document No. 1 of 2004 stated that motivating farmers to plant grain crops is the most vital aspect of food security so that increasing grain production capacity in the main production areas will ensure the overall control of grain production. As for the State Council Document No. 1 of 2008, it stipulated that the implementation of grain strategic engineering, focusing on the development a series of core grain growing (CGG) production areas characterized by sound basic conditions, high production levels and large grain transfer amounts should be considered critical for ensuring food security in China. Furthermore, at the 15th CPC Central Committee, it was decided that CGG areas should play a critical food security role through strengthening and improving State macroeconomic control over grain specialty goods, defending farmers' enthusiasm and guaranteeing the grain supply and basic grain production stabilization. Nowadays, China has 13 CGG areas [①], spread over 31 provinces of China that bear large food security significance due to their contribution to the total national grain output.

[①] Located in Hebei, Liaoning, Jilin, Heilongjiang, Jiangsu, Anhui, Jiangxi, Shandong, Henan, Hubei, Hunan and Sichuan Provinces and, Inner Mongolia Autonomous Region.

In term of food security, the result of those sector reforms was outstanding. Between 1949 and 1952, the 13 CGG provinces produced 59.2 percent and 65.3 percent of the total national grain production, respectively. From 1978 to 2000, the share of grain production from those 13 CGG provinces remained around 70 percent and that for a long period. From 2000 to 2009, grain production in the 13 CGG provinces significantly improved, rising to around 76 percent since 2010. For instance, from 1949 to 2015, the grain output in Heilongjiang and Henan increased from 5.78 million tons and 7.14 million tons to 63.24 million tons and 60.67 million tons(i.e. an increase of 9.9 times and 7.5 times). Respectively, in 2015, grain production in both provinces reached 60 million tons, which exceeded the national 1949 and 1952 total grain outputs.

In total, grain output in China increased 74 percent from 354 million tons in 1982 to 618 million tons in 2017, surpassing the growth of its population by about 34 percent.[1] Among the three major cereal crops grown in China for the country's food security, the self-sufficiency ratio of wheat, rice and corn is about 95 percent. In contrast, about 80 percent of consumed soybean and other agro-products, such as milk and sugar, are imported. China's agriculture is also an important engine for rural employment, absorbing and contributing to the income of 320 million farmers. In a global comparison, for the same interval, the proportion of China's grain production, compared to the total grain produced globally (2818 million tons), stabilized a level of about 29 percent. This indicates that China has now succeeded in guaranteeing grain self-sufficiency and in ensuring a near-absolute safety of food supply to meet the enormous grain demand of its population[2] . In some ways, current grain production, in fact, appears to be in a structural oversupply[3] . Therefore, protecting food security in the future should focus not only on the protection of the grain production capacity of CGG, but also on processing, retail and consumption.

At present, to sum up, grain production capacity in China, in term of quantity,

---

[1] Carter C. A., Zhong F., Zhu F. ,"Advances in Chinese agriculture and its global implications", *Appl. Econ. Perspect. Policy*, 2012 (34), pp.1–36.

[2] Huang J. et al .,"understanding recent challenges and new food policy in China", *Global Food Security*, 2017 (12),pp. 119–126.

[3] Wang D, et al .,"The implications on food security in China based on the reform of the agricultural supply– side structure", *Economist*, 2017.

has reached to about 600 million tons. As the ability to pay for food increases, net food imports also increase. Under the combined effect of those two factors, the situation of the food supply and demand on the China domestic market has been stable. For the future, due to improved varieties, as well as to the constant increase in irrigation effectiveness, the expansion of areas covered by plastic mulches, the improvement of agriculture mechanization, the increasing concentration of food production and the emergence of new types of agricultural management entities, altogether leading to economies of scale, China's food security conditions in term of quantity are promising.

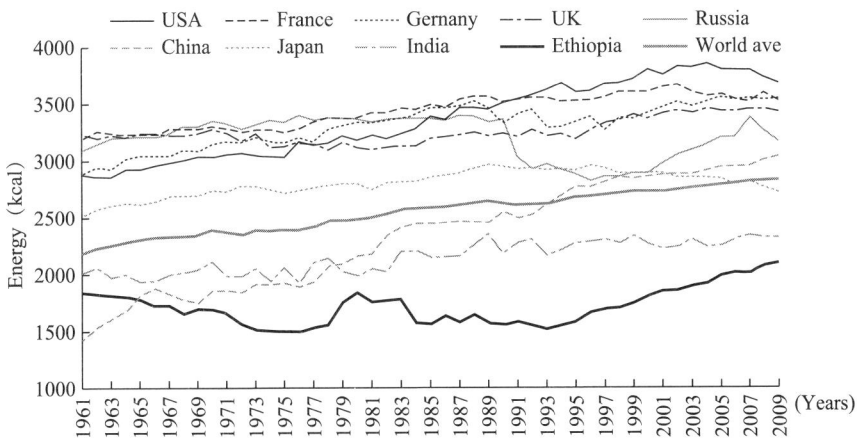

Fig. 1   Food self-sufficiency in selected countries between 1961 and 2009

However, to accomplish those outstanding agricultural production improvements, China paid a heavy price, including a current harmful state of agriculture lands NPS pollution [1] due to an over-application of agrochemicals' inputs and a problematic water situation due to low irrigation efficiency. [2] Furthermore, closely related to the over-use of synthetic fertilizers, notably nitrogenous fertilizers, straw burning and fuel consumption by the agricultural machinery, the carbon foot print of the agricultural

---

[1]   Agricultural land NPS pollution is mainly due excessive and inefficient use of chemical fertilizers, increasing 3 fold in the past three decades, with efficiencies averaging at 32 percent compared to world average of 55 percent.

[2]   China's available water supply per person is only 2050 m³ or 25 percent of the world's per capita average. Irrigation of rural crops accounts for 60 percent of China's total water demand with inefficient delivery of the Irrigation of rural crops accounts for 60 percent of China's total water demand with inefficient delivery of the order of 30–40 percent, compared to 70–80 percent for developed countries.

sector increased. Moreover, about one-sixth of the total grain produced in China is wasted annually in the production, processing and transportation of food because of poor equipment and logistical issues. Finally, high intensity grain production not only results in higher production, but also in high costs, notably due to increase in additional input costs. Those severe structural and eco-environmental issues caused by high intensity grain production require an urgent structural transformation of the grain production situation.

1.2 Food security challenges in terms of production

As of today, China product-level food security faces a series of challenges, such as increase in the price of labor, land, and inputs such as chemical fertilizers, pesticides, and the use of plastic films mulchings. The result of these cost increases is a decline in domestic food competitiveness compared to imports. Even if these three factors existed for a long time, this is an issue that agriculture in China has now to face.

China has gone beyond just providing adequate food and clothing to, nowadays, focusing on healthy eating. As result, the future of China's food security is mainly about the quality and safety of food. To ensure food quality and safety, China must:

i. Concentrate food production on fertile farmland to the maximum extent possible. This is one of the basic conditions for the production of healthy food;

ii. Address the challenges of over-transportation, over-storage, and over-processing to ensure food freshness in the market;

iii. Set up strict standards to eliminate the overuse of chemical fertilizers, pesticides and other agrochemicals; and

iv. Carry out effective supervision to gradually raising food quality to ensure that all foods entering the market meet at least the minimum food safety standards-so that all citizens can have access to reliable food. The monitoring of standards should remain the responsibility of the government.

1.3 Food security challenges in terms of land resources

Nowadays, the growing rate of farmland used for other commercial purposes and the increasing rate of conversion of farmland to non-agricultural purposes has led to a negative impact on food security at the resource level. Traditionally, agriculture in China has always seek to maximize food production, which was performed according to the following three main approaches: (i) intensively cultivating land that can produce food; (ii) intensively cultivating such land for grain production in the seasons in which the grain can be grown; (iii) intensifying cultivation based on the productive potential of the land.

However, in China, the land suitable for food production remains limited. In 2014, China's per capita farmland area was 0.08 ha, which was only 40 percent of the world average level.[1] In addition, farmland owned by smallholders mostly consisted in small-sized dispersed fields, of which 60 percent was below 0.1 ha.[2] Therefore, reclaiming marginal land and increasing the multiple cropping index for unilaterally seeking to improve grain production will inevitably causing food production to happen in places and seasons with poorly matched edaphic and hydrological conditions, resulting in long-distance water transfer, deep groundwater extraction, and other issues. Furthermore, since the natural fertility of arable land is also limited, chemical fertilizers and pesticides would have to be applied to meet the fertility and crops' nutrients' requirements, if the objective remains to unilaterally maximize grain yields. This may result in a series of problems, such as contamination of arable land and water bodies (including groundwater), and reduction of nutrients in the soil. If food safety at the product level is to be met by decreasing groundwater levels, increasing pollution of water bodies and farmland, and the reduction of soil nutrients, then the greater the pressure on natural resources would be. Therefore, China must abandon the traditional concept that all lands where grain could be grown must be cultivated, but focus on the grain production capacity of the land and the season when it is possible to plant and grow grain. This would require discarding the argument that lying land fallow at times for maintaining soil fertility would not be desirable.

The result is that, in the long run, it would be necessary to shift from the development of food production potential to the protection of the food production capacity, instead of increasing the pressure on natural resources for food production. As matter of fact, the

---

[1] Ge D. et al, "Farmland transition in its influences in grain production in China", *Land Use Policy*, 2018(7), pp.94–105..

[2] Xiao Y. et al., Optimal farmland conversion under double "restraints of economic growth and resources protection", *Journal of Cleanev Production*, 2017(142), pp.524–537.

lack of food supply can be solved through imports. The rational behind this approach is to purchase the right to use farmland and water resources from foreign countries.

1.4 Food security challenges in terms of ecological

Under the current China's agriculture context, both the carrying capacity of the ecosystem and the rehabilitation of the environment are limiting factors. If soil and water pollution caused by chemical fertilizers, pesticides, and plastic film mulching increase, then the ecosystems affected will no longer be able to continue to support the complex natural interaction between plants, animals, bacteria and fungi indispensable for continuously sustaining agricultural production. This situation will require correction measures. Sustainable food security should, therefore, be complemented by resources security and ecological security. Therefore, China must pay attention to both food security at production level and the ecological level of food security. While the first argument could easily be measured, the second one could not be easily assessed. If food security at the product level can be solved through domestic production and foreign imports, the ecological level of food production must be met by in-country measures. Therefore, food security at the ecological level is undoubtedly a vaster challenge that should require full responsibility and commitment from the government.

1.5 Food security challenges in terms of consumption

Food security is also related to consumption. With regard to food consumption in China, four problems could be mentioned: [1]

i. Large crop losses due to natural causes. The annual loss of grain caused by crop losses due to mildew, pests and rodents, etc. is as high as 25 million tons. In addition those pests are also affecting 17.5 million tons at post-harvest and grain storage stages;

ii. Large losses from processing. In 2011, the total rice grain production (paddy) was 20.8 million tons. However, due to excessive processing, the production in term of grain was only 12 million ton;

iii. Large degeneration loss. The total capacity of corn deep processing (from

---

[1] Li Zhou, "Four different aspects of food security", *Journal of China Social Science*, April 20, 2014.

which up to 2000 downstream products can be created) has been maintained at the stable level of about 77.5 million tons, which is equivalent to 47 percent of the domestic corn production. Deep processing can transform corn not only into non-food, but also converts some of the corn nutrients into pollutants causing high concentration of organic wastewater pollution, which require urgent treatment;

iv. Large consumption losses. Nowadays, food loss is significant in canteens, restaurants, hotels, factories, schools, as well as at the individual household's level. If relevant suitable measures were to be put in place, such losses could be reduced by 83.5 million tons. In addition, if there would be strict control over grain processing, it could be reduced by not less than 120 million tons per year. This is definitely a responsibility that would have to be performed at the level of each citizen.

2. Applying the Concept of Ecological Security to Food Security in China

Environmental issues caused by agricultural production such as those faced by China are currently attracting a wide concern over the world. Estimating environmental efficiency is an intuitive way to reflect the impact of agricultural production on ecological systems, which can make policymakers realizing the environmental costs of agricultural production and contributing to sustainable production.

There is a strong reliability between food security and ecological security. Ecological security is the foundation of food security, with the long-term security and safety of food depending upon ecological security. Ecological security should secure both food security and food safety. Therefore, food security, food safety and ecological security must be synergized. Promoting ecological security will, therefore, reduce pressure on factors impeding sustainable agriculture development, thus, alleviating food security and food safety problems.

2.1 Issues affecting food security in China

Called by the World Bank and the FAO, about 400 agricultural experts from around the world worked together to, after a six-year of survey, publish in 2008 a report called *Agricultural Development-related Knowledge, Science, and Technology for Global Certification* (FAO, 2008). The report pointed that the second "green revolution" of agriculture that was driven by chemical fertilizers, pesticides, irrigation and genetically modified crops has greatly increased grain production (and therefore food security), while also causing tremendous damage to the ecological environment.

In this context, China is not an exception. Similar problems also exist in other sectors of China.

The first problem is the loss of cultivated land. Agriculture land used either for non-essential crops (e.g. for export) or for other purposes, including a galloping urbanization and infrastructure development, which ran across the "Redlines" [1] may threaten 1.8 billion mu [2] (about 120 million ha) of cultivated land and 1.6 billion mu (about 106.7 million ha) of grain growing areas.

The second problem is soil erosion. According to estimations, based on the current rate of soil erosion, the black soil layer of 14 million mu (about 933,0000 ha) of arable land in the black soil region of northeast China will be lost during the next 50 years, with grain output going to decline by about 40 percent. Aside of that, the area of rock desertification area in the southwestern karst's areas will be doubled during the next 35 years.

The third problem is over-irrigation. In the Three-river Plain of Heilongjiang Province, the groundwater level dropped by an average of 2-3 meters during the past 10 years, up to 3-5 meters in some other regions. Over-exploitation of groundwater in the North China Plain covers an area of 90000 km^2, which is the largest groundwater zone in the world (including shallow and deep confined groundwater).

The fourth problem is excessive use of agrochemicals. In recent years, many major food-related public safety incidents have occurred, one after another, to the point that food insecurity has, nowadays, become a large public concern for many Chinese.

As a matter of fact, food production in China, characterized by an overuse of

---

[1] The Chinese government discussed ecological redlines as far as back as 2011 as a measure of success in implementing the ecological civilization targets. In early 2017, the State Council published a key document *Opinions on Defining and Protecting Ecological Redlines*, including rigorous regulations to fight pollution and contain environmental damages as a way to secure ecosystem services and manage conflicts.

[2] 1 hectare is equivalent to 15 mu.

agrochemicals for grain production is common in China, which also brought "undesirable outputs", such as, carbon emissions, pollution of soil and water, eutrophication, decrease in ground water supply, food poisoning etc. In 2011, CO_2 emissions in China from agricultural production were near to 90 million tons. For instance, the first national census of pollution sources stated that the total amount of nitrogen emissions from agricultural pollution sources accounted for 57.2 percent (2.7046 million tons) of the national-wide total, while the phosphorus emissions accounted for 67.4 percent (284700 tons). Undeniably, previous agricultural production efficiency measures did not consider those "undesirable outputs" in the analytical framework and, hence, neglected the negative impact of agricultural production on the environment.

2.2　The concept of ecological security

Ecological security refers to the integrity and health of ecosystems. It could be measured through indicators such as stability, sustainability of structure, and function of landscapes. What could also be measured is its resilience to stress. There are two main measures for the maintenance of ecological security, the first one being to eliminate ecological risks through conservation and the second by reducing its ecological vulnerability through development.

The International Institute for Applied Systems Analysis (IIASA, 1989) defines ecological security as referring to changes in human life, health, well-being, basic rights, sources of livelihood security, necessary resources, social order, and human adaptation capabilities to the environment. It includes natural ecological security, economic security, and social security. Ecological security is negatively related to ecological risks but positively related to ecological health. Therefore, ecological security can be defined in terms of ecological risks and ecological health.

2.2.1　Ecological risk

Ecological risk refers to the prospect that ecosystems are exposed to risks, disturbances or disasters that would damage ecosystems' structures, functions and resilience. The level of damages to ecosystems caused by specific risks is a function of its vulnerability, which may be affected by three aspects: first, the frequency and intensity of ecosystems' exposure to risks; second, the internal resilience of the ecosystem to deal with specific risks; and third, the external resilience of the ecosystem to resolve ecological risks.

2.2.2　Ecological health

Ecological Health Index (HI) = *System Vigor* × *Organizational Structure* × *System Resilience*. In this formula, the system vigor represents the system functions, and the organizational structure refers to the diversity of ecosystem components and approaches. Resiliency refers to the ability of the system to maintain its structure and functions when it is under stress. The system resilience can be measured from four aspects: (i) elasticity or time to return to pre-interference situation; (ii) plasticity or degree of allowable difference between the state of the system after restoration and pre-interference; (iii) amplitude or change of the recovery to original state after system interference; and (iv) hysteresis or the system recovery time after system disturbance disappears.

Ecological security is, therefore, a prerequisite to human survival and development. There are differences in the level of ecological security due to the degree of variability of ecological security in different places. Furthermore, the degree of ecological security is in a dynamic state, which means that ecological security may be changed with the improvement of social development and ecological needs. It is said that humans through conservation and development could also regulate ecological security. However, the maintenance of ecological security does have a cost. For those threats to ecological security that often come from human activities, large investments are needed to resolve those issues.

Ecological security has multiple characteristics (including but not limited to):

• *Integrity*. Partial ecological damages may cause problems to the entire ecosystem;

• *Comprehensiveness*. Factors for ecological security are mutually dependent and interacting;

• *Regional*. Issues affecting ecological security in different regions are different;

• *Dynamics*. The factors affecting ecological security in different periods are different;

• *Strategic*. The sustainable economic development and the development of the society as a whole depend upon ecological security.

2.3　Improving ecological security for food security at national level

Integrating ecological security into the national security system is an urgent pre-requisite for advancing the modernization of national governance systems and their capabilities, as well as for realizing the long-term stability of the country. If the central government is integrating ecological security into its national security management framework, then, such integration will be conducive to the establishment and modernization of a national ecological governance system with clear division of responsibilities, coordination and harmonization. When integrating ecological security into the national security system, particular attention should be given to at least the following three pre-requisites:

2.3.1 Strengthening the national legal system

Based on the needs of national ecological security, the first pre-requisite should be to strengthen law enforcement to ensure that any activity will follow *Redlines* or *Bottom Lines* [①] policy decisions of the government. There is also an urgent need to enhance people's awareness of ecological security, as to move towards good behaviors for both, enterprises and individuals.

2.3.2 Accelerating the establishment of national ecological security system and mechanism

Improving systematics, integrity and synergy. The second pre-requisite would be to integrate relevant organizations and clarify their individual responsibilities with regard to ecological security. Integrating relevant organizations would require building a coordination mechanism for ecological protection, economic development and improvement of people's livelihood as to maintaing a clear bottom line of the national ecological security. Then, an effective monitoring and accountability mechanism should be established to ensure the effectiveness and efficiency of the national ecological security strategy.

2.3.3 Establishing a national ecological security evaluation system

Establishing a comprehensive national ecological security database to analyze,

---

[①] The ecological redline is legally binding threshold. It refers to (i) the ecological protection boundary delineated by the central government, such as the boundary of the key ecological function zone; (ii) it refers to the legally binding values, such as the basic farmland area that cannot be broken and the water resource utilization that cannot be exceeded; (iii) it refers to acts that are subject to law. For example, wood must be harvested by certificate. The ecological bottom line is not legally binding. It is based on previous experience, scientific cognition, ecological carrying capacity, ecological threshold, etc., so that the scope, intensity and mode of ecosystem utilization do not cause devastating impact on ecosystem succession. The difference is that breaking the ecological red line will be punished by law, and breaking the ecological bottom line will eventually be punished by nature.

evaluate and predict the national ecological security situation and corresponding measures would be the third pre-requisite to ensure ecological security in China.

In a nutshell, on the one hand, "Ecological Redlines" should be used to regulate countrywide economic and social activities. On the other hand, incentive systems should be improved, such as ecological compensation, to encourage economic entities and individuals to consciously take actions to maintain ecological security. Ecological security would require joint policies, technologies, markets and the public to reduce the impact of threats to ecological systems (e.g., such those resulting from an overuse of agro chemicals).

2.4 Synergies between food security and ecological security

If the economic development in China has now entered a "new normal" stage with the Ecological Civilization, it is not just advisable and prudent to keep as is the grain production tasks of the CGG areas, and, at the same time, ignore ecological protection in those areas. Indeed, reducing the use of chemical fertilizers and pesticides has already been included in the national 14th Five-Year Plan and National Agricultural Long-term Development Plan. It would now be up to the central government to formulate a national overall strategic plan to reduce the use of chemical fertilizers and pesticides in China as soon as possible as to create concerted efforts to reduce the overuse of such agrochemicals, which are polluting soils and water. There is also an urgent need to formulate and improve relevant laws, regulations and policies for land and water conservation, to strictly control the use of various types of heavy metals, nitrates and antibiotics in animal feed, prohibit the use of organic fertilizer with excessive levels of nitrogen, heavy metals and antibiotics and regulate the use of groundwater, notably by improving irrigation efficiency.

II. Factors Affecting Ecological Security in CGG Areas

1. Chemical Fertilizers

1.1 Overview

Fertilizers are two types: organic, or natural fertilizers, and inorganic, chemical or synthetic fertilizers. Organic fertilizers are naturally occurring substances, and include bio-fertilizers, green manure, organic manure and compost. They slowly released essential nutrients into the soil to improve its overall fertility over time. Chemical fertilizers are man-made combinations of chemical substances., which typically combine nitrogen (N), phosphorus (P), potassium (K), calcium (Ca), magnesium (Mg) and other elements in different ratios. Chemical fertilizers, unlike their organic counterparts, are easy to use and are immediately releasing essential nutrients to the soil.

Chemical fertilizers are used in agriculture since the end of the 19th century and have paved the way to modern agriculture. By their impacts on crop yields, they were at the core of an agriculture revolution not seen before in human history. However, if chemical fertilizers do have far-reaching positive effects by supplying consistent amounts of precise nutrients to the soil unlike organic fertilizers that need to break down before absorption by plants, they do have, at the same time, long-term negative effects.

Chemical fertilizers contain acids, including sulfuric acids and hydrochloric acids. Indeed, those acids dissolve soil crumbs, thus damaging the natural structure of the soil by modifying its pH and killing beneficial microorganisms that convert plant remains into nutrient rich organic matter providing plants with natural immunity to diseases. When chemical fertilizers are used for prolonged duration, the result is a compacted surface that prevents rainwater from entering the soil. Nitrogen and phosphate based chemical fertilizers, leached after rainstorms into the groundwater, rivers, and lakes, increase eutrophication disturbing aquatic ecosystems. The use of chemical fertilizers increases nitrate concentration in the soil, which once converted into nitrites, may be linked to gastric problems and react with the hemoglobin in the human blood stream to cause methemoglobinemia (also called "blue baby syndrome"), which damages vascular and respiratory systems. Furthermore, chemical fertilizers produce vegetables and fruits with lower nutritional value and less flavor. Their repeated use may be source of toxic chemicals, like cadmium, arsenic and uranium to buildup in the soil, which can be ultimately be stored into vegetable and fruits that are consumed.

The result is that the over application of chemical fertilizers applied at farm level is, nowadays, the main source of non-point source pollution (NPS). The fact that fertilizers may pollute soils and water means that the plants do not take them up. Aside to being an environmental problem, their overuse may be a waste of money for the farmer. The solution is to get the plant to use the fertilizer that is applied. The ultimate paradigm is, therefore to provide plants with a balanced nutrition that can promote the rapid growth of the plants whose leaves and residues protect the soil from direct rainfall.

Therefore, the over-use of chemical fertilizers should be revisited to minimize their negative environmental problems while keeping in view the importance of sustaining crop yield levels and protecting farmers' incomes. Many solutions do exist from the application of slow-release fertilizers (physical coating of fertilizers' granules) to a shift in technology towards ecological agriculture management practices, including organic manure, compost, reduced tillage, soil conservation and erosion control measures, agroforestry and fertigation for high value crops, such as fruits and vegetables.

Chemical fertilizers' over-application is a problem that many developed countries are facing. To solve this problem, a safe fertilization standard of 225 kg/ha (equivalent) is proposed. According to the chemical fertilizer application amount and the total planted area, some Chinese scholars have calculated that the average chemical fertilizer application per hectare of cultivated land of 225 kg/ha resulted in over-application of chemical fertilizers in China's agricultural production. This calculation should help decisionmakers to realize the severity and danger of over-fertilization. But it does not solve the problem since this standard has been based on medium nutrient demanding (MND) crops such as cereals. The fact the matter is that this standard could not be adopted for high nutrient demanding (HND) crops, such as, vegetables and low nutrient demanding (LND) crops, such as soybeans.

1.2 Fertilizers application structure

Chemical fertilizers are not only used for crops on arable land used for grain production or for other agricultural crops, but also for fruit trees in orchards, gardens and reforestation, artificial grasslands and animal husbandry, and aquaculture. To find out the amount of chemical fertilizer used in grain production, the amount of chemical fertilizer used in forestry, animal husbandry, and fishery based on relevant parameters and statistical yearbooks of relevant departments should first be calculated.

The table 1 below, based on statistical data collected by relevant department is summarizing the evolution of chemical fertilizers used in China, between 1980 and 2016. During the past 40 years, as indicated in the table, the fertilizer application amount in China has increased from 12.694 million tons in 1980 to 59.841 million tons in 2016 (an increase of 3.7 times). With regard to the amount of compound fertilizer (NPK), its application rate increased the fastest by 80.1 times; as for the other fertilizers, the amount of potassium fertilizer increased 17.4 times, ranking second, phosphate fertilizer increased 2.0 times, ranking third, and nitrogen fertilizer increased 1.5 times, ranking fourth.

Table 1 Fertilizer application in China from 1980 to 2016

Unit: 10000 tons

Year	Chemical fertilizer	N fertilizer	P fertilizer	K fertilizer	Compound fertilizer
1980	1269.4	934.2	273.3	34.6	27.2
1985	1775.8	1204.9	310.9	80.4	179.6
1990	2590.3	1638.4	462.4	147.9	341.6
1995	3593.7	2021.9	632.4	268.5	670.8
2000	4146.4	2161.5	690.5	376.5	917.9
2005	4766.2	2229.3	743.8	489.5	1303.2
2010	5561.7	2353.7	805.6	586.4	1798.5

continued table

Year	Chemical fertilizer	N fertilizer	P fertilizer	K fertilizer	Compound fertilizer
2015	6022.6	2361.6	843.1	642.3	2175.7
2016	5984.1	2310.5	830	636.9	2207.1

As shown in the table 2 below, nearly 80 percent of chemical fertilizers used in China in 2015 should be attributed to the agricultural sector.

Table 2　Structure of fertilizer application in China from 1999 to 2015

Unit: 10000 tons

Year	National	Agriculture	Forestry	Fishery	Animal husbandry
1999	4124.3	3359.2	501.7	170.9	92.5
2000	4146.4	3457.1	421.1	175.6	92.6
2001	4253.8	3575.3	406.1	179.8	92.6
2002	4339.4	3615.9	446.5	184.5	92.5
2003	4411.6	3684.5	447.1	187.6	92.4
2004	4636.6	3826.0	528.2	190.2	92.2
2005	4766.2	3966.6	510.9	196.7	92.0
2006	4927.7	4043.2	591.5	201.1	91.9
2007	5107.8	4166.2	704.6	145.1	91.9
2008	5239.0	4291.8	686.6	168.7	91.9
2009	5404.4	4412.3	718.0	184.1	90.0
2010	5561.7	4525.2	760.4	188.4	87.7
2011	5704.2	4568.4	854.5	194.2	87.1
2012	5838.8	4635.6	919.4	202.5	81.3
2013	5911.9	4663.4	960.8	206.8	80.9
2014	5995.9	4563.2	1134.2	209.9	88.6
2015	6022.6	4736.7	996.9	212.7	76.3

1.3　Over time change in the amount of fertilizers used for cereal production

The decomposition of chemical fertilizers used for grain production since 1978 is indicated in the table 3. It is based on a differentiation of fertilizers used for high nutrient demanding crops (HND) such as cotton or vegetable, middle nutrient demanding crops

(MND) such as rice, wheat and corn and low nutrient demanding crops (LND) such as soybean or rape, grains and other food crops based on statistical data from the National Agricultural Product Data Assembly and the China Statistical Yearbooks.

Table 3   Decomposition of agrochemical fertilizer application for grain production 1978 to 2012

Unit: 10000 ha, 10000 tons, kg/ha

Year		1978–1982	1983–1987	1988–1992	1993–1997	1998–2002	2003–2007	2008–2012
Sown area	HND	1018.4	1267.1	1590.2	1834.6	2227.2	2584.3	2748.2
	Grains	8206.7	8069.9	8346.4	8301.6	8128.8	7783.1	8635.1
	Other food	3503.4	3089.6	2826.9	2809.9	2778.8	2534.7	2313.5
	LND	1968.9	1993.4	2004.1	2098.1	2439.6	2439.3	2328.2
Fertilizer amount	HND	122.3	213.2	326.0	612.7	804.5	1069.7	1175.4
	Grains	690.2	1017.6	1434.7	1799.0	2031.4	2152.8	2566.4
	Other food	176.9	235.1	293.5	347.0	371.7	386.3	391.8
	LND	53.5	82.5	110.7	236.1	276.6	328.5	353.2
Unit fertilizer application	HND	120.1	168.3	205.0	334.0	361.2	413.9	427.7
	Grains	84.1	141.7	171.9	216.7	249.9	276.6	297.2
	Other food	50.5	76.1	103.8	123.5	133.8	152.4	169.3
	LND	27.2	41.4	55.2	112.5	113.4	134.7	151.7
Non-adjusted		321.2	369.6	417.5	403.3	416.6	425.4	449.0

This table indicates that: (i) 2008–2012 the average fertilization amount per hectare of grain was 297.2 kg; (ii) 2008–2012 the average fertilizer application of vegetables is 427.7 kg/ha, about 32 percent higher than the safety standard of 225 kg/ha; and (iii) 2008-2012 the average fertilizer application of LND crops and other food crops was 151.7 kg/ha and 169.3 kg/ha, respectively, which did not exceed the safety level of 225 kg/ha.

Table 4   2002–2016 Application amount of fertilizer in China's cereals production

Units: kg/ha, 10000 ha, 10000 tons

Year	Initial average amount of fertilizer application			Sown area			Estimated amount	Actual amount	Adjusted average amount		
	Rice	Wheat	Corn	Rice	Wheat	Corn			Rice	Wheat	Corn
2002	317	309	314	2820	2391	2463	2405	2124	280	273	277
2003	315	284	314	2651	2200	2407	2214	2134	304	274	302

Year	Initial average amount of fertilizer application			Sown area			Estimated amount	Actual amount	Adjusted average amount		
	Rice	Wheat	Corn	Rice	Wheat	Corn			Rice	Wheat	Corn
2004	293	287	282	2838	2163	2545	2170	2143	289	283	279
2005	313	324	276	2885	2279	2636	2369	2153	284	294	251
2006	309	333	301	2894	2361	2846	2537	2236	272	293	265
2007	323	341	313	2892	2372	2948	2664	2318	281·	297	272
2008	309	344	305	2924	2362	2986	2625	2401	283	315	278
2009	309	348	321	2963	2429	3118	2761	2484	278	313	289
2010	323	377	338	2987	2426	3250	2977	2650	288	336	301
2011	321	377	338	3006	2427	3354	3013	2718	290	340	305
2012	320	381	344	3014	2427	3503	3094	2786	288	343	310
2013	324	381	350.3	3031	2412	3631.8	3173.2	2853.4	291	343	315
2014	329	405	364.7	3031	2407	3712.3	3325.9	2950.2	292	359	324
2015	333	406	364.5	3022	2414	3811.9	3375.8	3018	298	363	326
2016	339	410	372.3	3018	2419	3676.8	3383.6	3040	305	368	334
2015	333	406	364.5	3022	2414	3811.9	3375.8	3018	298	363	326
2016	339	410	372.3	3018	2419	3676.8	3383.6	3040	305	368	334

With regard to the estimated average amount of fertilizer applied to the planting area of the three main grains, the table 4 above indicates that it is about 10 percent higher than the actual amount of chemical fertilizers. According to this analysis, it is assumed that farmers used a small amount of chemical fertilizer for grain in their own vegetable fields and gardens. This is certainly not the main reason for making this adjustment: according to many years of surveys, farmers do not use more than 1500 kg/ha of chemical fertilizer. Assuming a mark down of 20 percent, the total unit chemical fertilizer should be about 300 kg/ha.

These over-application issues for grain and vegetable may be resolved by improving fertilizer application techniques, applying slow-released fertilizers (SRFs) techniques, soil testing and formula fertilization techniques; and organic fertilizers (vegetables) to not only reduce but improve the application efficiency of chemical fertilizers.

Based on those assessments, the task of solving the problem of over-fertilization is becoming more specific.

2. Agrochemical Pesticides

2.1 Excessive use of chemical pesticides and challenges

Herbicides, insecticides, fungicides, and rodenticides and other plant growth regulators are typical examples of agrochemical pesticides used in agriculture in order to protect plants and destroy unwanted agents such as fungi, weeds, rodents or insects that might otherwise reduce agricultural outputs.[1] Other industries utilize pesticides as well, to clear roadways from weeds, kill invasive species or to control algae in water bodies. By using pesticides, farmers are able to maximize crop yield and save money[2]. Pesticides are also used to protect human from vector-borne diseases such as malaria, dengue fever, schistosomiasis, etc.

The application of pesticides plays an important role in controlling pests and diseases and ensuring food production. According to statistics, the benefit from the application of chemical pesticides accounted for 1/3 of the world's total grain output. However, farmers generally overestimated the losses caused by pests, which inevitably resulted in excessive application of chemical pesticides. Pesticide pollution and pesticide residues in agricultural products caused by over application will not only directly harm the health of farmers and food safety, but also will lead to extinction of natural enemies of pests, reduction of biodiversity, and degradation of cultivated land and water quality.

However, there are many negative consequences of pesticide over use, which result in environmental and ecosystems degradation, particularly air (through volatilization), soil and water pollution, thus degrading biotic communities. For instance, pesticides contamination may result in fish and bird deaths. Other animal lives are suffering from nerve damage, such as amphibians, which resulted in population declines. There is now ample scientific evidence that eating and drinking pesticide-contaminated pollen and

---

[1] Recent statistical information (2017) estimate that, worldwide, 40 percent of pesticide use are from herbicides, 17 percent from insecticides and 10 percent from fungicides.

[2] Some estimates suggest that there is a 4-time return on pesticides.

nectar and water can chronically poison bees, thus affecting their crucial pollination roles. [①]

It has now been assessed those chemical pesticides are endocrine disruptors. As those pesticides pass into the food chain, they finally come to man, thus may be affecting human health from nerve damage to cancers [②] . As a matter of fact, residues of pesticides can be found in a great variety of everyday foods, beverages, animal feeds and even in breast milk. Within human and animal bodies, pesticides may be metabolized, excreted, stored and bio-accumulated in body fat. From Figure 2, it can be seen that from 1997 to 2013, the samples of fruits and vegetables containing multiple pesticide residues increased from nearly 15% to 27% in Europe and the United States. The highest number of pesticides residues in these samples increased from 8 to 26. The fact that fruits and vegetables consumed by consumers in Europe and the United States consume containing certain doses of pesticide residues, is an important reason why governments are paying attention to food safety in recent years.

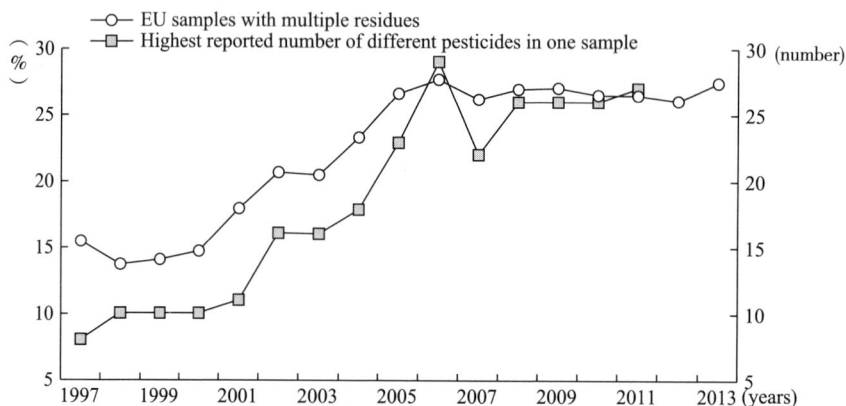

Fig 2   Pesticides residues in Food

In spite of the negative impacts of pesticides on the food chain and the environment, the level of concern for the negative effects of pesticides varies considerably

---

① According to a recent FAO report (2016), more than 70 of the 100 crops that provide 90 percent of the world food rely on bees for pollination available at: http://www.fao.org/news/story/en/item/384726/icode/

② WHO: *Agrochemicals, health and the environment: directory of resources*, 2017, available at: http://www.who.int/heli/risks/toxics/chemicalsdirectory/en/index1.html.

worldwide. [1] For example, in the U.S., if there are many laws regulating the use of pesticides used commercially (including the U.S. Toxic Substance Act) they, in general leave huge gaps in terms of their environmental and health effects. As for the EU, it has adopted a strategy in March 2012 (EU 284/2013) requiring pesticides to be effective and not harmful by setting maximum levels of pesticide residues in food and feed as well as to protect the aquatic environment [2]. NGOs have, however, criticized such pesticide legislation for containing too many exceptions with the pesticide industry arguing that such exceptions were indispensable. As for farmers, they are more concerned about the economic impact and administrative burden related to those rules.

Nowadays the use of pesticides is at the core of large policy (and media) debates with some researchers advocating that pesticide use is logical, when weighted against food security benefits. Others, however, suggest that this rationale is simply not founded, particularly when damages to the environment and human health are considered. Notwithstanding this current debate, environmental movements and a growing public concern for safe food have forced governments to start regulating the use of pesticides towards the introduction of preventive measures to decrease their use and related impacts by requesting farmers to apply pesticides only when the risk of pests is the highest rather than all year-round or by practicing crop rotation rather than monoculture, which drains resources and soil nutrients. Ecological farming practices, therefore, appear to be a compelling alternative to high pesticide use. In this type of farming, farmers rely on natural sources of fertilizers (such as manure and compost) and practice biological pest control. All that said, consumer demand for safe food products is not going away any time soon.

2.2   Pesticides application in China

In China, the data collection for pesticide application began in 1985. The collection of qualitative data includes the amount of pesticides used in crop farming, excluding the use of pesticides in forestry, grasslands, lawns, hygiene and disease control. In 2010–

---

[1] WHO: *The WHO recommended classification of pesticides used in agriculture*, 2009, available at: http://apps.who.int/iris/bitstream/handle/10665/44271/9789241547963_eng.pdf;jsessionid=1F8FD2E 4A52313191 1C979DC2CF3EB1A?sequence=1.

[2] The European Union will ban the world's most widely used insecticides (e.g. neonicotinoids) from all farmlands due to the serious danger they pose to bees. The ban, approved by all country members, is expected to enter into force by end of 2018.

2014, the average annual pesticide use was 317300 tons, of which, field crops (including rice, wheat, corn, cotton, oil-bearing plants, sugar-yielding crops, potato, and beans) accounted for 62.4 percent (198100 tons). The amount of average annual pesticides used in fruits and vegetables (excluding fruit trees managed by the Forestry Department) was 92500 tons, accounting for 29.2 percent; the amount of average annual pesticides used in other crops was 26700 tons, accounting for 8.4 percent. Nowadays, the proportion of bio-pesticides application is 7.83 percent. Based on the farmer households' national survey undertaken in 2012, in 2011, the pesticide application in rice, wheat, and corn crops reached 44400 tons, 21400 tons, and 39700 tons, respectively, representing an average of 14.8 kg/ha, 8.8 kg/ha and 11.8 kg/ha, respectively. As of today (2017), the utilization rate of pesticides for rice, corn and wheat in China reached 38.8 percent, which was 3.8 percent higher than in 2013. Accordingly, in 2017, the average pesticide application rate for rice, corn and wheat was 14.2 kg/ha, 8.5 kg/ha and 11.4 kg/ha, respectively, given an average chemical pesticide application of 11.6 kg/ha. It is about 50 percent higher than that of other developed countries (about 7-8 kg/ha).

Table 5　Use of Pesticides in crop production in China, 2010-2014

Unit:10000 tons, %

Year Pesticides' use	2010	2011	2012	2013	2014	Average
Amount	31.28	32.26	32.44	31.72	30.92	31.73
Field crops	20.13	19.37	20.53	19.82	19.18	19.81
Fruits and vegetables	8.56	10.27	9.18	9.16	9.07	9.25
Proportion of bio-pesticides	8.19	7.60	7.48	7.61	8.27	7.83

2.3　Main issues related to pesticides application in food production

From a general point of view, in China, increase in the cost of agricultural labor has increased farmers' dependence on pesticides. The decline of pesticide price also somehow stimulates the use of pesticides, such as in specific insecticides [1] . There are many farmers not following the instructions to adequately prepare and apply pesticides,

---

[1]　Pingali P. L., "Environmental consequences of agricultural commercialization in Asia ", *Environment and Development Economics*, 2001,6(4): 483-502.

thereby randomly increasing their dosage, or increasing the frequency of application and tending to use pesticides with high toxicity with obvious negative effects. [1]

From the government side, the following problems could be noted: inaccurate standards for pesticide residues, ineffective supervision, and insufficient publicity and training for the safe use of pesticides. Ryan E. Galt [2] pointed out that, there are "double standards" in pesticide regulation: strict control over the use of pesticides for agricultural exports to ensure that products pass the detection of pesticides in developed countries, while weak supervision over the use of pesticides in domestically consumed agricultural products remains [3].

2.3.1 Issues on application mechanization

As shown in the Table 6 below, pest control in food production in China is mainly based on manually spraying and knapsack sprayers (64.3-74.3 percent), with low pesticide utilization rate. China, however, counts nowadays about 3 million motorized knapsack sprayers and 600,000 boom sprayers, with higher pesticide utilization rates.

Table 6   Pesticide application equipment in China

	Amount (10,000)	Proportion (%)	Droplet diameter (μm)	Deposition ratio (%)	Utilization ratio (%)
Manual sprayer		4.3			
Knapsack sprayers	5,800	60~70	400~500	20~40	30
Motorized knapsack sprayer	300	35.7–25.7	80~150	50~60	50
Boom sprayers	60		150~250	50~70	55

2.3.2   Issues on business scale

As shown in the table 7 below, the larger operation scale, the smaller amount of pesticide applied per unit area is, and vice versa. In China, the operating scale of most rural households is less than 1 hectare, which is one of the reasons for the high pesticide application rate.

---

[1] Li Chuanyi, et al.,"The status quo and control measures of pesticide residues in vegetable bases in Chongqing City ", *Agricultural Environmental Science*, 2005, 33(6): 44-47.

[2] Ryan E Galt."Overlap of US FDA residue tests and pesticides used on imported vegetables: empirical findings and policy recommendations", *Food Policy*, 2009,34(5):468-476.

[3] Song Wencheng et al., Pesticide residue supervision status and promotion measures in China ", *Quality and Safety of Agricultural Products*, 2010(6):15-18.

Table 7   Pesticide application in rice production in Zhejiang Province (2011-2013)

Unit: Kg/ha

	Number	Operating area (ha)	2011	2012	2013	3-year mean
Enterprises, cooperatives or farms	82	67.47~263.29	11.33	11.19	12.02	11.51
Large scale households	114	19.39~22.67	11.82	15.57	11.35	12.91
Retail households	96	0.24~0.26	15.15	19.44	16.09	16.89
Average			12.91	15.41	13.02	13.78

2.4   Difference in pesticides application between China and other developed countries

A short assessment of the evolution of pesticides applications in developed counties is given in Appendix 1. From this assessment, when compared to the China's situation, the following could be theorized.

Differences in types of pesticides. In developed countries, herbicides application (notably glyphosate) accounted for more than 70 percent of the total pesticide application amount. Insecticides came second with a much lower percentage. However, in contrast, the proportion of herbicides in China was only 33 percent, while the proportion of insecticides was 40.1 percent.

Differences in pesticide application methods. Developed countries are focusing on prevention, with a considerable percentage of pesticides used in soil fumigation, disinfection, and seed coating. In contrast, in China, pesticides are mainly used to prevent and control harmful biological hazards.

Differences in pesticide utilization rates. Application of pesticides in developing countries, such as Brazil, tends to increase, and that of developed countries, such as the UK, tends to decline. Such changes are related to both the level of economic development, and the application of strict laws, regulations, standards and access systems for the production, sale and use of pesticides. Another factor to be considered is the progress of pesticide application technologies. Furthermore, most of the developed countries are using large-scale boom sprayer or aircraft spraying by professionals, with large-scale pesticide application and higher than 50 percent of pesticide utilization ratio. Meanwhile, in China, farmers are mainly using small-scale sprayers, with a ratio of 30 percent. In recent years, with the promotion of new spraying machinery, the implementation of specialized and unified regulations, the utilization ratio of pesticides has risen to around 36 percent.

Differences in pesticide utilization and management. Developed countries have sound laws, regulations, and standards for the production, sales, and use of pesticides, as well as strict access systems. However, China still has room to improve laws and regulations, market management, and standards.

Difference in the application amounts per unit area. Developed countries are more focusing on comprehensive prevention and control, large-scale control area, and efficient pesticide application machinery. However, at present, China has relatively simple prevention and control approach, with control area remaining rather small. As for application machinery, it remains simple, leading to higher amount of pesticide application per unit area [1].

Based on this assessment, to improve the use of chemical pesticides, the administration of pesticides use should be strengthened by formulating laws, regulations, and standards. In particular, farmers should have more knowledge and information on the use and issues related to chemical pesticides through publicity and training.

3. Water Resources

3.1 Excessive consumption of water resources and challenges

Food is not only a product based on cultivated land, but also a product based on water resources. For China, cultivated land accounts for less than 15 percent of the country's total land area, while water consumed by agriculture accounts for more than 60 percent of the total water consumed in the country. Therefore, the challenge to ensure food security, is not only to implement adequate land management and protection policies, including the control of fertilizer and pesticides overuse, but also to develop and implement policies aimed at sustaining the utilization of water resources, in particular in the agricultural sector.

---

[1] Shu Fang, Xiong Yankun, "Current status of pesticide production and the importance of pesticide use reduction in China", *China Pesticides*, 2016 (1).

3.2   Grain production in most CGG provinces depends on groundwater

Among the 13 major CGG provinces in China, only the five provinces of Jiangsu, Jiangxi, Hubei, Hunan, and Sichuan in the south have sufficient surface water resources. As a result, in those provinces, grain production does not require groundwater extraction. In contrast, in the north, eight provinces, namely Anhui, Henan, Shandong, Hebei, Inner Mongolia, Liaoning, Jilin and Heilongjiang face many surface water resources constraints. They have, to a large extent, to rely on the extraction of groundwater to meet the crop water demand. For example, the irrigation area from wells in North China covers 87.3 billion hectares, accounting for 56 percent of the total irrigation area of North China. As for the well-based irrigated area in the northeast region, it reaches 4.09 million hectares, accounting for 62 percent of the total irrigation area of his region. The well-based irrigated area in Shandong Province reaches 2.59 million hectares, accounting for 57 percent of this region's total irrigated area.

Those eight CGG provinces not only rely on the extraction of groundwater to meet crop water demand, but their dependence on groundwater is increasing steadily. The Hebei Plain represents the most serious water resources challenge, where more than 80 percent of the irrigation water in most agricultural areas is taken from groundwater. It is followed by the Huang-Huai-Hai Plain where the amount of groundwater extracted for agriculture accounts for more than 70 percent of the total local water use. In those areas, the decline of groundwater levels has become one of the most prominent environmental problems.

3.3   Analyses of the causes of excessive use of groundwater in North China

The project "Comprehensive Evaluation and Reasonable Development of Groundwater Resources in China's Main Grain Bases" completed by the China Geological Survey carried out a comprehensive evaluation of the dependency on groundwater and the ability of irrigating agriculture to support food production in the China's major food bases. The survey found that:

i. The groundwater level in the over-exploited area of the North China Plain decreased by "centimeters per day" (sometimes greater than 1.0 cm/day) during the main irrigation period while it only increased by "millimeters per day" during the non-irrigation period. These data are extremely significant as they show that irrigation for agriculture is the main reason for the sharp decline of underground water in the North China Plain;

The amount of groundwater pumped for irrigation in the North China Plain is generally above 180000 m^3/(year $\cdot$ km^2) with, in some agriculture areas up to 360000 m^3 (year $\cdot$ km^2) or even more. Worth to note is that those levels of extraction of groundwater represent about 3-time the amount of groundwater extraction considered sustainable. Experts indicate that such an amount of groundwater extraction compared to the sustainable use of groundwater is in a state of severe incompatibility with available water resources;

With regard to groundwater used, while irrigated wheat and other summer food crops account for more that 50 percent, corn and other autumn crops only account for 10–30 percent. Furthermore, the use of ground water for the irrigation of vegetable and fruit crops is rising sharply, and, nowadays represent in some areas up to 20 percent.

In general, there are two main reasons for the overuse of water resources in major CGG areas.

Recent expansion of irrigated agriculture. Many people in China believe that irrigated agriculture represents advanced agriculture while rain-fed agriculture represents backward agriculture. As a result, the current objective of agriculture development is to maximize the share of irrigated agriculture through the construction of irrigation infrastructure. Statistics show that China's effective irrigation areas increased from 15.9 million ha in 1949 to 44.96 million ha in 1978, and to 67.1 million ha in 2016, i.e. an increase of 22.16 million ha from the mid-seventies (or an increase of 51.2 million ha since the foundation of the PRC in 1949). It must be, however, pointed out that a major part of the effective additional irrigated area in the early stage of irrigation development was almost based on surface irrigation through the concerted joint efforts of farmers and mutual aid unions, or cooperatives during the people's commune period. However, a significant part of the effective irrigated areas added later was based on the extraction of groundwater, which was mainly the result of individual farmers' efforts. In fact, if irrigated agriculture and rain-fed agriculture are not highly differentiated, they are quite different in terms of their suitability according to different climatic characteristics. Developing agriculture based on local climatic factors will play an important role for the sustainable extraction and use of groundwater.

Decreasing sense of cooperative management, Since the dissolution of the People's Commune period in 1985, with the exception of a few villages that did not implement the household contract responsibility system, the level of village-based farmer cooperation no longer existed and, as a result, the surface water irrigation system gradually degraded due to the lack of farmers' cooperation required for its maintenance. As a result, farmers did not have had other option to resolve irrigation water problems than drilling individual wells. In order to achieve the scale of work required for the use of groundwater, some form of cooperation remained among small groups of farmers, but those were an exception. Of course, the improvement of well-drilling technology, the improvement of power supply, and the reduction of irrigation pipes weight made it easier to drill wells and extract groundwater. In addition, it should be noted that if well irrigation facilitate the extraction of groundwater, it also largely reduced water use conflicts among farmers, which is also an important reason why farmers choose well irrigation. In fact, to sustainably manage surface water irrigation, individual and cooperative management are both indispensable. The lessons from the above historical development indicate that absence of cooperative operation among farmers means, in general, that surface water irrigation will inevitably fall through. However, what can still be sustained are large-scale surface irrigation with districts responsible for the supply of irrigated water by state-owned enterprises.

Some scholars have linked the excessive use of water resources in China with the low rate of water availability per capita. This may be a plausible explanation since it is true that China is endowed with few per capita water resources availability, i.e. 1/3 of the world average in term of arable land per capita and 1/4 in term of water resources. As a result, if China's per capita water resources endowment will remain far below the world average, the per capita increase in water resource endowment can only come from many aspects such as resource utilization technology improvement, resource utilization structure adjustment, resource management system innovation, resource pricing improvement, etc. Since those improvements may have large potential, they may become more flexible indicators. In other words, instead of analyzing the reasons of the excessive use of water resources or proposing strategies to eliminate such excessive use, optimizing the per-capita resource requirements should be considered the priority.

4. Climate Change

Over the past several decades, global warming has occurred and caused more extreme weather/climate events in China, which leads to serious consequences for agricultural production. According to the projections of the Fifth Assessment Report of Intergovernmental Panel on Climate Change (IPCC AR5) from current Global Climate models (GCMs), global warming will keep going on for the 21st century, likely leading to positive as well as negative impacts on crop yields, notably more occurrences of frequent extreme weather/climate events in many CGG areas, especially floods and droughts.

4.1 Positive impacts of climate change on grain production

On the positive side, due to increase greenhouse gas emissions (GHG), it is likely that increased temperature, decreased freezing threat, increased total rainfall amounts and increased rainy days would be beneficial to agriculture by extending the length of the potential growing season and providing more water needed for crops.

4.2 Negative impacts of climate change on grain production

However, climate change may also impact negatively on crop productivity. If climate change may lead to gradual increase of the crops' growing season's length, it would also likely increase warmer daytime temperature and related evapo-transpiration that may also impact negatively notably on wheat and corn yields. Furthermore, as plant diseases and insect pollutions are strongly dependent upon temperature and humidity, traditional diseases and pests may increase accordingly. Furthermore, south crop pests may also migrate to north as the climate warms, resulting in possible additional annual grain harvest loss. Changes in precipitation patterns and amounts, and changes in temperature will also influence crop growth through changes in soil water content, runoff, erosion and soil organic matter, nutrient cycles, salinization, and biodiversity. In addition, climate change will have not only a direct impact on crop production, but also on soil water storage, likely putting increased stress on ground water availability for irrigation and, thus, groundwater levels.

Furthermore, due to the likelihood of increased occurrence of climate-related disasters, the overall resistance of existing farmlands to natural disasters may sharply decrease leading in the near future to much larger fluctuation in terms of crop production. As a matter of fact, agricultural production in CGG is already suffering from the continuous occurrence of many weather-related disasters. They include:

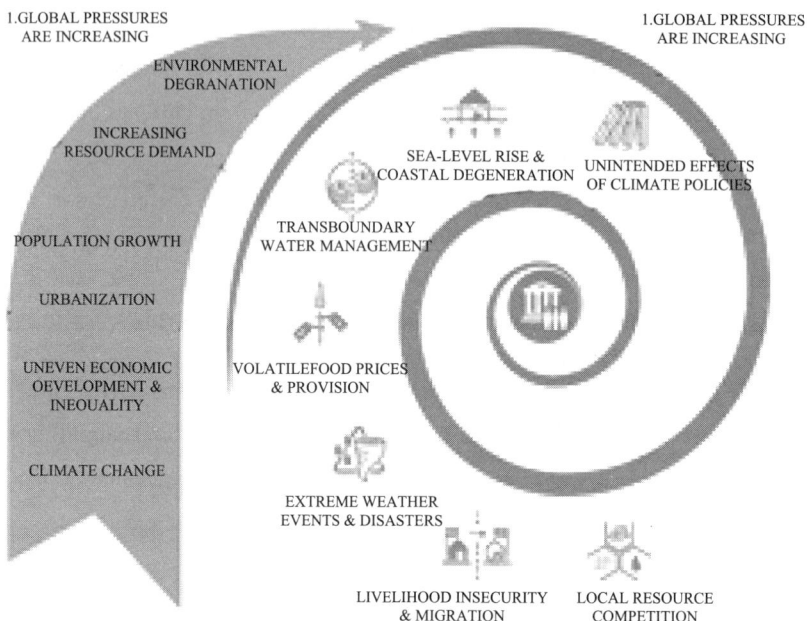

Fig 3   The Climate Change Nexus

i. Late spring and early summer hot and dry winds, particularly affecting wheat crops;

ii. Sandstorms/dust storms particularly affecting desertification-prone regions (sometimes limiting the visibility up to 1 km);

iii. Early summer droughts, particularly but not exclusively, early winter and early spring frost, cold spells and long snowy periods predominantly impacting on wheat productivity and quality;

iv. Floods due to intensive rainstorms generally occurring during the summer season; and finally;

v. Intense topsoil erosion, which may be further negatively affecting agricultural soil fertility in CGG.

Worth to note is that, in general, according to recent studies on the effects climate change on agricultural productivity in CGG areas, the frequency of heat waves, droughts, severe and extreme rainfalls, which may cause severe storms and floods are likely to increase in the future with high probability.

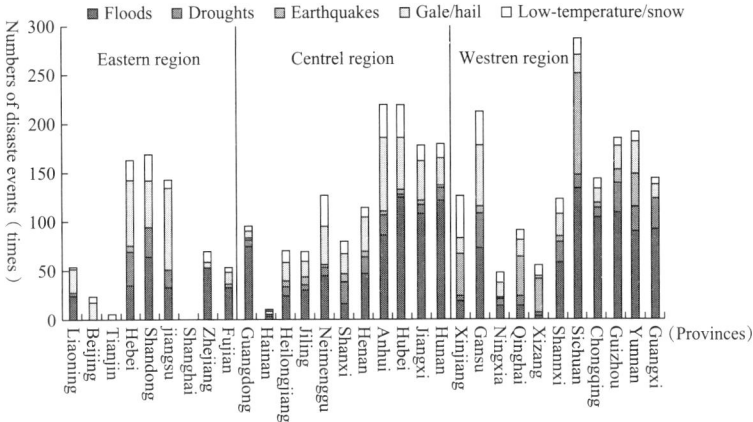

Fig 4   Number of disasters in China by province (2008–2010)

5. Afforestation Protection Forests

5.1   Recent reforestation efforts and ecological security in CGG areas

Major floods in the Yangtze River and the Yellow River basins in the late 1990s, regarded to be the consequence of forest loss, shifted forest policies and strategies towards rehabilitation of damaged forest ecosystems. As a result, the conservation of natural forests and tree planting became an urgent policy issue and massive reforestation campaigns began, exceeding by far any other countries' reforestation programs in the world. As a matter of fact, with the support of eco-compensation payments, China's agricultural regions witnessed an upsurge in tree planting following the development in the early 2000s of the "Six Priority Forestry Programs"[①] , which all together aimed at ecological restoration, sand and water erosion control and at boosting the production of commercial timber for supplying up to 40 percent of China's commercial timber consumption by 2015. These programs have been widely credited with generating

---

① Namely (i) the Sloping land Conversion Program (SLCP or Grain for Green); (ii) the Natural Forest Protection Program (NFPP); (iii) the Shelterbelt Network Development Project (Three North Shelterbelt Program); (iv) the Industrial Timberland Plantation Program (ITPP); (v) the Wildlife Conservation and Nature Reserves Protection Program (WCNRPP); (vi) the Desertification Control Project (DCP) around Beijing. Refer to: http://www.un.org/esa/forests/pdf/aheg/aheg1/China_case_study.pdf.

enormous positive environmental impacts in spite of the fact that they generally lead to the sole planting of monoculture forests without sufficient consideration given to managing or restoring natural forests.

In line with those new reforestation/afforestation initiatives, the forestry administration made concerted efforts outside CGG areas to develop agroforestry business opportunities to transform the state forest-based economy through various types of economic alternatives, such as dairy, cattle farming, growing minor, but high value non-timber forest crops, such as mushrooms, fruits, ginseng and collecting wild herbs, nuts and vegetables, which have all gained broad recognition, notably by private entrepreneurs. However, the financial support to farmers for the development of ecological forests under the policy of forest ecological compensation remains very small when compared to the environmental gains from those forests, which are now placed at high risk of conversion to commercial use, notably in remote areas.

As of today, China is said to have undergone a remarkable increase in tree cover over the past decades. according to the state forest inventory, China's tree cover reported in the inventory as "forest cover" has increased from 12 percent during 1977 to 1981 to 22.96 percent during 2014 to 2018. [①] bringing the country's total forest area to 208.3 million hectares with natural forests covering 121.8 million hectares, corresponding to a stock volume estimated at 15.14 billion m^3. As for the future, China's government has pledged to raise the total forest coverage of the country to 23 percent over the period 2016–2020. Such an increase in reforestation/afforestation is without precedent in such a short period of time in any other large nation. These increases are considered to be particularly attributable to the system of national reforestation and natural Forest conservation programs started in the early 2000 for timber and ecological benefits including the Natural forest Protection Program (NFPP) and the Sloping Land Conservation Program (SLCP). Planting trees has, therefore, become a key part of China's efforts to improve its environment and tackle climate change issues.

---

① According to the World Bank collection of development indicators, compiled from officially recognized sources.

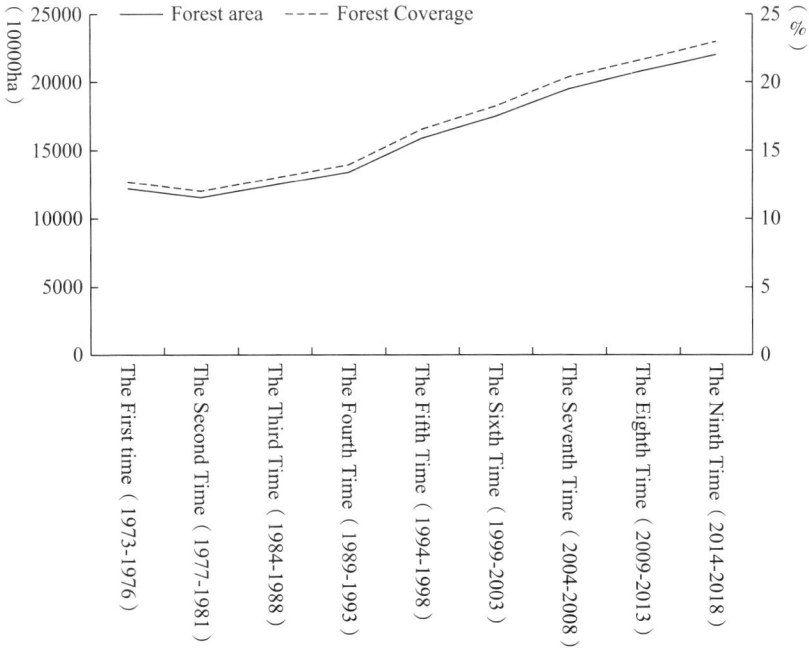

Fig 5   China Forest Change Area (in percent of land area) 2004 - 2016

5.2   Major reasons for the success of afforestation programs in China

The success of reforestation programs in China can be explain before all by two main reforms and policies: first, by forest land and tree tenure reforms process; and second by the gradual emergence and improvement of eco-compensation policies (payments for environmental services or PES).

5.2.1   Reform in forestland and tree tenure

Forestland in China falls into two broad categories of ownership – collective or state-owned. Collective forestland, owned by rural communities (i.e. villages) amounts to 180 million ha (or 60 percent of the nations' total), the rest (40 percent) being owned by the national, provincial and local /county governments.

The new wave of tenure reforms, emerging since 2004, is now recognized as a crucial driver in China's success in the development of reforestation forests. For the forest sector, this new tenure reform was aimed at alleviating rural poverty, improving forest conservation and stimulating local investments in forestry. Through Rural Land Contract, valid for up to 70 years, the reform has given expanded rights to individuals, including land transfer, inheritance and mortgaging, As a result, by 2011, 173 million ha of collective forestland, which accounts for 95 percent of the total collective forestland area of China, had been contracted to individual households, averaging 2.7–3.3 ha per household across the country. Forestland and tree tenure reform has however slowed down in recent years. With the rapidly expanding forest cover, the tenure transition mostly occurred through the increase of newly planted forests (rather than change of tenure rights in existing forest).

5.2.2 Eco compensation policies

Besides changes in tenure and property rights in forestlands, a coherent set of policy reforms has been implemented to support the involvement of farmers in tree planting. These policies, collectively termed as "eco-compensation" [1], include not only payments-in cash and/or in grain–to improve forest-related environmental services, but also an array of taxes, fees, and subsidies-including the central government removing or reducing forestry taxes to encourage tree planting and manufacturing of forest products. For their part, provinces and local governments have removed provincial taxes and some fees on forest products as well. Simultaneously, the government used transfer payments to support local governance organizations that were financed by forest taxes and fees. Eco-compensation payments were and still are nowadays major components of the six key forest conservation programs.

According to the Monitoring Report of Collective Forest Tenure Reform (SFA 2012), with farmers diversifying the use of their forestlands, eco-compensation measures lead to a significant increase in the rural per capita net income from forestry. However, more recent assessment studies on the socioeconomic impacts of eco-compensation payments indicate that reforestation under the SLCP (Grain for Green) has not increased the transfer of labor toward non-farming activities as the government expected. [2] Notwithstanding the above, the future impacts of current reforestation/

---

[1] Eco-compensation has its origin in the late 1990s Yangtze River floods, killing thousands of people and leaving millions homeless, when the government, realizing the importance of maintaining upstream forests for flood protection, introduce payments to farmers to protect or restore forests. Currently, China's eco-compensation payments, by which the principle of PES was built into China's forestry development, are centered mainly on non-commercial forests.

[2] Li Jie et. al.,"Climate Change in China: Policy Evolution, Action taken and Options Ahead January 2011", *Journal of Natural Resources Policy Research*, 2001(1),pp.23-35.

afforestation program associated to the logging ban in natural forests are going have global positive ecological security implications because they increase vegetation cover, enhance carbon sequestration, protect farmlands, improve the availability of water and decrease soil and water erosion.

5.3   Current issues affecting forestry-related ecological security benefits

However, recent remote sensing studies have indicated that this remarkable increase in tree cover was mostly due to the conversion of croplands to tree plantation, particularly to single species monocultures, used for the production of timber, fiber and other tree fruits, thus bringing very limited biodiversity and ecosystem services benefits, even in some cases harming wildlife. [1] Moreover, in the meantime, in many regions of China, the absence of concern for and measures related to the sustainable management of remaining natural forests and deficiencies related to the silvicultural treatments of existing plantation, including natural regeneration as a mean of restoring forests, is not encouraging.

Furthermore, despite China's commitment to mainstream sustainable forest management, promote multi-purpose forest management and enhance multiple environmental and socioeconomic benefits from reforestation, current forest management practices are slow in improving the ecological function of forests for the two main following reasons:

i. Plantation forests are still subject to age-class management with short rotation (ranging between 10 and 30 years), followed by logging and clear felling and replanting. Reforestation after planting requires the application of fertilizers as well as pesticides to control pests and diseases. Such management routines are not compatible with sustainable management practices and detrimental to biodiversity conservation; and

ii. Natural forests are often non-managed because of management restrictions under the Natural Forest Protection Program (NFPP) or classification as Ecological Welfare Forests (EPBF). Furthermore, selective forest management in natural forests often

---

[1]   Fang yuan Hua et al., "Tree plantations displacing native forests: The nature and drivers of apparent forest recovery on former cropland is Southwestern China from 2000 to 2015", *Biological Conservation*, 2018 (222), pp. 113-124.

located in remote regions remains practically restricted due to insufficient infrastructure, forest roads and firebreaks in particular, and adequate equipment.

Since 2010, however, the Forestry department has taken a series of measures and policies to overcome the above constraints and enhance sustainable forestry management. They include:

In 2011, SFA developed the *Forestry Development Plan 2011–2015*, which laid down basic sustainable forestry management principles, key targets and priorities;

In 2013, SFA formulates the *Guidelines for Plan on Building Ecological Civilization 2013–2020*, which specified mid-and long-term forestry strategies and major actions, such as ecological protection red lines and establishing key functional zones of ecological protection;

In 2013, SFA enacted the *Construction of Timber Strategic Reserve Production Base 2013–2020* focused on the development and management of fast-growing high yielding forests with large DBH, aimed at relieving the tension between the demand and supply of wood products;

In 2014, the State Forestry Administration issued the *National Forestry Poverty Alleviation Plan (2013–2020)*, focusing on forestry poverty alleviation in the Liupan Mountains, Qinba Mountains, Wuling Mountains, Wumeng Mountains, Yunnan-Guangxi-Guizhou Rocky Desertification, Western Yunnan Border, Southern Foothills of Daxinganling, Yanshan-Taihang Mountains, Luliang Mountains, Dabie Mountains, Luoxiao Mountains, Tibet, Tibetan areas in four provinces and three prefecture-level states in the southern part of Xinjiang. A total of 14 zones with 713 counties (cities and districts) were covered.

In 2016, the government enacted the 13th Five-Year Development Plan (2016–2020), the focus of forestry being (inter-alia) on stepping up mechanisms for the efficient use of natural resources, water in particular, pollution prevention, improving ecosystem functions, ecological restoration, biodiversity conservation, responses to climate change and ecological and environmental protection.

5.4 China experience with farmland protection forest and tree-crop intercropping

Almost half of the world's agricultural landscapes have at least 10 percent tree cover, suggesting that trees integrated within farms or into agricultural landscapes contribute to sustainable agriculture development. At the international level, integrating trees into farming systems is called "agroforestry" [①] but the term agroforestry in China is generally restricted to tree-crop intercropping systems. The potential of integrating trees into agricultural landscape to contribute to sustainable agriculture and adaptation and mitigation to climate change, and therefore sustainable economic development has been recognized in international policy meeting, notably by the *United Nations Framework Convention on Climate Change* (UNFCCC) and *the Convention on Biological Diversity* (CBD), justifying increased investments in its development.

Tree-crop intercropping agricultural practices has a long history in China. For instance, in the Henan Province, the tree-grain intercropping pattern, notably the Chinese red date-grain intercropping system, was used in farmlands on sandy areas along the old course of the Yellow River that needed protection from forest for more than a thousand of years. In this region, under the people's commune system, the range of tree-grain intercropping increased to include the development of farmland protection forest networks (also called "Four Sides"). As such, the "Four Sides" system remained unchanged until the late 1950s when a large amount of those protective farmland protection forests was harvested for iron and steel making. After this episode, under the People's Commune system, the scale of farmland protection forests not only tremendously increased but also become more uniform. But, as such, it remained unchanged until the enactment of the household responsibility system as a tribute to the legend that seeds would be blown out every year without the protection of farmland protection forests.

As of today, the following major types of agroforestry practices are currently recognized in main CGG regions include:

Farmland protection forest network (also called "Four Sides"), planted at farms' borders and/or along roads, railways, canals and ditches, and rivers as windbreaks,

---

① According to the World Agroforestry Center (ICRAF), agroforestry is a multipurpose land utilization system that combines perennial woody plants and annual crops and/or animals through space and/or timing arrangements, which can maximize complementarities or mutual benefits, including short-term and long-term economic and ecological benefits, while minimizing competitions for moisture, nutrients, light and space.

shelterbelts, and/or riparian forest buffers as wide-narrow lines of trees;

Tree-grain intercropping with Paulownia sp., Chinese date, Chinese ash or with fruit trees;

Fruit tree orchards;

Main forest belt (small shelterbelts) on sandy lands and green corridors notably along river banks, and roads;

Village woodlots, including economic or recreation or scenic forests.

Integrating tree into agricultural landscapes may, therefore, be conceived from tree planting in plots to on-farm tree planting or to off-farm lines of tree planting at the scale. At farm or village level, trees can be planted as household woodlots, along boundaries or roads or as recreation areas. Even at farm level, where it is generally believed that trees may compete directly with agricultural crops, experiments demonstrate that, in well-managed farms, trees have added value that would exceed any loss in crop production value. However, these outcomes are not guarantee, so attention must be paid to the type of tree plantation system and species selected.

5.5 Benefits from farmland protection forests and tree-crop intercropping

In CGG of China, farmland protection forests and tree-crop intercropping systems have the potential to address at least four key inter-related premises of ecological security.

Improving the agricultural productive environment. Based on long years of scientific field research, it has been proven that planting trees in and around farmlands was instrumental in improving farmland micro-climate, soil fertility, water conservation, air purification as well as decreasing risks associated to harmful weather such as dry-hot wind, spring cold, frost, sand storm, etc. Planting trees in and around farmlands also helped fixing carbon. The fact the matter is that, due to the ecological value of tree planting, both forestry and agriculture experts estimated that planting trees in and around farmland was contributing to improving crop yields by at least an average of 10 percent. For instance, it has been established that the ecological security benefits provided by on-farm and off-farm tree planting in the grain growing area of Henan was instrumental in raising the provincial crop production by 20.97 million tons in 1978 to 60.67 million tons in 2015. Past research in China also have demonstrated that forest intercropping systems are critical to bring back marginal/eroded land into production. Finally by reducing reliance on agrochemical inputs, forest-intercropping systems do potentially improve the production of safer food products. Furthermore, by combining crops with a tree component, it is possible to generate additional income from the sale of timber products in addition to agriculture.

Improving climate change mitigation and adaptation at farmland and landscape levels. Aside of mitigating greenhouse gases and sequestering carbon in leaves and roots, farmland protection forests and intercropping practices induce greater resilience against the effects of climate change by adding a high level of diversity within agricultural lands and, with it, an increased capacity for supporting numerous ecological and production services that impart resiliency to climate change impacts. Climate change risk management is difficult in annual crop monoculture systems due to the increasing uncertainty and volatility due to inter-annual variability in rainfall and temperatures;

Enhancing biodiversity. Farmland protection forests and tree-crop intercropping systems can also provide opportunities for increasing the diversity of airborne arthropods, small mammals and possibly birds within arable agriculture, in particular bees for pollination. The increased numbers of some pest predators or changes in microclimate can also lead to reduced numbers of some pests, such as grain aphids. Nevertheless, the presence of trees at farm or landscape levels would not by itself hamper research required to develop environmental-friendly pests and diseases control.

Improving the quality of life in rural areas and encouraging diversification of the rural economy. In addition to improving grain production, benefits from tree planting in and around farmlands also improved farmers' income through the sale of timber, round wood for pulp and paper (thus also driving provincial forest industrial development), wood fuels in addition to non-wood products such as fodder, flowers, fruits, etc. There are also many other socio-economic benefits of farmland protection forests and tree-crop intercropping systems. In brief, they include improved rural employment opportunities, diversification of local economies and products, and non-market benefits associated with landscape, aesthetics, recreation and other ecosystem services.

Economic analyses carried out under the Henan ADB-TA No 8962 PRC project in 2016 have demonstrated that farmers' income from forestry in CGG of Henan reached to CNY 918/ha on average in 2010. As a matter of fact, the theoretical economic analysis undertaken under the project on a couple of existing tree-intercropping composite models indicate quite positive results, as show in the table 8 below.

Table 8　EIRR from some model agroforestry practices in the Henan CGG area

Unit: %

S/N	Composite models	EIRR
1	Net of Farmland Shelterbelt of Poplar Tree Model	43
2	Paulownia Row Intercropping Model	35
3	Row Intercropping Model	N/A
4	Corridors Greening Model	N/A
5	Intercropping of Oil Peony and Walnuts Model	55
6	Under-forest Cultivation of Walnut Model	55
7	Planting *Bupleuri* under Walnut Model	55
8	Planting edible mushroom under the Poplar Forest Model	40

Moreover, farmland protection forests and intercropping systems can also contribute to the United Nations Social Development Goals (SDGs). To meet SDGs' expectations, land productivity in both agriculture and forestry lands will have to increase. With appropriate combinations of trees, crops and livestock, farmland protection forests and tree-crop intercropping systems may provide a range of goods, benefits, and services simultaneously, such as nutritious safe foods, renewable energy and clean water while conserving biodiversity and enhancing farm revenues.

Table 9　Positive and negative impacts of trees on crops under agroforestry systems [1]

Positive effects	Negative effects
• Improvement of microclimate	• Shading
• Soil fertility improvement	• Resource competition (nutrients and water)
• Maintenance of water quality	
• Recharge of groundwater levels	• Allelopathy (chemical interference)
• Carbon sequestration and greenhouse gas mitigation	

① Daizy Batish,Ravinder Kohli ,Shibu Jose, H. P. Singh,"Ecological Basis of Agroforestry", Boca Raton, FL,CRC Press, 2007.

continued table

Positive effects	Negative effects
• Ecological restoration	
• Phytoremediation	
• Weed and pest management	• Harboring of harmful pathogens and pests
• Biodiversity enhancement	• Invasive behavior of some introduced species
• Habitat for wildlife	

5.6 Issues affecting the conservation farmland protection forests in CGG areas

In spite of the inherent benefits of farmland protection forests and tree-crop intercropping on crop productivity as historically demonstrated, there are, however, a series of problems, constraints and barriers affecting the maintenance and expansion of farmland protection forests in CGG areas that should be addressed for ecological security reasons. These have been identified by farmers and forestry extension staff during the Henan ADB-TA No 8962 PRC project's assessment studies and the farmers' and extension staff's attitude survey towards existing farmland protection forests.

As for farmers, the most important barriers to the smooth conservation, maintenance and development of farmland protection forests include:

i. Too dense layouts and too narrow grids of farmland protection forests, thus hampering agricultural mechanization;

ii. Damaging tree border effects of farmland protection forests on crop productivity, due to shade, roots and competition for nutrients and soil moisture. The negative effect of farmland protection forests on crop productivity has not, so far, attracted enough research attention;

iii. Unclear tree ownership and inadequate management and harvesting regulations, which all together are acting as disincentives to farmers for their maintenance and development. The main problem related to the tenure of on-farm farmland protection forests is that the land where trees may be planted is classified as basic farmland where farmers could legally cultivate crops but could not plant trees;

iv. Decreasing prices and/or little marketing opportunities for timber and other specialty products derived from farmland protection forests. For instance, ten years ago in the Henan plain, if the price of larger diameter poplar timber reached more than CNY 1000/m^3, it has nowadays decreased to CNY 500-600/m^3;

v. Absence of adequate financial compensation measures leading to farmers' resistance to allocate farmland to forest protection forests. In effect, farmers are mainly concerned about revenues from agriculture. As a result, most farmers are considering that the costs of establishing and maintaining farmland protection forests for ecological security and compensation for the loss in productivity due to their border effects should be borne by the government. Therefore, the real challenge faced by the government is whether the level of financial compensation to be provided would be sufficiently attractive to engage farmers in rehabilitating, scaling up and maintain farmland protection forests for ecological security reason.

As for issues and constraints affecting the conservation and development of farmland protection forests mentioned by county level forestry and agricultural extension staff participating to the attitude survey, they can be summarized as follows:

i. Absence of an integrated inter-sectoral policy framework, specifically devoted to the role of farmland protection forests to improve farmland ecological security. They further attributed this absence of inter-sectoral policy framework to the current institutional fragmentation. Furthermore, the efficiency of the current institutional framework is hampered by weak horizontal and vertical collaboration between and within provincial rural organizations that should be aimed at jointly working at overcoming issues affecting ecological security in CGG areas in an integrated mode;

ii. Insufficient budget allocations for mainstreaming farmland protection forest for ecological security reasons in the agricultural landscape. Such insufficient budget allocations were even compelling some counties to borrow money from banks for the maintenance of existing farmland protection forests;

iii. Lack of adequate extension strategy, capacity and technical expertise especially devoted to ecological security, notably, absence of long-term training and capacity building at counties' level. For forestry extension, this situation is leading to both inadequate inter-personal skills and little knowledge of modern communication technologies for extension, awareness raising, outreach and education to disseminate up-to-date sustainable technologies;

iv. Absence of applied research work to help resolving both basic, process-level issues and applied management techniques to maximize the tangible short and intermediate term benefits provided by farmland protection forests. The greatest research need in CGG areas is to develop both region-wide analyses of the potential economic costs, benefits, and risks associated to farmland protection forests as well as on tree-crop environment interactions to provide a scientific basis for optimizing farmland protection forests' designs under the current changing climate environment. Demonstrating the positive environmental and economic linkages between farmland protection forests and crop productivity and economic growth remains a challenge that should be urgently addressed as well as making an economic case for farmland protection forests as a key asset for ecological security, national food security and food safety, and the improvement of farmers' livelihoods.

The above issues and constraints demonstrate the reason why, in spite of their inherent environmental and economic benefits and impacts on crop productivity as historically demonstrated, farmland protection forests and other tree-crop intercropping practices established during the collective time in CGG are facing a continuous deterioration. Furthermore, due to the current regulations pertaining to agricultural land conversion [1], the question of establishing and maintaining off-farm and on-farm farmland protection forests and other type of intercropping practices on basic farmland of CGG to improve the ecological security of CGG and increase crop productivity remains to be clarified.

Addressing the above constraints as stated by farmers and extension staff during the Henan plain's attitude survey would certainly be critical to their participation to the improvement of ecological security in CGG areas. One of the major challenges facing the inclusion of trees in the CGG agricultural landscapes for ecological security is, therefore, to endorse ways to facilitate farmers' adoption of off-farm farmland protection forests on basic and regular farmlands and, including in some specific areas [2], on-farm tree planting (i.e. on regular farmland), as to provide an adequate environmental protection for crop growing and, as a result, enhance national and provincial governments' food security and economic sustainability objectives.

---

[1] See : 1994 State Council regulations on basic farmland and 1999 Amendment to the Land Administration Law.

[2] Notably on sandy, erosion prone regular farmlands.

6. Farmland

6.1 Average level of pollution of cultivated land

The average level of pollution of cultivated land is higher than the average level of land pollution in the country. As shown in table 10 below, in term of pollution, 19.4 percent of cultivated lands have exceeded the national standard. Among them, the extent of slight, low, moderate and severe pollution levels is 13.7 percent, 2.8 percent, 1.8 percent and 1.1 percent respectively.

In comparison, if the average rate of polluted land is 16.1 percent, lands with slight, low, moderate and severe pollution levels represent respectively 11.2 percent, 2.3 percent, 1.5 percent, and 1.1 percent.

Table 10　Soil pollution in China

Standard rate of soil monitoring points	All lands (%)	Cultivated land (%)	Gap(point)
	16.1	19.4	3.3
Slight	11.2	13.7	2.5
Low	2.3	2.8	0.5
Moderate	1.5	1.8	0.3
Severe	1.1	1.1	0

Notes: The Third Survey of Soil Pollution in China (April 17, 2014). In this survey, the pollution level is divided into 5 grades: (i) no pollution if the pollutant level does not exceed the evaluation criteria; (ii) slight pollution if it exceeds the standard by 1 to 2 times; (iii) slight pollution if it exceeds the standard by 2 to 3 times; (iv) moderate pollution if it exceeds the standard by 3 to 5 times. With more than 5 times the grade represents a heavy pollution level.

6.2 Diminution of the black soil layer in Northeast China

Black soils in northeastern China are recognized as ones of the most fertile soils in the world. They cover an area of 103 million hectares, of which about 32 million hectares are arable lands that play an important role in safeguarding national food security. Current monitoring data show that the topsoil of farmland in the black soil region of northeastern China loses 0.3 cm-1.0 cm per year on average. As a matter of fact, the black soil top layer thickness of some parts of the cultivated land has decreased from 80 cm–100 cm at the beginning of the land reclamation period to a current 40 cm–50 cm, with, in some areas, down to 20 cm–30 cm. As a result, the soil organic matter content has dropped from 3-6 percent to a current 2-3 percent [①] .

The loss of black soil is particularly marked in Jilin and Heilongjiang provinces.In Jilin Province, which has 5.2 million hectares of black soil arable land, accounting for more than 70 percent of its cultivated area, the average annual loss of surface soil is 0.3 cm–0.7 cm, and the organic content of the cultivated layer has declined at an annual rate of 0.1 percent. Furthermore, the plowing layer of cultivated land has dropped from about 20 cm in the 1980s to 13 cm currently. This represents a decrease in soil fertility, which can, to a certain extent, result in an increase in crop disease frequency. [②] There are 15.93 million hectares of cultivated land in Heilongjiang Province. Due to improper use, the average thickness of black soil in cultivated land fell from 28.8 cm in 1982 (second survey) to 19.7 cm in 2012. In parallel, the average content of soil organic matter and total nitrogen in cultivated soil decreased from 4.32 percent in 1982 to 2.68 percent in 2012, respectively. As for the effective potassium content in the plowed layer, it also declined rapidly. Moreover, during the same period, the area of saline-alkali cultivated land in Heilongjiang Province increased from 233300 hectares to 566700 hectares, an increase of 143 percent. As the input of chemical fertilizers increased year after year, the contribution of organic matter also decreased year by year, while the amount of herbicides used increased, as well as the degree of soil compaction.

6.3 Heavy metal pollution

Heavy metal pollution of arable land in China results in a deterioration of the soil ecological environment. As of today, no official published data on heavy metal pollution in cultivated soils in China has been published. However, some partial survey results carried out in many regions have been published in domestic and international papers. Collecting and compiling those published data has allowed the development of a database of heavy metal pollution in cultivated land, which can be used to estimate the

---

① Jin Liang et al., "Treatment of black lands' 'anemia'", *Economic Daily*, July 28, 2015.

② Liu Weilin, "'The Green Butterfly' of the Black Land", *Peasant Daily*, September 14, 2017.

current status of heavy metal pollution in cultivated land in China [1] .

Based on the result of this analysis, the table 11 below indicates that 68.12 percent of cultivated lands in China are clean; 14.49 percent are slightly polluted; 15.22 percent have a low pollution rate; and 1.45 percent and 0.72 percent, respectively, are moderately and heavily polluted.

Table 11   Classification of Soil Pollution Degree

Level	Pollution index	Classification	Comments
1	$P \leqslant 0.7$	Clean	Safe
2	$0.7 < P \leqslant 1$	Slight pollution	Safe, but warning level
3	$1 < P \leqslant 2$	Low pollution	Soil quality exceeds national standard: crop would be polluted
4	$2 < P \leqslant 3$	Moderate pollution	Soils and crops polluted moderately
5	$P > 3$	Severe pollution	Soils and crops polluted severely

Among heavy metals, the probability of occurrence of cadmium (Cd) pollution is the highest, i.e. 25.3 percent-With regard to the probability of pollution in nickel (Ni) and mercury (Hg), they reach 5.17 percent and 3.31 percent respectively, while the probability of contamination in arsenic (As) and lead (Pb) elements is again 0.92 percent and 0.72 percent, respectively; soils are less likely to be contaminated by Zn, Cr and Cu.

With the exception of Inner Mongolia, all other 12 CGG provinces have serious heavy metal soil pollution issues. Some CGG areas also contain cadmium pollution.

In short, the problem of insecurity of arable land in China can be summed up as "Three Highs" and "Three Lows."

The "Three Highs " are related to: (i) a high proportion of middle and low-yielding fields, accounting to 70 percent of the total area of cultivated land; (ii) a large degraded area of farmland, accounting to more than 40 percent of the total area of cultivated land; (iii) a relatively large area of contaminated farmland reaching 19.4 percent.

As for the "Three Lows", they include: (i) a proportion of arable land with low content of organic matter of about 2.08 percent, 0.07 percent lower than the early 1990s'

---

[1]   The research team screened 138 articles from nearly a thousand retrieved documents, involving 26 provinces, 78 prefecture-level cities and 62 counties. It generally reflects the general situation of heavy metal pollution in cultivated land in China.

level; (ii) a low level of additional cultivated land of about 5 million mu/year, with lower fertility; (iii) a lower level of soil fertility, which is 20-30 percent lower than that of other developed countries.

Farmland heavy metal pollution has the following characteristics:

i. It is difficult to observe. Air pollution and water pollution can be perceived through the senses. However, soil pollution can only be determined through soil sample analysis, crop inspection, and even human and animal health evaluation. Soil pollution usually takes a long time from its start to the discovery of hazards;

ii. Soil pollution can easy build up. Contaminants in the soil have low mobility, difusibility, and dilution characteristics. They can, therefore, without difficulty accumulate in the soil;

iii. Soil pollution has a large variability. The nature of soils is quite different, making the distribution of pollutants in the soil not uniformed with large spatial variability:

iv. Slow degradation of soil pollutants. Heavy metals in the soil, like many organic pollutants, take a long time to degrade;

v. Difficult to treat. Soil pollution cannot be solved without cutting off the source of pollution. The treatment of soil is costly, long term, and complex.

New standards for soil pollution issued on July 10. 2018

As of August 1, 2018, new *China National Safety Standards for Soil Pollution* enter into force for the first time since 1995. The new standards differentiate between agricultural and construction land, with the former focusing on the safety of edible agricultural products with non-acceptable levels of cadmium, mercury, arsenic, lead and chromium in agricultural soils. For construction land, the standards address the health of those working in construction or in close proximity. They also consider the long-term consequences of exposure to toxins and carcinogens.

As specified in the new regulation, if the 1995 *China's Soil Environmental Quality Standard* played an active role in soil environmental protection, it has not been able to meet the current requirements of soil environmental management and food safety standards. In order to fully reflect the idea of risk management and control of "Ten Shi", the new "Agricultural Land Standards" and "Construction Land Standards" have been issued under the name of "Soil Pollution Risk Control Standards".

As for the "Agricultural Land Standard", its objective is to protect the quality and safety of edible agricultural products, taking into account the need to protect crop growth and soil ecology, and to develop soil pollution risk and control values. In particular, the new standard sets risk control values for five heavy metals such as cadmium, mercury, arsenic, lead and chromium on the assumption that, if the content of such pollutants in agricultural soils does exceed those values, the risk of land pollution would increase and agricultural products would not meet acceptable quality and safety standards, thus risking to affect human health.

6.4 Other factors affecting farmland security

6.4.1 Soil erosion

The first national water conservancy survey carried out by the Ministry of Water Resources from 2010 to 2012 showed that the loss of topsoil was more than 1 cm/year in the areas of the Loess Plateau, meaning that about 66700 ha of cultivated land are lost every year due to soil erosion.

6.4.2 Soil compaction due to conventional tillage

In practice, in order to absorb nutrients, the roots of the crops can reach 2 meters. However, as there is enough nutrients and water in the top 10cm–15 cm, the roots remain superficial, thus easily affected by soil pollution in absence of soil pollution management. Furthermore, due to conventional tillage, the soil below 15 cm is compacting to form a hard layer, resulting in the thinning of the soil cultivation layer.

6.4.3 Use of plastic films

The original national standard for agricultural film thickness is 0.008 mm ± 0.003 mm. As it is too thin, plastic film easily break, resulting in a large amount of labor to collect the abandoned agricultural film. As a matter of fact, farmers mainly abandoned those plastic films on the land or try to incorporate it into the soil, thus causing large white pollution. In response to this problem, China has formulated a new *Polyethylene blown mulch film for agricultural use standard,* which started to be officially implemented as of May 1, 2018. The standard stipulates that the thickness of the plastic film shall not be less than 0.010 mm with a deviation not higher than 0.003 mm–0.002 mm. This standard does not consider problems related to the degradation of plastic film.

6.4.4 Lack of supervision

The supervision of cultivated land is characterized by an absence of monitoring system for routine operation at municipal and countylevel due to lack of professional staff and equipment. In this respect, soil environmental supervision and law enforcement, risk early warning and emergency system are lagging behind. A coordinated monitoring mechanism for atmospheric, water, and soil pollution has not yet been established. Soil pollution prevention should involve agencies dealing with environmental protection, development and reform commission, science and technology development, industry, finance, land resources, housing, and agriculture. However, no coordination mechanism between such departments has yet been established.

III Government Policies Addressing Food Security Issues

In the 40 years since the implementation of the reform and opening-up policy in 1978, China's economy has grown rapidly, but for a certain period, no attention was paid to the long-term negative environmental impacts of development. Facing the major ecological challenges, the Central Committee of the Communist Party of China (CPC) is vigorously promoting the concept of "ecological civilization". Originally proposed at the 17th CPC National Congress, and incorporated into the Party Constitution at the 18th CPC National Congress (November 9-12, 2013), the concept of ecological civilization has been further elevated to a central strategic position in China's national development. The core objective of ecological civilization is to balance the relationship between people and nature, including the relationship between economic development, population, resources and the environment. The concept of ecological civilization, which aims to create a harmonious way of development between nature and human, stems from a reflection on the ecological dilemmas in the Chinese context, as well as from a critical reflection on Western industrialization.

As a result, China's government decisions since the early 2000s were paying a lot of attention to the development of comprehensive environmental protection policies and associated programs. As a matter of fact, the party has already accepted that the country's environmental conditions need urgent improvements, notably in term of air, water and soil qualities. That in the context of the Chinese Ecological Civilization concept (or Eco-civilization concept), which prioritizes green development, and notably pollution reduction, efficient use of natural resources, food security, climate change mitigation and adaptation to address development-related problems. More specifically, with the context of Ecological Civilization, environmental protection, sustainable rural development, food security and climate change have been placed firmly at the core of the agricultural policy development agenda of China-and related "National No 1 Policy Documents" issued since 2004, the National Climate Change Program, the China Biodiversity Conservation Strategy and Action Plan, the China Agenda 2030 and the 16 associated sustainability programs started in the late 1990s and early 2000s.

1. China Food Security Policy

1.1 The evolution of food security objectives

1.1.1 Increase the total grain output to meet the survival needs of residents

From 1949 to 1984, in term of food security, the main problem of China was its shortage in the total amount of grain needed to meet the survival needs of its large population. At this stage, the main goal of food security policy was to increase its total grain output and reverse the situation of short supply. Among them, the production measures taken at that time were focused on: (i) concentrating manpower, material and financial resources to build water conservancy, expand the scope of land reclamation for increasing the area of cultivated land, renovating farmland to expand the area under agriculture and building farmland shelterbelts; (ii) improving research to address scientific breeding technology and the promotion of hybrid varieties of rice, maize and dwarf wheat; (iii) improving grain production per unit area per year , e.g. 3000 kg/ha/year. Beyond the Outline, 4500 kg/ha/year across the Yellow River, and 6000 kg/ha/year across the Yangtze River.The management measures taken at that time were specifying that (i) more than 85 percent of the country's arable land should remain devoted to grain production; (ii) the policy of fixed production, order and sales was applied to the unified purchase and marketing of grain, cotton, oil and other important agricultural and side products; (iii) the grain, cotton and oil consumption of urban residents were supplied under a coupon system; (iv) the purchase, transportation and sales of grain, cotton, oil and other important agricultural as well as other side products were the responsibility of state-owned commercial departments.

1.1.2 Improving the incentive system for farmers to grow grain and increase grain output from agricultural land

From 1978 to 1998, the Chinese government adopted a series of reform measures around the central task of food security. They included: (i) reforming collective production and operation towards family production and operation. While this reform was encouraging farmers to increase their grain output above the fixed amount of national public grain and collective reserve, all grains produced by farmers were controlled by farmers; (ii) increasing the purchasing price of grain by 20 percent, This policy encourages farmers to increase their grain outputs, thus increasing farmers' income. The consequence of that measure was that farmers' revenues increased faster than grain outputs; (iii) increasing the purchasing price of grain that exceeds planned purchase quantity by 50 percent. This policy encourages farmers to sell more grain; (iv) the gradual reduction of the implementation scope and proportion of the unified purchase and marketing system as to let the market play an increasingly important role, thus leading to a "dual track system" of grain purchase and marketing, in which contract purchase and market purchase were coexisting; (v) the decision to implement a price policy based on "Keep the order quantity and price decided by the market".

1.1.3 Improving the stability of grain supply and demand balance to enhance the sustainability of grain supply

After 1998, China's grain supply and demand were basically in balance. The main task of China's food security policy was to reduce all risks associated to food supply and improve food production capacity and sustainability. The four main measures taken at that time were. (i) improving agricultural infrastructure as to reduce the risk of grain production reduction caused by extreme climate conditions; (ii) increasing provincial governors' responsibility as for them to fulfill the responsibility of stabilizing grain production; (iii) implementing the policy of minimum purchase price. When the supply of grain would exceed the demand, a minimum purchase price policy was implemented for rice and wheat as to stabilize farmers' grain income expectations; (iv) relying on agricultural technology innovation with a particular attention given to the improvement of the efficiency of agricultural input factors; (v) relying on standards for the application of chemical fertilizers and pesticides and advocating green production as to control agricultural chemicals inputs and irrigation water requirements within the scope of environmental and soil degradation and sustainable utilization of water resources.

1.2   The evolution of food security policy

With a food supply and demand situation changing from a shortage of supply to a balanced supply and demand situation with a food price mechanism changing from a government regulation to a market regulation, and a food consumption situation changing from meeting survival needs to improving the quality of life, the China's food security policy has undergone a profound evolution.

1.2.1   Grain subsidy policy

China initially implemented a grain consumption subsidy policy, notably targeting urban residents. With the abolition of the grain coupon system and the introduction of market grain price, this subsidy system was abolished, thus eliminating the heavy financial pressure on the government caused by both the increase in grain production and the increase of grain purchasing price as the sales price of grain remained unchanged. In 1985, the policy of the "three links" was implemented combining grain contract purchase with the supply of cheap chemical fertilizer and cheap energy (e.g. diesel oil) and the payment of advance purchasing deposit. This new policy was the starting point for granting new grain subsidies to agricultural producers. Following the implementation of the "three links", the content of subsidies gradually increased and the efficiency of subsidies gradually improved.

1.2.2   Grain circulation policy

From 1953 to 1984, under the policy of unified purchase and marketing, the grain price and grain management were fully operated by the government, with the consequence that it was strictly forbidden for individuals or enterprises to be involved in grain trading. From 1985 to 1997, with the double track system of contract order and market purchase, the state-owned grain enterprises could not only trade grain, but also assume the responsibility of macro-controlling the grain market organized by the government. For doing them, the state provided state-owned grain enterprises with a certain amount of financial funds. However, as of 1998, the food policy was modified to introduce the separation of government and enterprise, of reserve and operation, of central and local responsibilities, of new and old grain financial accounts, and the improvement of the grain price mechanism. This new food policy reform was called the "four separation and one improvement", leading to the transition from government's rules of grain circulation and grain price formation to marketization, as a first step towards the full liberalization of grain purchase and sale.

1.2.3 Grain Reserve Policy

In the early days of the founding of Peoples Republic of China, the purchase and sale of grain was adopted as a market rule. However, due to the fact that some private businessmen were bidding up the grain price, this situation led to various chaos in the grain market. As a consequence, the State adopted the strategy of establishing grain reserves to stabilize grain price fluctuation. Moreover, in order to ensure efficiency in the supply of grain and maintain social stability, the State established, between 1953 and 1954, the state-owned grain reserve system. The rural collective grain reserve system was established in 1965. With the implementation of the household responsibility system in the early 1980s, the rural collective grain reserve system gradually fails, the national special grain reserve system was further strengthened, and a "Regulations on the administration of central grain reserve" was promulgated and implemented. In order to resolve the farmers' problem of "difficulty in selling grain" and safeguarding their legitimate rights and interests in the main grain producing areas, a policy of temporary grain storage was formulated.

1.2.4 Grain trade policy

From 1950s to the mid 1990s, grain trading at the international level was the government's responsibility. It formulated annual import and export plans according to the domestic grain supply and demand situation based on the various provinces' food security situation. At that time, grain import and export trade were operated by the China grain, oil and food import and Export Corporation, the grain trade policy being to restrict imports and encourage exports. After the mid-1990s, the State gradually relaxed the control of international grain trade by reducing tariff rates, implementing a quota management policy for the import of agricultural products, notably for rice and wheat, implementing a tax rebate policy for key grain exports, and cancelling the railway transportation construction fund for rice and wheat.

1.3 Current food security policy

1.3.1 Main objectives of food security policy

Three following policy objectives underline the current food security policy: They include:

(i) improving and sustaining grain production capacity while maintaining at 95 percent the grain self-sufficiency rate as to increase farmers' enthusiasm for production, and improve the quality of ecological environment; (ii) improving the efficiency and benefit of grain circulation, including reducing administrative control, examination and approval procedures while providing more space for market players, and giving full play to the decisive role of the market in resource allocation; and (iii) stabilizing grain prices and safeguarding the interests of farmers and consumers.

1.3.2　Farmland protection policy

The following five points are characterizing China's farmland protection policy: (i) formulating land use planning. According to land use planning, non-agricultural use of agricultural land is forbidden. (ii) implementing a system of farmland occupation with compensation. Occupied agricultural land allowed by the State shall be cultivated in strict accordance with the occupied cultivated land area. If the quantity and quality of the cultivated land cannot reach accepted standards, reclamation fees can be claimed from the state. (iii) implementing a basic farmland protection system. Local governments at all levels shall take responsibility for the amount of cultivated land, protection of basic farmland, area, the overall land use plan and the implementation of the annual plan within their respective administrative areas. All agricultural producers and operators shall bear the corresponding responsibility for farmland protection in accordance with *The Regulations on The Protection of Basic Farmland*. (iv) stablishing farmland ecological protection areas. The cultivated land in the areas shall be protected and conserved more strictly to ensure soil fertility and quality, so as to prevent NPS pollution. At the same time, the incentive mechanism of cultivated land protection should be established to improve the enthusiasm of local governments for the protection of cultivated land and food production bases. (v) formulating and implementing laws and regulations on cultivated land protection. From 1978 to 1985, the state issued a series of farmland protection measures for farmland occupied by construction projects, but clear legal provisions were missing. As a result, in 1986, the state promulgated and implemented the *Land Management Law. Regulations for The Protection of Basic Farmland*. The Land Management Law revised in 1998 lists the details and measures of cultivated land protection in specific chapters. In 1997, for the first time, the destruction of cultivated land was included in *The Criminal Law*.

1.3.3 Grain science and technology policy

The grain science an technology policy include three aspects that could be summarized as follows: first establishing and improving research and development system for the deepening of the reform of grain science and technology system as to form a modern scientific research system. The goal of improving the grain science and technology research and development system is to establish the main body of public welfare research for the development of a combination of studies and applied basic research programs focused on production as well as to provide guidance for innovation and enhance marketing efficiency. Second, establishing and improving the grain science and technology system. In order to optimize the microenvironment for the extension of grain scientific and technological achievements, the promotion of scientific and technological research and development include the development of training and demonstration bases in the main grain producing areas, and the organization of one grain scientific and technological demonstration household in each village. And third, improving farmers' ability to use advanced and appropriate technology. In that context, operation rules for the development of grain production technology suitable for large-scale extension were established as to facilitate the extension of agricultural science and technology results at the countryside level, and thus improve yields.

1.3.4 Grain circulation policy

As for the basic characteristics of grain circulation policy, they were characterized by the following three measures: (i) fully liberalizing the grain purchase price and the grain market as to make the competition fairer and deeper, with grain prices fully depending upon market forces; (ii) promoting a healthy grain market cooperation mechanism by establishing a grain price warning mechanism to control the grain price within a specific range as to maintain the balance between grain supply and demand; and (iii) improving laws and regulations system related to grain circulation, grain information, grain market supervision and early warning system to improve the level of grain administrative law enforcement and standardize grain circulation.

1.3.5 Grain subsidy policy

As for China's grain producers' subsidy policy, it includes two parts. The first one is subsidies, which is referred as the "four subsidies" including financial subsidies, comprehensive agricultural subsidies, improved seed subsidies and agricultural machinery purchase subsidies for all grain farmers. These subsidies are calculated according to their cultivated land area. The other one is grain subsidies to guaranty a minimum purchase price of grain. This grain subsidy system means that the government entrusts grain enterprises with certain qualifications to purchase part of the grain produced by farmers when the grain price is lower than the minimum market price. The implementation of these grain subsidy policies hus played a positive role in improving farmers' eagerness for growing grain, for increasing farmers' income and for ensuring China's grain output increase and, thus, the stability of food security.

1.3.6 Grain Reserve Policy

Three decisions were characterizing the grain reserve policy. First, the establishment of a reasonable reserve scale depending upon China's grain output, market supply and demand, and the dynamics of international grain market, suitable reserve varieties and reserve locations. Second the optimization of the grain reserve system at central, provincial and county levels. And third, the establishment of a grain reserve network that would radiate over the whole country with convenient dispatching and handling characteristics.

1.3.7 Grain trade policy

Three measures were considered by the government to improve Chain's grain trade policy. First, making use of the comparative advantages of different countries and regions to reduce total import costs of grain while, at the same time, considering the regional market potentials. For example, southern China imports all kinds of crops and animal feed, while northern China is more focused on the exports of corn, wheat and other agricultural products. Second, the State implemented a quota management system for bulk agricultural products. In that sense, the State fixes the amount of import and export according to both the supply and demand of main grain at home and their availability abroad. As for the third measures, China imposes high tariffs on grain imports exceeding quotas.

2. Strategic Policy System of Food Security in the New Period

The CPC Central Committee, when formulating *The Fourteenth Five Year Plan for National Economic and Social Development and The Long-term Goals for The*

Year 2035, which was adopted at the Fifth Plenary Session of the 19th CPC Central Committee, pointed out that solving the problems of agriculture, rural areas and farmers should still be considered a top priority. In that sense, the Fourteenth Five-Year Plan acknowledges that food security and related farmers income are the core issues of agriculture, rural areas and farmers. Consequently, resolving those core issues requires building a new policy system of food security strategy based on the following principles:

2.1 China's grain industry is facing a new situation and new requirements

The current international and domestic situation is complex, and the pattern of economy, science and technology, culture, security and other fields is undergoing profound adjustments. In order to solve the problem of food security in such a changing environment, it is necessary to recognize and consider the new changes of development at home and abroad, analyze and determine the new requirements under the new situation from all aspects, and recognize and consider the new situation and requirements of China's food industry from increasing production to improving quality.

2.1.1 The consumer demand is moving towards new demands

With the improvement of living standards year after year, the consumer demand for green, organic, healthy and other high-quality food has increased from "eat enough" to "eat well" and "eat healthy". In contrast, for a long time, the yield increase of China's grain industry mainly depended on the extensive use of chemical inputs such as synthetic fertilizers and pesticides. As of today, this high use of synthetic fertilizers and pesticides cannot meet the demand of most of the population for high-quality and safe nutritional agricultural products.

2.1.2 Resource and environment constraints are instigating new pressure

Since the reform and opening up, China's agricultural development has made great achievements, to the point that China, achieving its goal of food security and being basically self-sufficient in grain, has become the world's largest grain producing country. After decades of rapid development, China's economic, scientific and technological strengths have been constantly improved, with the consequence that China's modern agriculture has steadily advanced. But at the same time, with the increase of food quality pollution, other problems have surfaced in the agricultural sector. Based on the current situation and looking forward to the future, China's grain industry is facing increasing constraints of resources and environmental issues.

2.1.3 The complex international market environment presents new challenges

Affected by the COVID-19, new geopolitical factors leading to the instability of the world economy have increased significantly. In this context, food security has become again the focus of the world attention, notably due a world food market environment becoming more and more complex and more and more instable. Indeed, this situation is posing new and great challenges to China's food security.

2.1.4 Technological innovation has brought new impetus

In 2019, the contribution rate of China's total factor productivity has reached 59.2%. Technology, system and organization innovation have become the key factors leading to the increase in grain yield and the improvement of grain quality. Based on the current development of scientific and technological innovation in China's grain industry, there is an urgent need to further improve the supporting role of scientific and technological change in grain production, make full use of new advances in the information technology, biotechnology, consumption reduction, and equipment technology to accelerate the high-quality development of China's grain industry.

2.1.5 Institutional and organizational innovation provides new vitality

With the development of agricultural modernization in China, the industrial organization of grain production has been developing uninterruptedly and a number of new types of food production management organizations, such as cooperatives and family farms, have emerged.Those diversified industrial organizations are more conducive to the high quality and sustainable development of grain industry in China.

2.1.6 Macro policy change provides new opportunities

China's grain industry support policies play an important role in the development of China's grain industry, but there are still many problems to address, such as rising policy implementation cost. In the current complex new environment, it is urgent to speed up the reform of grain industry support policies and build a new China's strategic policy system for food security in this new era.

2.2 The specific objectives and ideas of constructing China's strategic food security policy system for the new era

On the whole, the following three goals should be considered in building the future strategic food security policy system of China's. The first is to stabilize the grain production area and yield level and accelerate the improvement of grain quality; The second is to significantly improve the efficiency of production factors and relieve the pressure on water, soil and other natural resources; The third is to enhance the competitiveness of the grain industry, control import risks from foreign countries, and steadily increase farmers' incomes from grain production. When formulating its future strategic food security policy system, China must put a particular attention to those three goals as to finally form a new food security system adapted to the new era.

2.2.1 Create structural adjustment policies and optimize the existing supporting policies

Adapting the requirements to boost national economy and people's livelihood, ensuring food security should be considered as the bottom line by improving the agricultural support and protection system. On the premise of ensuring domestic grain production capacity, the urgent need io establish and stabilize in the short-term basic grain production subsidies, and gradually increase the intensity of grain production subsidies in the medium and long term. First, there is a need to support the adjustment of production structure through improving quality and efficiency as the basic direction. On the premise of ensuring an effective supply of output, the need is to optimize the production structure, take the market as the guidance, and actively guide farmers to make appropriate cropping decisions. The second need is to reform and optimize existing supporting policies and give full play to the role of market resource allocation. At the same time, additional measure should be taken to stabilize or increase the support from agricultural machinery purchase subsidies, financial insurance, resources and environmental protection, as to significantly expand the "green box" policy space, speed up the creation of structural adjustment support policies, and transform the existing land subsidies into direct income subsidies for scaled production operators, Furthermore, China should expand its pilot fallow subsidy policy system in appropriate areas.

2.2.2 Improve the support strength of R&D and speed up the cultivation of new entities

Strengthening the top-level design and clarifying the strategic layout of grain industry research would be required to fully integrate the resources of scientific research institutions, build an integrated scientific research sharing platform, as to avoid conflicts, and improve the success rate of adaption of scientific research results. Improving the support to R&D will also require Increasing the support of central and local financial funds for scientific and technological research for the development of grain industry, and explore a reasonable profit distribution mechanism. Other factors to take into consideration is to give more attention to the training of scientific research personnel, encourage and support universities and scientific research institutions, the improvement of the efficiency of relevant education courses, the improvement of talent exchange mechanism, the strengthening of the scientific research exchange and cooperation between international and domestic universities and colleges, the improvement of cooperation and exchange between scientific research institutions and grain enterprises and farmers, and the improvement of the practicability of scientific research achievements.

2.2.3 Reforming the grain reserve mechanism and establishing a multi-level grain reserve system

In recent years, the main body of grain storage in China has shown a trend of diversified development, but due to the fact that the state mainly subsidizes the storage enterprises according to the amount of grain stored, the interests of storage enterprises were more focused on the amount of grain stored in warehouse, thereby giving less consideration to the overall grain circulation efficiency in the country, all those factors making the reform of grain storage mechanism imminent. As for the reform of the grain storage mechanisms, the first need is to establish a reasonable purchase quota in the direction of marketization, as to ensure national food security as the core goal. The second need is to learn from the experience of developed countries as to request relevant domestic grain enterprises to focus on grain storage only. To support such reform, the state should give a certain amount of subsidies, build a multi-level grain storage system composed of the state, professional grain storage enterprises, grain enterprises and other main bodies, construct a nation-wide information exchange platform based on big data and other information tools, and enhance the capacity of the high-speed rail and other means of transportation to improve the efficiency of grain allocation throughout the country. The third need is to further enrich the implication of grain reserves by: (i) considering the supply and demand situation, storage pressure, ecological requirements and other factors as to stabilize yield and ensure a local production capacity, so as to realize "grain storage in the land"; (ii) accelerating the progress of science and technology, improving the level of science and technology in grain production, steadily improving the level of grain yield per unit area and the efficiency of resource utilization in China as to realize "storing grain in technology"; and (iii) carry out publicity and improving the education for farmers as to enhance their own reserve capacity, reduce the amount of waste caused by improper storing operation, and realize "grain storage by farmers".

2.2.4 Enhancing the competitiveness of grain industry and strengthening the support of brand building

As a big country of grain production, consumption and trade, China does not have a high voice at the international grain market level. The fundamental reason is that the international competitiveness of China's grain industry remains low in product quality and grain efficiency. Therefore, to overcome such situation, there is, firstly a need to speed up the construction of the whole grain industry chain. This would require first adhering to local conditions, implementing policies enhancing the role of local enterprises, promoting industrial integrated value-chain operation, industrial agglomeration, industrial integration, and post-delivery service driven modes, building a smooth information transmission bridge between farmers, cooperatives, enterprises, and consumers, guiding the effective multiple links allocation of resources, strengthening the scientific and technological support to the industrial chain, and improving coordination, health, and sustainable development efficiency of the grain industry. The second requirement would be to strengthen the brand building of the grain industry. On the one hand, branding can increase the value-added of the grain industry chain; On the other hand, branding agricultural products can increase the popularity of China's grain products and improve the influence of China's grain industry at the level of the international grain market.

2.2.5 Actively utilize overseas markets and diversify import sources

In the face of the new global environment, China needs to scientifically identify import countries of important grain varieties while scientifically determining the domestic security level of important grain varieties, as to improve China's food supply security. First of all, the need is to control the pace of import, following the basic idea of supplementing gaps in the domestic market and maintaining the stability of the domestic market as to avoid unnecessary imports. the second need is to strengthen negotiation and communication with other countries to ensure an effective control of the scale of imports. In the future of multilateral trade negotiations, China should adhere to the basic principle of not reducing the tariff protection level. While giving priority to surrounding countries, China should diversify the distribution of import sources with a priority given to its scarcity in specific grain varieties while reducing the unstable factors in the trade process. All that together while gradually promoting the liberalization of the domestic market. China's market volume is so enormous, meaning that it would have a great impact on the world food market. In order to avoid excessive impact on the international and domestic markets, China should adhere to the principle of gradual liberalization, and speed up the improvement of the competitiveness of the domestic food industry while using the international market to supplement domestic food supply.

2.3 Promoting sustainable green production in an all-round way

2.3.1 Cultivated land quality conservation action

Many action plans should be considered when implementing the national farmland protection project. They include the conservation of black soil and the improvement of organic matter in Northeast China, the maintenance of soil fertility in the dry land of north China, the recovery of farmland residual film in northwest China, improving soil fertility and water conservation in the Southwest drought-prone region, and the reclamation of saline alkali land in the Huang Huai Hai area.. One of the most salient point of those action plans would be to conserve the fertility of black lands as to consolidate the northeast granary. More generally, agricultural practices such as no tillage, less tillage, straw and stubble mulching and other conservation tillage methods should be adopted to improve soil structure and fertility, enhance soil water retention, improve drought resistance and resilience to erosion, and reduce soil wind and water erosion. Under abundant rainfall, deep tillage should be promoted to break the plough bottom, reduce soil hardening and improve the storing of rainwater.

2.3.2 Restoring and conserving the fertility of farmland

Many cultivated lands in China are experiencing other problems, such as over cultivation, over exploitation of groundwater, aggravation of non-point source pollution and so on. Depending on the level of gravity of pollution and land degradation, four measures should be recommended for restoring farmland soil fertility and maintaining its fertility level overtime. They include physical measures for separating and removing soil contaminants through various physical processes; the use of chemical agents for adsorption, precipitation, and complexation to remove or reduce the toxicity of pollutants; biological measures, including phyto-remediation, microbial remediation, combined biological repair technologies, and agronomic measures referring to the adjustment of soil physical and chemical properties through deep plowing, deep sub-soiling, proper management of water, and application of functional fertilizers. Conservation tillage or no-tillage, precise fertilization, and pesticide application practices to control and eliminate the negative impact of heavy metals pollution on farmland should be part of the agronomic measures required to improve and maintain the fertility of farmland. The objective of all those agronomic measures is to lessen the risk of agricultural land pollution. Furthermore, introducing crop rotation and fallow system, in association with the adoption of multiple cropping systems to conserve land fertility should be considered as key basic measures for implementing a strategy based on sustainable farmland management. However, with crop rotation and land fallowing, there may be production shortfalls due to the multiple cropping systems, which will affect, in one way or another, grain production and farmers' income. As a result, balancing actual food security and farmers' short-term revenues with longer-term food security objectives would be required. In this respect, the government should play a critical role in formulating appropriate compensation policies (subsidies) as for helping farmers to sustain their incomes. Other key rationale for implementing crop rotation and fallow system include groundwater saving, reduction of heavy metal pollution, and the improvement of the production capacity of thin top layers' soils.

2.3.3　Moving towards green farming

Controlling fertilizer input, reducing energy consumption and non-point source pollution, replacing chemical fertilizer by organic fertilizer or using large quantities of different types organic materials on regular basis-animal manures, composts, tree leaves, cover crops, rotation crops that leave large amounts of residues, etc.routinely keeping soil covered with green manure or crop residues to reduce ineffective evapotranspiration, adopting reduced tillage, or minimum tillage, or no-tillage practices, adopting crop rotation, introducing plant associations, including adopting holistic landscape management practices enhancing crop yield stability, such as agroforestry, windbreaks, shelterbelts, river buffers, insect strips, living fences, woodlots, etc., controlling the amount of synthetic pesticides within the allowable range or using biological pesticides, and enhancing biological management of pests and weeds should be considered the basic elements governing ecological or green farming practices. Moreover, adopting dry farming, drought-resistant varieties and introducing water-saving technologies will improve the efficiency of irrigation, reduce crop water demand and, as such, stabilize the total amount of agricultural irrigation water. All those actions are basically aimed at providing the most favorable soil and microclimate crop growth conditions, particularly by managing organic matter and enhancing soil biological activity that will improve soil physical structure, soil fertility and soil water retention capacities.

2.3.4 Trial for the implementation of food safety standard system

There has been a growing trend of consumer interest for microbial food safety, notably for agricultural products that are marketed under "natural", "environmentally friendly", "organic" or "healthy" labels. In order to develop interventions that would match new consumer expectations, there is an urgent need to not only formulate credible regulatory system for food safety, including safety standards of food production and product quality standards but also a system able to enforce quality and safety supervision, inspection and testing systems covering the whole process of food production, processing, storage, transport and marketing. Ideally, such food safety standards should be developed in accordance with internationally-recognized eco-labeling and/or certification standards such as HACCP safety protocol, green agricultural products, organic agricultural products, geographical indication of agricultural products, etc.. In the process of improving and extending food safety standards in China's domestic environment, a few basic policy recommendations should be considered to enhance public health and improve consumers' confidence. They include: (i) improving local (county) government's management responsibility and ability to monitor, supervise and audit the quality and safety of agricultural products, including their origin of production and supply chains; (ii) ensuring clear and accurate labeling; (iii) improving agricultural extension capacity to boost farmers' competence for the safe production of food: (iv) enhancing the awareness, self-discipline of producers, processors and marketing operators and enforce strict liability for negligence; (v) expanding the training of officials and food safety extension workers participating in the supervision, monitoring and audit of food safety for the delivery of factual information, education of and advice to consumers; (vi) broadening the channels for the public to participate in the supervision, monitoring and audit of food supply chains; and (vii) investing in food safety research to enhance microbial, chemical and physical safety of food and detection methodologies for food borne contaminants and illnesses. It is on this basis, that a pilot food safety certification system for agricultural products should be tried out. This trial should be established at counties level under local government's management responsibilities. Its objectives would be to improve local government's ability to improve the quality and safety level of agricultural products and the enhancement of food safety awareness and self-discipline of producers and supply chains' operators through extension, monitoring and supervision operations, as to And improve consumer satisfaction with the safety of edible agricultural products.

3. Food Security in the China's Concept of Ecological Civilization Green Regulatory Reforms

3.1 *The National Sustainable Agricultural Development Plan (2015–2030)*

Under the concept of Ecological Civilization, China is now proactively considering to achieve food security through a balance of resource management, environmental protection and sustainable agricultural development. *The National Sustainable Agricultural Development Plan (2015–2030)* is providing the framework for revising/adapting agriculture development policies and institutional mechanisms to the Eco-civilization and Agenda 2030 concepts. *The National Sustainable Agriculture Development Plan (2015–2030)* underlines six key interlinked areas of intervention linked to China's food security and food safety contexts.

A primary focus is on science and technology to enhance agricultural productivity, notably in CGG areas.

A second focus is on protecting arable land and promoting the sustainable utilization of farmlands. This includes the prevention of pollution of arable farmland and the establishment of a soil classification system for agriculture areas.

The third focus is on increasing irrigation water use efficiency and ensuring the safety of agricultural water. This includes maintaining irrigation water reserve at 372 billion m^3.

The fourth focus is on curbing environmental NPS pollution and improving the agricultural environment. This focus understates that both the volume of chemical fertilizers and pesticides should, at least, remain stable and efforts should be made to increase the use of organic fertilizers (e.g. Zero-Growth in fertilizer and pesticides use by 2020).

The fifth focus is on restoring agricultural ecology and enhancing the ecological function of the rural environment. This focus also refers to restoring grasslands and aquatic ecosystems and protecting biodiversity.

The sixth and last focus is on expanding forest coverage for improving the country's timber supply and concomitantly, ecological security.

China's agricultural policy goals are further detailed in the State Council Document No. 1 of 2017 and 2018, which both prescribe the implementation of core grain growing (CGG) areas characterized by sound ecological basic conditions, high productivity and large grain transfer capacities. The objective of those CGG is to guarantee China's food security with a grain production capacity in excess of 75 percent of China's grain production.

The tool to leverage the objective of the National Sustainable Agricultural Development Plan are further expanded in the 2017 and 2018 Document No. 1, which further specify that:

In term of food security, the bottom line for the Chinese Government remains "absolute security" in the area of staple grains (i.e., rice, corn and wheat). Rice and wheat area planted should remain stable in the foreseeable future while corn area planted should continue to decrease in "non-essential" regions, that is, regions not ideally suited for corn production. Furthermore, to ensure food security, both the 2017 and 2018 Document No. 1 stressed that "functional" optimal growing regions for grain production that covers rice, wheat and corn crops will be identified. For other key commodities, mainly soybeans, cotton, rapeseed, sugar cane, and natural rubber, the country shall establish preservation regions that would be dedicated to those specific crop production, that in order to maintain basic self-sufficiency. Under this framework, at least 53 million hectares of new high-quality farmland will be created by 2020, which will be highly productive to ensure stable yields, be cultivated in an environmentally friendly manner and be able to withstand the impacts of weather anomalies due to climate change, notably floods and droughts.

In term of food safety, both the 2017 and 2018 Documents No.1 acknowledge that Chinese farmers use a much higher level of agrochemicals in crop and animal production than farmers in other developed countries. The over-application of agrochemicals has not only contaminated soils, surface and groundwater, but has also create safety issues for human health. As a result, the two documents call for the establishment of green production mode protecting soil and water resources as to raising efficiency in the use of natural resources, thereby preventing resources from over-exploitation; the improvement of agricultural product quality and safety standards and the adoption of sustainable development practices such as Good Agriculture Practices (GAP). In this respect, the government vows to enhance surveillance on chemical application and crack down on excessive use of illegal drugs. It also stressed that future focus should be on establishing a traceability system for agricultural products. Under this framework, the government objective is also to increase forests' and wetlands' coverage, notably by converting more farmlands into forests and pastures.

In term of agriculture technology, the government is continuing to place high importance on agricultural R&D and the transfer of technological innovations to advance the processing of agricultural products and e-commerce to promote agricultural products as well as on developing rural human resources through training while continuing to carry out campaigns of poverty eradication. Furthermore, resource-sharing platforms on agricultural technology would be established with independent development and innovation, notably the seed industry being a priority.

In term of structural adjustment, the emphasis is on increasing farmers' income by further strengthening rural reforms and stimulating endogenous development drivers through revising price setting mechanisms for grain and other agricultural products, improving the agricultural subsidy system and reforming fiscal input mechanism for agricultural support (including refining risk compensation mechanisms), and last but not least improving the reform of the rural collective ownership system.

In term of the economic development of rural areas, the emphasis is on channeling more funds to poor farmers to start business in their hometowns and/or to find off-farm jobs in nearby regions, the integrative development of primary, secondary and tertiary industries in rural regions, the construction of irrigation programs, the provision of safe drinking water, electricity and a better rural road infrastructure to improve industrial convergence in rural areas, as well as to the development of wholesale produce markets.

In conclusion, while food security remains a top priority, the focus of China's agricultural policies will now gradually be shifting from quantity to quality, which is also at the core of the so-called supply-side structural reform programs. In other words, the government encourages farmers to improve product quality or to produce commodities that meet the increased demand from local consumers for better, safer and more varied agricultural products. For example, the government encourages farmers to expand areas of feed crops, such as silage corn and alfalfa in order to increase grass-fed cattle and sheep production. For the future, increasing the production of food-grade soybeans, tuber crops and coarse grains are also encouraged.

3.2   The National Climate Change Program (2014–2020)

Food production systems are particularly vulnerable to adverse impacts of climate change and it is one of the key factors that may be affecting food security in China. Indeed, climate change in China may have mixed results on grain production. While it may lower yields, it may also generate abundant heat resources, providing alternative agricultural opportunities. However, rising temperatures may also reduce the growth period of grains, leading to average reductions in yields, while frequent seasonal drought may place stress on the water supplies available for irrigation. In China, in effect, some experts estimate that climate change-driven seasonal drought may lead to substantial losses by 2030 in yields of three the main crops despite adoption of water-saving techniques. Out of the three grains, corn yields are likely to suffer the most, with projected drop of nearly one-fifth of total production, followed by wheat, with a 4 percent decline, and rice, 1.5 percent. Safeguarding food security, particularly food production systems, from the adverse impacts of climate change is now considered a fundamental priority of the *2015 Paris climate agreement.*

In response to climate change impacts on food security, *the National Climate Change Program (2014–2020)* is a comprehensive government strategy that covers mitigation, adaptation, scientific research and public awareness measures for overcoming the impacts of climate change on China's sustainable development. In a nutshell, the 2020 plan's physical targets include: (i) stabilizing GHGs emissions; (ii) cutting carbon emissions per unit of GDP by 45 percent from 2005 levels; (iii) increasing the percentage of non-fossil fuels in primary energy consumption by 15 percent; (iv) adopting climate-resilient cropping practices; and (v) increasing the proportion of forest areas by 40 million ha from the 2005 baseline.

National Climate Change Program (2014–2020) intervention axles in support to food security

i. Celeration and promotion of the transformation and modernization of agricultural production patterns, including preventing measures to minimize the impacts of weather-related disasters.

ii. Enhancing overall climate resilience through the promotion of conservation tillage (including inserting crop resides to stimulate their microbial decomposition and increase organic matter), water-saving irrigation, dry farming, soil moisture increase, soil testing technologies and formulated fertilization (in conjunction with the Zero-Growth in fertilizer and pesticides use by 2020).

iii. Adjusting cropping patterns, strengthen agricultural infrastructure, deferring sowing time to avoid high-temperatures or drought, promote water-saving techniques to increase the efficiency of water, and adopt mulching technology to prevent frost in late spring.

iv. Accelerating the construction of farmland irrigation and water conservancy, including the rehabilitation or construction of water canals, drainage stations and wells, the treatment of water loss and soil erosion.

v. Enhancing sustainable forest management and afforestation, and promote tree planting, including shelterbelts and windbreaks, to protect farmland and increase carbon sinks.

vi. Strengthening monitoring and early warning systems for extreme weather and climate events and accelerating work on flood control and drought relief to respond to climate change weather-related anomalies.

vii. Reinforcing researches on climate change mitigation and adaptation.

viii. Strengthening related education and training.

3.3 The China Biodiversity Conservation Strategy and Action Plan (2011–2030)

Looking back at a history of more than 7000 years of agricultural production, Chinese agriculture had succeeded in supporting China's ever-increasing human population without changing the stability of the traditional biodiversity-friendly agro-landscape, which incorporated various elaborate techniques such as the use of organic manure, traditional integrative farming approaches, such as rice-fishery systems, crop rotations and tree-crop intercropping as well as the preservation of traditional agricultural landscapes including diverse natural and semi-natural elements. These systems were developed to maintain agricultural landscapes with healthy soil quality, a complex structure and diverse habitat composition, which favored the sustenance of diverse species and a stable ecosystem functioning.

However, due to the lack of past efficient policy support, the habitat loss caused by increasingly severe land degradation has been significant: 90 percent of China's natural grasslands and 40 percent of its wetlands have recorded significant degrees of deterioration, and the area of primary forest has, over many years, decreased annually by about 50000 km^2. Furthermore, agricultural intensification through increasing use of agrochemicals and cropland expansion has caused severe problems of soil erosion and pollution and subsequent degradation, water contamination and air pollution associated with a rapid loss of semi-natural habitats and the subsequent loss of natural enemies of agricultural pests. These changes have had remarkable negative impacts on both biodiversity and China's socioeconomic development[①].

In response to those deterioration, the *China Biodiversity Conservation Strategy and Action Plan (2011-2030)* addresses three main food security issues: (i) further improving policies, regulation and systems to conserve biodiversity; (ii) mainstreaming biodiversity conservation into development planning processes; (iii) strengthening capacities building to conserve biodiversity; (iv) improving in-situ and ex-situ biodiversity conservation; (v) promoting sustainable development and use of biological resources; (vi) improving benefit-sharing of biological and genetic resources associated to traditional knowledge; (vii) improving the capacity to respond to new threats and challenges to biodiversity; (viii) raising awareness of public participation and strengthening international cooperation and exchange in biodiversity conservation. However, in spite of the fact that intensification of agriculture has been (and still is beyond dispute), a major driver of biodiversity loss and agriculture ecosystem degradation, a series of initiatives have been initiated to conserve biodiversity while protecting ecosystems, restoring damaged agriculture ecosystems and improve the rural environment as part of China's ecological civilization vision.[②]

China Biodiversity Conservation Strategy and Action Plan (2011–2030) **intervention axles in support to food security**

---

i. The strict protection of the ecological functions of ecologically sensitive or fragile areas to safeguard ecosystem functions in support of socioeconomic development, notably food security (ecological redlines areas).

ii. The implementation of ecological restoration projects[①].

iii. The improvement of the rural environment program through the development of demonstration projects aimed at strengthening environmental protection to improve the ecological conditions of rural areas and the building of "beautiful villages". Such demonstration projects include, *inter-alia*, the adjustment of the agriculture cropping structure, the development of a circular economy in the agriculture sector, managing agricultural related NPS pollution, and improving the quality and safety of agricultural products.

iv. The induction of ecological provinces, ecological counties ecological cities and ecological villager.

---

① The MEP (2009) estimates that the economic losses caused by environmental damage range between 4.5 and 18 percent of GDP.

② the Natural Forest Protection Project, the Returning Grazing Land to Forest (Grain for Green) and the Returning Grazing Land to Grass Lands.

3.4 China's 16 Priority Environmental Sustainability Programs [①]

In parallel to the above policy reforms, to response to the emerging environmental challenges, China dramatically enlarged investments in 16 major sustainability programs initiated from the late 1970s and the early 2000s. Their major foci were to reduce erosion, sedimentation and flooding in the Yangtze and Yellow Rivers, conserve forests in the northeast, mitigate desertification and dust storms in the dry north, and increase agricultural productivity in central and eastern China. Environmental objectives of those programs were typically complemented by strong socioeconomic objectives, such as poverty reduction, rural economic development and national food security. Investments in those environmental sustainability programs from 1978-2015 totaled US$ 378.5 billion (in 2015 US$). The box below is summarizing their respective aims.

China's 16 Priority Environmental Programs

P1. Shelterbelt Development Program. Three North (1978–2050). Control the expansion of sandy/desertified land in northern China through forest plantation, mountain closure, and sandy areas regeneration

P2. Soil and Water Conservation Program (1983–2017). Control soil erosion, improve farmers' livelihoods and agricultural production through ecological regeneration, plantation and cultivation measures

P3. Shelterbelt Development Program – Five Regions (1987–2020). Arrest environmental degradation in the Yangtze and Pearl rivers, the Plain and Taihang mountains through artificial plantation, mountain closure, aerial seeding and establishing shelterbelts

P4. Comprehensive agricultural Development Program (1988–2020). Raise rural quality of life, income and food security through land reform and management ecological construction, agricultural infrastructure using sciences and technology

P5. Soil and Water Conservation Program, Yangtze (1989–). Reduce sedimentation and improve the health of the Yangtze rive , ensure the safe operation of the Three Gorges Dam by controlling soil erosion in the upper reaches

P6. National Land Consolidation Program (1997–2020). Increase the area of cultivated land and revenues through consolidation, reclamation construction of high-quality cropland and improving land use and management

P7. Natural Forest Conservation Program (1998–2020). Halt logging, deforestation and protect natural forests for ecological/carbon benefits through mountain closure, aerial seeding and artificial planting. Create new business opportunities for traditional forest enterprises

P8. Grain for Green Program (1999–2020). Prevent soil erosion, mitigate flooding, store carbon, and improve livelihoods through increasing forest and grassland cover on cropped hill slopes and converting croplands, barren hills and waste lands to forests

P9. Fast-growing, High-yielding Timber Program (2001–2015). Remedy to the decline of timber supply without affecting natural forests through the establishment of fast-growing, high-yielding timber plantations

P10. Forest Ecosystem Compensation Fund (2001–2016). Conserve natural forests, protect species and ecosystems through restoration and management of forests that have important ecological, biodiversity, sustainable economic and social values

---

① Brett A. Brian et al., "China's response to a national land-system sustainability emergency", *Springer Nature*, 2018(559).

continued table

China's 16 Priority Environmental Programs	
P11. Sandification Control Program: Beijing/Tianjin (2001–2022). Reduce desertification and dust storms and improve the environment of Beijing/Tianjin areas through reforestation, grassland management and water conservation	P14. Rocky Desertification Treatment Program (2008–2020). Curb rocky/karsts desertification, improve the environment and increase incomes through protecting and establishing vegetation, promoting sustainable land use, farmland construction and water conservation
P12. Wildlife Conservation and Nature Protection Program (2001–2050). Conserve key animal and plant species and natural ecosystems by expanding the number of nature reserve and promoting sustainable development	P15. Grassland Ecological Protection Program (2011–2020). Mitigate grassland degradation by grazing ban and enhancing grassland vegetation cover/biomass, including increasing herders' incomes through promoting sustainable development of pastoral areas
P13. Partnership to Combat Land Degradation (2002–2023). Improve management of land and water resources, reduce poverty, protect biodiversity and combat climate change in western China by bringing agencies to work together in partnership	P16. Cultivated Land Quality Program (2015–2020). Enhance food security and the quality, safety and ecological sustainability of agricultural production through addressing soil acidification, salinization, nutrient imbalances, pollution, fertility and shallow topsoil

Worth to note is the fact that, in spite of urgent requirements, only a few of the above programs, addressed to improve environmental sustainability, are dealing with food security, in particular food production issues. There is, therefore, an urgent need to address ecological security in CGG areas and address food production issues in those critical areas.

IV Technical Measures to Improve Ecological Security in CGG Areas

1. The Issues of Agricultural Production Over-reliance on Chemical Fertilizers

In 2011, China's grain harvests passed the 550 million tons mark, achieving the five years of successive growth in half a century. Harvests have been at more than 1 billion tons for five years in a row and are already at the level originally planned to be reached in 2020.

Alongside overuse of agrochemicals, there is misuse, which also lowers uptakes rates. Only 30 percent of the fertilizer China applied actually does any good, much lower than the 40 percent rates in Western nations. A survey by agricultural authorities in Henan found that only one-third of the three million tons of fertilizer used in the province was actually absorbed by crops. Experts say misuse of fertilizers and pesticides has now reached a tipping point.

Economic factors push farmers towards using more chemical pesticides. Although biological pesticides have a lesser effect on the human body, they are not as effective and are more expensive and, as a result, farmers don't want the extra expense, so there is no market for the biological alternative.

2. Safe Fertilization Application Standards

Above all, there is a need to clearly understand the average fertilizer application amount for grain production in China. As of today, researches have concluded that, if the actual application of chemical fertilizers for grain production exceeds by 30-40 percent the safety level of 225 kg/ha, such over-fertilization in reality does not have an effect of production increase and consequently on food security level. Such views are obviously biased. As a matter of fact, farmers need to pay for the surplus amount of chemical fertilizers they use, even if it has no impact to grain yield. Overusing fertilizers years after years would obviously put them into an impossible situation. Therefore, in order to achieve a safe level of application of chemical fertilizers in China's grain production, a series of precise chemical fertilization and organic fertilizer replacement technologies that would increase the efficiency rate of chemical fertilizers must be adopted, against simply reducing the application amount.

2.1 Promotion of slow-release fertilizers (SRFs) and controlled release fertilizers (CRFs)

Experimental studies have shown that the use of slow-release fertilizers (SRFs) and controlled release fertilizers (CRFs) can increase fertilization efficiency by 10-30 percent, while increasing the average nitrogen fertilizer utilization efficiency by 22.8 percent. Therefore, promoting SRFs and CRFs would be an important guarantee for improving the utilization efficiency of chemical fertilizers. Promoting SRFs and CRFs would, therefore, be an effective way to ensure agricultural productivity, consequently, national food security.

Table 12   Comparison of the yield and nitrogen use efficiency between equivalent amount of SRFs and ordinary quick-release fertilizers

Unit: %

Location	Crops	Yield increase	Increased use of nitrogen
Qing'an, Heilongjiang	Rice	10.5	17.0
Xiaoshan, Zhejiang	Rice	16.0	16.2
Zhumadian, Henan	Corn	16.2	25.3
Gongzhuling, Jilin	Corn	11.2	18.6

continued table

Location	Crops	Yield increase	Increased use of nitrogen
Hulan, Heilongjiang	Corn	11.9	17.6
Zhumadian, Henan	Wheat	12.0	26.2
Suiping, Henan	Wheat	13.9	28.5
Huanggang, Hubei	Cotton	26.2	36.6
Zhijiang, Hubei	Rape	14.9	16.5
Xianju, Zhejiang	Citrus	37.6	25.5
Average		17.0	22.8

SRFs and CRFs have a series of advantages, such as, increasing fertilizer utilization efficiency, eliminating chemical fertilizer pollution, and reducing farmers' labor input for fertilization. The reasons behind promoting SRFs and SRFs are as follows:

i. The solubility of SRFs in water is small. The slow release of nutrients in the soil reduces nutrients' losses;

ii. Fertilization can be done in one go. The slow release of nutrients from SRFs will not cause damages to crops such as "burning of seedlings" due to high soil salinity caused by excessive release of nutrients. Moreover, cost savings can be achieved due to less fertilization application;

iii. The amount of fertilizer can be reduced. This would also reduce additional inputs' needs, such as coal, electricity, and natural gas needed for fertilizer production. The reduction in inputs will also reduce environmental pollution.

China has developed a long-acting coated ammonium bicarbonate in the late 1960s. Subsequently substantial progresses have been made in the development and application of SRFs during the past 10 years. Nowadays, CRFs have also reached similar qualities as foreign products. In 2015, CRFs production was 3.3 million tons, of which, 90 percent were used for grain crops, 5 percent for flowers and lawns, accounting for 5 percent of compound fertilizers applied in China, while the remaining 5 percent were exported. After ten years of development, CRFs leading companies in China led the development of international standards for SRFs and CRFs, thus improving the international influence of Chinese CRFs.

At the same time, there is a need to realize that in China, issues such as CRFs and SRFs high production costs and weak international competitiveness still do exist.

To this end, it is necessary to revamp production technologies, system reformation and agricultural extension mechanism, improve international competitiveness, and increase farmers' awareness of slow-release fertilizer products.

2.2   Improving soil testing formula fertilization

In China, agricultural soils, in general, include 40–80 percent of nutrients needed for crop production, but this stock is not an inexhaustible "nutrient pool". In order to ensure that the soil has sufficient nutrient supply capacity and strength and keep the availability of soil nutrients constant, the balance should be achieved through fertilization. The so-called "soil testing and formula fertilization", derived from soil testing and on-field trials based on the nutrient requirements of crops and soil nutrient supply performance, has been developed to supplement nutrient elements needed by crops, achieve a balanced supply of various nutrients, meeting crop nutrients, eventually improve fertilizer utilization efficiency, and reduce the fertilizers' application amount and cost savings.

In response to the problem of over-fertilization, the 2005 Central Document No. 1 clearly stated that it would be necessary to implement scientific fertilization, promote soil testing and formula fertilization, and increase soil organic content. Accordingly, the Ministry of Agriculture, with the support of the Ministry of Finance, launched a soil testing and fertilizer application subsidy program in 2005. By 2015, a total of CNY 7.8 billion has been invested to promote scientific fertilization. The various elements considered in the Chinese scientific fertilization concept include:

i. Carrying out soil testing. In the past 10 years, a total of 17.98 million soil samples have been collected and a corresponding 124 million analyzes performed. This to determine soil nutrient status over 1.4 billion mu [1] of cultivated land in 1857 project counties (fields);

ii. Conducting fertilizer testing. It was up to each project county to organize each year field fertilizer efficiency tests and calibration tests on one to two major crops. As a result, the cumulative number of tests reached more than 330000, through which it has been possible to basically ascertain the requirements of fertilizer demand for rice, wheat,

---

[1]   Equivalent to approximately 93.3 million ha.

corn, potatoes and other major crops;

iii. Promoting soil testing and formula fertilization. In the past 10 years, in order to guide farmers in rational fertilization, regional fertilization formulas for fertilizers have been formulated in various places. A total of 920 million copies of fertilizer recommendation cards have been distributed, 494000 trainings performed and 136000 on-site observations organized.

In China, the socioeconomic conditions applied to the soil testing formula fertilization and its related impacts could be summarized as follows:

i. Crop yields and farmers' income have both increased in parallel. According to farmer households' surveys, with the application of soil testing and formula fertilization technology, the yield per mu [①] of wheat, rice, and corn increased by 3.7, 3.8, and 5.9 percent respectively, while the income increased by more than CNY 30; at the same time, the average income from vegetable production increased to more than CNY 100;

ii. Production costs and resource consumption achieved "double savings". The use of soil testing and formula fertilization can save up to 19.83–34.65 kg/ha of nitrogen fertilizer and reduce nitrogen and phosphorus loss by 8 to 30 percent;

iii. The structure of fertilizer application and the industrial structure of fertilizers achieved "double excellency". First, the soil testing formula fertilization is optimizing the structure of fertilization, second, it has initially preset the demand for nitrogen, phosphorus and potash fertilizers that guided fertilizer companies to produce formula fertilizers, thereby adjusting the structure of the fertilizer industry; and

iv. The level of fertilizer and fertilizer utilization efficiency achieved "double increasing". According to surveys, about 70 percent of farmers, after demonstration, adopted the soil testing and formula fertilization techniques. As a result, fertilizer utilization efficiency in China increased by 5 percent.

2.3 Fertigation technology

Fertigation technology is an agricultural technology that integrates irrigation and fertilization. By using pressurized pipe irrigation system, solid fertilizers or liquid fertilizers are mixed with irrigation water, and evenly and accurately transported to the

---

① One mu is equivalent to 0.067 ha.

crops' root system. Such technology can provide water, nutrients and trace elements required by crops quantitatively and regularly during the whole growing period, while providing them directly to the crops. The root system absorbs the nutrients from the fertilizer while absorbing water. Undoubtedly, this technology can save water, increase fertilization efficiency and save labor.

Fertigation technologies are, so far, mostly used for the production of vegetables and fruits. They include fixed water spray fertilization mode and mobile spray fertilization mode. The fixed fertilization mode is suitable for irrigating lands with water field delivery pipelines, which have a small spraying radius. The mobile fertilization mode is suitable for larger fields and has larger spray radius. Nowadays, the cumulative application area using fertigation technology is reaching 25 million mu (1.75 million ha), including 7 million mu of corn, 2 million mu of wheat and 1 million mu of potato. Available monitoring data show that this technology can reduce nitrogen, phosphorus and potassium fertilizer application by 20, 10 and 20 percent respectively.

2.4 Improvement of organic fertilization

It is estimated that adding 4.5–7.5 tons/ha of organic fertilizer into cultivated land can reduce the application amount of chemical fertilizer by 15–20 percent.

Due to the rapid increase in the price of agricultural labor, the application of organic fertilizers must be as convenient as chemical fertilizers as for farmers to use them. Their benefit for grain production is relatively low, and the quality difference of the grain that uses organic fertilizer or not is difficult to be recognized by consumers. Therefore, the conditions for applying packed commercialized organic fertilizer are not yet met. Conversely, the vegetable and fruit production, which results in comparatively higher income, do meet basically the conditions for applying packed commercialized organic fertilizer. Worth to note is the fact that consumers can easily identify the difference in the quality of vegetables and fruits when using organic fertilizers. Moreover, the monitoring system for vegetables and fruits is more comprehensive than for cereals. It is, therefore, possible to reduce the over-application of chemical fertilizers in vegetable production. In China, vegetables and fruits production area reached 35 million ha, which are using a considerable amount of chemical fertilizers. As a result, the demand for organic fertilizers in this sub-sector is increasing rapidly.

To sum up in a nutshell, by combining these three technologies, i.e., SRFs and CRFs, soil testing and formula fertilization, and fertigation, the chemical fertilizers application for cereal production can be reduced by more than 35 percent, thereby, eliminating over-fertilization issues; in addition, for vegetable production, organic fertilization can also be used to replace chemical fertilizers. As a result, promoting the application of organic fertilizers in cereal production should be given high priority.

2.5 Establishing an industrial chain for the production of organic fertilizers

Large-scale livestock and poultry production has become one of the major sources of agricultural non-point source (NPS) pollution in China due to the increasing scale of livestock and poultry farming. Facing this situation, the Environmental Protection Department has required that, in each large-scale livestock and poultry farm, manure treatment facilities should be built. However, due to the financial costs for waste treatment, which is more than the income from livestock production, most of the waste treatment facilities could not be operated profitably. Therefore, it should be more appropriate to set up eco-industrial parks in livestock and poultry breeding counties, including the joint establishment of an eco-industrial chain for agricultural production, large-scale livestock and poultry farming, organic fertilizer production, slaughtering and processing, and feed based on slaughtering and processing residues.

Large-scale livestock and poultry breeding companies could obviously gathering together to supply sufficient raw materials for the organic fertilizer plant: under such situation, all manure from the livestock farms could be used by the organic fertilizer plant. This would solve waste problems that individual livestock company cannot manage. Biogas generated during the treatment process can be used as energy for the farm, and the organic fertilizer produced could be used by the surrounding farmland. Furthermore, slaughtering and meat processing plants could be built in several large agriculture counties adjacent to each other. Besides the production of main products, feed can be processed based on the residue from slaughtering and meat processing. In overall, worth to note is that this approach could help achieving zero C-emissions from livestock.

Keys to the establishment of such eco-industrial park is to formulate eco-industrial park planning, including a stakeholder coordination mechanism to ensure cooperation between large-scale livestock and poultry farms, organic fertilizer plants, slaughtering houses, processing plants, feed mills, and farmers' organizations and achieve a win-win solution in the end.

Based on the technical requirements of a demonstration project for the comprehensive utilization of livestock and poultry manure in Sichuan Province, establishing an organic fertilizer raw material plant or processing plant would require a production capacity of 110000 to 220000 pig equivalents in the breeding area respectively (assuming that an individual pig could produce 0.1 tons of manure per year and can produce 0.075 tons of organic fertilizer). This is very close to the scale of the livestock-and poultry-breeding park that has been established in Xiaoshan, Zhejiang Province. A slaughtering house and feed mill may require 3–5 livestock parks to support organic fertilizers' production.

2.6 Effects of fertilization on the quality of agricultural products [1]

Effects of organic fertilizers. Research conducted by the Ministry of Agriculture's research group on more than 20 species of plants showed that application of organic fertilizers can improve the quality of agricultural products, such as an increase of 2–3.5 percent of protein in wheat and corn, an increase of 1.4–3.6 percent in gluten, an increase of 0.3–0.48 percent in the eight essential amino acids; an increase of 0.56 percent of fat in soybean, and an increase of 0.31–0.92 percent respectively in linoleic acid and oleic acid. Conversely, the nitrate content decreased by 33–35.5 percent for leafy vegetables.

Effects of nitrogen fertilization. Studies have shown that, straight application of nitrogen fertilizer to sweet melon reduces fruit sweetness and increases nitrate content. Over-fertilization of nitrogen fertilizer will also affect the color of the fruit, delay ripening and make the ripening period uneven.

Effects of phosphate fertilization. Studies have shown that, when mustard-type rape is extremely deficient in phosphorus, its oil content is reduced from 33 percent to 23 percent.

Effects of potash fertilization. Application of potassium fertilizer will not only increase the wheat weight but also improve the flour baking properties.

---

[1] Song Wei, Xu Qi, "Rational Fertilization and Quality Safety of Agricultural Products", *Henan Agriculture*, 2011(9).

Effects of trace element fertilization. Application of manganese fertilizer can increase the vitamin content of agricultural products. The amount of manganese and molybdenum in food and feed is an additional important quality standard for agricultural products.

3. Measures to Eliminate Pesticides' Over-application

Reducing the excessive application of pesticides will help to improve the quality and safety of agricultural products, protect the agricultural ecological environment, and increase farmers' income. China began to implement the policy for reducing pesticides application in the late 1990s. In 1997, *the Regulation on Pesticide Administration* and *the Measures for the Implementation of the Regulation on Pesticides Administration* were issued. According to the lessons learnt from international experiences, regulating pesticide market management and pesticide application standards are the most critical measures aimed at reducing the amount of pesticide applications. The following six measures are recommended to lessen or reinforce the efficiency of pesticides application.

3.1 Improving pesticide application techniques

The Hubbell's research shows that, as a prerequisite to materialize the effects of prevention and control, the use of advanced spraying equipment, such as electrostatic spray and circulating spray, can reduce the application amount of pesticides by 50–95 percent.

3.2 Increasing the price of pesticides

The price of pesticides is negatively related to the application amount. Existing subsidies for both, the production and the application of pesticides should be adjusted as to eliminate price distortions in the prices of pesticides and reduce the use of pesticides.

3.3 Developing environmental-friendly pesticides

Lessening the quantity or increasing the efficiency of pesticides application-would require developing green and environmental-friendly pesticides, carrying out piloting projects for low-toxicity bio-pesticides, and subsidizing farmers for using such bio-pesticides, as well as encouraging and promoting the application of low-toxicity bio-pesticides. Moreover, applying biotechnology to control pests and diseases is certainly an additional method able to reduce the use of chemical pesticides.

3.4 Strengthening publicity and training

Recent studies in China have demonstrated that many farmers are insensitive to pesticide over-use. Moreover, pesticides can be dangerous for those who use them, their families, trade and the environment, if incorrectly applied or managed. There is, therefore, an obvious need to both increase their awareness of farmers of the dangers associated with the use of pesticides and receive adequate and up-to-date training and refreshing courses in both using pesticides safely and be skilled in pesticides application works. In many developed countries, the use of pesticides required a "certificate of competence (UK)" or an "accreditation (EPA-USA)" for pesticides use in agriculture, horticulture, and forestry.

Training themes should generally include: the relevant legislation; risks, associated with the use of pesticides (notably on the environment); safe working practices (pollinators' protection); application parameters, safety training; emergency actions in case of pesticides spillage, contaminated person, fire or other incidents; pesticide disposal and storage rules; using equipment for applying pesticides; etc.. In China, such type of training is already dispensed under the Green Farmer Training Program implemented in partnership with Walmart-China, however at a limited scale.

3.5 Expanding the scope of food production insurance

Insurance subsidies for major grain crops financed by the central and provincial governments and the insurance coverage and risks protection level should be revisited to replace "subsidies with rewards" and provide subsidies for premiums.

3.6 Expanding the scale of farmer operations

Currently, more and more rural households are reluctant to engage in small-scale agricultural production. This may, however, be an opportunity, not only to promote rural land use transfer to gradually expand the production scale of farmer households, but also to increase pesticide application accuracy, hence reducing the application amount of pesticides.

4. Measures to Overcome the Over-use of Groundwater

4.1 Overview

Due to secular huge deposits, the groundwater reserve capacity is much larger than that of surface water. Evidently, such deposit should not arbitrarily be wasted, as it would be critical for the role it could play in response to climate change risks. Specifically, there would be dry years with decreasing availability of water, flat years with constant availability of water, and replenishment years with abundant water. All together those years should be critical for maintaining a deposit's dynamic balance. In fact, the decrease in groundwater levels is a new problem that has emerged in recent decades. For example, in the North China Plain, where groundwater extraction is currently a most serious issue, farmers traditionally used surface water to irrigate. Aside of the management problems mentioned above, because of the high groundwater level, which was associated with waterlogging and salinization as well as because of increasing damages to surface water irrigation systems associated with increasing water needs, farmers began to extract groundwater. In actual fact, the decrease in groundwater levels will bring the following two problems: First, the cost of pumping will be steadily increasing while the amount of available groundwater will be decreasing; Second, groundwater extraction is leading to a series of serious consequences, including the evaporation of wetlands, river depletion, land subsidence and seawater intrusion. In particular, land subsidence can cause damage to, for instance, the rupture of water pipelines. Land subsistence may also cause damage to infrastructure, or even trains to derail. Moreover, over-exploitation of groundwater may result in seawater intrusion, rendering water unusable for irrigation or for drinking. What is even more serious is that, once all groundwater pumped out, it would be intricate to maintain agriculture.

In order to ensure the sustainable use of groundwater resources, it would, thus, be necessary to adopt a series of measures such as scientific regulation of agricultural water use, optimization and adjustment of planting structures, extensive application of water-saving technologies, notably the establishment and improvement of water-saving systems.

4.2   Scientific regulation of agriculture water use

Overcoming the overuse of groundwater resources requires a series of five measures: (i) expanding the area of low-water-consumption food crops according to local precipitation; (ii) improving irrigation methods to increase water use efficiency; (iii) strengthening regional water conservancy infrastructure and making full use of surface water in regions concerned; (iv) transferring water across regions to increase the supply of water resources; and (v) strictly implementing groundwater use system by controlling the amount of groundwater withdrawal within the scope of its sustainable use.

Improving irrigation methods. In China's CGG areas, extensive irrigation methods still occupy the larger percentage. Improving irrigation methods will, therefore, take a long time, since, for the time being, evaporation remains high and irrigation efficiency low, even, in some places, leading to alkalinization of arable land. Therefore, it becomes urgent to promote water-saving irrigation and reduced transpiration technologies. In addition, promoting biological water-saving technologies would be of great practical significance for resolving issues related to the over-exploitation of groundwater.

Water-saving irrigation technology. Relevant studies have shown that the conversion of flooded irrigation to low-pressure pipelines irrigation would save up to 30 percent in water loss by using sprinkler irrigation to increase the uniformity of irrigation and enable deeper seepage on uneven farmland as to reduce water leakage by 30–50 percent.

Reduce transpiration technology. In many parts of northern China, the amount of water evaporation is greater than 1100 mm. If film mulch is used on farmland during spring and summer time, the reduced amount of ineffective evaporation can reach 28–46 percent of the total crop water consumption. Farmland cover-crop technology includes plastic mulching and straw mulching, i.e. leaving crop residues on the ground. Their essence is to set up a layer of micro-breathable mulch on the surface of farmland, which would inhibit the evaporation of water into the atmosphere, thereby strengthening the water cycle in the soil-crop system and reducing the amount of ineffective evaporation. The dew condensation on the mulch can block the passage of long heat waves, preserve the latent heat taken away by evaporation of water, and transport it under the mulch layer to increase the temperature of the ground and facilitate crop growth. With this type of technology, it can save up to 25–42 percent of groundwater water used compared to conventional irrigation.

Soil fertility technology. The specific measures include: increasing organic fertilizers, planting green manure returning straw to the field to improve soil physical structure, soil water storage, and water supply capacity. Those measures should go together with a rational use of chemical fertilizers to increase fertility levels. Increasing the utilization rate of soil water by balanced fertilization could increase soil water saving rate by up to 28–49 percent.

Biological water-saving technology. The so-called biological water-saving technology refers to the use of the plant's own physiological and genetic potential[1]. It requires high drought-tolerant super-species able to increase the efficiency of plant water use, so as to obtain more food production under the same water supply conditions. Biological water saving requires three developments: genetic improvement[2], population or group adaptation[3] and physiological regulation[4]. Studies have shown that through the biological water saving technology, optimal regulation of photosynthetic rate and transpiration rate, can improve crop drought resistance and save water up to more than 30 percent.

---

[1] A large number of research results at home and abroad and evidence from field experiment evidence show that many crops support moderate drought at a certain stage of development. If water shortage does not exceed their adaptation capacity, their yield would not be affected.

[2] *Genetic improvement* is the breeding of drought-resistant and water-saving varieties, which is the basic path for biological water saving.

[3] *Group adaptation* is to optimize the allocation of water resources according to the water demand characteristics of soils and water consumption characteristic of crops, so as to achieve the goal of saving water without reducing production.

[4] *Physiological regulation* is based on the principle that a moderate water deficit can produce a compensatory effect, in case of inadequate irrigation.

4.3   Adjusting the structure of food crops

The CGG areas in China are rich in arable land resources and have relatively good rain water resources. Even in the CGG provinces in northern China, rainfall is enough to produce the expected seasonal grain production. For example, in Henan and Hebei provinces, the cultivation of corn does not virtually require irrigation. In such provinces, however, growing winter wheat with low rainfall requires groundwater irrigation. In order to alleviate the severe trend of over exploitation of groundwater, a "one season fallow, one season rain fed" mode should be implemented as to modify the "two harvests a year of wheat and corn to one harvest" or to replace the high water consumption wheat by another lower water consumption crop such as potato to maintain the level of grain production and reduce the demand for groundwater. This, not only to achieve the goal of "reserving the grain in the ground" and gradually increase land fertility, but also to solve the series of problems such as excessive use of fertilizers and pesticides, land subsistence and sea water intrusion.

4.4   Strengthening the scale of management and cooperation

The smaller the scale of agricultural operations and the smaller its impact on agriculture income is, the lower is the degree of farmers' households' attention to agriculture. Therefore, achieving a certain scale of agricultural operations is a necessary condition for improving irrigation efficiency. Surveys have shown that the efficiency of water use in large farms is significantly higher than that in small farms. In China, agriculture is currently transitioning to a modest scale of operations, but issues such as short-term leases associated with high rents need to be resolved. The gradual decline of some surface water irrigation systems in China's rural areas after implementation of the household contract responsibility system indicates that the effective operation of surface water irrigation systems needs to be supported by the cooperation of farmers and households across farming communities. In recent years, China's agriculture has resumed cooperation with management, but it also faces a series of problems that need to be resolved.

4.5 Establishing a water right trading market

Some scholars believe that the main reason for excessive groundwater pumping is that water fees are too low or missing. Of course, water fees could be increased to resolve the problem of excessive groundwater pumping. However, this should not be considered the most appropriate method to solve the issue of groundwater over-extraction as it would artificially worsens food production conditions, aside of the fact that it would further constrain farmers' support already spending money to extract groundwater. It can be seen from Figure 6 below that, in 2005, the average irrigation cost per mu of arable land in Hebei was already CNY 55, which was more than twice the national average.

A more appropriate approach would be to develop water-trading rights on the basis of clearly defined farmers' water rights, so that farmers would have a series of choices. Specifically, water rights could either be earned through the selling of grain or from income that can be obtained through the alienation of such rights. How much water-trading rights owned by farmers would be used for irrigated grain production and how much would be used for trading would depend upon the comparison between grain prices and water rights' prices. The responsibility of the government (and non-governmental organizations) would be to purchase water rights corresponding to the overuse of groundwater according to the market price of water rights. The industrial sector, which is operating with higher water use efficiency, and thus be able to pay for higher bids, already obtains water rights in such a way. Such market mechanism should be used to determine the price of water use rights. Therefore, using market mechanisms would be a better solution than the practice of the government using its administrative authority to increase the price of water resources. Not causing any harm to farmers, such mechanism will certainly be popular among them. In other words, if the government claims that farmers should pay for the full use of waterand anticipates that it would be the best strategy for resolving the issue of over-extraction of ground water-such a solution may be appearing the simplest solution, but not the most practical one.

Most importantly, the fact the matter is that China has already basically developed the conditions for water rights trading. Since recent years, China's groundwater management is adopting a measurement model of *"one well, one meter, one household, one card"*, through the installation by the government in each well of a smart water meter. As a consequence, each farmer has already to purchase water according to its own water rights. To get a pre-defined amount of water, farmers should insert an IC card into the smart water meter to start pumping. Accordingly, the amount pumped is deducted from the card up to a ceiling that cannot be exceeded. At present, 420000 wells in Shandong and 380,000 wells in Henan provinces are operating under such conditions.

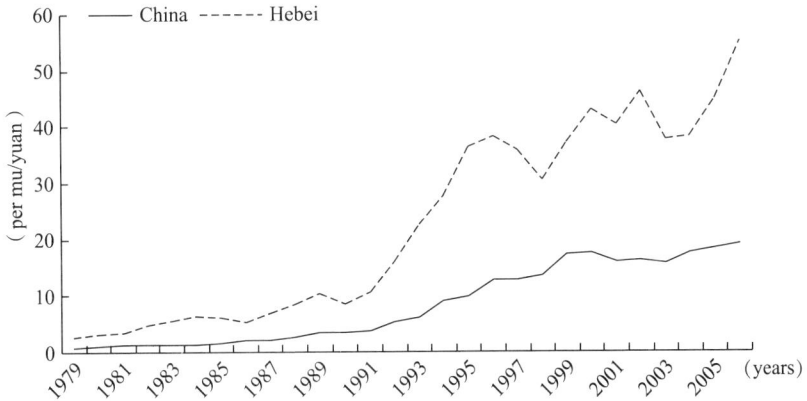

Fig 6   Changes in average irrigation cost per mu of wheat in Hebei province and China

Moreover, as to assess the amount of electricity needed for groundwater extraction, pumping tests have been established to assess how much groundwater can be pumped out at a time, Based on such assessment, water and electricity conversion coefficients for different groundwater levels have then been assessed. Then, the electricity amount required for pumping (corresponding to the amount of farmer's water rights) is sold to farmers. In such a way, electricity consumption is controlled as well as the amount of groundwater pumped. Furthermore, the remaining electricity on the farmer's IC card is multiplied by a hydropower conversion factor, which corresponds to the tradable water right amount. Under such condition, farmers would remain free to extract less groundwater, on the assumption that farmers will pump less groundwater assuming that the incentive created by the trading of water rights would be attractive to farmers. In this way, through the traded price of water rights, the problem related to the over-extraction of groundwater could be resolved. In addition, it may be anticipated that the government may be given farmers ecological compensation to provide additional incentives to farmers to trade water rights. Another benefit of using this method is that it no longer needs to establish a water fee collection system. Of course, this mechanism needs coordination between ecological security and food security.

4.6　Strengthening water resources management

Four governance measures should complement the above technical recommendations.

Improving water use planning. In the planning of water resources, a red line (bottom line) for demarcating groundwater resources should be defined such as the *red line* for the cultivated land, which specifies that 120 million ha (1.8 billion mu) of basic farmland should be should be strictly protected to ensure grain security. Such red line should not only include measures to control the decline of groundwater level, but also measures to gradually restore the groundwater level. Through strict planning and management and water quota management, it should be the responsibility of local governments to supervise adjustments to the planting structure of crops with the goal of preventing the decline in groundwater levels. The goal of recovering groundwater levels should be considered as an integral part of the construction of the Ecological Civilization.

Improving water resources related laws and regulations. Improving water resources related laws and regulations should require, at the same time and in a coordinated fashion, the drawing up a new legal system with a particular focus on the improvement of law enforcement as to strengthen the legal responsibility for the protection of water resources and the supervision and administration of implementation plans. Strengthening the responsibility system for law enforcement should also improve the mechanism for the mediation of water disputes as well as mechanism for dealing with emergencies. Furthermore, capacity building for improving on-site law enforcement capabilities and ability to respond to sudden water disputes should be considered full part of improving the legal cadre related to improving water resources use efficiency.

Improving water resources management policy. The state of water resources is an important indicator of a country's ability to promote sustainable development. In order to continuously improve the status of water resources and achieve their sustainable utilization, exploring systems and mechanisms that are conducive to the rational development, optimal allocation, efficient use, comprehensive conservation, effective protection, and comprehensive management of water resources is a prerequisite to the establishment of a water supply and efficient water use system. Furthermore, improving mechanisms for integrating public participation, expert consultation, and government decision-making should be considered another prerequisite and a complement to all conditions above to ensure a scientific and democratic decision-making process regarding water resources management.

Education. public notice and awareness raising should also be considered critical in the above context. Such activities should be carried out in a flexible and diverse manner with the objective to raise farmers' awareness for water laws and regulations, including the risks of water shortages as well as benefits from water conservation and environmental protection. The rationale behind education, public notice and awareness raising is to increase initiatives related to protecting water resources based on the concept of a legal access to water resources with paid use as to give up improper behaviors and unauthorized construction of water projects.

In reality, if the severity of air pollution can be felt immediately, the severity of the decrease in groundwater level is much harder to detect. As a result, it is recommended that a display device, which would reflect the groundwater level situation, should be established at village level so that farmers could, individually and commonly, assess how far the water table is from the red line. This in order to guide them and enhance their cooperation in the development of water-saving agriculture, improve their capacity related to groundwater conservation and take common actions.

5. Measures for Improving Forest Plantation Management

5.1   Silvicultural management requirements

One of the major problems experienced with the classical monoculture forest plantation models established under the Grain for Green program is its lack of ecological and structural stability, its limited flexibility and its inability towards addressing natural and anthropogenic disturbances, notably those due to the effects of climate change. This prompted forestry scientists to look for alternative forest management approaches, the more, that nowadays forestry has grown into a broader range of benefits' provision, other than serving exclusively the supply of timber. Increasingly, highly praised forestry policy functions such as environmental protection, ecosystem protection, biodiversity conservation, recreation, and social values are, aside of timber production, increasingly been considered as major policy objectives. Consequently, if the economic and technical efficiency of timber production still remain to be prioritized, ecological and social parameters should be progressively taken into account to enhance the multi-use function of forests.

For all these reasons, forest management strategies have evolved overtime towards new silvicultural approaches that bear the words "nature" and "ecology" as alternative to plantation forestry. Those silvicultural approaches are attempting to emulate natural processes in forest management to minimize disturbances, such as invasion of non-native plants, insects, pathogens, wild animals, the effects of climate change and/or human impacts that the plantation silviculture cannot appropriately alleviate. This approach, advocated by Pro Silva in 2012, can be summarized by the term "nature-based silviculture" or "close-to-nature forest management" or "close-to-nature silviculture (CNS)". The basic fundament of CNS is to incorporate structural qualities and functional features of natural forest ecosystems into sustainable forest management principles (i.e. integrating regeneration processes to enhance the structural heterogeneity of natural forest ecosystems in forest management activities).

The Close to Nature Forest Silviculture Principles

The Close-to-Nature Forest Silviculture (CNS) concept has its origin in Central and Eastern Europe, where forest cycle models have been successfully applied since the late nineteenth century. They all were based on the selection forest principle focused on sustainable wood production. In the 1980s, new forestry paradigms emerged, which, in contrast to the previous silvicultural approaches, viewed as "far-to-nature" silvicultural systems, emphasized the potential to manage forests for ecosystem values, such as biodiversity over larger scales, in addition to more traditional forest commodities.

Such silvicultural approaches included the Single-Tree Selection model-e.g. Dauernwald concept in Germany (Möller, 1922), Plenterwald in Switzerland (Biollet, 1920); the Group Selection model (e.g. gap cutting model or Femelschlag in Germany and Switzerland); and also the irregular Shelterwood model. A common feature of these approaches, although considered as man-made approaches, was to meet evolving societal objectives, while avoiding even-age system, and particularly clear felling systems and enhancing species mixtures and irregular-age structure.

The CNS refers to a management approach treating forest as an ecological system performing multiple functions. Close-to-Nature-Silviculture (CNS) tries to achieve management objectives with a minimum necessary human interventions basically aimed at accelerating the processes that nature would do by itself more slowly. In other words, the CNS is widely held as an approach that optimizes multiple forest functions at small spatial scales. The CNS approach is particularly focus on:

i. Creating optimal conditions for natural regeneration by maintaining the permanent forest climate and refraining from clear-felling;

ii. Promotion of natural and/or site-adapted tree species, often based on their assumed potential natural regeneration;

iii. Stability improvement and risk diversification (resilience) through the creation of uneven mixed forest stands (of diverse vertical and horizontal structures) with site-adapted species;

iv. Active stand improvement through frequent but weak thinning;

v. Protection of natural equilibriums among forest organisms, including pests, with the aim of promoting biodiversity and avoiding the use of pesticides;

vi. Avoidance of clear felling

However, CNS is not an approach with a commonly agreed definition. It is rather a compilation of several silvicultural principles, which are given different weights depending upon different edaphic conditions (i.e. soil nutrients, structure, porosity, moisture), topography, exposure, climate and species composition.

Compared to CNS, the mono-specific plantation approach leads to less robust forest stands. The weakness of the plantation approach focusing on monoculture of timber species in short rotation is that it neglects most forest ecological, social and cultural functions. Therefore, due to its integrative flexibility, CNS is able to fulfill different management goals since it allows to gradually adjust the course of management practices to address the ever-changing objectives and aspirations of the society.

The table 13 bellow illustrates the difference between the traditional plantation management, the CNS and the strict nature protection approaches [1] .It indicates that the plantation approach, focusing mainly on timber production in short rotation and neglecting most ecological and social values, is rather inflexible in its goal fulfillment.

---

[1] Jørgen Bo Larsen, *Close to Nature Forest Management: The Danish Approach to Sustainable Forestry*, University of Copenhagen, Denmark, 2012, https://www.intechopen.com/chapters/36975.

In addition the plantation approach generally leads to less robust forest stands. In comparison, the integrative ability and flexibility of the nature-based silviculture to fulfill different management goals,including timber production but to a lesser extent than the plantation approach-explain why the nature-based silviculture approach to sustainable forest management has been developing in many European countries. Also because the flexibility of the nature-based approach, allows forest managers to gradually adjust the course of management to address the ever-changing objectives and aspirations of the society.

Table 13   Different forest management approaches and their respective fulfillment of specific management goals

Management Approach	Plantation (production) approach	Nature-based (CNS) approach	Nature protection (conservation) approach
Specific management goals	Focus on timber production and direct economic outcome	Flexible wood production, nature protection and recreation	Strict forest reserves, following natural structures and processes
Production of timber	5	4	1
Economic outcome Long term	3	5	1
Economic outcome Short term	5	3	1
Production of quality timber	4	4	1
Ecosystem integrity	1	4	5
Biodiversity protection	1	3	5
Aesthetic qualities	1	5	5
Landscape integration	2	4	5
Space for public recreation	2	4	2
Resiliency to climate change	1	4	5
Flexibility to changing goals	1	5	1

Notes: The scale is 1 to 5, 1 is indicting low goal fulillment; 5 is indicting high goal fulillment

5.2   Improving plantation forests adaptive capacity

The following six adaptation management principles and silvicultural practices are generally recognized when it comes to improving plantation forest adaptive capacity and resilience to climate change. They are listed below without grading them according to their relative importance, as it would depend upon the type, situation, past management history and adaptive capacity of already existing plantation forest stands.

Increasing tree species richness at the stand level because there is a strong evidence that mixed stands are more resistant than pure stands to climate-related disturbance, such as drought or storm and more resilient once a disturbance has occurred.

Increasing structural diversity in term of trees of different ages and sizes to improve overall resistance to biological (e.g. insects, pests) and physical (e.g. winds, fires) agents of disturbances. Structural diversity can be achieved through uneven-aged silvicultural systems (single tree selection) leading to irregular stand structure. Generally increasing structural diversity (through e.g. under-planting) is done in association with increasing tree species richness as to create structurally diverse forest mixed stands.

Increasing genetic variation within tree species. Increasing genetic variation consists in enriching existing populations with locally adapted species or tree species from other provenances, for instance with provenance from warmer and/or drier climates.

Increasing resistance to biological and physical stresses as individual tree can exhibit different resistance to stress. This could be done through heavy thinning from above (at the pole stage) leading to increasing soil volume for root systems and pruning to eliminate branches leading to large-crowned trees.

Replacing stands at high risks of being damaged by disturbances such as wind storms, forest fires or insects, or stands already destabilized by logging by replacing them with less vulnerable stands using modified clear-cutting or group or strip felling or transformation to uneven-aged structure.

Keeping average growing stock low as high growing stocks are generally correlated with increased damage susceptibility. Reducing growing stocks can be implemented by heavier or lighter thinning depending on local risks-related situations. However, reducing growing stocks implies less carbon sequestration, therefore, less climate change mitigation impacts.

6. Measures for Improving Farmland Ecological Security

6.1 Establishing an arable land quality survey system

The productivity of arable land is affected by a number of factors such as its spatial location, climate, multiple cropping index, and inputs. According to the difference in the annual crop yield of arable land, in China, the arable land is divided into 15 quality index, which have important limitations. To take hold of dynamic changes in the quality of cultivated land, it is required to build an investigation system to assess the quality of cultivated land, carry out detailed inspections on a regular basis, understand and apprehend the changes in the soil quality of cultivated land, and their effects on yields and quality of agricultural products. At the same time, a comprehensive evaluation system for arable land quality, including a database of arable land topography, land area, soil, infrastructure, and a data analysis method system should be established to evaluate changes in arable land quality and propose countermeasures.

China's experience with land quality assessment

From 1999 to 2014, the Ministry of Land and Resources completed a geochemical survey over a total of 15.7 million hectares of land, of which 92.4 million hectares were listed as arable land, accounting for 68 percent of the country's total arable land. Within the surveyed area:

• 2.23 million hectares of arable land exceeded basic standard pollution;

• 2.26 million hectares were declared slightly polluted or exceeding the basic arable land pollution standard;

• Soil organic matter in some areas declined;

• Soils in the north had a tendency to alkalization, and soils in the south had a tendency towards acidification.

In 2012, the Ministry of Agriculture launched an additional survey of soil heavy metal pollution in agricultural production areas, over 10.82 million hectares. *The 2016 National Cultivated Land Quality Monitoring Report* released by the Ministry of Agriculture complemented the results of those two surveys, indicating that:

• 65.5 percent of the country's monitoring sites had a shallow plowed layer, which was less than the thickness of the suitable plowing layer (20cm) while 25.9 percent of the monitoring sites had a smaller soil volume than the standard for suitable crop growth;

• The contents of soil organic matter, total nitrogen, available phosphorus and available potassium have improved overall;

• The levels of middle-level elements and trace elements remain relatively low;

• Regional soil acidification is increasingly noticeable.

After more than 15 years of investigations and high-precision testing of more than 600000 soil, water, and biological samples through 54 indicators, more than 30 million data across the country and its 31 provinces (including autonomous regions and municipalities) have been compiled. Altogether, those surveys allow the identification of the characteristics and the assessment of the patterns of the main pollutants of cultivated soils in China.

6.2 Formulating policies, laws and regulations for the protection of cultivated land

Cultivated land is the basis for human survival and development, and it is related to the country's food security and food safety, agricultural stability, and sustainable development. Current, arable land security protection standards include:

Basic cultivated land area protection. The basic farmland protection regulation includes strictly controlling the conversion of arable land to non-cultivated land; promoting the rehabilitation of degraded and abandoned land; regulating farmland use right circulation, preventing "non-grainification" (land to be used for non-grain production purpose) and prohibiting "non-agriculturalization" (land to be used for other purpose rather for agricultural production). The objective of the basic farmland protection is to strictly abide 120 million ha (1.8 billion mu) of cultivated land to "red line" standards.

Cultivated land quality protection. The objectives of farmland quality protection measures are to prevent problems such as soil erosion and arable land desertification, salinization, and depletion of cultivated land as well as to take measures to rehabilitate arable land and solve problems such as farmland pollution as well as the current decline of farmland plowing depth.

Cultivated land use protection. The objectives of cultivated land use protection are to formulate and implement standards for the use of chemical fertilizers and pesticide and agricultural plastic films, as well as for irrigation water quality and groundwater withdrawal, etc. to eliminate the adverse impacts of excessive applications of chemical fertilizers and pesticides, and the use of agricultural films, sewage irrigation, and groundwater depletion which are causing farmland insecurity.

Implementing the objectives of the responsibility system for cultivated land protection. The objectives, tasks, measures, and responsibilities for cultivated land protection are to be implemented at all levels of the people's government including administrative departments, agricultural enterprises, rural community leaders, and farmersusing targeted, quantitative, institutionalized management methods, and accountability mechanisms as to clearly define the responsibility of such entities.

To improve farmland security, the following four objectives should be considered in terms of policies, laws and regulations.

Improving the legal system of cultivated land protection. Even though *Land Administration Law*, *Law on the Contracting of Rural Land*, and newly revised *Environmental Protection Law* involve provisions for the protection and rational use of farmland if they all have their own particular emphasis they are neither practical nor operational. Therefore, the government shall formulate a specific law on the protection of cultivated land based on the relevant provisions of these laws, to form a legal system that take cultivated land protection as a core, and link with above-mentioned laws. This new law should guide the government, enterprises and farmers in view of regulating the protection of arable land accordingly.

Formulating farmland protection regulations. With the power of laws and regulations, all administrative regions are required to use more than 80 percent of cultivated land as basic farmland in accordance to the requirements of the 1.8 billion mu (120 million ha) of cultivated lands red line and land use control. Priority should be given to high-quality cultivated land, especially land that is easily occupied in the outskirts of towns and along roads. Such land should be designated as permanent basic farmland [1], with the basic farmland protection zone defined by townships as basic unit, so that the red line of 1.8 billion mu (120 million ha) of arable land should be expanded from the "physical" red line to the "quality" red line.

Improving farmland quality standards and policy systems. Improving farmland

---

[1] Basic farmland refers to agriculture land specifically restricted to food grain, cotton, oil crops and vegetable production and to land with good irrigation, drainage and erosion control as well as to agricultural scientific research, experiments and teaching fields. Under basic farmland regulations, the conversion of basic farmland to alternative agricultural land uses (e.g. forests, pastures, cash trees, fishing pounds, etc.) or other land use types (e.g. tombs, sand digging, mining, etc.) is strictly forbidden. When conversion is unavoidable, it must be approved by provincial governments if the conversion is below a threshold amount of 500 mu (around 33 ha or by the State Council if the conversion is above that threshold. Those standards were further tightened by the 1999 Amendment to the Land Administration Law. Those regulations do not apply to regular farmland.

quality standards should include the formulation of arable land quality grades and soil environmental standards for arable land; guidance for arable land evaluation and arable land compensation; specifications relevant to arable land soil monitoring and assessment, risk management and control, treatment and remediation technologies. It should also include revising the thresholds of hazardous and harmful substances included in fertilizers, feed, and irrigation water; control standards for pollutants; the formulation of bio-degradable agricultural plastic film standards, and the revision of agricultural plastic film and pesticide packaging standards, and the specifications of cultivated soil standard samples;

Enhancing ecological security effects from farmland protection forests and tree-crop intercropping. Farmland protection forests at farm and agriculture landscape level and tree-crop intercropping were historically instrumental in providing an ecological security environment favorable to agricultural productivity, notably in devising a micro-climate favorable to crop yields, protecting farmland against weather related anomalies associated with climate change and soil erosion, enhancing soil nutrient cycling, carbon sequestration, biological diversity and the production of valuable products as timber, food, fodder, medicinal plants, essential oils and materials for local industries. In effect, the current degradation of farmland protection forests, if not reversed, may lead to catastrophic changes in the ecosystem services they were historically providing. Since most farmland protection forests systems are developed either at farm and/or at agricultural landscape level, inter-sectoral policy and institutional coordination remains a matter of improvement due to the current institutional segregation between agriculture, forestry, nature conservation and the environment.

6.3   Formulating an action plan for the prevention and control of arable land pollution

Since 1949, China's overall economic development mode has been extensive and still face serious challenges with regards to environmental protection for reasons such as unreasonable industrial structure and high level of pollution discharge. Farmland, as one of the ultimate receptors of pollutants, has been severely affected. The implementation of farmland pollution prevention and control action plans is a major policy measure to be promoted to eliminate these adverse impacts.

Physical goals of the action plan. In 2016, the State Council issued *Action Plan for Soil Pollution Prevention and Control*. The goal of this plan is that 90 percent of the contaminated farmland should be rehabilitated and safely used by 2020. By 2030, the targets will more than 95 percent. The 13 CGG provinces also formulated provincial "Soil Pollution Prevention Action Plans".

Classification control and strategic objectives. The objectives of the prevention and control of cultivated land pollution should also include the safety protection of cultivated land for the production of safe food and human environmental security. To put protecting and improving the quality of cultivated land at the core of the strategy, classified control and comprehensive measures should be adopted. According to the degree of pollution, the agricultural land should be divided into three grades, and priority measures should be given to the protection, safe use and strict control. Measures for the protection, control, and restoration of both unpolluted and contaminated soils should be separately proposed and implemented.

Establishing a system for prevention and control of arable land pollution. The implementation of this system should be led by the government, clearly identifying the responsibility of enterprises, encouraging public participation, and accepting public supervision. Safe cultivated land is the basis for human survival, and arable land security is something that everyone should pay attention to. Therefore, there is a need to give full play to the legal system, technology support, reform and innovation and market guidance, and the participation of all social forces, which should be mobilized to make concerted efforts, and play a critical role through enterprises and public participation. It should be pointed out that in recent years, as the country has continuously increased the support for rehabilitation of cultivated land, the scale and the role of the soil remediation industry are increasing year by year through market mechanisms.

6.4 Implementing arable land remediation and improvement projects

The implementation of the arable land remediation projects would be a major measure to reverse the degraded trends. their overall goal would be "Two increasing and One improvement". Among them, "Two increasing" refers to (i) an increase of 0.5 grade of basic productivity of farmland through the construction of high standard farmlands; (ii) an increase of 0.5 percent of soil organic matter content.

"One improvement" means improving soil properties and quality of cultivated land by rehabilitating soils affected by acidification and salinization. This could be done through the following three measures.

Formulation of plans for arable land remediation and improvement. The improvement of arable land can be handled through the following stages: investigation and assessment, feasibility study, project design and preparation, construction, and project acceptance. The investigation and assessment includes the identification of pollutants, pollution degree and scope, pollution risk, and the set up of targets, etc.; the feasibility study and project design include selection of technology, determination of process parameters, estimation of engineering quantities, feasibility assessment, construction drawing, environmental management plan, etc.; project acceptance will be the results of the monitoring of the project impacts.

The development of pilot projects for the treatment and rehabilitation of farmland soil pollution. Piloting projects should be carried out to demonstrate technologies used as to promote the remediation of soil pollution in a step-by-step manner. The objective of pilot projects would be to identify and adopt a series of measures to control soil erosion, increase organic matter content, improve soil fertility, and to increase by 0.5 grades or more farmland basic productivity, increase soil organic matter content by 0.5 percent or more by 2020, and achieve the required thickness of the plowed layer.

Promotion of comprehensive technology systems. It includes conservation farming, precision fertilization, fertigation, and the control of chemical fertilizers and pesticides, notably to control and eliminate the negative impacts of heavy metal and organic pollution on arable land.

6.5   Improving cultivated land restoration techniques

Polluted and degraded cultivated land can be rehabilitated using physical, chemical and biological and agronomic measures.

Physical measures. They refer to the technique of removing or separating contaminants from the soil through various physical processes; including soil and land method, thermal desorption, soil gas phase extraction, mechanical ventilation and so on. Their advantages are that those repair measures are efficient and fast. Their disadvantages are that their costs are high.

Chemical measures. Chemical remediation measures include the use of chemical agents for adsorption, precipitation, and complexation to remove or reduce the toxicity and bioavailability of pollutants, therefore, reduce the risk of arable land pollution. Their advantages are that the remediation efficiency is high and the remediation speed fast. Their disadvantages are that adding chemicals may cause secondary pollution.

Biological measures. Biological technologies include phyto-remediation technologies, microbial remediation technologies and combined biological repair technologies. Such measures are based on the unique biological ability to absorb or decompose toxic and harmful substances, reduce or remove pollutants in the soil, and gradually restore farmland to produce safe agricultural products. The main measures are to adjust the planting structure or return farmland to forests and grasslands. Their advantages are that they do not destroy soil organic matter and soil structure, while their costs remain low. However, their disadvantages are that they take long time to meet the expected results.

Agronomic measures. Agronomic measures refer to the adjustment of soil physical and chemical properties through deep plowing, deep sub-soiling, proper management of water, application of functional fertilizers and other measures to reduce the risk of agricultural land pollution.

Worth to mention is the fact that the two latter measures require relatively low inputs, and are easy to operate. They are suitable for the remediation of soils contaminated by heavy metals of medium and low concentrations over large areas.

6.6 Promoting agriculture land fallow systems

The crop rotation and fallow system is not only a measure to improve the quality of cultivated land affected by reduction of the soil layer and of the tillage layer, soil acidification, degradation, pollution due to excessive heavy metals, and the increase of non-point source pollution, but also a measure for the protection of arable land and a guarantee of long-term food security. It is also a measure of agricultural transformation required for the sustainable development of China's agriculture. Therefore, crop rotation and fallow should be adopted not only for the protection of development areas, but also for the optimization of development areas.

The crop rotation and fallow system is a cultivation system of fertility maintenance, which will improve the productivity of the farmland, and which does not affect grain yield significantly. The rice-wheat rotation experiment showed that organic carbon content in soil has increased significantly by returning 75 percent of straw to the soil for five consecutive seasons. Sequestering carbon in agricultural soils is an important climate change mitigation measure [1] . In addition, available phosphorus content also increased, thus, microbial communities in the soil have been improved as well as nutrient availability, and soil permeability improved. By effectively preventing secondary soil acidification, crop rotation would, without doubt, prop up the sustainable use of cultivated land in China [2] .

The implementation of a crop rotation and fallow system, jointly with a reduction of the area of cultivated land or the adoption of multiple cropping systems for gradually recovering land fertility should be considered as one of the basic measures for implementing a strategy based on sustainable farmland management. China's grain production capacity has currently stabilized at the level of 600 million tons, and there are abundant grain reserves. The international grain supply and demand situation is also, for the time being, in a good situation, which is providing a series of favorable conditions for the implementation of the crop rotation and fallow system. The implementation of the crop rotation and fallow system can also not only improve the international competitiveness of Chinese agricultural products, but also promote the Chinese agricultural subsidies policy to move from the "Amber (yellow) Box" to the "Green Box".

With crop rotation and land fallowing, there may be, however, production shortfalls due to the multiple cropping system of cultivated land or because of the need to return more farmland to forests or grasslands, which will affect, in one way or another, grain

---

[1] There are currently a general consensus among scientist and practioners that increasing soil carbon is key to improving agro-ecosystems productivity as soil carbon plays important roles in maintaining soils structure, improving soil water-holding capacity, fostering soil microbial activity and providing fertility for crops. While some uncertainties remain with regard to the potential of agricultural soils to act as carbon sink in the longer term, a vast amount of co-benefits of soil carbon sequestration should be considered as incentives to modify agricultural practices to increase soil carbon. See Appendix XX on soil carbon sequestration and its impacts on agricultural productivity.

[2] Xu Jianglai et al.," Effects of continuous straw returning on cropland soil nutrient and carbon stocks in rice-wheat rotations", *Soils*, 2016 48(1).

production. As a result, there is a need to balance actual food security and farmers' short-term revenues with long-term food security objectives. In this respect, the government should not only play a critical role in formulating appropriate compensation standards, ensuring that farmers' interests would not be lost, but also play a role in improving market mechanisms, guiding and helping farmers to get hold of off-farm employment, and in optimizing planting structure through the development of specific laws and regulations and accountability mechanisms. Other key rationale for implementing the crop rotation and fallow system include groundwater saving, reduction of heavy metal pollution areas, and improving the production capacity of the thin layers' soils zone.

6.7 Enhancing the ecological benefits from farmland protection forests.

In view of the various, but inestimable benefits that can be derived from "agroforestry" practices, the interpretation of the current degradation situation pertaining to farmland protection forests as well as the attitude of farmers towards reintroducing trees into the agricultural landscapes of CGG lead to the following conclusion: the role of farmland protection forest should yet become a general social objective and the maintenance and development of farmland protection forests a conscious action of farmers.

According to *the European Commission's Rural Development Policy* (RDP) 2014–2020, agroforestry systems have the potential to contribute to the objectives identified in the Europe 2020 Strategy for Smart, Sustainable and Inclusive Agricultural Growth in the following ways:

- Contributing to biomass production;
- Improving water quality by increasing infiltration and slowing down the leaching of nitrates;
- Improving soil quality and fertility;
- Contributing to restoring the production potential of degraded farm lands due to an excessive use of mineral fertilizers, pesticides and herbicides;
- Controlling erosion by providing permanent soil cover with litter;
- Adapting and mitigating effects of climate change, by preventing forests from fire damages and limit evaporation of water;
- Contributing to carbon sequestration;
- Enhancing the positive effect of biodiversity in natural landscapes.

The main production objective of CGG areas in China is agriculture, not forestry. When planning and developing farmland protection forests systems, it should be the forestry sector's objective to positively respond to this objective, not only for the benefits of farmers but also for that of the sustainable agriculture objective, notably for food security reason. In that sense, the goal of the forestry development should be to contribute to that objective rather than solely maintaining and enhancing the status of the forestry sector in CGG areas. In order to meet the food security strategic needs of the country and the income of farmers, the planning of farmland protection forest system must refer to the following two principles:

i. The main function of farmland protection forests should be to protect national food security. In that sense, the positive and negative effects of farmland protection forests on grain production should reach a marginal equilibrium while taking into consideration climate change-related weather anomalies and hazards;

Minimizing farmland protection forests' land occupation and their negative impacts on grain production. In that sense, the grid of farmland protection forests should not be too dense. There is no reason to occupy more land than what the protective function of farmland protection forests requires to impact positively on crop production.

Based on the above two principles, it has been anticipated that improving grain productivity and ecological security in CGG areas, will depend upon four layers of farmland protection forests systems building on the past success of the "Four Sides".

i. A first protection layer already established (or in a stage of improvement and/ or expansion), which will consist of afforestation programs in the hills and mountains surrounding CGG areas, in particular under the Grain for Green program.

ii. A second protection layer, which will consist of the rehabilitation and expansion of tree lines planted on both sides of highways as well as along counties', townships', and villages' roads.

iii. A third protection layer will encompass the rehabilitation and development of village woodlots. At present, in most villages, there are certain areas devoted to economic forests, timber forests, recreation areas or scenic forests, etc..

iv. A fourth protection layer, which should include the planting of farmland protection forests along service and access roads, canals and ditches located at farm boundaries. Since the turn of the century, the government, which is paying more and more attention to food security, is promoting the scale of agricultural land consolidation in CGG areas including land leveling, the digging of wells for irrigation, canals and drainage and electrification.

The continuous increase of grain production in CGG areas during the past decades could be explained by three factors including: (i) access to improved varieties, (ii) advantageous fertilizer and grain price support policies, (iii) the positive role played by the farmland protection forests ("Four Sides" mentioned above). To build on this success, the future development of farmland protection forest system in CGG areas should further be based on the following principles.

i. A transition from small grid to larger grid to reduce the negative impacts of farmland protection forests due to the tree root system and shade and meet the requirements of mechanized operations;

ii. A transition from symmetry to asymmetry; In the past, farmland protection forests were regularly implemented in small regular grids, thereby hampering irrigation and mechanization and increasing losses in crop yields and often creating neighborhood problems and discontents with other farmers having to bear their negative influence. As a result, it is recommended that farmland protection forests be, as far as possible, located in priority along roads, and canals and between roads and canals, and to a lesser extent at the boundaries of farmland;

iii. A transition from singletree species to many tree and shrub species for at least three reasons. First, replacing singletree species with multiple tree species, and mixing then with shrubs and grasses represents the major advantage to increase biological diversity, and improve the forest landscape. Second, selecting tree species with tall trunk and large crown would reduce or even eliminate the crop yield losses from trees. Third, it would improve management flexibility and diversify farmers' income from trees.

iv. A transformation from the self-consistent system into an open integrated system in order to avoid the negative influence of trees on infrastructure such as, for instance, irrigation and maintenance of roads and canals. In that respect, since the planning of farmland protection forests should be an organic part of land use planning in rural areas, it would be essential for the forestry department to collaborate with other relevant departments directly and indirectly involved in agricultural development in CGG areas.

The government should, therefore, clearly identify the policy and institutional conditions require to maintain and further develop farmland protection forests, where appropriate tree-crop intercropping, notably to enhance soil fertility of degraded and/or polluted agricultural land. This would require putting in place an innovative governance system required to take into account the multifunctional nature of farmland protection forests (and tree-crop intercropping where useful) and their inter-sectoral requirements. Moreover, for getting the full participation of farmers, which would be critical not only for the maintenance of existing farmland protection forests and their further development, such innovative governance system should include financial incentives (such as payment for environmental services or eco-compensation), or monetary support through loans or grants that should be made available to offset the costs of maintaining and developing farmland protection forests, in particular in respect of their ecological security role. Clarifying and securing tree (and land) tenure conditions as well as regulations pertaining to the development and management of farmland protection forests, notably those planted along infrastructures such as roads, canals, ditches, etc. and other farmland trees should also be considered a policy prerequisite to the full participation of farmers.

Finally, to improve farmers' participation towards tree planting on CGG farmland, at least the following six social, economic, policy and institutional prerequisites should be considered for promoting farmland protection forests and, in some specific case tree-crop intercropping. They include:

Economic justification. Farmers, as well as extension staff of concerned institutions, will have to understand the benefits that could be derived from farmland protection foresters and tree-crop intercropping, and notably their ecological, economic and financial justification. This will require both agriculture and forestry institutions to plan for training, workshops and even demonstration for the farmers to see and experience how "profitable" farmland protection forests and tree-crop intercropping will be compared to mono-cropping systems. Demonstrating the "multi-function profitability" of farmland protection forests and tree-crop intercropping will, however, require time.

Overcoming farmers financial constraints. This would require specific loans or grant incentives through, for instance, eco-compensation payments at least during the initial implementation stage of farmland protection forests and tree-crop intercropping systems. In particular, farmland protection forests with stronger public welfare should be given more development and maintenance subsidies. However, such subsidies would not be suitable for all trees planted as farmland protection forests or tree-crop intercropping systems. For instance, it should remain the farmers' responsibility to plant trees at the edge of his farmland, either to protect his farmland or to utilize his land more efficiently to get more income or to rehabilitate degraded or polluted soils. Defining all trees as farmland protection forest and taking exactly the same management policy for all of them would not be the best strategy as they would respond to different usages. The full justification, scope and procedures of introducing eco-compensation payment for the development and maintenance of farmland protection forests remain, however, to be worked out.

Availability of an integrated technical assistance. The lack of knowledge and the lack of efficient combined agriculture and forestry extension programs hinder the adoption of farmland protection forests. This is why the combined training of local technicians is vital for the maintenance and development of farmland protection forests and tree-crop intercropping: the presence and contact with technical people able to disseminate objective, transparent and commercially oriented "agroforestry" information about the wealth created by farmland protection forests and tree-crop intercropping would be an effective tool for promoting the adoption of farmland protection forests and tree-crop intercropping.

Improving tree (land) tenure security. This prerequisite applies in particular to farmers who may be involved in on-farm tree planting and tree-crop intercropping and maintenance or do not possess long-term land use certificates. In such case, the absence of ownership rights over land and/or trees may act as a hindrance to farmland protection forests development. In addition, the absence of land or tree tenure clarity would make it difficult the access to credits and other forms of financial support such as eco-compensation payments or subsidies.

Forestry regulations. Encouraging farmers to invest in on-farm and off-farm tree planting for ecological security reason with a long-term perspective would require creating a new enabling forestry regulations' environment. Many conflicts have aroused in getting felling permits for trees grown in existing farmland protection forests. Those regulations may act as a disincentive to tree planting and maintenance on non-forestland for ecological security reasons. For instance, on regular farmlands, farmers who preferred trees with value added may be relieved from strict forestry felling rules.

Monitoring and evaluation. The attitude survey carried out in 2016 in the CGG areas of Henan Province highlighted that, contrary to farmers' opinion, forestry officials always emphasize the importance of farmland protection forest for its positive general impacts on crop yield, thus minimizing problems related to the reduction of yield in areas adjacent to tree belts. Furthermore, the attitude survey also indicated that agriculture officials were not well informed of the scope of benefits of farmland protection forests and tree-crop intercropping. Overcoming farmers' reluctance towards farmland protection forests and disbelief from agriculture staff underscores the importance of establishing an objective supervision and monitoring system. Equally important, would be the development of information systems, which should include provisions for the collection of data necessary to answer key questions regarding farmland protection forests and tree-crop intercropping economic and environmental impacts. Such supervision and monitoring system should be combined with the proposed arable land quality supervision system.

6.8 Strengthening arable land quality supervision

Since the quality of cultivated land is the most important basis for the quality of grain, the supervision of cultivated land quality must be focused on the control of cultivated land pollution, and the improvement of the quality of cultivated land. The treatment of cultivated land pollution is a long term and phased work for decades to come, as the improvement of cultivated land quality is a permanent work that has to be done. As of today, arable land quality supervision in China has focused on contaminated farmland only.

The risks of arable land pollution include affecting the quality of agricultural products, endangering human health, threatening ecological security; affecting the normal functions of soils and the growth and reproduction of plants, animals (such as earthworms) and microorganisms (such as rhizobia), and soil nutrient conversion and fertility maintenance. The conversion and migration of pollutants in soil may cause pollution to surface water, groundwater, and even drinking water sources. Therefore, establishing a comprehensive supervision system for the quality of cultivated land is an urgent need. It should include an accountability system for a lasting quality of cultivated land, including the control the behaviors of indiscriminate use and abuse of chemicals as to prevent new farmland pollution from becoming a reality.

Strengthening arable land supervision should include:

Farmland pollution risk supervision. Farmland pollution risk supervision should use probabilistic methods to assess arable lands' hazards potential. The risk of life caused by pollution refers to the possibility of contaminated food and other agricultural products endangering human and animal health. In parallel, ecological risk refers to the possibility of harming the ecosystem or its elements.

Land use regulations. Heavily polluted arable land cannot grow safe edible agricultural products, as it would not ensure the safe use of cultivated land and the security of food and agricultural products. Land use regulations, therefore, should include formulating plans for the safe use of contaminated cultivated land and eliminating risk of non-compliance through measures such as agronomic regulations and crop adjustment. Heavily polluted arable land can be planted with other agricultural products or returned to forests or grasslands.

Supervision of cultivated land remediation processes. It would take a long time to restore polluted arable lands. An arable land remediation monitoring network should be establihed to measure dynamics changes and supervise arable land remediation processes. Such supervision system will also have a positive impact on the development of a cultivated land remediation market.

Comprehensive supervision of the quality of cultivated land. The safety of cultivated land depends not only on the safety of cultivated soil, but also on the water and atmospheric environments that affect it. Therefore, a comprehensive supervision system, including the supervision of cultivated land and soil environment, the supervision of the water environment of cultivated land, and the supervision of cultivated land atmospheric environment should be established.

V The Way Forward: Towards an Ecological Security Strategy for the China's CGG Areas

1. Basic Foundation for Scaling up Ecological Security in China's CGG Areas

Agriculture in CGG areas is nowadays a victim of its past successes, especially based on the successes of HRS policies, agricultural incentives, technological improvements and implementation of farmland protection forests. If it is nowadays cereal centric and input intensive, the issue of sustainability of current production systems has emerged. In particular, challenges for the future have surfaced prominently, such as factor productivity; soil fertility degradation and pollution as well as groundwater and surface water pollution due to the excessive use of chemical fertilizers and pesticides; decreasing level of groundwater availability for irrigation; decline in soil organic matter; increased cost of inputs and related decline in farm profits, degradation of the protective functions of farmland protection forests; and, last but not least, the increasing risk of adverse impacts on agricultural productivity from weather anomalies and the increased incidence of pests and diseases due to climate change.

Environmental degradation is, therefore, one of most important issues facing today's CGG areas, notably because soil and water pollution, impacting on food safety, represent an important and increasing threat to human health. In China, a combination of soil pollution due to chemical fertilizers and pesticides over-application, decreasing availability of water resources in terms of quantity and quality and an increasing food safety risks are gradually affecting a large part of the population. It is important, therefore, that issues threatening food safety such as combined fertilizer and pesticide residues, heavy metal pollution and irrigation inefficiency are being addressed to reduce risks to human health.

Responding to environmental degradation in CGG areas requires improving ecological security for increasing crop productivity, notably by growing less water-requiring crops, increasing the availability of irrigation while promoting water saving measures, promoting landscape-based production systems reducing the application of chemical fertilizers and pesticides while facilitating large-scale adoption of ecological farming practices, including proven dry farming technologies and support for new innovations such as new fermentation technologies for the promotion of organic fertilizers' supply and application.

Scaling up ecological security in CGG areas requires, therefore, overcoming key challenges affecting the sustainability of the current agriculture production, notably those affecting crop production in CGG areas, with a particular attention given to overcoming the negative impacts of the continuous and persistent NPS pollution of agricultural soils and groundwater due to an over application of synthetic fertilizers, pesticides, and other agro-chemical inputs [1]; the continuous decrease of availability of water for irrigation due to an over exploitation of available groundwater resources; the impending impacts of climate change, notably due to both changes in precipitation pattern leading to changes in soil water content, runoff and erosion, nutrient cycles, salinization, biodiversity, and soil organic matter and the probable increasing frequencies of extreme climate events; and the deterioration of the protection benefits of farmland protection forests due to a series of problems, constraints and barriers, which are currently affecting their maintenance and continued existence, not to mention a general reluctance of farmers for preserving them due to their negative border effects on crop production and decreasing financial returns in absence of government financial support.

When addressing the above issues, it is expected that improving the ecological

---

[1] As synthetic fertilization is a major source of methane gas emissions and contamination of land and water, the reduction in their use will lower the risks of soil and water pollution as well as specific health problems associated with their inappropriate use (with farmers often ignoring or misunderstanding labels).

security of CGG areas would help achieving multiple sustainability objectives through integrated practices, supported by coherent cross-sectoral policies addressing the economic, environmental and social dimensions of CGG areas food systems. In this respect, ecological security underlies holistic solutions to the complex inter-related and multi-sectoral challenges notably related to poverty, hunger, environmental degradation and climate change. Moveover, ecological security requires innovation in policies, extension and rural institutions and partnerships, as well as in the production, processing, marketing and consumption of food as anticipated by the China 2030 Agenda, which aims at providing a national framework for achieving integrated sustainable development in its three environmental, social and economic dimensions. China 2030 Agenda calls, in particular, for much better policy, institutional and technological consideration given to ecological security related improvement in the food and agricultural sectors. It also calls for all people to be critical agents of change in the process.

1.1   Challenges and opportunities in scaling up ecological security in CGG areas

In scaling up the ecological security concept in CGG areas, the following challenges should be considered:

Lack of awareness of ecological security among farmers' communities, in particular the lack of awareness of the potential of ecological security to contribute to the multiple challenges facing today's conventional high-inputs agriculture.

Current absence of economic support to prioritize sustainability approaches in the agricultural sector. There is currently a lack of political support to catalyze national policies in support of more sustainable food production systems through innovative and integrative agricultural systems, such as ecological farming practices, which should respond to multiple economic, social and environmental challenges.

Absence of an enabling policy environment. Enhancing farmers' adoption of agricultural practices meeting ecological security requirements would require providing positive incentives to help them buffer against risks while they adapt their production systems to ecological security requirements, which may take time to realize their full benefits.

Lack of cross-sector coordination and collaboration in policy and governance. Ecological security requires greater interaction among sectors, disciplines and actors to achieve its multiple objectives. Sector policies need to be integrated across sectors and scales (from local to regional, to national) to achieve coherence. In particular, ecological security demands governance solutions that can coordinate actions at both individual farms and landscape levels. But so far, current policy and institutional frameworks have always privileged sector-specific interventions in governance mechanisms, regulatory systems and accountability.

Current research, education and extension systems do not yet respond to the need of ecological security. Meeting ecological security requirements in CGG areas requires the development of farming systems able to maximize the synergies between their production factors, such as soil, water, trees, biodiversity, climate, human behaviors etc. to deliver greater resource-use efficiency and resilience. Managing these interactions depends on both local conditions and farmers' knowledge. However, as of today, current research, education and extension systems mainly focus on single sector discipline and approaches, primarily focusing on crop yields improvement of single commodities and top-down technology transfer models. To scale up the ecological security concept, research, rural and scientific education and extension should be reoriented towards different modalities of knowledge creation and alternative extension pedagogy combining scientific knowledge with farmers' knowledge with the objective to maximize the configuration of biological and technological component of the farming systems based on ecological principles.

However, when scaling up ecological security, the following opportunities should be considered:

There is a widespread recognition among scientists that farming practices based on high-inputs and resource intensive farming systems have reached their limits. According to FAO[1] (2017), "high-inputs, resource-intensive farming systems, which have been instrumental in improving crop yields and food security during past decades, but which have also caused massive soil depletion, water scarcity, deforestation and high levels of GHG cannot anymore deliver sustainable agricultural production. Needed are innovative farming systems, such as ecological farming practices that would protect the resource base, while increasing productivity".

Solutions to improve ecological security in CGG areas do exist in policies and practices.

[1] FAO: *The future of food and agriculture: Trends and challenges*, 2017.

They all refer to conservation agriculture, climate-smart agriculture, organic agriculture, and in particular ecological agriculture, which represent a different, innovative, knowledge intensive, environmentally friendly, socially responsible way of farming, which depends on skill labor. They all have in common the replacement of, at least, some agrochemicals with organic inputs, diversified crop rotations, improved nutrient and water use efficiency, agroforestry and minimum tillage to reduce soil erosion and increase the soil capacity to hold water and sequester carbon while increasing productivity [1] .

Moreover, due progress made with information and communication technology (ICT), rural areas are not yet any more isolated. Therefore, the scientific knowledge require to improve ecological security may rapidly be available to farmers throughout CGG areas. Undoubtedly, this new development in ICTs presents new opportunities for exchange of knowledge between various state and non-state actors as well as the sharing of experiences among farmers.

Farming practices such as those developed under conservation agriculture, ecological agriculture, climate-smart agriculture, tree-crop intercropping, and organic agriculture are also addressing climate change adaptation and mitigation. Agroforestry, for instance, by diversifying crop-tree-livestock associations is increasing resourceuse efficiency and resilience to climate change. At the same time, maintaining and developing farmland protection forests as an integrated part of ecological farming practices will improve the vegetation and soils' capacity to sequester carbon, while providing additional off-and on-farm benefits.

A growing public demand for diversified and healthy food. There is, all over the world and China alike, an increasing demand for healthy food and diversified diets as a result of malnutrition and obesity. Integrated ecological farming practices can address this demand, while simultaneously improving soil health, reducing environmental degradation and lowering water irrigation needs. Again throughout China, innovative markets for organic agriculture products are gradually emerging at local and regional levels in synergy with diversified agriculture production systems.

---

[1] However, available meta-analysis confirm that yields under ecological agriculture can take several years to reach comparable yields under high-input agriculture using optimal applications of chemical inputs. Policy incentive measures such as subsidies would therefore be required to ease the transition period and avoid to compromise national food security objectives.

1.2 Public policies to promote ecological security in CGG areas.

While ecological security approaches to improve crop productivity, food safety, mitigate and adapt to climate change threats, and enhance farmers' livelihood are increasingly gaining support from scientists and consumers alike, most agricultural activities in CGG areas still focus on conventional, high-input solutions that rely on agrochemical inputs and fail to advance food security based on nutritional and environmental sustainability. Therefore the urgent need is to create economic and social policies that will enable farmers to make the transition to ecological security. Enacting such policies would require change in policy development and reorientation to cross-sectoral approaches and from on-farm approaches only to landscapes approaches.

Between 2014 and 2015, FAO organized a series of regional *International Symposia on Agro-ecology for Food Security and Nutrition* on the premise that meeting ecological security in the agriculture is a critical way to reduce dependence on fossil fuels and the negative impacts of conventional high-input agriculture has had on society and the environment. For promoting ecological security in CGG areas, the following four policy recommendations:

Agricultural policies meeting ecological security requirements should be inclusive and cross-sectoral and developed in collaboration with social movements, scientists, educators and others.

Realizing the full potential of ecological security would require not only policies relating to crop production, but also incentive policies and policies addressing issues such as poverty alleviation, health (food safety), education and environment conservation.

Farming practices meeting ecological security requirements should be largely based on context-specific and locally adapted knowledge of complex dynamic ecological and human systems. This would require the need to foster the co-creation of knowledge between farmers, extension agents, scientists and local decision-makers as well as among farmers.

Ecological security policies should recognize the potential of ecological farming practices for climate resilience and mitigation. The fact the matter is that ecological farming systems can play an important role in mitigating the effects of climate change through carbon storage solutions based on enhanced biodiversity and increase organic content in soils; and finally.

For ecological farming practices to be successful, it would be critical to improve market access for agro-ecological products through the creation of value chains establishing direct producer-consumer relations; public procurement policies oriented towards agro-ecological products; and the promotion campaigns focused on the nutritional value of agro-ecological products.

2. Main Features of the Proposed Ecological Security Strategy

2.1 Ecological security strategic functions

Three strategic functions should be ascribed to improving ecological security in CGG areas. They include:

First, actions to improve ecological security should be designed to secure or even improve crop productivity capacity as to enhance and even improve CGG areas food security role;

Second, actions to improve ecological security should aim at eliminating the negative factors affecting crop productivity and food safety and controlling negative externalities, such as of soil and water pollution, decrease in groundwater availability, and climate change;

Third, actions to improve ecological security should aim at improving farmers' livelihood.

2.2 Strategic lines of actions to improve ecological security in CGG areas

Addressing the negative factors affecting sustainable agriculture in CGG areas would, therefore, require four strategic lines of actions to be implemented in an integrated fashion. These strategic lines should be complemented by a series of policy and governance measures. There are no such single groups of actions that can individually reach the final goal of improving ecological security in CGG areas of China.

The first strategic line of action would refer to, the establishment of an agricultural NPS pollution control system. Lessening the use of chemical fertilizers and pesticides and, thus decreasing agricultural NPS pollution would require the reform of the current system of agricultural input subsidy policies, including the enactment of preferential subsidies for the application of environmentally friendly fertilizers and pesticides strict control of the use of synthetic fertilizers and pesticides through the issuance of quota, the development of new fermentation technologies for the promotion of organic fertilizers' supply and application system that would make more convenient their use, emphasizing the complementarity between NPK and micro nutrient-enriched fertilization and organic fertilization to meet nutrition needs of crops through soil testing as to reduce the amount of chemical fertilizers, the establishment of crop diseases and insect pests biological control systems and the extension of mechanized of mechanized pesticide spreading technologies for reducing the use synthetic pesticides.

The second strategic line of action would refer to, the development of a water resources conservation system with the following four-fold objectives:

Enhancement of water-saving technologies to increase the efficiency of reservoir, canal and irrigation infrastructure systems, including the issuance of marketable water coupons to encourage farmers reducing their own water irrigation consumption. Adjustment of the planting patterns to natural soil moisture and water resources availability according to seasons, soil characteristics and location; and Promotion of dry-farming techniques, including no-tillage farming and plastic film coverage technologies to reduce evaporation of soil moisture, top soil erosion and improve beneficial insects and soil microbes.

The third strategic line of action should include, the rehabilitation and expansion of the farmland protection forests systems adapted to local conditions, including rehabilitating and expanding farmland protection forests based on four layers of protection, including:

The first layer of farmland protection refers to reforestation, forest management, grazing restriction, the building up of soil and water conservation forests, nature reserves and recreation forests in the hills and mountain forests surrounding CGG areas; The second layer of protection refer to the establishment of forest belts (windbreaks, shelterbelts, riparian buffer forests, etc.) planted on both sides of highways, railways, provincial/municipal and county roads, rivers and canals; The third layer of protection includes the rehabilitation and development of new village forests and various kinds of economic forests, timber forests, and recreation and scenic forests should characterize the third layer of protection; and finally, establishing farmland protection forests in the framework of the development of high-standard farmland should be considered the fourth layer of protection. This fourth layer of protection may also include tree plating along roads at township and village levels as well as, where suitable tree-crop intercropping practices, notably for the rehabilitation of degraded and/or heavy polluted agriculture lands.

As for the fourth strategic line of action, it would refer to, the development of ecological farming field practices at farm level. Transforming conventional high-input agriculture is going to be a tremendous challenge and work on various fronts as the transition process towards more sustainable agricultural systems respecting ecological security standards would be complex, requiring changes in field practices, day-to-day management operations at farm level, planning and marketing. The objectives of promoting ecological farming practices would be three-fold: (i) enhancing the beneficial biological interactions and synergies among the components of the agro-biodiversity systems as to enhance ecological services, rather than focusing only on mono-crops species; (ii) incorporating the concept of long-term sustainability into the overall agro-ecosystem design and management; and (iii) most highly valuing the overall health of the agro-system rather than the outcome of a particular cropping system. The following principles can serve as general guidelines for inducing the change process at farm level. [1]

Emphasizing in an integrated manner the conservation of soil, water and energy and biological resources.

Optimizing the use of nutrients and energy at the farm level for providing the most favorable soil condition for plant growth. Optimizing nutrients at farm level would require: (i) enhancing the recycling of biomass with a view of optimizing organic matter; (ii) minimizing losses of energy, water, nutrients and genetic resources; (iii) using large quantities of different types of organic materials on a regular basis (animal manures, compost, tree leaves, cover crops, and rotation crops that leave large amounts of residues); and (iv) avoiding (or minimizing the unnecessary use of agrochemicals that may affect the environment and human health.

Improving water harvesting efficiency.

Reducing soil compaction by reducing tillage or adopting no tillage technology.

---

① FAO, "Agro-ecology for Food Security and Nutrition; Proceeding of FAO International Symposium", *Rome*, 2014.

Diversifying species and genetic resources (at field and landscape level) to strengthen the agricultural systems auto-immune capacities by enhancing biological management, which can prevent pests and disease rather than instead of "controlling" them with chemical inputs such as synthetic herbicides.

Respecting local knowledge and experience of farmers in agro-ecosystems design and management.

3. Implementation Arrangements

3.1 Policy support requirements

Implementing with success the above four strategic lines of action require the support of three groups of policies aimed at improving ecological security. They include compulsory policies, incentive policies and coordination policies as described below:

Compulsory policies. They should include the enactment of new agricultural laws and regulations focused on ecological security requirements with due respect to conserving soil fertility, controlling soil erosion, improving irrigation efficiency, strictly controlling the use of synthetic fertilizers and pesticides for the protection of soil and water from pollution and eutrophication and promoting the protection of farmland through the establishment and maintenance of farmland protection forests and, where required, ecologically and financially attractive on-farm tree-crop intercropping systems.

Incentive policies. Three types of incentive policies would be required: first, the enactment of regulations including the payment of bonus to farmers who use chemical fertilizers less than fixed quota; second, the issuance of marketable water coupons to encourage farmers reducing their own water consumption; and third, eco-compensation measures to encourage farmers to protect their ecological environment as well as develop and maintain farmland protection forests.

Coordination policies. In addition to compulsory and incentive policies, enhancing ecological security in CGG areas will require the coordination of economic, technical and resource management policies. In that sense, it should be anticipated that all product subsidies should be adjusted to ecological requirements: (i) existing agricultural subsidy policies should be discontinued, while preferential subsidies should be ordained for the application of environmentally friendly fertilizers and pesticides; (ii) irrigation water saving technologies should be promoted as to decrease pressures on groundwater; and (iii) the management, development and maintenance of farmland protection forests should be stimulated through better policy coordination between agriculture and forestry departments as to improve the conditions for the development of ecological farming practices. In this respect, their configuration should be adjusted to uneven arrangements depending on local farming conditions and protection requirements. Such uneven arrangements should include trees of various species, characteristics and ages, keeping in mind the need to reduce their negative border effects on crop production.

3.2 Inter-sectoral coordination requirements

On the institutional front, successful implementation of ecological security in the CGG areas would require cross-sector cooperation among those departments that are mandated by the government to implement their own sector development strategies. These institutional crucial actors need to go beyond isolationism and commit themselves to policy collaboration and coordination among their departments (horizontal collaboration) and with other decentralized institutions (vertical collaboration with county and township authorities as well as with other actors such as farmers' communities and NGOs). However, as of today, current integrated policies aimed at improving ecological security in CGG areas are tragically flawed due to sector institutions' predisposition to lean towards sectoral programs instead of more broad-based approaches aimed at improving the type of horizontal and vertical collaboration needed to improve the ecological security in CGG areas.

Therefore, one of the major institutional prerequisites to improve ecological security in CGG areas refers to the need to promote mutually consistent interdepartmental collaboration. Meeting this prerequisite will require four requirements: (i) the first would be to enhance a sense of cooperation, stimulate collaborative demands, and emphasize complementary advantages to eliminate the many disadvantages of sector resource allocation; (ii) the second is to regulate inter-departmental coordination while ensuring symmetry of participant's rights, responsibilities and benefits; (iii) the third one is to accelerate information exchange, making it more efficient and more comprehensive as to make respective services more open, more transparent and more useful; and (iv) the fourth is to lessen collaborative risks by establishing exit mechanism and punishing uncooperative behaviors.

To be specific, the ecological security strategy calls for five levels of collaboration/ cooperation. They include:
- Collaboration/cooperation between government sector agencies;
- Collaboration/cooperation between government sector agencies and local government institutions;
- Collaboration/cooperation between the local governments and villages; and
- Collaboration among farmers;
- The cooperation between third-party monitoring and evaluation agencies and stakeholders.

3.3 Monitoring and evaluation requirements

The setting up of an inter-sector ecological security monitoring and evaluation system (M&E) should complement the above four strategic lines of actions and institutional coordination requirements. It should be aimed at monitoring and evaluating measures taken to control groundwater level, agricultural NPS pollution and soil quality as well as the efficiency and effectiveness of the four level of forest protection. Monitoring and evaluation should be organized as a three-tier system with expertise from relevant departments, farmers and external M&E experts. Monitoring and evaluation methods should be simple, cheap, and effective. Monitoring and evaluation indicators should have simple, accurate and stable features, which can easily be monitored with the analysis of remote sensing data, fixed sample survey, random sampling checks. Finally, the M&E system should be complemented by an information disclosure system.

To lead to effective the proposed M&E system requires efficient cooperation between the third party M&E, government institutions and farmers.

3.4 Eco-compensation requirements

China has been officially piloting eco-compensation projects since the early 2000, notably through the development of the 16 priority ecological protection projects, (e.g.

Natural Forest Protection Program), ecological damage restoration projects (e.g. Beijing-Tianjin Sandstorm Control Program), ecological grants and subsidies (e.g. Conversion of Cropland to Forest and Grassland Program [①]). All these programs have four features in common that should be emphasized when promoting eco-compensation payments to improve ecological security in CGG areas.

The primary driver of eco-compensation is the State and, the main source of financing with market mechanisms remaining for the time being at an incipient stage, though the government recognizes that the participation of market actors should be mobilized to alleviate pressure on government financial resources.

The participation to eco-compensation programs should be mandatory, after negotiation with intended beneficiaries/farmers.

Existing eco-compensation transfer payments should be both vertical (central government to provinces) and horizontal (provinces to municipalities/counties to beneficiaries).

Eco-compensation system design should largely depend on local situations, thus creating a diversity of measures governing how eco-compensation payments would be allocated to intended beneficiaries/farmers and how they should be used.

Notwithstanding those definitions, in practice, eco-compensation in China is a de facto subsidy system paid as a conditional transfer form governments to private actors to promote environmental actions to improve externalities in the production of basic goods (e.g. environmental conservation, hydroelectricity, carbon offsetting, agriculture productivity, etc.). To be more explicit, from an economic efficiency viewpoint, eco-compensation payments concentrate on actors who should (or would) modify their behavior for environmental conservation as a direct consequence of the incentive proposed and exclude those whose practices do not threaten the productive capacity of the environment. Accordingly, not paying/rewarding people who do not threaten the environment should not be seen as unfair, since their livelihoods are not affected by conservation restrictions, nor are they incurring conservation costs.

[①] The SLCP is a compendium of environmental policies and instruments including fiscal reforms using a series of conditional transfers (CTs) alongside wider policies promoting off-farm income to encourage ecological restoration and contribute towards China's vision of "eco-civilization". As of 2015, investments totaled US$ 69 billion.

3.5   Objectives of compensation programs in CGG areas

Eco-compensation payments should demonstrate that they would contribute to specific environmental program objectives as well as to the well being of people. In other words, eco-compensation payments should not be limited to environmental objectives, but should encompass poverty reduction objectives. In this respect, eco-compensation programs that seek to change behaviors towards positive environmental actions (e.g. improving ecological security) may use different incentive packages that may be including a mix of cash and in-kind rewards.

Furthermore, eco-compensation programs in CGG areas should have three major functions in common: (i) to stimulate ecological protection in accordance to local situations; (ii) to promote social equity through the positive internalization of externalities; and (iii) to promote regional cooperation and coordinated development. In its context, ecological compensation basically includes three types of stakeholders: beneficiaries, in particular farmers, the sector departments concerned and environmental protection organizations. Those three stakeholders also explain the reasons why ecological compensation measures may have diversified features.

With due consideration given to the above three functions, since CGG areas have the dual function of producing agricultural crops for food security and of providing ecological services, it is of chief importance to bring them into the scope of an eco-compensation policy. For doing so, a special attention should be paid to the following points:

i. First, eco-compensation should only be paid for ecological security and environmental protection activities that could not be paid by the market;

ii. Second, eco-compensation should be linked to the value of ecological services resulting from environmental protection activities;

iii. Third, eco-compensation should be based on either the ecological service value of ecological protection or the opportunity costs of it;

iv. Fourth, while it would not be wise to link eco-compensation with production loss due to ecological protection measures that should be contemplated as part of opportunity costs. However, those production losses should be considered as the basis for the calculation of eco-compensation payments.

As a result, the chief principle governing eco-compensation in CGG areas would be that those who would benefit and those who would be affected by ecological security construction should be the beneficiaries of eco-compensation. Furthermore, such eco-compensation system should ensure symmetry of rights and obligations, be related to incremental ecological services, be linked to effective supervision mechanisms and, above all, be dependent of a scientific performance monitoring and evaluation system. In order to eliminate unintended inflation of eco-compensation payments, the amount of compensation payments shall be calculated according to the actual price of grain harvest.

3.6   Eco-compensation measures to be promoted in CGG areas

To advance ecological security in CGG areas, eco-compensation payments should primarily be addressed to the construction of farmland protection forests, Within the context of the proposed four layers of protection, they should focus on both: (i) reforestation in mountains or hills surrounding CGG areas (first layer of protection); and (ii) farmland protection forests to be established in the framework of the development of high-standard farmland and along lower level country-side roads and canals (fourth layer of protection). They both could be used in parallel or aside or in complement to standards, regulations, fiscal instruments, prohibitions, and infrastructure development and/or education programs.

For the reforestation of hills or mountains surrounding CGG areas, eco-compensation standards should be in line with those established under the Grain for Green Project, i.e. based on opportunity costs or the maximum benefit farmers could get from their farmland if the land is used for forestry-related ecological security purpose.

For farmland protection forests to be established as part of the construction of high standard farmland, individual eco-compensation measures should be based on tree-planting compensation according to the number of trees planted on farmland and their respective plantation, management and maintenance costs; and production loss compensation calculated on the basis of production loss due to the border effects of farmland protection forests.

In both cases, eco-compensation payments should be made to address the positive and/or negative environmental externalities imparted by the maintenance and scaling up of reforestation and farmland protection forests (in cash or in-kind or mixed) on the premises that those forestry structures will enhance ecological security in CGG areas or protect specific ecosystem services. Those payments could be made in parallel or aside or in complement to standards, regulations, fiscal instruments, prohibitions and/ or education programs that would be promoted by central or provincial governments to enhance ecological security in CGG areas.

When organizing such eco-compensation program, it would be imperative that finance, forestry, agriculture departments and farmers' representatives jointly approve the purpose of ecological compensation and their related standards. Moreover, ecological compensation payments must directly be paid to concerned households after verification and public posting. Furthermore, beneficiary farmers must participate to the monitoring and evaluation of the efficiency and effectiveness of eco-compensation disbursements/payments.

For farmland protection forests to be established along infrastructure (second layer of protection), no eco-compensation measures should be foreseen as the land devoted to farmland protection forests to be established along large infrastructure is already under the jurisdiction of related institutions and, as such, developed by those institutions. As for the greening of villages (third layer of protection), conditional transfer payments relative to their development costs should be preferred to eco-compensation payments.

Transfer payment for biodiversity conservation in Swiss grssslands

Increasing biodiversity in agricultural landscapes in one of the goals for the Swiss Federal Constitution and one of the tasks of multi-functional agriculture. Forty percent of Switzerland is comprised of agricultural grassland. Due to this large area and the strong effect of management intensity on biodiversity, grassland management is crucial for species richness of the entire country. In 1993, the Swiss government with the aim to reverse species decline introduced an agri-environmental program. Within this program, the farmer needs to manage at least 7 % of the farm's utilized agricultural area (UAA) in accordance with rules laid down for ecological compensation areas (ECA). In return the farmer will receive basic payments per year and per ha subject to cross-compliance. More recently. the Swiss Parliament enacted a new direct payment system which, from 2014, assigns societal objectives to each kind of payment, paying tribute to the Tinbergen principle according to which each objective has to be followed by at least one instrument. Payments for Ensuring Food Supplies, for example, will be paid per hectare dependent on the production capacity; *Biodiversity Payments* will be paid only for land with a lot of species on it. Animal-based payments, which still play an important role today are being abandoned. Although the new system is neither changing the amount of money transferred to farmers nor expected to rapidly change the structure of Swiss agriculture, it is argued that the system change may well be historic, because it makes societal transfers to agriculture more prone to critical analysis and evaluation and because it shows for the first time what the application of the Tinbergen principle to multifunctionality policy design could look like.

3.7 Eco-compensation best practices

Many useful lessons can be drawn from worldwide PES experience [1] , including from the SLCP eco-compensation program. They were all pointing to the crucial and inextricable link between institutions and incentives. For eco-compensation measures to succeed, the following critical rules should apply:

Enhancing farmers' ownership of the eco-compensation programs. This would require linking social protection and ecological conservation to increase farmers' commitment to environmental management and conservation. In this respect, the eco-compensation program should be sensitive to local heterogeneity in term of both environmental considerations and local economic situation. In this regard, poverty reduction in the context of local economic development and environmental restoration' needs should be given a particular attention when targeting eco-compensation payments. Targeting the most disadvantaged communities, notably those affected by environmental degradation and a strong focus on the creation of off-farm alternative livelihood options in nearby towns would be key to enhance farmers' participation [2] .

Scaling up eco-compensation programs of large scale would require an intense focus on planning, managing, demonstration and piloting. In this respect, large scale eco-compensation programs should encourage the formation of groups of farmers or intended beneficiaries through, for instance, agglomeration bonuses. Such groups of farmers could

---

[1] For more details, refer to *Ecosystems, poverty alleviation and conditional transfers: Guidance for practitioners* (edited by Ina Porras (IIED) and Nigel Asquith (Fundacion Nature). The full document is available under http://pubs.iied.org/pdfs/16639IIED.pdf.

[2] Duan et al.,"The effects of the SLCP on poverty alleviation in the Wulin Mountainous Areas",*Small Scale Forestry*, 2015, 14 (3) pp. 331-350; Li et al.,"Assessing the decadal impact of China SLCP on household income", *Forest Policy and Economics*, 2015, (61) , pp. 95-103; Wang et al., "Impacts of regional payments for ecosystem service program on livelihoods of different rural households*", Journal of Cleaner Production,* 2017 (164) , pp.1058-1067.

apply together to the intended eco-compensation program.

Obtaining a strong political support to the eco-compensation program and ultimately the availability of sustainable financing means would both be decisive, as they would define whether the eco-compensation program could reach sufficient scale. This requires government to have a clear and long-term strategy to generate sufficient funding for eco-compensation. In this respect, a particular attention should be given to the creation of independent trust funds as well as the diversification of the portfolio of economic instruments for capitalization.

What would also be required is the establishment of an independent M&E systems focused both on the impacts on the eco-compensation program on the quality of the environment and livelihoods, notably on poverty reduction. Such M&E systems should be considered as one of the necessary tools to improve the adaptive capacity of eco-compensation programs in the long run as to, for instance, minimize conflicts among group of participating farmers.

Finally, enhancing capacity building bringing scientific advances in modeling, planning, implementing and monitoring eco-compensation programs to better understand conditions for behavioral changes would be critical in scaling up eco-compensation programs. As for extension, a particular attention should be given to the "training of trainers" to improve the capacities of the various stakeholders involved in the eco-compensation program.

3.8 Systems and tools for the effective implementation of the eco-compensation in CGG areas

Based on the above recommendations, the development and maintenance of farmland protection forests with the support of ecological compensation measures should respond to at least the following basic requirements.

A clear identification of intended beneficiaries and capacities, in particular with reference to local socioeconomic and environmental conditions.

A clear identification of eco-compensation payment types. They can vary from cash rewards by direct transfers, to in-kind rewards, to mixed rewards. In kind rewards may include investments at community level reflecting the fact that improving ecological services of farmland protection forests would require group actions and that their impacts go beyond individual farm while mixed rewards could include investments for community infrastructure and/or education in combination with cash transfers; In case of cash transfers, direct and faster payments to beneficiaries through established financial institutions should be preferred.

A clear and efficient cross-sector institutional setup including management/ supervision and monitoring [①] systems when operating at large scales, notably coordination across different sectors, i.e. between forestry, agriculture, social affairs an environmental department.

The availability of a local technical managerial capacity. This would require matching farmers' and extension staffs' capacity and training activities at various levels (including at village level) and, when needed, re-deployment of extension staff;

Clarity of land and tree tenure security as an intrinsic but essential factor of the capacity of eco-compensation manager to enforce conditionality.

A clear identification of protection needs. Farmland protection forests or tree-crop intercropping should only be established where needs arise notably in view of restoring soil fertility, decreasing adverse impacts of weather-related disasters, stabilizing (or increasing) grain yields; improving farmers' incomes; etc..

Meeting protection efficiency. The design, setting and composition of farmland protection forests should maximize their protection efficiency and effectiveness, in particular with regard to improving grain yields and farmers' incomes.

Not being harmful to surrounding farmlands and households.

4. Food Security in the Context of China Agenda 2030

4.1 *Transforming our World: the 2030 Agenda for Sustainable Development*

In September 2015, in line with the Ecological Civilization concept. China endorsed the U.N. Agenda 2030 at the United Nations Sustainable Development Summit.

---

① Hu Zhentong ," Grassland Eco-compensation in China: What can and what cannot ne monitored?", China Institute for Rural Studies, Tsinghua University (5th International Conference on Eco-compensation).

Transforming our World: the 2030 Agenda for Sustainable Development [①] is aimed at providing guidance to national and international cooperation, dwelling momentum towards the implementation of concrete actions addressing various global challenges, speeding up the economic and ecological transformation. As a matter of fact, the 13th Five-Year Plan approved by the 12th National People Congress in 2016 contains a strong commitment to the active implementation and integration of the Agenda 2030's 17 Social Development Goals (SDGs) and 169 Targets, thus achieving the synergy between the 2030 Agenda and the PRC's mid-term and long-term development strategies as specified in the context of the eco-civilization concept. Provincial, autonomous regions and municipalities' development plans [②] are or will complement such national commitment.

With regard to agriculture, most, if not all, Agenda 2030's SDGs are directly or indirectly connected with farming, conferring a special multi-dimensional status to agriculture. In effect, the SDGs cross the whole range of sustainable agriculture policy areas. Those Agenda 2030 Goals are intended to be a guideline for sustainable agriculture development for all governments, governments of developed and least developing countries alike. If some goals are mainly socioeconomic in nature (1, 4, 5, 8–11, 16, 17), others focus on biophysical systems, in which sustainable agriculture for food security plays a clear role. Notwithstanding this distinction, these two realms define together human capacity to manage food production and agriculture ecosystem services and mutually depend on each other: for achieving goals with a socioeconomic focus, the associated dynamic behavior of ecosystems need to be taken into account, while for achieving a goal with an ecosystem focus, one should consider socioeconomic aspects.

Table 12   U.N. 2030 Agenda's Relevance to Food Security in China CGG areas

U.N. Agenda 2030's Goals	Agenda 2030's Targets Relevant to Food Security
Goal 1&2: End poverty hunger, achieve food security, improve nutrition and promote sustainable agriculture	Concerns the development of agricultural policies focused on poverty reduction and increasing investments in agriculture research, extension services and technology, which would be key to improving agricultural productivity
Goal 3: Ensure healthy lives and promote well being	Concerns the reduction of health hazards due to hazardous chemicals and air, soil and water pollution

---

① See: *Transforming our World: the 2030 Agenda for Sustainable Development*, https://sustainabledevelo pment.un.org/post2015/transformingourworld.

② See: *China's National plan on Implementation of the 2030 Agenda for Sustainable Development*, Sept, 2016, http:// www.fmprc.gov.cn/mfa eng/zxxx 662805/w020161014332600482185.pdf.

continued table

U.N. Agenda 2030's Goals	Agenda 2030's Targets Relevant to Food Security
Goal 6: Ensure availability and sustainable management of water and sanitation for all	Concerns the improvement of irrigation efficiency and water quality through the reduction of NPS pollution and the protection of water-related ecosystems
Goal 8: Promote productive inclusive and sustainable economic growth, productive employment and decent work to all	Concerns farmers' access to financial services and insurance and improvement of resource use efficiency
Goal 9: Build resilient infrastructure, promote inclusive and sustainable industrialization and foster innovation	Concerns farmers and agriculture SMEs' access to financial services and compensation to improve ecological security and in case of weather-related disasters (droughts, flooding) and their integration into value chains
Goal 11: Make cities and rural settlements inclusive, safe, resilient and sustainable	Concerns greening of agricultural landscapes including villages' and rural settlements
Goal 12: Ensure sustainable consumption and production patterns	Concerns efficient use of natural resources (soils, water, biodiversity), environmentally sound management of agrochemicals, the development of climate-smart agriculture and the reduction of environmentally harmful subsidies
Goal 15: Protect, restore, and promote sustainable use of terrestrial ecosystems, sustainably manage forests, combat desertification and reverse land degradation and biodiversity loss	Concerns the sustainable use of available soil and water resources, the promotion of sustainable forest management, the restoration of degraded soils, combating desertification and the prevention of biodiversity loss.
Goal 16: Promote peaceful and inclusive societies for sustainable development, and build inclusive institutions at all levels	Concerns efficient integrated cross-sector institutions, improvement of horizontal and vertical institutional cooperation, notably with local governments (agriculture, forestry, environment, infrastructure, etc.)

Placing the eradication of poverty and hunger as the first key intervention areas, the China's commitment to Agenda 2030 reflects the primacy given by China to sustainable agriculture and food security. Furthermore, putting hunger nutrition, poverty, eco-security, learning, innovations and sustainability issues among the key indicators of growth support the critical role played by agriculture in China's sustainable economic development. The nine key intervention areas highlighted in the table 12 above also indicate that sustainable agriculture needs to be "farmers' centered" and "knowledge-based" so that the full potential of farmers, both men and women, including small holders and agriculture commercial entities, can be harnessed in making food security and sustainable development a reality. Clearly speaking, sustainable agriculture development will not only depend on policies or institutional arrangements, but, primarily, on the actions and behaviors of land users such as farmers or forest managers. As a result, the

Agenda 2030 presents real challenges to China's agriculture in its various policy arenas and institutional frameworks.

2016 was the first year of implementing the Agenda 2030 in China. *The China's Progress Report in Implementation of the 2030 Agenda*, published in August 2017, which is highlighting China Agenda 2030 priority intervention areas in the context of sustainable agriculture development, is emphasizing the relationship between the objectives of China Agenda 2030 and ecological security in CGG areas, i.e. between intervention policies and institutional mechanisms, structural change, innovation, access to healthy soils and clean water (as critical natural resources), climate change and agricultural productivity. Those intervention policies and institutional mechanisms should be considered the key drivers of productivity growth and sustainability in CGG areas. More specifically, the report reaffirmed that improving ecological security in CGG with the effective participation of farmers would be facilitated by four groups of incentive policies.

Economic stability and trust in institutions (security, property rights, justice), which are essential to attract farmers' participation and investment.

Public and private investments that would ensure sustainable uses of natural resources (soils and water in particular), facilitate the adoption of innovation, in particular ecological security measures, and access to markets, capital and knowledge.

Capacity building, notably to increase extension services efficiency would facilitate the adoption of ecological security measures and innovations, and improve farmers' skills needed to accept innovation and improve resource use efficiency.

Agricultural sector-specific policies for structural change, sustainable resource use, incentives for innovation and risk management, should include: (i) economic policies: adjustment of subsidies and enactment of regulations responding to ecological security needs; (ii) incentive polices to encourage farmers to contribute to ecological security needs; and (iii) technical and resource policies to enhance the efficiency and effectiveness of agro-environmental measures.

4.2 Ecological security in the context of China Agenda 2030

Ecological security is central to both food security as anticipated by the policy documents related to sustainable agriculture development, climate change and biodiversity conservation and, as a result, the China 2030 Agenda. As mentioned earlier, ecological security is critical to the sustainable development of human society, which includes air security, land security, water security, resource security, biological security, environmental security, food security, and social order, etc.. As such, it can be best defined as the maintenance of dynamic equilibriums in continually evolving relationships among human societies and key components of the ecosystems in which human activities are embedded. In other words, ecological security refers to the capacity to addressing situations that are threatening human survival, health, food security and food safety, social security, and social order. In practice, ecological security assessment does reveals various challenges caused by land degradation, deforestation, desertification, water and air pollution, energy shortage, greenhouse gas emissions, and global climate change. As a result, the objective of an Ecological Security Strategy is to propose the development and implementation of appropriate ecological policies and governance frameworks aimed at both preventing the negative impacts of these problems on agricultural productivity, food security, food safety and livelihoods and, when and where needs arise, restoring already damaged ecosystems.

However, the high-input type of agriculture developed in CGG areas during the past decades has required the use of a wide range of physical, biological and chemical inputs, including irrigation, tractors, chemical fertilizers and pesticides, the breeding of high yield varieties, and the development of fast growing cultivars that has allowed, during the past decades, the doubling or even the tripling of crop productivity. While this high-input agriculture has been a highly beneficial approach to increase food production, and, as a result, China's food security, it had a number of drawbacks in terms of high capital investments' and high water and energy requirements leading to the rapid depletion of groundwater, NPS agriculture pollution due to excessive use of chemical fertilizers and pesticides, top soil and organic matter erosion, the development of pest resistance to chemical control measures and last but not least the degradation of existing natural biological resources and of the farmland protection forests established during the collective time.

The table 13 below is summarizing the relations between the policy objectives of U.N. Agenda 2030 and recommended ecological security measures to improve long-term agricultural productivity in CGG areas.

Table 13　The Relation of Sustainable Goals and Food Security Goals

SDG Goals \ Food and Ecological Security	Improve cropping productivity for food security	Decrease agriculture soil and water NPS pollution	Improve irrigation efficiency and control groundwater levels	Improve soil water storage capacity	Enhance the protective effects of farmland protection forests	Enhance carbon storage in soils and mitigate emission of GHGs	Decrease impact of weather anomalies on crop production	Provide raw material	Restore and manage soil fertility and enhance nutrients cycles	Regulate agricultural pests and diseases population	Improve aesthetic and promote recreation	Reform unfavorable structural, and economic policies and enact compulsory policies to enhance ecological security	Provide incentive policies and environmental compensation	Revise inadequate sector policies	Improve inter-sectoral horizontal and vertical collaboration and cooperation collaboration/cooperation	Improve extension effectiveness and efficiency
End poverty in all forms	×		×		×		×	×	×	×		×	×	×	×	×
End hunger, achieve food security and improve nutrition	×	×	×				×		×	×				×	×	×
Ensure healthy lives and promote well being	×					×	×	×	×	×	×					
Ensure equitable and inclusive quality education and provide life-long learning opportunities																×
Achieve gender equality and empower woman																
Ensure availability and sustainable management of water and sanitation for all		×	×	×	×											
Ensure access to affordable, reliable and sustainable energy						×		×								
Promote productive inclusive and sustainable economic growth, productive employment and decent work to all	×	×	×				×	×								

continued table

Food and Ecological Security / SDG Goals	Improve cropping productivity for food security	Decrease agriculture soil and water NPS pollution	Improve irrigation efficiency and control groundwater levels	Improve soil water storage capacity	Enhance the protective effects of farmland protection forests	Enhance carbon storage in soils and mitigate emission of GHGs	Decrease impact of weather anomalies on crop production	Provide raw material	Restore and manage soil fertility and enhance nutrients cycles	Regulate agricultural pests and diseases population	Improve aesthetic and promote recreation	Reform unfavorable structural, and economic policies and enact compulsory policies to enhance ecological security	Provide incentive policies and environmental compensation	Revise inadequate sector policies	Improve inter-sectoral horizontal and vertical collaboration and cooperation collaboration/cooperation	Improve extension effectiveness and efficiency
Build resilient infrastructure, promote inclusive and sustainable industrialization and foster innovation								×						×	×	×
Reduce inequalities within and among countries																
Make cities and human settlements inclusive, safe, resilient and sustainable	×	×		×	×	×										
Ensure sustainable consumption and production patterns	×	×	×	×	×	×	×	×	×	×		×	×	×	×	×
Take urgent action to combat climate change and its impacts					×	×	×		×							
Conserve and sustainably use oceans, seas and marine resources																
Protect, restore, and promote sustainable use of terrestrial ecosystems, sustainably manage forests, combat desertification and halt and reverse land degradation and halt biodiversity loss	×	×	×	×	×	×	×		×			×	×	×	×	×

288 | 中国粮食主产区生态安全研究

continued table

Food and Ecological Security / SDG Goals	Improve cropping productivity for food security	Decrease agriculture soil and water NPS pollution	Improve irrigation efficiency and control groundwater levels	Improve soil water storage capacity	Enhance the protective effects of farmland protection forests	Enhance carbon storage in soils and mitigate emission of GHGs	Decrease impact of weather anomalies on crop production	Provide raw material	Restore and manage soil fertility and enhance nutrients cycles	Regulate agricultural pests and diseases population	Improve aesthetic and promote recreation	Reform unfavorable structural, and economic policies and enact compulsory policies to enhance ecological security	Provide incentive policies and environmental compensation	Revise inadequate sector policies	Improve inter-sectoral horizontal and vertical collaboration and cooperation collaboration/cooperation	Improve extension effectiveness and efficiency
Promote peaceful and inclusive societies for sustainable development, provide access to justice and build inclusive institutions at all levels														×		×
Strengthen the means of implementation and revitalize global partnership for sustainable development						×									×	

5. An Action Plan for Integrating Farmland Protection Forests in CGG Areas Basic Features of the Action Plan

The rationale behind the development of an Action Plan for the integration of farmland protection forests (or four sides) in CGG areas lies to the fact that the protective effect of trees, notably farmland protection forests, which were historically instrumental in providing an ecological security environment favorable to agricultural productivity, notably in protecting farmland against weather related disasters, declined over the recent years-notably due to the reluctance of farmers in absence of eco-compensation measures aimed at maintaining or developing on-and off-farm farmland protection forests' systems in spite of their in-built benefits. In effect, the degradation of farmland protection forests, if not reversed, may lead to catastrophic changes in the ecosystem services CGG areas have historically provided.

The aim of the proposed Action Plan is to translate into specific and concrete actions eco-compensation payments aimed at maintaining and scaling up existing farmland protection forests to improve ecological security in CGG areas. It is based on the following prerequisites.

The first prerequisite is that, if farmers and farmers' community should be considered the primary development actors for the improvement of ecological security in CGG areas, they should also be considered as the primary development actors for the maintenance and scaling up of farmland protection forests.

The second prerequisite is related to the existence of an eco-compensation program to encourage farmers to participate in forestry-related activities aimed at improving ecological security and crop productivity in CGG areas.

The third prerequisite is related to the clarification of farmland protection forests' land/tree tenure and specific management conditions considering the ecological security objectives of those forestry structures.

The fourth prerequisite is that provincial institutions involved in agriculture and forestry development in CGG areas should be able to work much more closely together and share more information and resources with each other than nowadays.

The fifth prerequisite is related to the availability of a three-tier Ecological Security Monitoring and Evaluation (M&E) System, involving related sector institutions, farmers and external independent M&E experts. This three-tier Ecological Security M&E System should be considered a critical management tool to track progress, notably with regard to the relevance and fulfillment of the ecological security strategy's objectives, efficiency, effectiveness, impacts and sustainability of proposed development activities, notably the efficiency and effectiveness of eco-compensation measures directed towards the maintenance and scaling up of farmland protection forest structures.

The sixth prerequisite implies that the design and implementation of farmland protection forest structures aimed at improving ecological security (including farmland protection forests and tree-crop intercropping practices) should respond to and be adapted to local conditions and markets.

The seventh prerequisite refers to the development of applied regional and site-specific inter-disciplinary action research activities to help improving the design of farmland protection forest structures. In selecting and designing applied research projects, priority should be given to: (i) the reduction of the negative impacts of tree roots, shade or trunks on crop productivity; and (ii) the quantification of the direct and indirect economic costs, environmental benefits and risks associated to the building of farmland protection structures for ecological security.

The eighth prerequisite implies the use of modern ICT tools and applications in extension activities that could help fostering linkages between extension professionals and farmers as well as among farmers to foster stronger coordination and engagement with farmers as to increase the adoption of ecological security remedial practices.

5.1 The Six Action Plan Goals

Based on the above prerequisites, the Action Plan has been structured around six main goals that need to be implemented in an integrated fashion. When and if addressed correctly, implementing those goals should lead to a wider adoption and maintenance of farmland protection structures for ecological security. Policymakers should view this Action Plan as a set of actions and tools that would create favorable conditions for the development of such ecological security activities, notably those aimed at maintaining and scaling up farmland protection forest structures. This Action Plan should in clude the following goals:

Goal 1: Raising awareness.The primary aim of raising awareness would be to reverse the current trends of farmland protection forests degradation. This ill-fated situation is due to both a lack of incentives leading to farmers' reluctance to maintain them in proper conditions. Therefore, raising farmers' and decision-makers' knowledge and awareness of the benefits of farmland protection forest structures for ecological security through the development of outreach and training activities would be critical as to make the development of forestry-related activities in CGG areas the work of every farmers and farmers' communities involved in agriculture.

Goal 2: Creating an enabling policy and institutional environment.The building of ecological security in CGG areas is the common task of multiple provincial government departments and stakeholders (including farmers and farmers' communities), who needs to join efforts for its development. However, so far, government agencies were (and still are) operating in CGG areas on a sector basis. More specifically, with regard to the development of forestry-related investments for ecological security, unfavorable legal, policy and institutional arrangements are too often impeding farmers' involvement in their maintenance and expansion to the point that they are continuously degrading. Nor are the ecological security benefits of forestry-related investments sufficiently addressed in provincial policy-making, land-use planning and rural development and land consolidation programs currently principally focused on (irrigated) mono-cropping, industrial agricultural crops and mechanized farming. The general aim of this second goal is, therefore, to overcome institutional fragmentation by (i) improving inter-agency vertical and horizontal coordination/collaboration for better coherence and synergies; (ii) reforming unfavorable forestry and agriculture regulations and legal restrictions that may hamper a genuine farmers' participation; (iii) clarifying legal land and tree tenure conditions; (iv) setting up of a joint-monitoring and evaluation system (M&E) to assess the performances, outcomes and impacts of and lessons to be learned from mainstreaming forestry-related protection structures in CGG areas; and (v) improving budget allocation for ecological security extension at various decentralized scales.

Goal 3: Providing incentives.The main objective of this goal would be to develop and implement a clear policy context for the development of eco-compensation measures aimed at improving farmers' participation. For the time being, if farmers are hoping to get the best ecological services from farmland protection forest structures, they do not want to pay for the ecological protection provided or do not want farmland protection forests interfering on their contracted farmland and related revenues from agriculture. As a result, the aim of this Goal would be to entrust research institutions to conduct systematic researches on the design of a specific eco-compensation and conditional payment transfer program adapted to CGG specific local conditions, and, through consultation meetings, involving relevant parties, to jointly determine the scope, content and implementation modalities of the proposed eco-compensation program for the development of forestry related protection structures for ecological security in CGG areas.

Goal 4: Communicating the know-how. Without a functioning public/private integrated ecological security-related extension system, it would not be possible to successfully rehabilitate and expand forestry-related protection structures to improve ecological security in CGG areas as current overdependence on conventional agricultural and forestry extension methods, inadequate consideration given to ecological security and ecological farming approaches have restricted and still restrict the interest of both policy-makers and farmers for ecological security. Recently, current extension and research efforts were so far mainly focused on mono-cropping systems or reforestation with not sufficient attention given to the potential role of tree species in improving ecological security and sustainable agriculture. This situation was often made worse by a lack of investment in adaptive action-research aimed at improving the productivity and profitability of farmland protection forests' systems. Furthermore, conditions for improving ecological security systems are not yet included in the curricula of agriculture or forestry schools and universities. Therefore, the main objective of this goal is to improve institutional capacity for mainstreaming forestry-related protection structures into the agricultural landscape of CGG areas. This goal, therefore, implies making forestry development for improving ecological security the work of every institution and farmers' communities by improving extension efficiency and effectiveness though education of extension professionals and farmers' communities to bridge forestry and agriculture disciplines, disseminate improved technical knowledge to overcome issues and constraints affecting ecological security and build strong community-based partnerships to enhance ecological security objectives. Actions to be developed under this goal would, therefore, have the dual objective to (i) formulating forestry-related ICT extension strategies that would support the mainstreaming of forestry-related investments for ecological security in the agricultural landscape of the Henan's plain; and (ii) developing capacity building and training program at institutional and individual levels to enable extension professionals to efficiently use modern ICT tools to provide technical, educational, financial and marketing assistance to farmers and farmers' communities.

Goal 5: Advancing the knowledge of forestry for ecological security.Farmland protection forests and other forms of tree-crop intercropping technologies have been used and promoted in China for many centuries as an improved form of land management aimed at improving crop productivity and controlling environmental degradation and weather anomalies. However, overtime, farmland protection forests have very significantly degraded and agro-ecological farming practices abandoned by farmers for agricultural mono-cultural practices. Therefore, developing participatory applied researches to disseminate the anticipated benefits from forestry-related investments and, at the same time, tackle and resolve the main environmental, economic and sociological constraints/issues that would hamper the participation of farmers in the rehabilitation and expansion of forestry-related investments would be critical to the building of ecological security in CGG areas. The main objective of this goal is to improve the ecological and economic efficiency and effectiveness of various customized forms of forestry-related protection structures for ecological security through the development of inter-agency and multidisciplinary applied researches connecting farmers, practitioners, scientists and technical advisors. This, in order to improve the availability of information on the tangible impacts of forestry-related protection structures and their positive linkages between farmland protection forests and ecological security, crop productivity and economic growth.

Goal 6: Adapting forestry-related structures to local environments. The main object of this goal is to improve ecological security in selected priority CGG areas through the planning of investment projects related to the physical development of various types of forestry-related protection structures, notably networks of farmland protection forests. The primary aim of this goal would be to elaborate a priority integrated investment program including the development of forestry-related protection activities to respond to specific local ecological security issues and existing challenges as to create a healthy environment for agriculture production at county, township and village levels. The preparation of such investment program should include: (i) the location of priority areas for intervention based on ecological and climate change/weather-related risks; (ii) the assessment/identification of the respective scope of the above forestry related activities and their related investment and maintenance costs; (iii) the design of support activities tailored to respond to local ecological, socioeconomic and market conditions Such support activities should notably include awareness raising and information campaigns, the identification of extension activities based on an incremental use of ICTs, the development of site specific eco-compensation programs, and a training program aimed at improving the intervention capacities of extension agents.

It has been anticipated that addressing those six goals outlined above in an integrated fashion at counties' level will contribute to the formulation of coherent, interactive and proactive ecological security public strategies that would support the development of forestry-related investments, notably farmland protection forests, aimed at improving ecological security in the CGG areas of China.

VI Implementing Ecological Security Strategies and Improving China Food Security

Nowadays, many people will be distracted by the Covid-19 pandemic and serious associated economic consequences, but climate change and the crisis in the global environment have not diminished in importance or in urgency in this critical year. It will matter greatly what pathways to recovery governments and the society choose as the pandemic recedes.

The COVID-19 pandemic affecting the society as whole should even further reinforce the ecological security recommendations for the building of resilient food system included in the book (for China as well as for other developed and underdeveloped counties). As of today, food produced through the overuse of chemicals and water, in monoculture cropping systems, and intensive animal farming on land (and seas) are degrading soils, water and other natural resources faster than they can reproduce. Moreover, those agricultural practices cause a quarter of all man-made greenhouse gas emissions, with livestock responsible for a half of that. Too many people today suffer from the disruption of the water cycle, soil and water pollution, deterioration of ecosystems, the vertiginous drop in biodiversity, desertification and unsanitary urban concentrations. Issues affecting today food systems may expose the society to ever-larger heath and financial shocks as climate change and population grow.

Moreover, the pandemic has shown that sectors crucial to food security do not operate independently. For decades, thinking and strategies around food systems have developed in silos, with little coordination between communities working in agriculture, water, environment, forest, health, climate, trade and transport. Integrating these seemingly distinct domains would be crucial to emerge stronger from the pandemic.

Taking an integrated thinking system view, as proposed in this book, would allow policy-makers and the society to tackle complex questions, such as: How can food systems ensure abundant harvests meeting nutrition food for people in China by 2050 sustaining natural habitats and healthy ecosystems? How can water used for irrigation be more ecologically sound? How to reduce NPS pollution from agricultural activities? How can trees and forests integrated into agricultural landscapes benefit agricultural production in a changing climate environment? How can farmers be empowered to adapt to and help fight climate change? How can food systems help eliminate diet-related diseases? How can food systems improve farmers' livelihood? How to articulate and adopt integrated plan for food system transformation?

The rebuilding of economies after the COVID–19 crisis, therefore, offers, a unique opportunity to rethink the current food systems and the way we produce, distribute and consume food as for food production system to become more resilient to future shocks-that are likely to happen due to climate change, to build a healthier world and to ensure environmentally sustainable and healthy nutrition to all.

In 2008, the Asian Development Bank (ADB) issued a *Long-Term Strategic Framework 2008–2020* (the ADB Strategy 2020) to firmly set the institution's goals towards 2020. Although focused on three critical strategic agendas: inclusive economic development, environmentally sustainable growth and regional integration, the ADB Strategy 2020 is addressing a broad range of sustainable development issues and challenges faced Asian and Pacific countries. It notably stresses the fact that, if poverty eradication remains a central challenge for Asian and Pacific countries, their rapid economic growth is putting severe strains on the environment, notably due to the widespread pollution of air, soils and water, the destruction of the natural resource base and climate change. Undoubtedly, these severe strains are (and will be) undermining governments' efforts to improve agricultural productivity and food security.

With regard more specifically to China, the ADB's Board of Directors endorsed, on February 2016, a new Country Partnership Strategy (CPS) for the period 2016–2020. The aim of this CPS is to support the government of China's reform agenda, notably addressing climate change and the environment issues, knowledge cooperation and institutional and governance reform. For the CPS, most of the climate change and environmental challenges facing China's agricultural sector are of such seriousness that transformational responses are urgently needed. In effect, estimates of the costs of water and soil pollution and ecosystem degradation in China, although difficult to assess, range from 6 percent to 9 percent of the gross domestic product (GDP). According to a recent study[①] , air, soil and water pollution and ecosystem degradation are not only undermining agricultural productivity and other resource-based industry but also were contributing to 1.2 million premature deaths in 2010. Furthermore, China is exposed to significant and increasing climate change risks. Climate change projections for 2100 indicate that temperatures are expected to increase by up to 4.5 degrees in the north and in the west, and up to 3 degrees in the southeast. As for precipitations, if they are likely to increase by up to 20 percent in the northeast with southeast receiving minimal or no increase, their variability is of major concern. Of the 120 million hectares of agricultural land, the average area currently affected by crop failure due to climate-related disasters such as severe storms, droughts, floods, and landslides is currently estimated at approximately 39.17 million hectares.

1. China Food Security Challenges

1.1   The food security concept

The concept of food security was first proposed at the time of the 1972–1974 world food crisis. In 1974 when the Food and Agriculture Organization of the United Nations (FAO) pointed out in the International Undertaking on World Food Security that food security should be considered as a basic survival rights to human beings. This definition is based on the fact that the availability, at all times, of adequate, nourishing, diverse, balanced and moderate world food supplies of basic foodstuffs should be considered when sustaining a steady expansion of food consumption and off-setting fluctuations in production and prices. During the past 40 years, the meaning of food security has gradually evolved from a quantity-based towards a quality-based concept, i.e. from food security to food safety, resource security and ecological security.

---

① Horton R., "Global Burden of Disease Study", *The Lancet*, 2012(380).

From a global perspective, agriculture in the 21st century, with a population expected to increase up to about 9.1 billion people by 2050, is facing multiple challenges. Globally, the world has to produce more food to feed a growing population with a smaller labor force, more feedstock for a potentially huge bioenergy market, while contributing to the overall development, adopting more efficient and sustainable production methods and adapting to climate change. This implies that feeding a population of 9.1 billion people would require raising overall food production by some 70% between the 2005/2007 level and 2050. According to FAO [①] , meeting the above food security challenge will require: (i) investments in sectors strongly linked to agriculture productivity growth, such as rural infrastructure (roads, power, storage and irrigation systems); (ii) investments in institutions to improve farmers' environment (research, extension services, land tenure systems, veterinary and food safety control systems and insurance); (iii) non-agricultural investment to bring about positive impacts on human well-being, including targeted food safety nets, social programs and cash transfers to the most needy.

1.2 Food security in China: four decades of consecutive growth

Agriculture in China was, over three thousand years, mostly traditional and focused on responding to the need of food in terms of quantity of agricultural products. During those immemorial times, agriculture developed mainly through advances in four areas: (i) farmland improvements, notably through the use of human and animal manure as fertilizers, soil enriching plants or green manure crops; (ii) improvement in agriculture techniques, such as the introduction of crop rotation, seed selection, and/or the breeding of new strains; (iii) the improvement of farming implements, notably for land preparation (e.g. the use of curved mold board) and irrigation tools (e.g. animal-powered water wheels); (iv) compliance with local conditions, notably farming seasons. In spite of those improvements, agriculture productivity during those immemorial times remained highly dependent upon historical events, notably natural disasters-floods, droughts, frost in particular-and wars.

---

① FAO, *Global agriculture towards 2050*, http://www.fao.org/fileadmin/templates/wsfs/docs/Issues_papers/ HLEF2050_Global_Agriculture.pdf.

As a matter of fact, with regard to food security China's limited space for farming has always created significant challenges throughout its history, notably by leading to chronic food shortage and famine. Due to this strong contrast between a large population and limited availability of arable land resources, China experienced numerous food shortages, and then remedied them by implementing a quota system (1955–1993) and a land contract reform (1981) that incentivized farmers. Today, China feeds 21 percent of the world's population on 8 percent of the world's agriculture lands, which works out at about an average farmland availability of 0.09 ha per person, which is only 40% of the world average level. [1] In addition, farmlands owned by smallholders mostly consisted in small-sized dispersed fields, of which 60% were below 0.1 ha. [2]

In spite of those adverse conditions, China has, nowadays, basically resolved the problem of insufficient food supply. In 1996, the government issued a White Paper on grain production issues that established a 95% self-sufficiency objective for staple crops, including rice, wheat and corn. In 2008, in order to further strengthen food security, the No. 1 Document of the Central Committee of the Communist Party of China proposed to implement the "Grain Strategic Project" and developed specific measures to create a number of core grain growing (CGG) areas with good basic conditions, high production levels and large volume of transfers. *The Decision of the Central Committee of the Communist Party of China on Several Major Issues Concerning Agriculture and Rural Work* adopted by the Third Plenary Session of the 15th Central Committee of the Communist Party of China clearly pointed out that CGG areas should play not only an important but a critical role for strengthening food security at national level. As a result, major CGG areas were created in 13 provinces, namely Hebei, Liaoning, Jilin, Heilongjiang, Jiangsu, Anhui, Jiangxi, Shandong, Henan, Hubei, Hunan and Sichuan Provinces and Inner Mongolia Autonomous Region.

In term of food security, the result of those sector reforms, associated with the successful implementation of Household Responsibility System (HRS) policies, agricultural incentives, technological improvements and the implementation of farmland

---

[1] Ge D. et al.," Farmland transition in its influences in grain production in China", *Land Use Policy*, 2018 (70), pp. 94-105.

[2] Xiao Y. et al.," Optimal farmland conversion under double restraints of economic growth and resources protection", *Cleaner Production*, 2017(142), pp. 524-537.

protection forests was outstanding, with agriculture production in its CGG areas vastly increasing to reach 618 million tons of grains in 2017, surpassing the growth of its population by about 34 percent [①] . Among the three major cereal crops grown in China for the country's food security, the self-sufficiency ratio in wheat, rice and corn is now about 95 percent. In contrast, about 80 percent of consumed soybean and other agro-products, such as milk, meat [②] and sugar, are still imported. China's agriculture is also an important engine for rural employment, absorbing and contributing to the income of 320 million farmers. In a global comparison, for the same interval, the proportion of China's grain production, compared to the total grain produced at the world level (2818 million tons [③]), stabilized a level of about 29 percent. This indicates that China has now succeeded in guaranteeing stable crop self-sufficiency and in ensuring a nearabsolute safety security of food supply to meet the enormous grain demand of its population [④] . Moreover, in fact, current grain production appears to be today in a structural oversupply [⑤] . For the future, due to the development of improved varieties, as well as the constant increase in irrigation effectiveness, the expansion of areas covered by plastic mulches, the improvement of agriculture mechanization, agriculture consolidation leading to an increasing concentration of food production and the emergence of new types of agricultural management entities, leading to economies of scale, China's food security conditions in term of quantity should be considered promising. [⑥]

1.3　Challenges facing food security in China

However, the excessive pursuit of gross domestic product (GDP) growth by over management and irrational development during the past decades has also heavily

---

① China Ministry of Agriculture, *China Agriculture Yearbooks*, China Agriculture Press, Beijing, China: 1982-2017; Carter C.A. et al," Advances in Chinese agriculture and its global implications ", *Economic Perspectives and Policy,* 2012, 34(1), pp. 1-36.

② China customs data shows that it imported 9.91 million tons of meat in 2020, up 60 percent on 2019.

③ World Bank, *World Bank Open Data*: available online: https://data.worldbank.org.cn.

④ Huang J. et al .," Understanding recent challenges and new food policy in China", *Global Food Security*, 2017(12), pp. 119-126.

⑤ Wang D., et al., "The implications on food security in China based on the reform of the agricultural supply side structure", *Economist*, 2017.

⑥ Zhun Xu et al., "A Decade of Consecutive Growth or Stagnation?" *Monthly Review*, 2014 (66), https://monthlyreview.org/2014/05/01/chinas-grain-production/.

exploited the country's natural resources and damaged environment conditions. This resulted in a series of serious ecological and environmental problems challenging food security, notably in CGG areas as well as in plain agriculture in general. They include:

Non-point-source chemical soil pollution (NPS) due to an excessive application of chemical fertilizers and pesticides leading to a harmful state of diffuse agriculture lands pollution level[①] . Such NPS soil contamination may lead to at least 3 consequences: impairment of the mass balance (regulation function); defects in plant growth (production function); and health risks to human and animals through the contamination of harvested products, polluted ground water and the direct intake of soil and water. As a matter of fact, during the past 40 years, the fertilizer application amount in China has increased from 12.694 million tons in 1980 to 59.841 million tons in 2016 (an increase of 3.7 times). With regard to the amount of compound fertilizer (NPK), its application rate increased the fastest by 80.1 times. With regard to pesticides, their use skyrocketed for the same period from less than 1 million tons to 3.7 million tons giving an average application per hectare of grain in China in 2017 of 11.6 kg (i.e. 50% higher than the amount of pesticide used per hectare in developed countries or about 7–8 kg).

Point source soil pollution, notably from atmospheric deposition and heavy metal and other harmful substances, in dumping areas and wastewater ponds around industrial mining areas, transport infrastructures and urban centers. Among heavy metals, the probability of occurrence of cadmium (Cd) pollution is the highest (i.e. 25.3%), followed by nickel (Ni), mercury (Hg), arsenic (As) and lead (Pb) pollution respectively.

The compaction of agricultural soils inducing surface water runoff and thus, soil erosion. Soil compaction occurs, for example, when soil is handled or driven over by excessively heavy agricultural machines or vehicles.

An increasing rate of farmland topsoil erosion, in particular erosion of the highly fertile black topsoil layers in Northeast China and rock desertification in the Southwestern karst region. Current monitoring data show that the topsoil of cultivated

---

① Agricultural land NPS pollution is mainly due excessive and inefficient use of chemical fertilizers, increasing 3 fold during the past three decades, with efficiencies averaging at 32 percent compared to world average of 55 percent. Modern-day agricultural practices often require high levels of fertilizers and pesticides, leading to high nutrient and chemical surpluses that are transferred to soils and water bodies through various diffuse processes. Excessive nutrient concentrations in water bodies, however, cause adverse effects by promoting eutrophication with an associated loss of plant and animal species.

land in the black soils lose 0.3—1.0 cm per year, with the thickness of black soil layer of some cultivated land reducing from 80–100cm to 40–50cm or even 20–30cm. Along with the diminution of top layers, the content of organic matter, which was in the order of 3%–6% fell to a current 2%–3%.

Declining surface and groundwater resources for irrigation due to low irrigation efficiency [1] leading to water scarcity in some regions. The declining availability of groundwater for irrigation can be explained by both the expansion of irrigated areas (in China, effective irrigated areas increased from 15.9 million ha in 1949 to 44.96 million ha in 1978, and to 67.1 million ha in 2016) and the increased dependence of China's farmers to groundwater due to the constant improvement of well-drilling technology, the availability of power supply, and the reduction of irrigation pipes weight, which, altogether, played a critical role as they make it easier to extract groundwater. The use of groundwater also largely reduced water use conflicts among farmers, which is also an important reason why farmers prefer well irrigation. As a matter of fact, water consumed by agriculture in China nowadays accounts for more than 60% of the total water consumed in the country.

The use of too thin and too friable agricultural film mulches leading to the white pollution of agricultural fields. Agricultural films in use currently are too thin, extremely fragile, and the amount of labor used to collect discarded agricultural film after harvest too large. As a result, abandoned agricultural films are incorporated into the soil, thus causing white pollution. As of today, aside of the fact that soils become enriched with plastic residues, the effect of plastic pollution in terrestrial environment remain largely unknown.

A continuous loss of agricultural land due to the development of urban and peri-urban centers, infrastructure and industries. Since 1984, the speed and scale of China's urban growth and infrastructure has been driven by many important factors such as economic reforms in the late 1970s, withincountry migration policies, increasing urban–rural income disparities, surplus agricultural labourers, and massive conversion of farmland for urban use that could threaten its rural and urban food security. The fact

---

[1] China's available water supply per person is only 2050 m³ or 25 percent of the world's per capita average. Irrigation of rural crops accounts for 60 percent of China's total water demand with inefficient delivery of the order of 30–40 percent, compared to 70–80 percent in developed countries.

the matter is that, between 2001 and 2013, the total urban area increases from 31076 km² to 80887 km², an annual growth rate of 13.36%. During this period, this widespread urban expansion consumed 33080 km² of agricultural land [①]. The consequence is that effective policies and strategies are currently and should continue to be implemented to mitigate urbanization-related agricultural land loss in the context of China's rapid urbanization.

A decreasing ecological benefit from farmland protection forests established during the collective time. Farmland protection forests and tree-crop intercropping have a long history in China. Farmland protection forests do, in practice, provide many positive impacts on crop productivity. They include interalia providing an enhanced microclimate, improving soil fertility, maintaining water quality while restoring groundwater levels, sequestering carbon and mitigating GHG emissions and providing additional revenues from timber and associated specialty products. However, in spite of those inherent benefits on crop productivity, as historically demonstrated, there are a series of constraints and barriers, which have affected overtime their maintenance and expansion by farmers in agricultural landscapes. They include too dense layout, damaging tree border effects on agricultural production, unclear tree ownership and inadequate management regulations, decreasing prices of wood products and marketing opportunities and, above all, absence of adequate financial support to compensate farmers for the costs of establishing and maintaining them for ecological security reasons as well as for the loss in crop productivity due to their border effects. Eradicating or letting degrade farmland protection forests in order to increase cropping areas is likely to have the downside effect of degrading soils, increasing the likelihood of flash flooding and greatly reducing the potential for groundwater recharge [②].

Forest ecosystem degradation, associated to a general loss of biodiversity. Prior to 1998, excessive logging and neglected forest management led to a substantial decrease in the area of natural forests leading to an increase in runoff, flooding risks disasters and erosion, and a reduction in rainfall and moisture, surface and groundwater resources,

---

① Kaifang Shi et al., *Urban Expansion and Agricultural Land Loss in China: A Multiscale Perspective in Sustainability* 2016.

② David Ellison, Background Study prepared for the 13th session of the United Nations Forum on Forests in UNFF- Forests and Water (April 2018).

plant and animal biodiversity and ecological protection of arable lands. Further to the devastating effects of the major floods in the Yangtze River and the Yellow river basins in the late 1990s, regarded to be the consequence of forest loss and erosion, China undergone a remarkable increase in tree cover over the past four decades, through the development of six key forestry programs [①] aimed at reducing environmental degradation, and supplying its enormous demand for forest products. According to the state forest inventory, China's tree cover has increased from 14 percent of the country's terrestrial area in 1981 to 22.16 percent in 2015 bringing the country's total forest area to 208.3 million hectares with natural forests covering 121.8 million hectares. However, recent remote sensing studies have also indicated that this remarkable increase in tree cover was mostly due to the conversion of croplands to tree plantation, particularly to single species monocultures, used more for the production of timber, fiber and other tree fruits, than for biodiversity and ecosystem services benefits. Moreover, in many regions of China, the absence of concern for and measures related to the sustainable management of remaining natural forests and deficiencies related to silvicultural treatments of existing plantation, including natural regeneration as a mean of restoring forests and their biodiversity and improving the environmental protection of agricultural landscapes remain an issue to be addressed urgently by the government; and last but not least,

The vulnerability of current cropping patterns to the effects of climate change. Published in October 2018, the last IPCC report specifies that unless global temperature rise was maintained below 1.5 degree, planetary conditions for human and natural ecosystems will face great difficulties. Climate change is therefore, one of the key factors that may affect food security in China. If climate change may lead to a gradual extension of crop-growing periods, the increase in temperature and related evapotranspiration may also have a negative impact on grain production, notably on wheat and corn production. Furthermore, climate warming may increase the risk of usual pests and diseases and cause southern crop pests to migrate northward to create new pests and diseases, thus

---

① Namely (i) the Sloping land Conversion Program (SLCP or Grain for Green); (ii) the Natural Forest Protection Program (NFPP); (iii) the Shelterbelt Network Development Project (Three-North Shelterbelt Program); (iv) the Industrial Timberland Plantation Program (ITPP); (v) the Wildlife Conservation and Nature Reserves Protection Program (WCNRPP); (vi) the Desertification Control Project (DCP) around Beijing.

likely to be leading to reduced food production. New studies suggest that yield lost to insect pests for the three most important grain crops – wheat, rice and corn-may increase by 10%-25% per degree of warming. Climate change will not only affect crop yields, but also water availability for irrigation, which will, in turn, increase the pressure on irrigation water. Furthermore, due to the likelihood of increased occurrence of climate-related disasters-as already experienced during the recent past decades-the overall resistance of existing farmlands to natural disasters may sharply decrease leading in the near future to much larger fluctuation in terms of crop production.

The result of those issues is that the ecosystem functions of agriculture lands are degrading fast with critical consequences on agricultural productivity and, thereof, food security and food safety. As a matter of fact, if China is nowadays paying a heavy price to the past decades' enormous increase in agriculture production through intensification and irrigation, the current ecosystem degradation and environmental pollution are threatening and undermining the country's economic development and social growth, as well as its food security situation[①] . In a worst-case scenario, the chemical and physical impacts of agrochemicals on soils and water described above are either irreversible or can only be reversed at very high costs. Therefore, it is highly recommended that the government of China should adopt a precautionary principle as an absolute necessity in agricultural landscape protection. In view of this current situation, in order to ensure that agricultural soils remain able to fulfill their life-sustaining functions, a sustainable and integrated land management approach that take all natural resources functions into account, soil and water in particular, is an absolute requirement.

All the issues mentioned above are not confined to China only. About a quarter of the world's arable land is degraded[②] , a degradation compounded with environmental degradation, such as forest ecosystem degradation, land-based pollution, soil nutrient degradation, and soil salinization creating a widening gap between the demand for natural resources, for food production and the environment's ability to provide and replenish those resources. In South Asia, for instance, while about 43% of total agricultural land is already degraded, with 31 million ha already highly degraded,

---

①   Hongii Zhang and Erqi Xu , "An evaluation of the ecological and environmental security on Chinas, terrestrial ecosystems", *Sci Rep*, 2017 (7), p. 811.

②   FAO: The State of Food and Agriculture 2014; Innovation in Family Farming, Rome, 2014.

water availability for irrigation is more and more endangered by the rapid depletion of groundwater aquifers due to unregulated extraction and increased competition for scarce water between agriculture and industry, between industrial and domestic use, between rural and urban residents. Altogether those issues are leading to damage to both land and water resources resulting in severe production and income losses [1] , which are further threatening prospects for increased food security, continued economic growth, and poverty reduction. Consequently, maintaining the natural capital must also be a crucial goal for all Asian countries. [2]

1.4　The China food security policy context

Since the early 2000s, the government of China was paying a lot of attention to the development of comprehensive environmental protection policies and associated programs. As a matter of fact, since the turn of the century, the party already accepted that the country's environmental conditions needed urgent improvements, notably in term of air, water and soil qualities. More specifically, within the context of Ecological Civilization [3] , environmental protection, food security, sustainable use of natural resources, pollution reduction, sustainable rural development, and climate change mitigation and adaptation have been placed firmly at the core of the agricultural policy development agenda of China. *The China's National Plan on Implementation of the 2030 Agenda for Sustainable Development; the National Sustainable Agriculture Development Plan (2015–2020)* (and related Documents No. 1), *the National Climate Change Program (2014–2020); the China Biodiversity Conservation Strategy and Action Plan (2011–2030); the 2017 China Rural Revitalization Strategy*; and the 16 associated sustainability programs started in the late 1990s and early 2000s bear witness of this commitment.

Moreover, in September 2018, the State Council released a new *Strategy Plan for Rural Revitalization (2018–2022).* This new policy document is outlining key tasks to be

---

① M. Khor., *Land degradation causes $10 billion loss to South Asia Annually*, 2013, http://www.twnside. org.sg/title/land-ch.htm.

② ADB, *Environment Operational Directions 2013–2020: Promoting Transitions to Green Growth in Asia and the Pacific.* Manila 2013.

③ UNEP, *Green is Gold*: *The Strategy and Actions of China's Ecological Civilization* 2016.

achieved towards the goal of building rural areas with thriving business, pleasant living environments, social etiquette and civility, effective governance, and prosperity. This new strategy embodies a roadmap for China reaching the following three goals in terms of rural revitalization: By 2020, to establish an institutional and governance framework to achieve rural revitalization; By 2035, to complete the modernization of rural areas agriculture; By 2050, completing the rural revitalization project by having equalized livelihood standards between the countryside and urban areas.

This strategy, in particular, stressed that resolving issues relating to agriculture, rural development and rural people (San Nong in Chinese) are fundamental to China as they directly concern the stability of the country, food security and people's well-being. As a result, it prioritizes the development of both agriculture and rural areas. With regard to agricultural transformation, the strategy provides a clearer pathway and aims to consolidate and improve the basic rural operation system. It advocates reform of the rural land system and improve the systems for separating the ownership rights and contract rights and management rights for contracted rural land. In that respect, it confirms that the rural land contracting practices will remain stable and unchanged on a long-term basis by extending it for another 30 years upon expiration of current contracts. This strategy also emphasizes that China should always have control over its own food security. In that sense, it would be critical for China to establish industrial, production and business operation systems leading to a modern agriculture adhering to green development, notably ecological farming practices. In parallel, governance system for supporting and protecting agriculture would have to be improved, emphasizing the overall protection of mountains, water, forests, farmlands, lakes and grasslands. This strategy also stresses the importance of environmentally sustainable development through, in particular overcoming the negative aspects of non-point-source pollution (NPS), the sustainable use of surface and groundwater resources and rural waste altogether to improve agricultural products' safety and quality. Accordingly, the strategy requests local government to strengthen farmers' awareness of the protection of their ecological environment so that they can deeply realize that a good ecological environment in their agricultural landscape will not only benefit their production and their own livelihood, but also the national food security.

2. Changing Perspectives: Adopting the Concept of Ecological Security for Food Security in China

2.1 Ecological security in China: an emerging concept

Ecological security refers to the integrity and health of ecosystems. [1] It could be measured through indicators such as stability, sustainability of structure, and function of landscapes. What could also be measured is the resilience of ecosystems to stress. The maintenance of ecological security is, therefore, requiring two measures, i.e. the first one is to eliminate ecological risks through conservation, and the second is to reduce the ecological vulnerability of ecosystems through development. Ecological security is, therefore, a prerequisite to human survival and development. There are differences in the level of ecological security due to the degree of variability of ecological security in different ecosystems. Furthermore, one should admit that the degree of ecological security is in a dynamic state, which means that ecological security may be changed with the improvement of social development and the state of ecological conditions. That said, humans through conservation and development could regulate ecological security. However, the maintenance of ecological security does have a cost. For those threats to ecological security that often come from human activities, large investments are needed to resolve those issues.

In China, because of the magnitude of ecological and environmental problems affecting food security, the need for integrating socio-ecological aspects of natural resource problems have become increasingly important, as, within the scope of the concept of Eco-civilization, traditional national security outlooks have gradually expanded to include environmental and human security concerns. An overview of six main stressors of ecological security – food security, ecosystem degradation, energy, water, urbanization, and climate change-that affect security in China reveals that current

---

[1] The International Institute for Applied Systems Analysis (IIASA, 1989) defines ecological security as referring to changes in human life, health, well-being, basic rights, sources of livelihood security, necessary resources, social order, and human adaptation capabilities to the environment. It includes natural ecological security, economic security, and social security. Ecological security is negatively related to ecological risks but positively related to ecological health.

policies need to be reformed. As a matter of fact, China's ecosystems remain subject to widespread natural resources degradation, food supply stress, a growing demand for energy. conflicts over water quality and quantity, a rapid urbanization proceeding without sufficient environmental and social concerns, as well as increasing climate-change impacts projected to intensify. To resolve such security issues, China's policy makers must depend less on technological solutions and should instead craft adaptive management reforms to address ecological security through interdisciplinary problem-solving, improved institutional capacity, and gaps between policy and implementation.

2.2 Ecological security and food security: an evident synergy

If it is nowadays, in CGG areas, cereal centric and input intensive, the issue of sustainability of current production systems has emerged. In particular, challenges for the future have surfaced prominently, such as the decline of agriculture productivity growth as a result of soil fertility degradation and pollution as well as groundwater and surface water pollution due to the excessive use of chemical fertilizers and pesticides; decreasing level of groundwater availability for irrigation; decline in soil organic matter; soil compaction, increased cost of inputs and related decline in farm profits, degradation of the protective functions of farmland protection forests; and, last but not least, increasing risks of adverse impacts of weather anomalies on agricultural productivity and the increased incidence of pests and diseases, both due to climate change.

Indeed, under current climate change scenarios, agriculture in China faces a triple challenge. To meet food security needs, agriculture productivity has to increase, notably by closing the gap between actual and attainable yields, whilst at the same time adapting to climate change and reducing its environmental impacts. Given the increasing risk of extreme weather, this cannot come at the expense of production resilience only. Increases in productivity, sustainability and resilience to climate change are required at the same time. This will require significant investments, as well as improved cross-sector collaboration.

Scaling up ecological security for food security, therefore, requires overcoming key challenges affecting the sustainability of current agriculture production, notably those affecting crop production. In that sense, ecological security depend upon overcoming the negative impacts of the continuous and persistent NPS pollution of agricultural soils and groundwater due to an over application of synthetic fertilizers, pesticides, and other agrochemical inputs [①] ; the continuous decrease of availability of water for irrigation due to over exploitation of available groundwater resources; the impending impacts of climate change, notably due to both changes in precipitation pattern leading to changes in soil water content, runoff and erosion, nutrient cycles, salinization, biodiversity, and soil organic matter and the probable increasing frequencies of extreme climate events; and the deterioration of the protection benefits of farmland protection forests due to a series of problems, constraints and barriers, which are currently affecting their maintenance and continued existence, not to mention a general reluctance of farmers for preserving them due to their negative border effects on crop production and decreasing financial returns in absence of government financial support.

When addressing the above issues, it is expected that improving ecological security at the level of agricultural landscapes would help achieving multiple sustainability objectives through integrated practices, supported by coherent cross-sector policies addressing the economic, environmental and social dimensions of food production systems. In this respect, ecological security underlies holistic solutions to the complex inter-related and multi-sector challenges notably related to poverty, hunger, environmental degradation and climate change as anticipated by the China 2030 Agenda, which aims at providing a national framework for achieving integrated sustainable development in its three dimensions: environmental, social and economic. Furthermore, ecological security requires innovation in policies, extension and rural institutions and partnerships, as well as in the production, processing, marketing and consumption of food. The China 2030 Agenda calls, in particular, for much better policy, institutional and technological consideration given to ecological security related improvement in the food and agricultural sectors. It also calls for all people to be critical agents of change.

2.3 The ecological security's seven main challenges

China claims an agricultural culture stretching back five millennia. But, while

---

① As synthetic fertilization is a major source of methane gas emissions and contamination of land and water, the reduction in their use will lower the risks of soil and water pollution as well as specific health problems associated with their inappropriate use (with farmers often ignoring or misunderstanding labels).

in the past, this culture worked in accordance with nature, now everything relies on chemicals and over-use of water resources. Before 1979, farmyard manure was used as fertilizer, and water pollution was very rare. *The Soil Pollution Prevention Law*, aimed at legislating for the use of fertilizers and pesticides and preventing soil pollution, has long been in the works. But there is still no sign that the current legislation actually impacts positively on ecological security. Actually, it is economic factors and input subsidy policies that are pushing farmers towards using more chemical fertilizers and pesticides. With regard to pesticides, if biological pesticides have a lesser effect on the human body, they are not as effective. Furthermore, they are more expensive. Those two factors explain that farmers do not want to pay extra expense, with the consequence that there is currently no readily available market for biological alternatives.

In response to the seven major challenges facing food security in the future (namely, the challenge of rural non-point source pollution caused by excessive application of chemical fertilizers and pesticides, the challenge of declining groundwater levels caused by overuse of groundwater resources, the challenge of total grain yield and quality caused by soil pollution, soil thinning and occupation of arable land, the challenge of declining protective function of farmland protection forests caused by fragmentation of forest belts and forest networks, the challenge of declining agricultural competitiveness caused by the rapid rise of agricultural labor costs, the challenge of an aging agricultural workforce caused by the migration of young and middle-aged rural laborers to urban areas, and the challenge of increased probability of extreme weather events caused by climate change), China has taken the following measures. Drastically reducing the significant impacts of food systems on ecosystems – land, soils, water and biodiversity–due to over-commutations of synthetic agricultural inputs while adapting to climate change and mitigating greenhouse gas emissions as to increase their resilience in dealing with increased number of natural disasters and emergencies; Striving for "nature positive" food systems that maintain or even restore agricultural ecosystems and the natural resources and ecosystems services on which food security depend; Fostering an integrated approach by thinking in term of "eco-agri-food systems" that encompass food production, natural resources protection and the ecosystem services they offer as part of food security policies and institutions; Promoting an integrated food security governance system, notably by mainstreaming environmental protection in food security policies at landscape or watershed level, as to promote and maintain complex multifunctional agricultural landscapes to would increase agriculture production as well as ecosystem services; Developing process for sector policy coordination and increasing the capacity of policymakers to work across multiple sectors – vertically, horizontally and temporally to support the transformation of intensive agriculture based on chemical inputs toward more resilient eco-agri-food system and address future crisis. Endorsing positive incentives–from regulation to market-based and normative incentives–to impact the production choice made by farmers for the development of sustainable, nature-positive food systems. Improving the efficiency of agriculture extension system governance by improving extension management through training, procedures, incentives and monitoring and evaluation and, notably by using digital tools improving interaction with farmers (e.g. providing the right information to farmers in a timely and appropriate manner).

3. Towards an Ecological Security Strategy to Improve Food Security in China

Food security vulnerability begins with biophysical effects at the level of individual farms, including in CGG areas. With many of the resources needed for sustainable food security already stretched notably population increase, accompanied with unprecedented rates of urbanization and industrialization, farmland pollution, decreasing availability of water and destruction of natural habitats, the food security challenges in countries such as China are huge and the multiple stresses linked climate change will make it even harder to overcome them. Altogether, they will have considerable impacts not only on agricultural productivity and, by consequence on food security, but also on the socioeconomic conditions of millions.

As illustrated above, promoting ecological security at the levels of farms and agricultural landscapes in China through the adoption of ecological agriculture practices to decrease NPS pollution, restoring the fertility of degraded and heavy polluted soils, improving groundwater management through more efficient irrigation systems, conserving soil moisture, organic matter and nutrients in association with the promotion of drought resistant varieties and the reintroduction of trees at farm and landscape levels would increase the resilience of food security systems, with an emphasis on improving the socioeconomic conditions of farmers. However, in China, like elsewhere in the developed and developing world, farmers alone cannot deal with the magnitude of threats, which are likely to affect food security in the near future. They need to be supported by government.

In the context of the China's food security, addressing ecological security negative factors affecting sustainable agriculture at farmland and landscape levels would, therefore, require six strategic lines of actions to be implemented in an integrated fashion. There are no such single groups of actions that can individually reach the final goal of improving ecological security at both farm and landscape levels.

3.1 The promotion of an ecological protection system at agricultural landscape and farm levels

The promotion of an ecological protection system at agricultural landscape and farm levels would aim at improving farmland security. Its objective is and would not only be at controlling land degradation and erosion at landscape levels but also at providing crucial support to agro-ecosystems' functions, agriculture production, the conservation and enhancement of the benefits of existing biodiversity, the improvement of farmers' livelihood conditions and the revival of agricultural landscapes and its touristic attractiveness. The first phase of the establishment an eco-security protection system started in the 1970s with the launching of "Ten" forest protection systems, notably the Three North Shelterbelt Project, the Seven Major Rivers' Forest Protections System, the Coastal Protection Forest system and the Farmland Forest Protection System aimed at controlling land erosion and desertification. The second phase of this program, which started in the late 1990s, included and still includes the Natural Forest Protection Program (NFPP), the Sloping Land Conversion Program (SLCP), the Returning Grazing Land to Grassland Program and the Wetland Protection and Restoration Programs. The implementation of this recent tranche of ecological protection programs is still in progress and still due to be implemented over a period of 20 to 40 years.

One of the essential constituents of this sustainable land management system would be the beneficial ecological security role plaid ecological protection structures such as farmland protection forests, buffer strips, ecological corridors and wetlands to protect natural habitats and biodiversity niches as to provide nesting opportunities for pollinating insects. In China, integrating trees in agricultural landscapes was historically instrumental in providing an ecological security environment favorable to agricultural productivity, notably in devising a micro-climate favorable to crop yields, protecting farmland against weather related anomalies, hot wind and drought in particular, controlling soil erosion, enhancing soil nutrient cycling, carbon sequestration, biological diversity and the production of valuable products as timber, food, fodder, medicinal plants, essential oils and materials for local industries. Moreover, the integration of trees and the conservation of natural habitats into the agricultural landscapes should be considered the keystone in building climate change resilience across all scales, as well as enhancing carbon sequestration. A recent study by the World Bank even suggests that, among the range of ecological farming practices, "trees in agricultural landscapes by far have the highest carbon sequestration potentials".

However, when implementing those ecological protection structures, attention should be paid to the combination of trees and shrubs with crop systems as to both minimize the possible negative impacts of trees on crop productivity while not affecting the operation of agricultural machinery. Since most of those ecological protection structures are to be developed either at farm and/or at agricultural landscape level, inter-sector policy and institutional coordination remains an important matter of improvement. Other inter-sector issues to be considered include:

i. Clarifying land and tree tenure rights and management obligations notably for farmland protection forests established at landscape and farm levels, which are currently acting as disincentives to farmers' participation in their development and maintenance.

ii. Adopting adequate financial compensation (eco-compensation policies in the China' context) to further enhance farmers' participation in the development and maintenance of those ecological protection structures.

iii. Adopting nature-based forest management approach to improve the ecological and structural stability of existing forest plantations established under reforestation programs, their flexibility and ability to address natural and anthropogenic disturbances, notably those due to the effects of climate change.

3.2 The establishment of an agricultural non-point-source (NPS) pollution control system, at the same time, improving farmland soil fertility.

Lessening the use of chemical fertilizers and pesticides and, thus decreasing agricultural NPS pollution and improving farmland fertility and the production of safe food products will require four types of measures. They include:

i. Strictly controlling the use of synthetic fertilizers and pesticides through the issuance of quota and the promotion of slow and controlled release fertilizers, fertigation and organic fertilization in accordance to existing soil testing and formula fertilization. Improving the supply and use of organic fertilizers will, however, require the establishment of eco-industrial chains, which can operate on the basis of raw materials produced by large-scale livestock and poultry breeding companies.

ii. Restoring the fertility of polluted and already degraded farmlands through physical, chemical, biological or agronomic remediation measures depending upon the level of gravity of farmland pollution or degradation.

iii. Enhancing both the use of eco-friendly pesticides and application techniques. Improving the use of eco-friendly pesticides would require intensifying the development of pilot R&D projects for the development of low-toxicity bio-pesticides, as well as training and subsidizing farmers for accelerating their uses and their safe application.

iv. Improving mulch film standards and relevant quality control mechanisms to increase to decrease white pollution. Heightening R&D for the development of light-weight biodegradable mulch film and multi-functional equipment that can be used regularly during farming operation for the collection and recycling of residual mulch film.

3.3 The management, control and reclamation of point source pollution at the level of industries

The management, control and reclamation of point source pollution at the level of industries should be established at town and township levels. This would require two main measures: (i) the closing down of the fifteen most polluting small enterprises such as cement factories, leather factories and coking processing enterprises; (ii) establishing a county level integrated point source pollution control system to assess scattered enterprises' pollution risks, levels and remedial measures in case of needs. The objective of this point source pollution control system would be to create a polluted free county-level industrial estate. Those two measures are already currently under implementation as per the Soil Pollution Prevention Action Plans.

3.4 The development of a water resources conservation system

The development of a water resources conservation system should include the following four measures aimed at lessening the use of groundwater and promoting water-saving irrigation technologies. They include:

i. An increased used of low-pressure pipelines, sprinklers and drip irrigation (instead of flooded irrigation), able to save up to 30-50 percent in water loss aside of increasing the uniformity of irrigation and enabling deeper seepage on uneven farmland thereof reducing water leakage.

ii. The introduction of water quota systems in connection to the issuance of marketable water coupons and the development of a water rights trading market to encourage farmers reducing own water consumption. Since recent years, China's groundwater management is adopting a measurement model of "one well, one meter, one household, one card", through the installation by the government in each well of a smart water meter to give farmers the opportunity to purchase water according to their respective own water rights or sell it through the alienation of such rights.

iii. The adjustment of planting patterns (i.e. adopting a "one season fallow – one season rain fed" mode as to reduce the "*two harvests a years of wheat and corn to one harvest*") and the structure of food crops to seasonal characteristics, soil moisture and water resources availability (e.g. increasing the use of low-water consumption crops and/or adopting dry farming practices).

iv. The further extension farmland cover-crop technologies, including plastic and straw mulching.

3.5 Adopting ecological field farming practices

Transforming conventional high-input agriculture to improve farmland security is going to be a tremendous challenge and work on various fronts as the transition process towards more sustainable agricultural systems respecting ecological security standards would be complex, requiring changes in field practices, day-to-day management operations at farm level, planning and marketing. The objectives of promoting ecological farming practices would be three-fold: (i) enhancing the beneficial biological interactions and synergies among the components of the agro-biodiversity systems as to enhance ecological services, rather than focusing only on mono-cropping systems; (ii) incorporating the concept of long-term sustainability into the overall agro-ecosystem design and management; (iii) most highly valuing the overall health of the agro-system rather than the outcome of a particular cropping system.

3.6　Build a farmland ecological landscape system

A few management rules are governing ecological farming practices. They are basically aimed at providing the most favorable soil and microclimate conditions, particularly by managing organic matter and enhancing soil biological activity through four main agronomic measures to be promoted to improve ecological security at farm and landscape levels. They involve:

i. Moving from single cropping to multiple cropping system aimed at providing the most favorable soil and microclimate conditions, particularly by managing organic matter and enhancing soil biological activity through using large quantities of different types of organic materials on a regular basis.

ii. Using large quantities of different types of organic materials on a regular basis–animal manures, composts, tree leaves, cover crops, rotation crops that leave large amounts of crop residues on fields.

iii. Encouraging crop rotation and fallow systems and holistic farmland management practices enhancing crop yield stability, such as tree-crop intercropping, windbreaks, shelterbelts, river buffers, insect strips, living fences, woodlots, etc..

iv. Routinely keeping soil covered with living or crop residues–cover crops, sod crops in rotation-and adopting reduced tillage or minimum tillage or no tillage.

v. A continued support to genetic improvement of crop varieties.

4. Mobilizing Policy and Institutional Support for Improving Ecological Security in Agricultural Landscapes of China

Improving the ecological security in agricultural landscapes of China, including in CGG areas, will require four governance prerequisites, namely, (i) establishing an enabling policy environment, including compulsory, incentive and coordination policies; (ii) strengthening inter-sector coordination mechanisms; (iii) establishing inter-sector monitoring and evaluation mechanisms to assess the performances of ecological security measures; (iv) revising the mandate and improving the efficiency of agricultural extension.

4.1 Building an enabling policy environment

Investing to improve ecological security in agricultural landscapes, in particular in CGG areas, with a long-term view shall be necessary to guarantee a transition from high intensity agricultural systems to sustainable agricultural systems that overcome climate change threats to food security and reduce soil and water pollution and the use of fossil energy. However, meeting the above objectives require an enabling governance framework. Three types of policies should complement the above four governance prerequisites.

Compulsory policies, laws and regulations for the improvement of ecological security at agricultural landscape level and the protection of arable land at farm levels. Their aims would be at protecting arable land, conserving soil fertility, controlling soil erosion, improving irrigation efficiency, and strictly controlling the use of synthetic fertilizers and pesticides for the protection of soil and water from pollution and eutrophication. In this respect, four types of integrated policy actions should be considered:Reforming the current system of agricultural input subsidy policies with a particular attention given to the adjustment of input subsidies to ecological requirements and the enactment of preferential subsidies for the application of environmentally friendly fertilizers and pesticides.Strengthening laws and regulation for the strict control of the use of synthetic fertilizers and pesticides through the issuance of quota and promote the use of micro-nutrient enriched organic fertilizers.Strengthening laws and regulations to enhance the conservation of water resources and the introduction of water saving technologies. Establishing crop diseases and insect pests biological control systems, notably at CGG areas' level in conjunction with the extension of mechanized pesticide spreading technologies, both to reduce the use synthetic pesticides.

With regard to the protection of arable land at farm level, even though *the Land Administration Law, the Law on the Contracting of Rural Land,* and the newly revised *Environmental Protection Law* involve provisions for the protection and rational use of farmland, they are neither practical nor operational. It is, therefore, recommended that the government shall formulate a specific law on the protection of cultivated land based on the relevant provisions of these laws and ecological security requirements. The objective of this new law shall be the establishment of a legal system that takes farmland ecological security at its core, with linkages to farmland existing regulations. This new law should guide the government at various administrative levels, enterprises and farmers in view of regulating the protection of arable land in terms of regulations focused on (i) the establishment of 120 million ha of permanent basic farmland protection zones; (ii) new thresholds for hazardous and harmful substances included in fertilizers, feed, and irrigation water; and new standards for bio-degradable agricultural plastic films and the revision pesticide packaging standard; (iii) new standards to prevent soil erosion, desertification, salinization, soil compaction and bareness of cultivated land such as conservation tillage or no-till; land restoration measures to address issues such as farmland pollution and the thinning of top soils; standards for the use of agrochemicals and irrigation water quality, etc.; (iv) new regulations to enhance the ecological security benefits from farmland protection forests and tree-crop intercropping. In effect, the current degradation of farmland protection forests, if not reversed, may lead to catastrophic changes in the ecosystem services they have historically provided. Inter-sector policy and institutional coordination remains a critical matter of improvement due to the current institutional segregation between agriculture, forestry, nature conservation and environmental protection.

Incentive policies to encourage farmers to improve ecological security at agricultural landscape level and protect arable land at farm level. Three types of incentive policies would be required: first, the enactment of regulations including the payment of bonus to farmers who use chemical fertilizers less than fixed quotas; second, the issuance of marketable water coupons to encourage farmers reducing their own water consumption above what is required for grain production; third, eco-compensation measures to encourage farmers to protect their ecological environment as well as inducing them to develop and maintain farmland ecological landscapes.

4.2   Promoting eco - compensation policies

When elaborating a new incentive policy framework, a particular attention should be given to eco-compensation policies. Eco-compensation is one of the eight mechanisms designed to bring "eco-civilization" into practices encompassing environmental fiscal reforms, e.g. revising taxes, subsidies, prices in line with the beneficiary and polluter pays principles, financial transfers to change behaviors and custom-made programs to respond to the needs of key functional areas. China has been experimenting for many years eco-compensation as a way to redress market signals for ecosystem services. [1] More specifically, advancing ecological security in agricultural landscapes of China would require eco-compensation measures.

Achieving full compliance with reduced agrochemicals application standards.

Controlling and reducing irrigation water use in accordance to local climatic and edaphic conditions to ensure sustainable grain production.

Promoting the use organic fertilizers and bio-pesticides for the gradual improvement of soil fertility.

Improving the farmland ecological landscape, including the protection benefits from reforestation and agroforestry on barren slopes of mountains/hills surrounding CGG areas and the greening of plain agricultural landscapes, with a particular attention given to the establishment and maintenance of farmland protection forests, where suitable.

Improving R&D programs aimed at improving ecological agriculture system for sustainable food production in a sustainable manner.

Coordination policies to improve cross-sector effectiveness. Enhancing the multi-functional role of ecological security in agricultural landscapes will require the contribution from economic, financial, agriculture, forestry, land resource management and climate change policies. Typically, the ministry of agriculture alone would not be sufficient in fulfilling this function. As experience shows. the efficiency of sector specific

---

[1]   As of 2015, investments for eco-compensation in the form grain subsidies, conditional transfer payments, in-kind rewards, such as investments at community level, or mixed rewards totaled US$ 69 billion.

policies is mutually enhanced by inter-sector coordination. Meeting ecological security requirements is, therefore, calling for specific national governance and coordination mechanisms between the different ministries, public administration and concerned farmers, the more that policies and ecological farming practices and remedial actions required to improve ecological security in agricultural landscapes should be implemented in an integrated fashion.① Therefore, strengthening inter-sector coordination mechanisms would be an important prerequisite for improving ecological security strategy in agricultural landscapes. This would require four complementary measures.

i. The first one would be to enhance a sense of cooperation, stimulate collaborative demands, and emphasize complementary advantages to eliminate the many disadvantages of sector resource allocation.

ii. The second is to regulate inter-departmental coordination while ensuring symmetry of participant's rights, responsibilities and benefits.

iii. The third one is to accelerate information exchange, making it more efficient and more comprehensive as to make respective administration more open, more transparent, more efficient and more useful.

iv. The fourth one is to lessen collaborative risks by establishing exit mechanism and punishing uncooperative behaviors.

4.3 Inter-sector monitoring and evaluation mechanisms to assess the performances of ecological security measures

A third-party inter-sector and independent monitoring and evaluation systems (M&E) ensuring transparency shall be considered an important inter-sector coordination tool. Its objective would be to assess and demonstrate the impacts of policy, institutional and technological measures promoted to improve ecological security in agricultural landscapes as well as at farmland levels. In this framework, one key recommendation would be to embed in such M&E system environmental impact assessment studies (EIA) to ensure the long-term sustainability of policy, institutional and technological

---

① For instance, the development management and maintenance of a farmland ecological landscape should be stimulated through better policy coordination, notably, but not exclusively between agriculture and forestry departments as to improve conditions for the development of ecological farming practices, including, where suitable, farmland protection forests.

measures and their benefits to farming communities. When designing such M&E system, a particular attention should be given to assessing and monitoring the impact of eco-compensation measures on ecological security and their impacts on poverty reduction. Monitoring and evaluation should be organized as a three-tier operating system with expertise from relevant departments, farmers and external M&E experts.

Revising the mandate of agriculture extension. Ecological security to sustain and even improve food security and food safety is a major challenge for China. In that context, farmers need to acquire new adequate knowledge and information in order to understand current issues affecting ecological security and their consequences on food security and food safety. Meeting the objectives of ecological security shall, therefore, require the development of ecological security-related extension services, including critical access to the knowledge, information and technology that farmers should acquire to improve ecological security at their farm and at landscape levels to improve the quality of their agricultural production with a particular attention given to food safety standards while improving lives and livelihoods. It is hence crucial to provide farmers with the knowledge and information on ecological security in the best possible quality and timely way.

Nowadays, the unprecedented speed of adoption of Information and Communication Technologies (ICT),[1] notably mobile smart phone technology, has raised general expectations about their potential contributions to the spread of innovative sustainable farming technology, as well as for improving farmers' knowledge and awareness with regard to other relevant knowledge and information.[2] Therefore, apart from traditional extension methods, another means to communicate to farmers and other stakeholders in agriculture has gradually emerged based on the use of telecommunication and computer networks. In one-way or another, ICTs are now increasingly being used in agricultural extension in many countries over the world. However, if the importance of dissemination information about agricultural practices to enable farmers to learn new practices is well recognized, less acknowledged is the

---

[1] Information and Communication Technology (ICT) is an umbrella term that includes any communication device or application, encompassing cellular phone, radio, television, computer and network hardware of software, satellite EO systems, etc. as well as various services and applications associated with them, such as videoconferencing and distance learning (Webinars).

[2] Karen Vignare, Options and Strategies for Information and Communication within Agricultural Extension and Advisory Services, *USDA/Feed the Future*, 2013.

value inherent to establish a multi-directional communication, particularly between farmers, researchers, extension agents and policy makers.

In spite of some progress already made in China with the introduction of ICT based services in agriculture and forestry, there are still many barriers to the further development, deployment and utilization of ICT based information dissemination models. [1] As a result, the following five strategic points should be considered in order to identify the most efficient ICT tools and infrastructure adapted to the promotion of ecological security for food security.

Establishing an appropriate ICT governance structure. Promoting ICT extension for ecological security in agricultural landscapes would not be feasible without specific governmental support, notably to foster integration and coherence across agricultural themes, sector disciplines and commodity that would enable a successful adoption of ICTs to benefit ecological security.

Involving universities and research centers on key issues affecting the adoption of ICT in rural areas. Agricultural universities and associated research centers, the traditional role of which being to create, store and diffuse knowledge, should play a significantly broader responsibility and act as local facilitators in promoting ICT for ecological security;

Developing capacity, in terms of human skills to manage, share, exchange and use scientific and technical knowledge for the adoption of ecological security-related measures. Extension staffs need to be trained on how to use ICT as an extension tool and methods because too few extension staff are currently aware of it.

Improving investments for the use of ICT in extension. Extension budgets, without which almost nothing could be done, should be reviewed accordingly. With regard to extension, these budgets should not focused on the purchase of basic ICT devices, but on the purchase of packaged services on behalf of the farmers from network companies providing technical supports so that farmers could have free access to such information. In parallel, farmers also must also be aware of ICT potential, and it should be the responsibility of the extension service to pass on this information to farmers. Once farmers' awareness would be raised on the role of ICT tools for ecological security extension, the next step would be to train them on how to make an efficient use of ICTs; and

---

[1] Yun Zhang et al., Agricultural information dissemination using ICTs: A review and analysis of information dissemination in China, https://www.sciencedirect.com/science/article/pii/S2214317316000020#s0200.

Setting an adequate institutional infrastructure for ICT extension. Another key point is to have a proper extension infrastructure if ICT should be used as an extension tool for the promotion of ecological security. As of today, basic ICT devices like computers, laptops and mobile phones, etc. are not used for extension or not always available in a suitable format to extension staff and farmers as well. This would require identifying how to "integrate" information and communication management in the work of ICT-based extension organizations through appropriate policies, strategies, resources allocation, capacity development, and organizational structures and process.

4.4 Conclusions

China's unprecedented economic growth, which has lifted millions out of poverty has, however, been putting a heavy pressure on the eco-systems, land, soils, water, biodiversity, on which food security and food safety depend. Increasing unsustainable production and consumption patterns have led to worsening air, soil and water pollution, water scarcity and the generation of waste. All those are threatening food security and the environment as well as human health. Increased demand for chemical agricultural inputs and natural resources, intensive agriculture requiring are causing environmental degradation and biodiversity loss. With the Ecological Civilization and the Rural Revitalization Strategies, China is nowadays acting towards a green growth path but, despite increased investments for example in ecosystem rehabilitation, reforestation or renewable energy, the exploding demand for food risks undoing past food security gains. And this situation may be exacerbated by adverse climate change effects and the risks of an increasing number of natural disasters, which may be causing devastating human and financial losses. Extreme climate events are now projected to become the new normal.

Moreover, the COVID-19 pandemic, which causes widespread losses in livelihood and incomes, threatening food security, health and nutrition, in particular for poor and marginalized people, has brought some momentum and lessons to increase resilience, health and the sustainability of food security through a better integration of human food systems with ecosystems.

This book identifies the challenges facing China's food security, reveals the drivers of agroecosystem degradation, and proposes eight courses of action to address these challenges, including the establishment of an agricultural non-point source pollution control system, a water resource protection system, an ecological protection system, an ecological agriculture system, a policy support system, an intersectoral coordination mechanism, a cross-sectoral ecological security monitoring and assessment system, and an ecological compensation system for major grain-producing areas, as well as seize opportunities to promote eco-agricultural practices, smart agricultural practices, and quality agricultural production practices, and carry out innovations in agricultural policy systems, farmland protection forestry systems, and sectoral coordination systems to make China's food system more inclusive, more efficient, more sustainable, healthier, and more resilient to future shocks.

Seven main challenges for the future of food security in China could be learned from the Book.

Drastically reducing food systems significant impacts on ecosystems, land, soils, water and biodiversity, due to over-commutations of synthetic agricultural inputs while adapting to climate change and mitigating greenhouse gas emissions as to increase their resilience in dealing with increased number of natural disasters and emergencies.

Striving for "nature positive" food systems that maintain or even restore agricultural ecosystems and the natural resources and ecosystems services on which food security depend.

Fostering an integrated approach by thinking in term of "eco-agri-food systems" that encompass food production, natural resources protection and the ecosystem services they offer as part of food security policies and institutions.

Promoting an integrated food security governance system, notably by mainstreaming environmental protection in food security policies at landscape or watershed level, as to promote and maintain complex multifunctional agricultural landscapes to would increase agriculture production as well as ecosystem services.

Developing process for sector policy coordination and increasing the capacity of policymakers to work across multiple sectors – vertically, horizontally and temporally- to support the transformation of intensive agriculture based on chemical inputs toward more resilient eco-agri-food system and address future crisis.

Endorsing positive incentives from regulation to market-based and normative incentives – to impact the production choice made by farmers for the development of sustainable, nature-positive food systems.

Improving the efficiency of agriculture extension system governance by improving extension management through training, procedures, incentives and monitoring and evaluation and, notably by using digital tools (ITC) improving interaction with farmers (e.g. providing the right information to farmers in a timely and appropriate manner).

There is, among agronomists, environmentalists, sociologists, economists and health specialists, a growing consensus that none of options underlining the Ecological Security Strategy can be tackled successively in isolation as they are interlinked. In China, improving food security must happen in a sustainable manner to protect China's already scarce natural resources, soil, land, water, and eco-systems from further depletion and degradation while providing stable incomes to farmers' and ensuring well-functioning markets to distribute food to all consumers at affordable prices. Meeting the objectives of the Ecological Security Strategy in the context of a changing climate, will, in particular, require two additional, but complementary, strategic objectives: (i) continuous cross-sector and cross-scale research efforts and development for new technologies and innovation to, at the same time, enhance eco-agri-food systems and Agricultural Total Factor Productivity according to challenges ahead; (ii) helping farmers to adapt to the greater uncertainties associated with climate change by improving their knowledge of fundamental agronomic, ecological and economic mechanisms underlying eco-agri-food systems through recurrent training and post-training programs.

Developing these eco-agri-food system technologies and bringing them to scale will, hence, require significant financial investments. Therefore, meeting the goals of the Ecological Security Strategy may be difficult to achieve, but putting Ecological Security Strategy at the core of China's food security should be considered by the Government of China a indispensable objective.

Appendix 1   Changes in Worldwide Pesticide Use in Major Countries

Major European countries

France: In 2002, the annual application amount of fungicides was 40,000-60,000 tons, and it was reduced to 25000 tons in 2011; the amount of herbicides used was 30000-40000 tons before 2000, and reduced to 22000 tons in 2010; in 1990s, the annual amount of insecticides used was about 10000 tons, and reduced to 2000-3000 tons in 2000; affected by climate change, the annual used amount of those three types of pesticides in 2013 has increased to about 30000 tons, 30000 tons and 3318 tons, respectively.

Spain: Before 2010, the annual application of fungicides, insecticides and herbicides was around 10000 to 15000 tons. In 2013, the annual amount of fungicides used was 32000 tons, more than double than that of in 2010. The annual amount of herbicide used was approximately about 15000 tons, with an increase of 50 percent, while the amount of insecticides was 7000 tons, with a decrease of 50 percent.

United Kingdom: Before 2005, the annual amount of herbicide used was 20000-25000 tons. In recent years, due to the use of higher activity herbicides, the annual amount has decreased to approximately 7500 tons between 2011 and 2013. While the amount of fungicides has remained stable, with an annual average of 5000 to 6000 tons, the amount of pesticides used in 2000 was around 1500 tons. It decreased to about 600-700 tons in 2011.

Germany: Herbicides are one of the main pesticides used in Germany, with an annual amount of 15000 to 20000 tons. Fungicides, with an annual consumption of about 10000 tons followed. As for insecticides, their annual amount was about 1000 tons. There was little change in the amount of pesticides used during those years, while the herbicide use has slightly increased in recent years.

Italy: In 2008, the annual amount of fungicides was 50000 tons. In 2013, this amount reduced to 32000 tons, with a decrease of 36 percent. However, the amount of insecticides and herbicides did not change much between years to about 10000-12000 tons. The amount of herbicide used was 7000 to 10000 tons.

The Netherlands: Due to the significant reduction in the amount of soil disinfectants, the use of pesticides per unit area was reduced by 50 percent in the mid-1990s compared to the mid-1980s. In recent years, the annual application of fungicides, herbicides and insecticides was about 4000 tons, 3000 tons and 266.9 tons, respectively. The amount of pesticides used has decreased from 5 kg/ha before 2008 to about 4 kg/ha in 2013.

Major Asian countries

South Korea: in South Korea, control of pesticide started from 1996 and began to decline in 2001. Annual use of pesticides, fungicides and herbicides decreased from 9880 tons, 9332 tons and 6380 tons in 2001 to 6403 tons, 6324 tons and 4479 tons in 2013, respectively. The average pesticide use has decreased from 13 kg/ha in the 1970s–90s to 9.6 kg/ha in 2013.

Japan: The use of pesticides has declined since the 1990s. The amount of pesticides used in 2000 was about 80000 tons. It reduced to 52000 tons in 2013, with a decrease of 35 percent. In the same period, the annual amount of fungicides used decreased from 40000 tons to 23000 tons, with a decrease of 42.5 percent; the annual amount of pesticides used reduced from 27000 tons to 17000 tons, with a decrease of 37 percent; the annual amount of herbicides used was stable at about 11000 tons.

Major countries in the Americas

United States: The annual amount of pesticides used is about 300000 tons, of which agricultural use accounts for about 80 percent. The annual amount of herbicides used is in the order of 200000 tons. As for the annual amount of pesticides used, if it was about 100000 tons before 2000, it has been reduced in recent years to about 75000 tons, while the annual amount of fungicides has remain stable at about 20000 tons.

Brazil: The amount of pesticides used was about 50000 tons in 1990 and 350000 tons in 2013. In 1990, the annual amount of herbicide used was 22000 tons, while in

2013 it was 240000 tons, representing an increase of more than 10 times. In 1990, the amount of insecticides used was 18000 tons, while, in 2013, it was 70000 tons, an increase of about nearly 3 times. In 1990, the use of fungicides was 8000 tons, while in 2013, it was approximately 44000 tons, an increase of about 4.5 times.

Mexico: The annual amount of fungicides used was 20000–30000 tons before 2006, 50000–55000 tons in 2007–2011. Thereafter, it stabilized at about 40000 tons in recent years. As for the annual amount of herbicide, It remained stable since 2005 at about 30000 to 35000 tons. If the annual amount of pesticides used was about 15000 tons before 2005, it increased to 20000–25000 tons in 2005–2010 and 30000–40000 tons in recent years.

Canada: If the annual amount of herbicide used was about 30000 tons before 2006, it increased to 58000 tons in 2012, an increase of 93 percent. As for the annual use of fungicides, it was about 3500 tons in 2006, then increased to 7546 tons in 2012, a 100 percent increase. The annual use of insecticides was stable at about 3000 tons.

The above information shows that:

• The overall pesticide application rate in a country generally increased at first, then decreased (or inverted U-shaped curve). This could be explained by the fact that the application of pesticides in developing countries, such as Brazil, tends to increase, and that of developed countries, such as the UK, tends to decline. Such changes are related to both the level of economic development, and the application of strict laws, regulations, standards and access systems for the production, sale and use of pesticides. Another factor to be considered is the progress of pesticide application technologies;

• Due to climate change and other factors, the level of pests and diseases during different periods may have varied. Therefore, the long-term decline trend in the amount of pesticides application is depending upon short-term upward and downwards fluctuations, such as in France and Germany; and

• The situation of agricultural pests and diseases varies from countries to countries. As a result, there still are large differences in the amount of pesticides applied by countries even with similar level of economic development, as for instance, between the Netherlands and South Korea.

Appendix 2　Swiss Agricultural Policy Direct Payments to Farmers[*]

General. In Switzerland, the Federal Government's exclusive responsibilities is to the military, international trade and agriculture sectors. Switzerland's 26 cantons have substantive powers in most other policy areas, but, within the agricultural policy, cantons are primarily implementers. With regard to agriculture, the federal level sets the budget, payment rates and much of the details of the policy.

Biogeographic adaptation of the Agricultural Policy. Swiss farms range from the pluvial plains through rolling hills (Jura) to alpine pasture. Swiss agricultural policy accounts for these differences by defining and differentiating between those three biogeographic regions. Cantons also have a role in setting local priorities with regard to thematic programs.

Direct payments to farmers. One of the main supports provided to farmers in Switzerland is market price support (MPS) resulting from important trade barriers applied at the Swiss border, i.e. payments per area to secure food supplies. Overtime, the MPS has been reduced from 80% to around 50% of total support to farmers, though domestic price for agricultural products were on average 60% above average world prices (in 2013–2015).

---

[*]　The Swiss direct payment system to farmers summarized in this Appendix refers to the 2014-2017 Swiss agricultural policy framework. Such direct payments to farmers were extended until the end of 2021 (Agricultural Policy 2018-2021 (PA 2018-2021). On February 12, 2020, the Swiss Government announced its plan for the future development of the Agricultural Policy from 2022 (PA 2022), which foresees the promotion of an even more sustainable and value-creating agriculture. It is expected that this new agricultural policy will be presented to the Swiss Parliament in early 2022.

Aside, Switzerland provides important direct payments to farms (all subject to environmental cross-compliance) in the form of payments to maintain farming in less favored ecological conditions and in the form of payments to farmers who voluntary apply stricter farming practices related to environmental (e.g. ecological agriculture practices) and animal welfare objectives. The role of direct payments has been increasing overtime and while it represented around 20% of total support in 1980s, it has increased to around 50% in the current years. This, to compare with China, where direct payments are paid only to grain producers.

Quality matters as much as quantity. The requirement to have 7 percent of farmland managed for biodiversity is the most eye-catching part of Swiss agriculture policy. But many in Switzerland doubt its efficacy as farmers can place that 7 percent where they want, rather than where it would have been the most effective. As a result, inappropriate areas are often allocated; such as where soil fertility or the effects of shading are too high.

Providing advice. Much of the discussion about improving the Swiss system focused on the need to build the capacity of farmers around public good delivery. The linchpin of this was the advisory services that are publicly supported and coordinated through a federal agency.

The OECD ranked Switzerland as the country with the highest Producer Support Estimate (PSE) in its 2016 Agricultural Policy Monitoring and Evaluation. PSE is the total amount of transfers from consumers and taxpayers to agricultural producers including direct support (subsidy) and border protections. The latest policy, Agriculture Policy 2014 (PA14, available only in French and German), repurposed the sizeable federal agricultural budget to create 8 direct payment programs [1] for Swiss farmers to apply for. They include, in particular (but not restricted to):

A. Payments for the security of food supplies;

B. Payments for the conservation of cultivated landscape;

C. Payments for biodiversity conservation;

D. Payments for the quality of the agricultural landscape;

E. Payments for the production system;

F. Payments for the efficient use of resources;

---

[1]   Payments for animal production and animal welfare have not been considered in this summary.

G. Payments for special crops;

H. Transition payments (not considered in this document).

To access any support, the farmer must first provide "Proof of Ecological Performance" (PEP) which was an inspiration for the EU's (less robust) cross-compliance and greening support to agriculture. In other terms, Swiss farmers must meet the following PEP requirements before accessing any support:

i. *Crop rotation*, Have a minimum of four crops in rotation. Includes limits for each crop.

ii. *Water and soil protection*, Farmers must have soil cover after August 31 and have identified measures to reduce soil erosion (where necessary).

iii. *Biodiversity area*, 7 percent of the farmland must be allocated as a biodiversity habitat (15 eligible habitats are defined).

iv. *Animal welfare*, Retaining relevant veterinary records and demonstrating 'good disease management.

v. *Pesticide use*, Requiring a farm specific integrated, pesticide management plan, sprayer testing and competence certificates as well as buffer strips next to watercourses and roads.

vi. *Nutrient balance*, Nitrogen and Phosphorus must be balanced at farm level (+/- 10 percent).Decadal soil analysis is also required.

If farmers agree to meet PEP across their farms, they can then access the available direct payment programs. Three of these are primarily income support. The remaining programs provide additional funding for biodiversity, landscape features and specific production systems (such as high animal welfare, or low chemical input).

A. Payment for the security of agricultural supplies

Basic contribution:

Basic payment rates	CHF ① / (ha · year)
Utilized agriculture area for food production	900
Open farmland and perennial cultures	400
Grasslands	450

---

① Swiss franc (FCH) and US$ are more or less at parity

No contribution are made for crops that are not used for food production.

The basic contribution is distributed as follows on the basis of areas eligible for payments to farms:

Cultivated areas	Reduction of the basic rate
Up to 60 ha	0
60-80 ha	20%
80-100 ha	40%
100-120 ha	60%
120-140 ha	80%
More than 140 ha	100%

Additional contributions for farming in difficult ecological situations:

Zone	CHF/ (ha · year)
Plain	0
Hills	240
Alps I	300
Alps II	320
Alps III	340
Alps IV	360

B. Payments for the conservation of the cultivated landscape

(Contribution for an open agricultural landscape)

The contribution to an open agricultural landscape is distributed by zone. No contribution is foreseen for the plain region, nor for hedges, the small forests and riparian forests along rivers. Agricultural land must be used as to prevent forest rejuvenation.

Zone	CHF/ (ha · year)
Plain	0
Hills	100
Alps I-IV	230-390

C. Payments for biodiversity conservation

General. Farmland areas devoted to the promotion of biodiversity (APB) surfaces must be exploited for a minimum commitment period of 8 years.

The contribution to biodiversity is paid according to two quality levels. For quality level I, the lower level requirements must be fulfilled. Contributions are paid cumulatively. This means that for quality level I, and quality level II's contributions are paid.

Contributions of quality level I are granted at most for half of the areas eligible for contributions. Surfaces and trees that are the subject of contributions for quality level II are not subject to the limitation.

Conditions for the quality level I.

i. No fertilizer should be applied to APBs;

ii. There is a need to fight again problematic/invasive plants;

iii. No pesticide product should be used. The treatments by plant or group of plants are allowed for problem plants, if it is impossible to fight them reasonably by mechanical means,

iv. The product of the mowing must be evacuated. The heaps of branches and litter are allowed where it is desirable for the protection of nature or in the part of a networking project,

v. Grinding and use of a rock cutter is forbidden,

vi. For seeding, only seed mixtures recommended by agriculture extension can be used;

vii. Small, unproductive structures present in extensive grasslands such as along a watercourse, litter surfaces and riparian grasslands along a watercourse give right to an additional biodiversity payment on 20% above the area considered.

Conditions for the quality level II

i. The APB has a floristic quality or structures favoring biodiversity;

ii. The use of conditioners is not allowed;

iii. Survey methods to assess quality level II are set by the canton administrations.

Quality contributions. They apply in particular to (but not restricted to): (i) extensive grasslands, (ii) litter areas, (iii) little extensive grasslands, (iv) extensive grazing lands; (v) wooded grazing lands; (vi) wooded riparian areas, (vii) fallow lands, (viii) rotational fallows, (ix) grasslands along rivers, (x) fruit tree orchards, (xi) tree alleys and (xii) flower strips for pollination. Payments for animal production have not been considered in this summary.

Extensive grasslands

Zone	CHF/ (ha · year)	
	Quality I	Quality II
Plain	1080	1920
Hills	860	1840
Alps I–II	500	1700
Alps III–iV	450	1100

Note: (i) Quality I: surfaces must be mown once a year for the production of fodder. The fodder must be evacuated; (ii) Quality II: indicator plants of nutrient-poor soil and species-rich vegetation are met regularly.

Litter areas

Zone	CHF/ (ha · year)	
	Quality I	Quality II
Plain	1440	2060
Hills	1220	1980
Alps –II	860	1840
Alps III–IV	680	1770

Note: (i) Quality I: litter areas cannot be mown before September 1. The fodder must be evacuated; (ii) Quality II: indicator plants of nutrient-poor soil and species-rich vegetation are met regularly.

Little extensive grasslands

Zone	CHF/ (ha · year)	
	Quality I	Quality II
Plain, hills and alps –II	450	1200
Alps III–V	450	1000

Note: (i) Quality I and II: a fertilization of up to 30 kg of N per hectare is authorized in the form of manure or compost.

Extensive grazing lands

Zone	CHF/ (ha · year)	
	Quality I	Quality II
All regions	450	700

Note: (i) Quality I: grazing lands must be pastured at least once a year. Cleaning cuts are allowed and grazing land poor in nutients are excluded; (ii) Quality II: indicator species-within a nutrient-poor grazing lands-favoring biodiversity are met regularly

Wooded grazing lands

Zone	CHF/ (ha · year)	
	Quality I	Quality II
All regions	450	700

Note: (i) Quality I: farm manure, compost and non-nitrogen fertilizers can only be used with the consent of the forestry extension service. Only the grass areas give the right to payments; (ii) Quality II: same regulations as extensive grazing lands.

Hedges, woodlots and wooded riparian areas

Zone	CHF/ (ha · year)	
	Quality I	Quality II
All regions	2160	2840

Note (i): Quality I: A strip of grassland or litter area with a width of 3 to 6 m must be kept on both sides along the hedges, woodlets and riparian banks. The strips of grassland or litter areas must be mowed at least every three years, respecting the mowing season of extensive grazing land, which can be grazed between September 1 and November 30. The covered area of woody plants must be managed every 8 years according to rules.

Note. (ii) Quality II: Hedges, woodlots and wooded riparian banks are exclusively composed native woody species (trees and bushes). They should include at least 5 different woody species per 10 m.

Floral fallow lands

Zone	CHF/ (ha · year)	
	Quality I	Quality II
Plain and hills	3800	0

Note: Quality I:

(i) Before being sown, fallow lands must have been used as or for perennial crops.

(ii) The floral fallow land must be maintained for at least 2 years up to at least a maximum of 8 years.

(iii) No plowing are allowed until February 15 of the year following the year of payment.

(iv) After a fallow period, the same parcel can be reallocated for this purpose only from the fourth growing season after plowing.

(v) As early as the year following the floral fallow establishment, floral fallow can be mowed only between October 1 and March 15 and only half of them.

(vi) A cleaning cut is allowed during the first year in case invasion by weeds.

Rotational fallows

Zone	CHF/ (ha · year)	
	Quality I	Quality II
Plain and hills	3300	0

Note: Quality I:

(i) Before being sown, the surface must have been used as or for perennial crops.

(ii) After a fallow, the same parcel can be reallocated for for perenial crops from the fourth growing season after plowing.

(iii) Surfaces must be sown between September 1 and April 30.

(iv) One year's rotational fallow must be maintained until February 15 of the following year of contributions.

(v) Biannual or triennial rotational fallow must be maintained until September 15 of the second or third year of payments.

(vi) Rotational fallow area can only be cut off between October 1 and March 15.

(vii) After a fallow, the same parcel can be reallocated to perennial crops from the fourth growing season after plowing.

Grassland along rivers

Zone	CHF/ (ha · year)	
	Quality I	Quality II
All zones	450	0

Note: Quality I:

(i) Surfaces must be mowed at least once a year.

(ii) Unless otherwise agreed, surfaces may be grazed between September 1 and November 30.

(iii) Grasslands along rivers should not be more than 12 meters.

Fruit tree orchards

Species	CHF/tree/year	
	Quality I	Quality II
Fruit trees	13.50	31.50
Walnut	13.50	16.50

Note (i): Quality I

i) Payments are made for pome and stone fruit trees and walnuts, as well as chestnuts in managed chestnut groves.

ii) No contributions for high-stem fruit trees not found on owned or leased farmlands.

iii) Payments are granted from 20 trees giving entitlement to contributions per farm.

iv) Payments are made for up to 120 pome fruit trees and per hectare, except for cherry trees.

v) Payments are made for up to 100 cherry trees, walnut trees and chestnut trees per hectare.

vi) Trees should be planted at appropriate intervals for growth and their performance capacity.

vii) High-stem fruit trees can be manured.

vii) By fruit tree being manured on an extensive meadow, it is advisable to exclude from the right to payment area less to 1 are.

ix) Fruit trees must have a minimum height of 1.2 m, that of other trees 1.6 m minimum.

x) No herbicide can be used at the foot of trees. Exception: for trees less than 5 years old.

Note (ii): Quality II

i) The surface of high-stem fruit trees must be 20 ares and must include at least 10 high-stem fruit trees.

ii) Density of trees: at least 30 and at most 120 fruit trees per hectare.

iii) With regard to cherry, walnut and chestnut trees, the maximum density is 100 high stem trees per hectare.

iv) The interval between each tree is at most 30 meters.

v) The trees should be pruned in accordance with the state of the art.

vi) For high-stem fruit trees, they should be planted at a distance of up to 50 m

Tree alleys

Payments made are up to 5 FCH/tree. Trees must be planted at 10 m distance. No fertilization permitted in a radius of 3 m around the tree.

Flower strips for pollination

Zone	CHF/ (ha · year)	
	Quality I	Quality II
Plains and hills	2500	0

Note (i): Quality I

i) Before being sown, the surface must have been used as or for perennial crops.

ii) Surfaces must be sown before May 15.

iii) The different surfaces must not exceed 50 ares.

iv) The flowering strip must be used in accordance with prescriptions during at least 100 days.

v) A cleaning cut is allowed in case of strong pressure of invasive weeds.

vi) Annual flower bands taken into account for pollinators and other useful organisms can not represent more than half of the biodiversity promotion area.

D. Payments for the improvement of the landscape quality

With the contribution to landscape quality of the landscape, the government supports cantonal projects for the preservation, promotion and development of diversified cultivated landscapes.

Project landscape objectives should be based on existing regional concepts. In view of the implementation of landscape projects, measures should be agreed for a contractual term of 8 years.

Contributions are fixed for each measure on the basis of cost and the value of this measure. The canton fixes the amount of the allocated contribution for each measure.

The Confederation supports at most 90 percent of the following amounts per project and per year:

i. CHF 360 per ha utilized areas (UAA); and

ii. CHF 240 per unit of the usual charge agreed under an agreement.

The Confederation makes every year available to the cantons at most 120 FCH per hectare of utilized area and at most 80 FCH per unit of usual charge.

E. Contributions to the production system

Payments for biological agriculture.

All crops	CHF/ (ha · year)
Special crops	1600
Open land cultivation	1200
Other crops giving right to contributions	200

Note: (i) Refer to the law specifying the rules to be applied to biological agriculture.

(ii) Controls are made by an agreed organic certification organization

Payments for extensive cultivation

All crops	CHF/ (ha · year)
Payments to extensive cultivation	400

Note: (i) for extensive cultivation

i) Crops should be grown without the use of growth regulators, fungicides, chemical stimulators synthetic natural defenses insecticides (exception: kaolin for the control of meligethorn rapeseed).

ii) The requirements for extensive production must be respected in the whole farm for each crop.

iii) Included in extensive crops are all types of cereals; rapeseed; sunflower ; protein peas, faba beans and lupins as well as the meslin of these three legumes with cereals used for animal feed.

iv) The contribution for feed wheat is only paid when the variety of cultivated wheat is registered in the list of recommended varieties for feed wheat from Agroscope and swiss granum.

v) Extensive cultures should be harvested at maturity for the seed and should not be invaded by weeds.

F. Contributions to an efficient utilization of resources

They include: payments for (I) spreading techniques; (ii) agricultural techniques preserving agricultural soils; (iii) the use precise spreading techniques; and (iv) the reduction of pesticide products.

Payments for spreading techniques

All crops	CHF/ (ha · year)
Payments related to spreading techniques	30

Note (i):

i) The contribution is paid for spreading techniques reducing farm fertilizer and recycling fertilizer emissions.

ii) Contributions are paid until 2019.

iii) Are considered as spreading techniques reducing polluting emissions: (a) the use of a flexible hose spreader; (b) the use of a skid injector; (c) disc buriers; and (d) injection of slurry in depth.

Note (ii):

i) The contribution is limited to 4 slurry spreads per year.

ii) No contributions for liquid manure spreading between 15 November 15 and February 15.

iii) For each hectare and input of farm and recycling fertilizer with the aid of spraying techniques that reduce pollutant emissions, 3 kg of available nitrogen may taken into account in the balance sheet.

Payments for agricultural techniques preserving agricultural soils

All crops	CHF/ (ha · year)
Direct seeding	250
Line sowing	200
Sowing under mulch	250
Supplementary contribution for non-using herbicides	200

Note (i): Contributions are paid until 2021. No contributions are made for subsequent management of: (a) artificial grasslands by sowing under mulch; (b) green manure and intercrops; and (c) wheat after corn.

Note (ii):

i) Appropriate measures must be taken to reduce the risks associated with diseases, weeds and pests.

ii) Between the harvest of the previous main crop and the harvest of the following main crop giving right to contributions, it is not necessary to plow and

iii) The use of glyphosates must not exceed 1.5 kg of active substance per ha.

Payments for the use precise spreading techniques

All crops	CHF/ha
Sub-foliar pulverization By unit of pulverization	75% of purchasing cost to a maximum of 170 FCH
Anti-drift sprayer used in perennial crop By horizontal airflow sprayer (e.g. tangential sprayer)	25% of purchasing costs to a maximum of 6000 FCH
Anti-drift sprayer used in perennial crop By horizontal airflow adjustable sprayer and vegetation detector; or By tunnel sprayer with recycling air and liquid	25% of purchasing costs to a maximum of 10000 FCH
Anti-drift sprayer used in perennial crop with separate rinsing system	25% of purchasing costs to a maximum of 2000 FCH

Note (i): Contributions are paid until 2021 for the purchase of sprayer

Payments for the reduction of pesticide products.

Crops	CHF/ (ha · year)
Fruit trees-reduction of herbicides • Partial • Total	200 600
Fruit trees-reduction of fungicides	200
Sugar beets – reduction of herbicides • Mechanical weeding • No herbicides • No fungicides nor insecticides	200–400 800 400

Note: the contribution per hectare per year is paid for the reduction of pesticides in arboriculture and viticulture, as well as in the cultivation of sugar beet. Excluded are areas that give right to the contribution for organic farming.

G. Contribution to special crops and supplement for grain crops

Payments for special crops

Crops	CHF/ (ha · year)
Rapeseed, sunflower, oil squash, linseed, poppy and false saffron	700
Potatoes and corn seeds	700
Forage and leguminous seeds	1000
Beans, protein peas and lupines for animal feeding	1000
Sugar beets for sugar processing	2100

Supplemental payments for grain crops. The amount of the supplement is determined at the end of each year according to the allocated resources and the area under cereals.

H. Transition Payments

The resources made available for the transitional contribution correspond to the budget item for direct payments, minus the expenditure made for all types of contributions (contributions to the cultivated landscape, contributions to security of supply, contributions to biodiversity, contributions landscape quality, contributions to the production system and contributions to the efficient use of resources); and expenditures for projects for efficient use of resources and water protection.

I. Total Government's contribution to direct payments to farmers

In total, in 2017, the Government's direct payment contribution amounted to CHF 2806 million, which were paid for an area under cultivation of 1.022 million ha given in average about 2745 CHF/ha. The 1.022 million ha under cultivation include approximately 270000 ha of open land (field crops and perennial crops), 21000 ha of permanent crops such as for instance vineyards and fruit tree crops, and 731000 ha of grassland. The areas of field crops and perennial crops have increased by 3000 ha since 2014.

It should also be noted that direct payments for programs related to biodiversity, landscape quality, production systems and resource efficiency increased again slightly in 2017. Biodiversity promotion areas in the plain reached 77000 ha, far exceeding the target of 65 000 ha. As such, farmers currently exploit 40 percent of all biodiversity promotion areas as high quality and 75 percent of them are networked.

Under the pesticide action plan, since 2018, new incentive schemes have been established for partial or total non-use of pesticides in sugar beet, fruit and vine. A similar incentive program is planned for 2019 for other major crops.

The summary of the effective government's contributions to direct payments to farmers is given in the tablebelow. Note that for 2018, the figures quoted are related to the 2018 budget.

Table1 Direct payments to farmers-Government spending in FCH million

Year	2015	2016	2017	2018
Payments for the conservation of the cultivated landscape	504	507	523	535
Payments of the security of supplies	1094	1091	1086	1092
Payments for biodiversity	387	400	414	410
Payments for landscape quality	125	142	145	150
Payments to production system	450	458	467	468
Payments for an efficient use of resources	17	25	28	59
Contribution to the protection of water resources and sustainable use of resources	26	12	18	—
Transition payments	178	162	129	98
Reduction/ anticipated payments	−2	−4	−4	—
Total	2779	2792	2806	2812

Some preliminary conclusions based on discussions with farmers on direct payments related to environmental protection.

One of the tensions in Swiss agricultural policy is the extent to which farmers can become primarily public good farmers. As a matter of fact, the Federal Office for the Environment expresses some frustration that farmers are not able to make delivering biodiversity or other public goods the priority for their farm business. The barrier is a rule created by the Federal Office for Agriculture that limits total payments under environmental schemes to a percentage (either 50 percent or 20 percent) of the UAA (utilized agriculture area).

Officials in the Federal Office for Agriculture were unapologetic about the limits. The Swiss constitution includes food security as one of the three objectives of agricultural policy – for instance one of the three income support programs is titled "payment for ensuring food supplies" (the others are labeled "transition payments" and "farmland payments"). The Federal Office for Agriculture had therefore imposed this limit, as apparently "some farmers weren't producing anything". By which they meant any food.

Technically the direct payment programs are voluntary but economically most farmers have few options. The result is a Swiss farming sector, which, as one official told, "has yet to accept its role as a provider of public goods". Farmers muttered that they don't "want to be the gardeners of Switzerland".

Appendix 3 Principles of Slow-release (SRFs), Controlled Release (CRFs) Fertilizers and Production of Organic Fertilizers

Broadly speaking, SRFs and CRFs refer to fertilizers with slower nutrient release rates and longer release periods. In a narrow sense, SRFs refer to fertilizers with slower nutrient release speed than common fertilizers when applied to the soil. Most of them are monomeric fertilizers (nitrogen fertilizers); the release of such fertilizer depends on pH value, soil moisture content, soil types, microbial activity, irrigation water volume and other external factors, which are less controllable. CRFs are mostly compound fertilizers or total nutrient fertilizers supplemented with trace elements. It is based on pre-set nutrient release patterns, so that fertilizer nutrient release and crop nutrient absorption are basically synchronized, with strong controllability. The specific criteria are: at 25°C, the fertilizer nutrients release ratio within 24 hours does not exceed 15 percent; within 28 days does not exceed 75 percent; and not less than 75 percent thereafter within the specified time. The nutrient release curve is consistent with the nutrient absorption curve of the corresponding crop (Commission European Normalization, CEN).

In response to the inconsistency of the nutrient release ratio of fertilizers and the nutrient uptake ratio of plants, the concept of SRFs was proposed at the beginning of the 20th century. In 1955, SRFs began to be used for agricultural production. In the 1960s, the development of SRFs made significant progresses. In the 1980s, the development of nitrogen CRFs made rapid progress while in the 1990s, SRFs technology matured.

A polymer resin coating controls the nutrient release of CRFs. The CRFs surface of the membrane is filled with pores. After application of the fertilizer to the soil, the moisture enters through the membrane pores and dissolved nutrients, which are released through the membrane pores. When the temperature rises, the plants grow faster, the nutrient demand increases, and the nutrient release speed increases; when the temperature decreases, the plants grow slower or even remain dormant, and the release speed slows down or stops. When crops absorb nutrients, the nutrient concentration on the outer side of the membrane decreases, the concentration of nutrients inside and outside the membrane increases, and the nutrient release speed increases. Thus, the nutrient release curve is consistent with the curve of crop nutrients according to crop demand, thereby improving the utilization of fertilizer nutrients.

The main modes of organic fertilizers production include: (i) through the composting from livestock and poultry manure waste, crop straw and other wastes can be converted into non-toxic and harmless organic fertilizers; (ii) wastes, such as livestock and poultry manure, may be converted to non-toxic and harmless organic fertilizer; (iii) human and animal manure, mixed with crop straws, may be converted into non-toxic and harmless biogas residues digested through septic tanks.

Postscript

As long as the problem of food and clothing shortages was not solved, food security was the basis of ecological security. If food and clothing shortages would not be solved, ecological security could not be guaranteed. With the lifting of food and clothing issues, ecological security has become the basis of food security. Without ecological security, there can be no sustainable food security. For China, ecological security in the main grain producing areas of the country is of utmost importance. Based on this understanding, the author carried out relevant research and wrote this book entitled "Ecological Security in China's Main Grain Producing Areas".

This book is not only aimed primarily at all those involved in making food security policies in China, such as decision-makers, key policy advisers and civil servants and agronomists operating at national and provincial levels but also at all their counterparts operating in developed and developing countries. Their functions are to support an increased recognition of the need to address ecological security issues affecting agriculture ecosystems in the current climate-changing environment, and by consequence, the sustainable production of safe food products as well as the benefits that could be derived from technical, policy and institutional measures aimed at improving ecological security for food security reasons.

The study began in late 2015. After retiring in November 2015, the author joined the research group of "Strategic Research on Ecological Security System in the Core Area of Grain Production in Henan Province" headed by the Department of forestry of Henan Province, recommended by Professor Yuan Peng, Rural Development Institute, Chinese Academy of Social Sciences (CASS). This strategic research was financed by the Asian Development Bank. Once this project completed in 2018, Ms. Suzanne

Robertson, Project Officer at the Asian Development Bank, the sponsor of the project, suggested that Mr. Claude René Heimo (World Bank Retiree and Advisor of the Socio-Eco-Nomic Center, Geneva) and I should work together to further expand the research content of the Henan Ecological Security project, especially focusing on summarizing the Chinese experience and challenges in food security that could be used for reference in other developed and developing countries as a knowledge product. Accordingly, with support from the Asian development Bank, I applied to the Foreign Affairs Bureau of the Chinese Academy of Social Sciences for this new study, this time focusing on Ecological Security in China's main grain producing areas. In effect, this new project was approved, and financed by the Asian Development Bank. I wrote the Chinese version of the research report, which was later on translated in English by Ms. Zhou Lijun, a doctoral candidate of the China Agricultural University. Mr. Claude René Heimo fine-tuned the first version of the report and its English translation according to the habits of western readers with the goal of telling a good Chinese story. As a result, this book should be actually considered as a research achievement jointly completed by Mr. Claude R. Heimo and myself.

On the occasion of the publication of this study on Ecological Security in China's major grain producing areas, allow me, first, to thank all those who have contributed to the publication of this book. A particular thank you will go to Mr. Claude René Heimo for his meticulous work and selfless dedication, and Dr. Zhou Lijun for her support and devotion. I, also, would like to thank Professor Wei Houkai and Professor Du Zhixiong for their recommendations, the Academic Committee of the Rural Development Institute, and the Bureau of Veteran Cadres of the Chinese Academy of Social Sciences for their recognition, so as to give this publication the opportunity to be supported by the Research Fund for Retired Scholars of the Chinese Academy of Social Sciences. Finally, I would like to thank the responsible editor Mr. Xu Chongyang for his specific work related to the publication of this book.

Despite my efforts, there must be many unsatisfactory places in the book. Please don't hesitate to suggest corrections.

Li Zhou

October 5th, 2021